D1532008

Reprints of Economic Classics

MIDDLEMEN IN ENGLISH BUSINESS

MIDDLEMEN

IN

ENGLISH BUSINESS

PARTICULARLY BETWEEN 1660 AND 1760

BY

RAY B. WESTERFIELD

[1915]

REPRINTS OF ECONOMIC CLASSICS

AUGUSTUS M. KELLEY · PUBLISHERS
NEW YORK 1968

First Edition 1915

(New Haven: Yale University Press, Transactions of
The Connecticut Academy of Arts & Sciences, 1915)

Reprinted 1968 by
AUGUSTUS M. KELLEY · PUBLISHERS
New York New York 10010

FROM *A COPY IN THE COLLECTIONS OF*
THE NEW YORK PUBLIC LIBRARY
Astor, Lenox and Tilden Foundations

Library of Congress Catalogue Card Number

68-30551

PRINTED IN THE UNITED STATES OF AMERICA
by SENTRY PRESS, NEW YORK, N. Y. 10019

Middlemen

in

English Business

Particularly Between 1660 and 1760

BY

RAY BERT WESTERFIELD, Ph.D.

Instructor in Political Economy in Yale University

YALE UNIVERSITY PRESS
NEW HAVEN, CONN.
1915

PREFACE.

The purpose of this book is to present an historical sketch of the origin and development of the middleman organization that served English business before the Industrial Revolution. The period after that event is reserved for future study; in the throes of that great industrial and commercial upheaval it is very likely that the technique of business underwent great change. I find a comparative dearth of writings depicting business life and practice of the past. It may be that this contribution to the history of business may find reception in the business or scholastic world.

Three main classes of material have been used. One is political, social, and economic tracts published as polemics, dissertations, complaints, and opinions on the contemporary questions that stirred the tongue and pen in the years of the past. The Yale University Library has deposited with it, through the kindness of an alumnus Henry R. Wagner, an invaluable collection of many thousands of these tracts. Mr. Wagner, '84, is an earnest student of English and Irish economic history and is assembling what is probably the best collection of such materials anywhere existing. The collection, which now numbers above nine thousand volumes and is being continuously increased, covers the economic and social life of England and Ireland from the beginning of the sixteenth century and contains some very rare literature. I have found it a great and profitable pleasure to immerse myself in the practical questions of the past as they are revealed by these tractators, pamphleteers, and more extensive writers.

A second class is the published state, municipal and borough papers, including parliamentary reports and the statutes. To some of these papers I have not had direct access and have depended upon the validity of quotations by some other writers; in such cases the quoting writer is also cited. The third kind of material is local and county histories. This part of the work has been much facilitated by the excellent series of county histories now being published and known as the Victoria histories.

The citations will be found quite profuse, so that the reader will be aided to further study of any of the points raised. The citations in footnotes are much abbreviated; the full title of each will be found in an alphabetical list at the close of the book. Anonymous books and tracts are indicated by quotation marks.

I owe thanks without measure to Professor Clive Day for his extensive assistance in the preparation of this work. His guidance has been constant and inspiring and careful. He has been indulgent of my faults and patiently criticized in a stimulating way both the plan and content of the book. To him I tender my deepest thanks.

My thanks are due to Professor Charles McLean Andrews for having read the manuscript in a preliminary stage and given me most valuable criticisms and suggestions.

Messrs. Henry R. Gruener and Henry Ginter and the members of the economics division of the Yale Library staff have been very courteous and helpful. I thank them greatly.

RAY BERT WESTERFIELD.

Yale University, June, 1914.

TABLE OF CONTENTS.

CHAPTER I.

CHAPTER II.

CHAPTER III.

CHAPTER IV.

MIDDLEMEN IN THE MINERAL TRADES.

Coal

CHAPTER V.

MIDDLEMEN IN THE TEXTILES AND TEXTILE MATERIALS TRADES.

Wool and Woolens

Contents

CHAPTER I.

INTRODUCTION.

The three pillars upon which the classical economists erected the structure of political economy were land, labor and capital. These three categories of economic life neglect a fourth element which is equally important and sustains the relation of direction to the other three. This element is the organization and management of the means of production. Given the same capital and labor, the output of the shop and the supply gotten to market vary as widely as the genius of the captain of industry. In the processes of production, and between production and consumption, the agent of direction and the technique instituted by this agent constitute as important a factor of economic life as the labor and capital spent.

Histories of the labor movement have been written. The evolution of the laboring class has been traced through the mediaeval and modern periods. The organization of factory production and of domestic or household production has been treated. But the historical aspect of the technique of the market has been comparatively neglected. The agents and machinery wherewith the wares of commerce are collected and distributed are phenomena whose origin is dated from the feudal era. They have passed into a relatively orthodox type. There is much room for historical investigation into the origin and operations of the men of trade and commerce. The history of commerce might be written from this point of view. The growth of English commerce is not explained by a statistical account of manufactures produced, of mports and exports, of new markets abroad and of colonial expansion. The volume of production and the volume of consumption are entities related by the mechanism of business. The degree of perfection to which this mechanism is developed is one determining factor of the nature, volume, direction, and service of commerce.

It is the purpose of this work to sketch in some detail the origin and development of the middlemen and their functions in certain leading industries of England. Middlemen are understood to in-

119

clude the series of traders through whose hands commodities pass on their way from the maker or producer to the consumer. The period chosen to which greatest particularity is given is roughly defined by the dates 1660 and 1760. It is a round century marked off by great political, religious, commercial, and industrial events. The organization of any business must, from its very nature, develop by slow transformations; for this reason these terminating dates cannot be rigidly adhered to; the roots of some parts of the organization will be followed back of 1660, and the tendencies beyond 1760 indicated.

The year 1660 was a turning point in English and European history. England had passed through two decades of civil war, and had lived under the stern military and Puritanic government of Cromwell. She now returned to Stuart monarchy and entered the reactionary period of the Restoration. Abroad the Peace of Westphalia and of the Pyrenees and the accession of Louis XIV and the revocation of the Edict of Nantes were momentous events. Hereafter differences of religious creeds ceased to be even nominally a source of political activity. Theological liberalism came. The papacy ceased to be preëminent in European diplomacy. The traditional unity and dignity attaching to the imperial authority wasted as Spain and Germany declined. Louis introduced personal sovereignty and monarchic absolutism into France, and Charles tried it in England. Dynastic and commercial wars succeeded religious wars.

The doctrines of mercantilism and national power were revived and made ascendant. England began her contest for maritime supremacy over Holland and for the colonial mastery of the world. The Acts of Navigation, 1651 and 1660, and the prohibition of the export of wool initiated the policy of the economic self-sufficiency of the English nation. The Dutch wars were thrusts at her greatest competitor on the sea; retaliatory tariffs were used as weapons against France. The prohibition of the export of wool aided English woolen manufacturers, caused the decline of the Merchants of the Staple, and developed the exportation of cloth instead. The Navigation Acts tended to shift ship-building from Holland to England and her colonies.

The period of the Restoration was one of very rapid extension in economic respects. In spite of the Plague and Great Fire, 1665–6, and the foreign wars, there was a remarkable increase in wealth and population.[1] Commerce, foreign and domestic, quickly revived after the long period of civil commotion, and entered a new era.

Equally as important events in the political and economic world characterized 1760. England had just attained her greatest supremacy in colonial enterprise; India and America had been won. Holland was negligible, Portugal an economic dependency, and France conquered. At home she was just entering one of the greatest industrial revolutions in the annals of history. In the next few decades the introduction of machinery, steam-power, and the factory system transformed the whole system of production and distribution and multiplied the volume of commerce.

Neglecting the fluctuations caused by depressions during foreign wars, the century from the Restoration of Charles II to the accession of George III, was marked by a steady, continuous increase in the volume of foreign commerce. The statistics of commerce for this period are quite defective. The "Custom House Ledger" was not introduced until 1696, and the "Register General of Shipping" until 1701 and 1706. Consequently the figures of commerce in the seventeenth century are but approximate estimates of men contemporary or later. The custom house figures were also very defective in the eighteenth century; they gave only valuations based on prices existing in 1694. When no export duties were charged exporters, out of vanity or business purpose, exaggerated their shipments.[2] The tonnage was underestimated to evade tonnage taxes; ships were counted at each voyage; and prior to 1786 the tonnage was reported only at two-thirds the actual amount.[3] Besides, smuggling was carried on to a considerable degree, with or without the connivance of the customs officials. Making much allowance for all these defects,[4] a rough approximation may yet be had for the progress of commerce in the century. The following tables indicate a steady growth. The index number, based on the average annual total of exports and imports for 1700–04, points to a

---

[1] Contemporary notice was taken of it in Child, Discourse; Petty, Pol. Arith.; and Davenant, Works; Chalmers, Estimate, 46–7. Cunningham, Growth, II, 193–4; Anderson, Origin, II, 506, 536, 579, et seq.; Capper, 103–4; and Macaulay, IV, 119–120, conclude the same.

[2] Dowell, Taxation, IV, 432–3, gives an instance after the repeal of export duties on cottons and woolens, 11–12 Wm. III, Cap. 20.

[3] Chalmers, Estimate, CXXXV.

[4] Further defects are cited by Macpherson, III, 341–342.

four-fold increase. The paucity of data for the period of the Restoration may be supplemented by the table of the average annual customs duties collected, which indicate that commerce did not quite double in that period. The table of shipping cleared singularly substantiates a quadrupling of foreign commerce in the century.

TABLE A.

Foreign Commerce (*Annual averages*).

(Million pounds sterling.)

DATE	IMPORTS	EXPORTS	TOTAL	INDEX NO.
1662–63	£4.0	£2.0	£6.0	51*
1668–69	4.2	2.1	6.3	53†
1696–97	3.5	3.5	7.0	59‡
1700–04	5.1	6.7	11.8	100§
1705–09	4.3	6.5	10.8	106§
1710–14	4.9	7.3	12.2	103§
1715–19	6.0	8.0	14.0	119§
1720–24	6.4	9.0	15.4	130§
1725–29	7.1	10.6	17.8	150§
1730–34	7.4	11.5	18.9	159§
1735–39	7.6	11.8	19.3	163§
1740–44	7.1	11.6	18.7	158§
1745–49	7.4	12.0	19.4	165§
1750–54	8.1	14.0	22.0	186§
1755–59	8.8	13.7	22.7	192§
1760–64	10.0	15.7	25.7	217§
1765–69	11.6	14.2	25.8	218§

* Authority: Anderson, II, 478; Br. Mer., II, 334.
† Authority: Anderson, II, 496; Br. Mer., II, 334.
‡ Authority: Chalmers, Estimate, 234.
§ Authority: Anderson, IV, 692–4.

TABLE B.

Customs Duties[1] (*Averages*).

DATES	ANNUAL AVERAGE	INDEX NUMBER
1661–1664..........................	£485,000	100
1665–1669..........................	476,000	98
1670–1674..........................	550,000	114
1675–1679..........................	648,000	134
1680–1684..........................	709,000	147
1685–1688..........................	787,000	163

[1] Chalmers, Estimate, 49.

TABLE C.

Shipping cleared[1]

DATES	TONNAGE ANNUAL AVERAGE	INDEX NUMBER
	Tons	
1663–1669	143,000	45
1668	286,000	90
1696	175 000	55
1697	245,000	80
1700–1702	317,000	100
1709	289,000	90
1712	356,000	112
1713–1715	448,000	141
1718	444,000	140
1726–1728	456,000	144
1736–1738	502,000	160
1739–1741	471,000	150
1749–1751	661,000	209
1755–1757	525,000	163
1760	574,000	181

Statistical data for internal commerce are almost entirely wanting. The total consumption of the English people was variously estimated to be between 42,000,000 and 60,000,000 pounds sterling,[2] in the second decade of the eighteenth century. Of this, between 4,000,000 and 5,000,000 was imported; the ratio of the consumption of foreign and domestic goods was one-tenth or one-fifteenth. The ratio of exportations to home consumption, i.e. of the foreign and home markets was one-sixth. In 1760, Macpherson, stating the results of some one's else calculation, gave the ratio of these two markets as one-thirty-second.[3] The average annual coastwise coal shipment from the Tyne progressed from 336,000 tons in the decade 1661 to 1670, to 482,000 tons in the first decade of the eighteenth century.[4] The sheep brought to Smithfield yearly about 1731 were 568,000; in 1760 they numbered 617,000.[5] The cloth output of West Riding increased from about 27,000 broads in 1726 to 49,000 in 1760, and narrows, which were first manufactured in 1737,

---

[1] Chalmers, Estimate, 69, 234, 256–7.

[2] Br. Mer., 165, 167; Hobson, Mod. Cap. 12–13.

[3] Macpherson, Annals, III, 340 note.

[4] Surtees, 105: 260.

[5] Anderson, Origin, IV, 156.

mounted to nearly 70,000 pieces by 1760.[1] The Post Office receipts rose from 180,000 pounds sterling about 1725 to 229,000 about 1760.[2] Rough and incomplete as these data are, it seems fair to conclude that the domestic commerce underwent a still more rapid extension than the foreign commerce during the century 1660 to 1760. There is a general agreement among writers on this subject that with the exception of the "seven barren years," 1693 to 1700, England enjoyed exceptional prosperity until 1760.[3] "The first half of the eighteenth century—was one of great plenty, high profits, low prices, and increasing wages."[4] Statistics of woolen manufactures, of importation of woo and cotton, of the value of exports and imports in general, of shipping revenues, population and poor rates—all validate this conclusion.[5]

The causes of this increase were undoubtedly many: the complexity of its causation makes it impossible to trace the effect of any one element. The geographical distribution of commerce was changed and new areas included within the market. New products, wares and industries were introduced. The technical processes of production were improved. Better highways and vehicles of transport furthered communication. The policies of government with respect to trade were liberalized and devoted to its extension. Population increased, that of England and Wales rising from five and a half to nearly seven millions.[6] These and many other factors contributed to make England the commercial nation of Europe.

The thesis here proposed is that there developed a trading and mercantile class, a new kind of man—one who saw and created opportunities for trade at home and abroad—who took the initiative in new methods of organization, correlating and establishing a mutual interdependence between specialized producers and consumers—who influenced the policies of state to the furtherance of commerce—and who undertook activities new to the economic life then existent. It is believed that commerce and its growth are inexplicable if little or no countenance is paid to this active, thinking, constructive, organizing class. The class did not exist, except in embryo, in the medieval system of barter-market. Before the

---

[1] Anderson, Origin, IV, 146–7.

[2] Hemmeon, 245.

[3] See Hewins, Eng. Trade, 114; Tooke, Prices, I, 38–61.

[4] Rogers, Ec. Interpr., 247; see also p. 58.

[5] For such statistics of progress see Cunningham, Growth, 928, App. 4.

[6] See the estimates of Petty, King, Chalmers, and Davenant.

Industrial Revolution an orthodox system of middlemen had become an established fact, and the modern integrated-business system is just now beginning to divest itself, in some parts, of its hold. It is important to discover what were the activities of these new men, what were their relations to each other and to the producers and consumers, what were their functions in commerce, and what their connections with statesmen, national policy, and social life.

Practice confirms the economic theory that up to a certain degree specialization of functions economizes, giving equal results for less expenditure. The successive differentiations of middlemen, each class specializing in the performance of more limited functions, have contributed much to the progress of society. This contribution is too little recognized. Before the Industrial Revolution especially, the hand that turned the wheel of commerce was not the producing craftsman but the merchant and tradesman. After this Revolution, the successful manufacturer became to some degree a "commercant", organizing his own sales' department.[1] But a most significant feature of the period before 1760 was the almost absolute dependence of the producing class upon the trading class. It is proposed to seek out in part the specialization of functions, the means employed, and the method of action, by which the trading class performed commerce in this period.

The structure and life of four leading and representative trades have been studied separately somewhat in detail. This method of treating a combination of labor and capital devoted to one ware of commerce has the advantage of definiteness. The treatment consists in a sort of narration of the successive handlings of the ware; its progress toward and from the market is taken step by step. But the method has the disadvantage of dividing the market so much that the actual complex of interrelations existing there is little felt. It divides the market vertically and horizontally, so to speak, i.e., on the basis of ware and of agent. For instance, the corn factor at Bear Key differed from other factors with respect to the commodity handled and from other cornmen with respect to function. The fact of these double relations is likely to be overlooked and the actual intricacy of the market not appreciated.

Chapters II–VI consider the middlemen in these four groups of

---

[1] This change was noticed by contemporaries. For instance, manufacturers began to export their own goods and did the work of the merchant. Chalmers, Estimate, XXXVI.

industries; in each group that product in the handling of which the middlemen organization reached the highest development is selected for most consideration, and the other products of the group are briefly summarized. Throughout the work considerable attention is paid to the accessories of commerce which were originated, developed and employed by the middlemen in performing their business. The technique of commerce is not intelligible without knowledge of the various accessories which facilitated it and by means of which the middlemen agents performed their operations. The middleman was the correlating factor in a group of organically and genetically related businesses constituting the mechanism of commerce. To understand his position requires an interpretation embracing his relations to the transmission of wares, persons and intelligence; his relations to and employment of capital and credit; his situation geographically and socially. Chapter VII treats in a more general way the merchant and tradesman class as an economic, social and political element of the population. The writer realizes only too well that Chapter VII has less merit than the previous Chapters. Many of the topics are too general for definite and full treatment in the compass of this book; many lack the precision which makes detailed history possible; many are so mingled with social and political affairs that the economic phase can scarcely be extricated; many, as important topics as those given, are necessarily left untreated. Many generalizations are drawn for which comprehensive substantiating data are not given or cannot be had; the consequence is that they are more disputable. Writers are devoting much attention to social and economic correlations of political history, and this field will undoubtedly be quite fully developed in the near future. With a realization of these and many other shortcomings the seventh chapter is given more as a supplement than as an integral part of the book.

As will be shown in the last chapter the mercantile and trading class has been subject to much opposition from both the producers and consumers. National and municipal legislation joined with social usage to make the way of the middleman undesirable. The church and gild presumed to do his functions in a collective manner and render him unnecessary. Writers on social and economic questions were usually adverse to his interposition between producer and consumer. This was more particularly true of the medieval and Continental writers. The theory that middlemen were an unproductive and therefore an undesirable class did not gain much acceptance in English economic theory. Petty in 1662 was of the opinion that a "large proportion of these . . . . might be retrenched, who properly and originally earn nothing from the Publick, being onely a kinde of Gamesters," yet he recognized their services in being "veins and arteries, to distribute back and forth . . . . the product of Husbandry and Manufacture."[1] Locke also regarded middlemen "Brokers" as inconsistent with the public good,[2] because they retarded the circulation of money. But these opinions had but little effect and wasted in the eighteenth century before the tenet that the employment of population and labor was the fundamental riching power in a nation,[3] and that therefore goods ought to pass through as many hands as possible.[4] This theory, though resting on the economic fallacy of "making work," did favor the existence of middlemen and carriers, but hindered any change of organization which tended to reduce the number of middlemen or forced a change in their occupation. For instance, the introduction of the turnpike, stage-coach and canals was opposed by the vested interests. The doctrines of the period were therefore not opposed to the rise and perpetuation of middlemen.

Omitting the personal catering to human whims and fancies, the only justification which a middleman can offer for his existence is that by his intervention economies are realized which at least equal what he extracts from the trade for his expenses and profits. The test of this equality in a competitive market is determined by the effect his intervention in the handling of a ware has on the price of that ware. If he performs a real service to the trade the price is lowered; if he does not perform such a service the price is raised and he is eliminated. In actual trade the inertia of habit and the power of monopoly may long continue him as an unprofitable servant.

In a state of widely dispersed industry, with little local specialization, with poor means of communication and transportation, and with seasonal activity, there is excellent opportunity for the rise of a middleman class. Goods must be bought in small lots from domestic producers, and they must be sold to distant consumers in small lots. It is not profitable for each producer to carry his small product to the distant consumer; the cost of carriage and the waste of time prevent. Nor does he know nor have the means of learning where

---

[1] Petty, Treatise of Taxes, 11.

[2] Locke, Works, 11, 15.

[3] Palgrave, 1, 87; Defoe, Eng. Tr. 11, Chap. XXXVII.

[4] Defoe, Com. Eng. Tr. 11, 178, Chaps. XXXVII and XXXVIII.

consumers may be found. On account of the seasonal activity of both production and carriage, warehousing during a part of the year is necessary. Where such conditions exist a middleman may assume the function of buying from the many producers, warehousing the collected purchases, specializing in knowing the mutual wants of consumers and producers, and carrying to the distant consumers. Add to these conditions, the circumstance that foreign trade was practically limited to a few ports and was there concentrated in the hands of a few privileged merchants, and you have a presentment of the conditions existent under which the orthodox middleman class arose. As a functionary the middleman was necessary and useful: he effected economies that reduced prices to consumers and justified his intervention. As the century progressed this class increased in numbers, efficiency, and degree of specialization. The increase in the volume of trade was both cause and effect in respect to this increase.

But the middleman tends, by the development of his own efficiency, to eliminate himself from trade. He does this in several ways: as a speculator, the risks of trade are assumed by him and he specializes at reducing the very ignorance upon which speculation rears itself. He introduces better communication and cheaper transport; but this enables the producer to discover his consumers and carry his produce himself. These improvements make possible mass-production and quantity buying, travelling salesmen and mail-order business. Business is done on a bigger scale, capital is concentrated in fewer hands, and industries are integrated. The economic dependence of the producer on the middleman comes to jeopardize the producer's business by separating him from the market. The producer seizes the opportunity of dealing directly with the consumer, appealing to him by trade-marks and trade connections, learning more truly the nature of the demand for his goods, and gauging better the production of his mill. But it is apparent that the system of integrated industries was not possible until the domestic workshop had given way to the factory and production was done on a massive scale. That era was introduced by the Industrial Revolution. Until that time the tendency was for the middlemen to increase in numbers, efficiency and specialization. Since that time the economics of large production and wide distribution and the improved means of production and communication have caused a counter movement and tended to break down the orthodox system of middlemen.

The introduction of the middleman into economic life had a most profound influence in the social history of mankind. Instead of local self-sufficiency and separation, a broad economic interdependence and community of interests arose. A competitive system supplanted the medieval direct-exchange, public-market, fixed-and-just-price system. Supplies were equalized in times and places, and made less dependent upon the accidents of weather. Economic life acquired a speculative quality. The modern categories of economics arose. Business was born.

CHAPTER II.

MIDDLEMEN IN THE CORN AND CORN PRODUCTS TRADE.

The study of the middlemen handling corn and corn products covers a greater geographical part of England than the study of the dealers handling any other commodity. Of all the products of English soil corn was the most universally raised. Except for some minor parts, as the fens, the heaths, the mountains of Wales, etc., nearly every farm was in part devoted to corn. Being so closely linked with the food supplies, every farmer sought to produce enough at least for his household's consumption, and where opportunity of market existed he turned the surplus into the hands of the middlemen, on its way to consumers who were not producers and who resided principally in the cities and larger towns, or abroad.

The most characteristic phase of the general industry of England in the period, 1660 to 1760, antedating the Industrial Revolution, was the meager local specialization. By 1760 a few centers in Lancashire and Yorkshire had specialized at textile manufacturing to the degree that they gave over, comparatively speaking, agriculture and so devoted themselves to manufacturing as to become dependent upon adjacent districts for corn supplies. In other parts, as in the West of England and Norfolk, where manufacturing had long been seated, the specialization had not become so intense, and sufficient food-products were produced among the manufacturers to supply themselves.

The geographical distribution of the corn-producing regions in the century preceding the Industrial Revolution is presented in the accompanying table.[1] It is indicated that nearly every county had corn in the list of its products, and in many it was the chief crop. The counties of the South, the East, the Thames, the Severn and the Trent embrace the generality of the corn-area. The Thames district was particularly rich in corn. It was an age when agriculture was undergoing a revival after the Civil Wars and a transformation in the technical processes of cultivation and in the variety of crops; but if the testimonies of these observers can be trusted the corn area abided about the same throughout the century.

[1] See Appendix.

The present concernment is with the surplus only above the local consumption. Since the rural communities were essentially self-sufficient, this surplus did not, could not find a local market. Two outlets were open. One was exportation abroad; the other was the supply of the great cities, especially London. The study, therefore, is to trace the surplus corn from the raiser to (a) the purchaser abroad, or (b) the consumer in the great city London. One other phase suggests itself—part of this corn may be stopped enroute and manufactured into a corn product: this product and further sub-products are to be traced to the final consumer.

CORN AS A WARE.

Corn has many valuable qualities as a ware of commerce. It lends itself readily, except for weight, to transportation; it is very divisible, is durable, and has little tare. Accordingly, wherever any surplus corn finds tolerable means of transportation, it is carried to market. Its cost of carriage will be comparatively low. Its price will be more uniform over any area where communication exists than the price of most commodities. It can be warehoused; consequently when a system of business and of middlemen capitalists have arisen, there may be expected to be a more evenly supplied market and more constant prices. It can be graded and standardized, or samples can easily be carried to market: hence there may be anticipated a separation of the market into two parts, viz. the buying and selling place, and the place where the grain is actually handled. It is a prime necessity of life, and universally so; yet it is subject to the whims of the weather, its droughts and bumper crops; the dearth of one year must be equalized with the abundance of another: wherefore there is a peculiar fitness and opportunity for a speculative middleman. These various qualities— ease of handling in bulk, durability in storage, grading and classification, extensive demand, fluctuating supply but uniform demand— make corn especially subject to speculation, and occasion a class of specialized speculative traders in corn.

MARKETS.

In the manorial period the market for the surplus produce of the manor was somewhat peripatetic. The lord and his retinue moved from part to part and consumed *in situ* his portion. Besides this method of ambulatory consumption certain carrying services were required of manorial tenants.[1] Chief of these was the "averagium ad hospitium"

---

[1] Ashley, Ec. Hist. 44–5; Neilson, 19; Domesday of St. Paul, XLI et seq.

or carriage from manor to monastery. There were also the "averagium de manerio ad manerium" (from manor to manor) and "averagium ad mercatum et ad forum" (to market). No real markets existed in this intermanorial system. The system disintegrated with the break-down of the manor as a unit and as a group. Inequalities in the density of population and diversifications of occupation tended to cause territorial market areas. London was the first clearly distinct market. Its corn markets date very early: those for corn and malt brought by water were at Billingsgate and Queenhite; Graschirche and Smithfield were the markets for grain coming from the counties of Cambridge, Bedford, Huntingdon and from Ware. Those owners of corn coming from the West, "as from Barnet," sold on the pavement at Newgate. Such pavements were convenient for the deposit and exposure of their sacks. Stratford in Essex was a suburban corn-supply place for London: the corn was carried up by carts.[1] The rise of local markets is further indicated by the fact that in the Peasants Rebellion one demand was for free markets for their corn.[2]

Until the sixteenth century the metropolitan influence on the prices prevailing on the other markets of the Kingdom and consequently on the direction of corn movements was not marked. The chief reason was that its population was small and it did not exceed the other ports much in exportation. The Kingdom was divided into regular marketing districts whose conformations were determined by local facilities of transportation as river or port, by relative plentitude of corn, by nearness to foreign market, and by the numbers of the local consuming population. Prices in the upper Thames, the Severn and Cambridge districts were lowest; while in the counties of the far North and South-east they were highest. The outports as well as London exported to the continent: the Trent and Humber counties used Hull; the eastern counties Lynn Regis, Yarmouth, and Ipswich; the southern counties Chichester, Poole, and Weymouth; the Severn counties Bristol.

During the sixteenth and first half of the seventeenth century the population of London was nearly decupled and it so outran the rural parts that it could number a tenth instead of a fiftieth of the total

---

[1] Lib. Alb. I, LXXII.

[2] Rymer, VII, 317. The writer wishes to make due acknowledgment to Dr. Gras of Clark University whose excellent thesis on the early corn trade the writer has read. It is hoped that Dr. Gras will publish his work soon. In several places in this chapter the writer owes the opinions and the findings of facts to this thesis.

population of England.[1]   This remarkable urbanization had a marked effect upon the marketing of corn and the government policy relating to the corn trade.   London practically ceased exporting corn and began importing, especially in times of dearth.[2]   A corn-importing middleman organization was developed.   The metropolitan consumption necessitated the development of a coastwise corn-supply and a foreign corn-supply business.   The former sources of supply by way of the Thames and Ware and by land-transport proved insufficient.[3] Coastwise vessels at first came chiefly from Kent, but by the middle of the seventeenth century large numbers were listed in the London Port Books from Essex, Suffolk, Yarmouth, Lynn, Hull and New-castle-upon-Tyne, on the east coast, and from Southants, Devon, Cornwall and South Wales, on the south coast.   The total number of shipments more than quadrupled meanwhile.   This abnormal development of London caused a most important shift in the internal trade and markets.   Metropolitan prices became highest; prices on surrounding markets tended to vary inversely as the distance from London.[4]   The more localized markets tended to yield to the metropolitan influence.   Those counties with better facilities of transport to London found their prices rising and conforming to the London scale; as prices rose and as the means of carriage were improved the London market area was extended.

The Restoration period, 1660 to 1689, witnessed a reversal in the direction of foreign corn trade.   The necessity of importing corn for London's consumption ceased.   Instead, London became an exporting port.   The organization of importing merchants and distributors was supplanted by an organization of exporters.   The operations of exporters and importers are described under the head "Corn Merchant," below.   To whatever market or port the corn came it appears to have passed through practically the same series of middlemen; but, by reason of the larger volume of traffic, the middleman organization in connection with the London market was more extensive, clear-cut and specialized.   So for various reasons it will be more satisfactory to trace out with more detail the refinements of the system whereby London was supplied.

---

[1] See Estimates in Chap. VII; also, Blackwoods Mag. 1891: 495.

[2] Stow, Survey, 368.

[3] Rep. XVIII, 75b (17 Sept. 1573).

[4] This is evident by even casual glances at Haughton's prices 1691–1702 and might be statistically computed from these data, as Young did from data gathered some decades later: see Chap. VII on "Location" of the commercial classes.

CORNMONGERS.

From the middle of the thirteenth century there appear to have been cornmongers (bladers, bladarii) in London. They were mostly Londoners and resident there; some were mentioned from St. Albans, Fulham, Great Marlow, Stratford and other nearby towns. Though men of considerable wealth they did not obtain prominence in the city. The city offered them a varying recognition, sometimes encouraging them to buy in the country and to bring to the city, at other times laying restrictions on their dealings. One class of dealings seems to have been in the capacity of agents selling for country producers.[1] In the latter part of the fourteenth century the cornmongers were organized into a Mistery, which, apparently, lasted somewhat longer than a half century.[2] It was never an important company; the want of a monopoly of its ware—corn—was probably its greatest weakness. Cornmongers' gilds existed outside London also.[3] By 1600 a new nomenclature was arising; the terms badger, kidder, mealman, etc. displaced the more general term cornmonger.[4]

CORN BUYERS.

In some orders[5] issued by Charles I, 1630, "for . . . Preventing and Remedying of the Dearth of Graine and Victual ." . . there is, in the somewhat redundant language of public laws and decrees, a list of the middlemen concerned, at that date, in the corn trade. They are "Badgers, Kidders, Broggers, Carriers of Corne . . . Mault-makers, Bakers, Common Brewers or Tiplers . . . Buyers of Corne to sell againe . . . Buyers of Corne upon the Ground." In the Edwardian statute[6] against regrating, forestalling and ingrossing, 1552, the corn-buyers were included under the terms badger, lader, kidder, and carrier. These terms were redundant so far as the functions of the persons in the trade were concerned; for the badger was kidder, lader, and carrier, and so was each of the others, respectively. Real distinctions seem not to have existed at that time nor since, and whatever fact led a buyer to assume one appellation instead of another seems lost, for the most part, in the community of functions.

[1] Lib. Alb. I, 693, 697.
[2] Brewer, Records, 167; Unwin, Gilds, 162, 370.
[3] Gross, I, 47, 152; II, 383; Herbert, 28.
[4] Cf. Dyson, 374.
[5] See J. Massie, reprint, "Orders" 11.
[6] 5 and 6 Ed. III, Cap. 14, Sec. 7.

A. Badger.

A badger (variously spelled bager, bodger, budger) was one who bought corn or other commodities at one place and carried them elsewhere to sell;[1] an itinerant dealer who acted as middleman between the producing farmer and the consumer.[2] He was a traveling buyer, a carrier, and a seller in another market; these functions involved others such as capitalist, speculator, etc. Nor does he seem to have changed the scope of his activities in the seventeenth century; while in the eighteenth the name badger was less used and gave place to the simpler "buyer." He seems to derive his name from the "bag" or "bodge" in which he carried his grain, usually on horseback.

B. Kidder.

The kidder or kiddier performed the same function, viz. to buy from producers their provisions and carry them to some market to sell. In the legislation and decrees of the sixteenth, seventeenth, and eighteenth centuries, kidder was always joined with badger, lader, etc.—a group of terms meant to be inclusive of all who were known corn-buyers or ingrossers.[3] The origin of the name kidder is obscure. The business of a kidder is illustrated at Beverley market in Yorkshire about 1641, when on "calmedayes" "the Lincolnshire-men vente and sell a greate parte of theire oatemeale, which they carry and sell againe in Brigge Markette, and other markettes thereabouts."[4] They were inter-market dealers.

C. Lader.

A lader seems, as the name signifies, to have been one who lades. It appears by a statute[5] in 1542–3 that laders were corn-buyers who bought corn up the Severn, put it aboard "Picards" of 15 or 36 tun,

[1] New Dict.; s. v. Badger. Cf. French 'blatier;' Usher, Corn Trade.

[2] Note its use in the following years: 1641, Best, Farm Books, 101, "The badgers come farre, many of them; wherefore theire desire is to buy soone, that they may be goinge betimes, for feare of beinge nighted." 1674, Ray, No. Co. Words, s. v. Badger, "Badger, such as buy corn, or other commodities in one place, and carry them to another." 1695, Kennett, Par. Ant. Gloss., s. v. Carbody, Badger—"a carrier or retailer of Bodges or bags of corn." 1700, Gough, Myddle, 115, "His imployment was buying corne in one market towne and selling it in another . . . ."

[3] See Ray, S. and E. Co. Wds. s. v. Kidder, "Badger, Huckster, or Carrier of Goods on Horseback." (Cited in New Dict.)

[4] Surtees, 33:101.

[5] 34–5 Henry VIII, Cap. 9.

carried it down the river and harbor, and, outside the customs limits, met ocean-going ships onto which the wheat was transferred. This trade was carried on to such an extent that the ballast discharged as the corn was loaded on the latter ships was filling the channel and havens of Kingrod and Hungrod to the ruin of their commerce. From many references[1] it appears that the lader was essentially a freighter of vessels, and might or might not be master of the vessel used. His function seems distinctly that of freight-forwarder. In this capacity he was a buyer of corn to sell again, and a distinct middleman.

Another excellent illustration of the operations of a lader is found in Henry Best's method of selling his "Doddread Wheate" in Yorkshire in 1641. Samples of his wheat were sent by the salters (who were going that way) to the ship-master (or lader) and the price demanded for the wheat was stated. If they could arrive at a sale, a day was arranged for delivery of the wheat at a specified key. The lader then carried it to Newcastle or Cumberland for sale.[2] In this case the transition of the lader to the merchant is very evident.

D. *Brogger.*

Brogger (brager, bragger, broger) appears etymologically to be a corruption of broker,[3] suggesting that his function was originally as agent buyer for a principal. He was found in London in the thirteenth and fourteenth century. The corn-broker brought buyer and seller together and acted as lawful witness of the sale; by an easy step he acted as agent of one party or the other for a commission. The city government regarded him with suspicion and laid many regulations.[4] Agency for strangers was interdicted. It was a function of the Cornmongers' Mistery to elect the corn-brokers. But by the beginning of the seventeenth century this characteristic of agency was lost in the more general notion of corn-buyer and forestaller of the market. Brokers in the period 1660–1760 were classified into three classes, (a) brokers of exchange, (b) brokers of stocks, and (c) brokers of merchandise.[5] In each case broker has the sense of agent buyer, and brogger falls more nearly under the last of the three classes.

---

[1] See instances in Cart. Mon. de Ram., III, 146, 175, of the fourteenth century.
[2] Surtees, 33:100.
[3] Stowe (1754 ed.), II, V, XV; cf. 25 Hen. VIII, Cap. 1.
[4] Lib. Alb. I, 315, 586, 587.
[5] Hatton, Mer. Mag., 208.

E. *Carrier*.

The other corn-buyer mentioned in the statute against ingrossers was the carrier. There are recorded references of common carriers from the last decade of the fourteenth century.[1] At first they were engaged to carry cloth from towns, whose gilds produced surplus supplies, to colleges, etc. Their vocation gradually extended with the rising commerce of the fifteenth and sixteenth centuries to other commodities, and by this statute they were carrying corn. By the beginning of the eighteenth century it had become the general practice among the carriers to deal in the commodity as well as carry. A critic of the time (1718) said

It is also common, though a very ill custom, for Waggoners, Carriers, and others employed in conveying Provisions to London, by any sort of Carriage, not to content themselves with the reasonable Profit arising by such an Employ, but to turn Hucksters and Dealers in any kind of those Provisions, which it should be their sole Business to convey to the Market; they having by their quick and frequent passing and repassing between Town and Country, a better opportunity of knowing how the Markets are like to rise and fall; and by these means they easily draw off a considerable, though a very unjust gain, out of all Provisions of this kind.[2]

In the days when the means of communication were so poor that the dispatcher knew less of the market than the carrier, every opportunity was open to the latter to supplant his employer; he visited the markets, he carried the letters and reports of markets, sales and orders, he had the vehicles, and knew the routes: these conditions facilitated his rise to dealer. The steps were private-carrier, common-carrier, and dealer-carrier, successively. It was this quality of *dealer* that was condemned by the above-mentioned statute and critic.

LICENSE.

Before tracing farther the course of the corn in the market, it is fitting to view the general policy of internal commerce of corn and the restrictions laid on the corn-buyers. The laws, in this respect, that were in existence and service at the opening of the century to which especial attention is given in this study were the laws of 1552 and 1562, of Edward VI and Elizabeth respectively, against ingrossers, regraters and forestallers. The legislative ideal of the day was 'from farm and shop to consumer.' The legislator sought to eliminate

[1] Rogers, Ag. and Pr., 1, 660.
[2] "Essay against Forestallers," 17–18.

purchases of materials that were not to be immediately used in the
industry carried on by the purchaser himself, or consumed in his
household's sustenance.[1] The only justification of a purchase was
that the purchaser intended at once to improve or fit for use the thing
bought, or else consume it in his household. The old ideal is stated
in a pamphlet[2] thus:

> Then is this Trade most Fair and Regular, when Provisions pass from the first
> Producer of them to the last Consumer, through the hands of such Honest and
> Lawful Dealers and Manufacturers only, as are requisite to fit them for Consump-
> tion. Fairs and Markets are appointed as places of Resort or Rendezvous for the
> Parties concern'd, in which to Meet and Treat for the better carrying on of this
> mutual Exchange and Regular Circulation. Whoever therefore gets any of these
> commodities into his hands, without making them more fit for Consumption than
> they were before he had them, and without forwarding them to that End; or who-
> ever Diverts, Interrupts, or Molests any of those Meetings designed for this good
> purpose in furnishing the Public with Provisions, is most certainly an Enemy to
> this Trade, and consequently a Nuisance to his Country.

The regulations exercised over the London corn and victual markets
and customary at the opening of the fifteenth century aimed at this
direct exchange between producer and consumer. The victuals
markets were limited to special parts of the streets lest they be a nuisance to passage. Corn-buyers, called in contemporary legal French
"bladdiers," who brought corn to the city to sell were not to sell by
show or sample. They were to come to certain places established
in the city with their carts laden, and with their horses having the
loads upon them, without selling anything or getting rid of anything
until they reached these established places, as Graschirche. No corn
was to be sold till six o'clock in the morning. All ships and boats that
brought corn to sell at Billingsgate and other riparian markets were
to remain one whole day upon common sale, without selling anything
in gross. This was done so that the common people could buy what
they needed for their sustenance. There were buyers and brokers of
corn in the city who bought of the country folks who had brought it
into the city to sell. These buyers seem to have paid only part
down, the rest on credit, and frequently dealt fraudulently; heavy
penalties were inflicted for such frauds; the prevention of unfair dealing was probably the chief reason for the open public market. Forestalling was prohibited. Dealers, denizen or stranger, had to refrain

---

[1] See 4 Hen. VIII, Cap. 11; 22 Hen. VIII, Cap. 1; 5–6 Ed. VI, Cap. 7; 3–4 Ed.
VI, Cap. 6; 5–6 Ed. VI, Cap. 15; 5 Eliz., Cap. 8; 27 Eliz., Cap. 16.

[2] "Essay against Forestallers," 22.

from going to meet dealers coming by land or water with their merchandise and victuals towards the city to buy or sell. They were not to go to the Pool of the Thames to meet wines or other merchandise or go on board vessels to buy such. The ideal was to let victuals, etc. "stand for common sale by him who shall have brought the wares, that so the community may be served without regrators."[1] Thus the operations of the middlemen in corn were closely hedged about. Sales by sample and in any place out of public view were forbidden; the hours and days of purchase were prescribed. The mixture of good and bad corn "in deceit of the people," agency by way of option buying, regrating between foreign merchants in Graschirche and Newgate, forestalling goods coming by land or river—all these practices were rigidly prohibited. In addition to these direct regulations a system of customs burdened them: on the "small trades" a sort of octroi duties was levied—victuals were taxed, as were coal, timber, pottery, etc.—when they were brought into the city; and if the carrier set them down from his back, his horse's back or his cart an extra stallage fee was imposed.[2] Under all these burdens it is not surprising that mercantile life made little headway.

Regrating, however, was not unknown. There is evidence that the laws and regulations were not rigidly enforced against the regrator. After the good folks of the city "had bought as much as they had a necessity for their use" the regrator might buy up victuals.[3] Warehousing and selling in gross received some public sanction.[4] Aliens were allowed to warehouse their grain for forty days and "sell it in their storehouses and granaries." Regrators bought up grain and held it for higher prices, as modern speculators do.[5]

In provincial parts of the Island ingrossers sometimes found opportunity for business.[6] During the sixteenth century "some Ingrossers, who" bought "Wheat of the husbandman—and deliver(ed) it to the transporting Merchant" were operating in Cornwall.[7] The officers of the ports also made use of the public funds left in their hands by ingrossing corn. They were the occasion of grievous complaints by the farmers.[8]

---

[1] Lib. Alb. I, 260–271; III, 79–93; for further details, Lib. Alb. LXXXIII.
[2] Lib. Alb. III, 65–7.
[3] Lib. Alb. I, 270.
[4] Ibid., 261.
[5] Paris, V, 673; Rymer, 11, pt. 1. 597.
[6] Harrison, II, c. 18; Acts P. C., VIII. 108.
[7] Carew, Cornwall, 54.
[8] Cal. S. P. Dom. 1591–4, 362; Hist. MSS. Com. Rep. XIII. App., pt. IV, 29.

The statute of 1552 was not a new departure in trade policy[1] but was passed to supply the defect of "good Laws and Statutes against Regrators and Ingrossers" and to explain more definitely the meaning of "Forestaller, Regrator or Ingrosser."[2] This legislation was occasioned by the rapid growth of London. The Tudor corn-policy was dictated in no small degree by the consuming population as against the producing population. The supply of corn brought to the city by the medieval methods proved insufficient for her consumption. The city resorted to various devices for procuring and assuring a steady, dependable corn supply. In the twelfth year of Henry VIII London initiated the "prest and loone" or system of voluntary contributions of money by citizens for provisioning the city with corn. Lists were taken of those who contributed to this purpose.[3] Between 1578 and 1678 the city tried the system of imposing contributions of corn on the twelve livery companies; this method was spasmodically used and was at its acme about 1587; after this date it declined and was revived occasionally in times of dearth during the rest of the century of its existence. Henry VIII tried also the public granary system. The granary was known as the "Bridgehouse."[4] At first it was used by the city, king and private parties, but later was given over to the exclusive use of the city. The city somewhat intermittently bought up yearly supplies of corn for storage against dearth. This was abandoned in 1578.

The anxiety of the metropolis to attract corn to itself in the Tudor period is further illustrated in numerous ways; for instance, the supervision of the millers and bakers and the establishment of the assize of bread;[5] the removal of the town-tolls;[6] and the encouragement of foreign merchants.[7] Under Elizabeth and the early Stuarts the Justices of the Peace were ordered in times of dearth[8] to gather information as to the amount of surplus corn held by producers and buyers

[1] For biblical teachings on these methods of trade see G. A. Smith Dict. s. v. Jerusalem, 1, 316; for early London legislation and customs on the matter see Lib. Alb. I, 263, 270; III, 81–2; Lib. Cus.,312; for restrictions on the corn badger during the sixteenth and seventeenth centuries see Thornbury, II, 180; Rep. VI, 3b; XV, 132; XVII, 66.

[2] 5–6 Ed. VI, Cap. 14, Sec. 1.

[2] Rep. XI, 60; XL, 176, B; XIV, 350 b.

[4] 5 Henry VIII, Rep. II, 149 b; VII, 149–182.

[5] Rep. II, 140; IX, 74 b; XII, pt. 1, 125.

[6] Jor. C. C. XII, 370.

[7] Rep. V, 267; VII, 247.

[8] 1586–7, 1594, 1608, 1619–22, 1630.

in their several jurisdictions and to provide for its sale in the interest of the consumer.[1]

It was in line with this anxiety for the metropolitan consumer that Edward felt constrained to define more particularly who was forestaller, regrator and ingrosser, by this statute of 1552. It defined Forestaller as " . . . whatsoever Person or Persons . . . (a) buy . . any Merchandise, Victual or any other thing whatsoever, coming by land or by water toward any city, Port, . . . from Parts beyond the Sea to be sold . . . (b) make any Bargain or Contract or Promise for the having or buying the same . . . before the said Merchandise . . . shall be in the Market, Fair, City, Port, . . . ready to be sold; . . . (c) make any Motion by Word, Letter, Message, or otherwise, to any Person . . . for the inhancing of the Price . . . (d) dissuade . . . any Person coming to the Market or the Fair, to abstain or forebear to bring or convey any of the things . . . to any market, Fair, City, Port, . . . to be sold . . . "[2] Regrator was defined as "whatsoever Person or Persons . . . shall by any Means regrate, obtain, or get into his or their Hands or Possession, in any Fair or Market, any Corn, Wine, Fish, . . . that shall be brought to any Fair or Market . . . to be sold, and do sell the same again in any Fair or Market holden or kept in the same Place, or in any other Fair or Market within Four Miles thereof . . . ."[3]

Lastly, it defined Ingrosser as "whatsoever Person or Persons . . . shall ingross or get into his or their Hands, by buying, contracting or promise-taking . . . any Corn, . . . Butter, Cheese, . . . to the Intent to sell the same again . . ."[4]

The statute prohibited all three practices under severe penalties. But the exceptions[5] specifically allowed to these general prohibitions bring out the purpose of the law. For instance, a person might buy corn to convert into malt or oatmeal in his own house; a fishmonger, butcher or poulterer might buy materials used in his craft if he sold them at reasonable prices; likewise innholders and other victuallers. A list of prices for the different grains was fixed in the statute,[6] at or under which it was lawful for any person (not forestalling) to buy,

---

[1] For illustration of such order see Acts P. C. XIV, 338; Leonard, 318–26.

[2] 5–6 Ed. VI, Cap. 14, Sec. 2.

[3] Ibid., Sec. 2.

[4] Ibid., Sec. 3.

[5] Ibid., Sec. 7.

[6] Ibid., Sec. 13.

ingross and keep corn in his granary. Another exception was made in favor of certain badgers and drovers who were to be licensed to ingross and regrate but not to forestall. This license system was the new feature of the law, and the origin of the huckster's license now so common.

These licenses[1] were to be issued to badgers, laders, kidders, and carriers of "Corn, Fish, Butter or Cheese." The issuance was committed into the hands of three Justices of the Peace of the county wherein the candidate badger lived. They enabled the licensed to buy and sell in open and regular market unrestrained by the laws against regrating and ingrossing; to transport corn freely from one port or place within the realm to another provided the grain be shipped within sixty days after its purchase with reasonable expedition to the place the cockets named as destination, and a certificate be gotten at the unlading place from the Customer of the Port directed to the Customer of the Port clearing the grain.

It was made evident by these exceptions and the license system introduced that it was not designed to stop the wheels of trade that had been started, but rather to regulate it, and make the food supply more constant and sure by removing and restraining certain practices which seemed like harmful excrescences on the customary course of trade, and by forcing the wares of trade to go through the open public market and fair. That the system did not repress trade intolerably is evident.[2] Without doubt the law confining the sale of corn to market towns worked serious injury to the small husbandman. In 1623 Nottinghamshire complained against this restriction. Many of the small agriculturists did not have the horses wherewith to convey their corn to these distant markets; the townsmen badgers were thus given an advantage over the husbandmen, who preferred to market nearer home.[3] But it appears that the farmers added to their sales at the weekly market by selling "at home to their neighbors the rest of the weeke."[4] The Justices seem to have issued licences freely in some parts and the clamors for local equality of treatment tended to draw others to the same practice. Bishop Hooper in the year the law went into effect said:

[1] 5–6 Ed. VI, Cap. 14, Secs. 7, 12.

[2] Cf. opinions of Faber, 66, and Naudé, 20. The restraint on the coastwise trade in the fourteenth and fifteenth and sixteenth centuries was really only one of supervision, to guard against shipping abroad under guise of coastwise trade.

[3] S. P. Dom. Jas. I, CXL, 10; V. C. H., Nott., II. 288.

[4] Carew, Carnwall, 54.

The Statute of Regrators is so usid that in many quarters of these partes it will do little good; and in some parts, where as license by the Justices will not be grauntyd, the people are mouche offended, that they should not, as well as others, bagge, as they were wont to do.[1]

So many licenses were issued that ten years later the statute was amended and further limitations laid by way of qualifications for those eligible to license. The amendment states that

Such a great Number of Persons seeking only to live easily, and to leave their honest labour, have and do daily seeke to be allowed and licensed to the said Offices and Doings, being most unfit and unmeet for those purposes, and also very hurtful to the Commonwealth of this Realm, as well as by the inhauncing of the Prices of Corn . . . . as also by diminishing of the Number of good and necessary Husbandmen.[2]

These allegations have scarcely a pith of economic truth in them as reasons for reducing the number of badgers; nevertheless, on the basis of these assumptions, hereafter no one was to be licensed who had not lived the previous three years in the county in which he would be licensed, who was not married, and who was not a householder rather than a servant or retainer to another person. The time of the license was restricted to one year,[3] and provision was made whereby a badger might procure a *special* license for buying "Corn or Grain out of open Fair or Market to sell again" but this license had to contain "special and express words . . . that he . . . may do so."[4] A slight fee was charged for the license and a register kept of all licenses issued.

Such was the legislation which existed a century later, in 1660. During this century the system seems to have operated quite uniformly, trade fell in with the license system, custom mollified the erratic features, and the business of the market and fair was done in general[5] in the prescribed public and open way. But immediately after the Restoration the system began to break and lose its customary grip. In 1663 Charles II enacted a law[6] for the encouragement of agriculture, (a) permitting exportation of corn when the prices of

[1] Strype, Cranmer, II, 628.

[2] 5 Eliz., Cap. 12, Sec. 3.

[3] Ibid., Sec. 4.

[4] Ibid., Sec. 7.

[5] The law was not rigidly enforced. In times of dearth a sort of public recognition was given the regrator; see Book of Orders, extensive quotations from which are given in Leonard, 318–26.

[6] 15 Chas. II, Cap. 7.

corn at home fell to certain prices listed;[1] and (b) permitting the ingrossing of corn when it fell to certain prices listed.[2]

Hereafter, while wheat was 48*s* or lower anyone might engage in
the trade, buying and storing it, or buying and exporting it.   Many
who had not the qualifications that would entitle them to a badger's
license were now free to badge when they saw fit.   Hence the statute
of 1663 virtually repealed the statutes of 1552 and 1562 intermittently,
that is, every time the abundance of wheat or other events forced the
price down to 48*s*.   It not only repealed it intermittently but
locally also, since the price at certain ports might be lower than at
others.   Confusion was thus introduced into the system.

Besides the badgers could only be licensed at the Quarter Sessions;
if out of or between these sessions the price of wheat rose above the
legal 48*s*, according to law those not licensed would have to stop buying and selling till the sessions opened, and those not qualified to
take out licenses would have to stop indefinitely.   It is idle to suppose
that either was done, nor would it be desirable.   Those who had involved their capital in the trade could not and would not thus readily
leave it off; and their experience in the trade would have made them
most competent to conduct it.[3]   The Act of 1663 was therefore an
opening wedge in the rigid restraint laid by law upon the middlemen
of the corn trade.

Another dissolving element was a practice newly resorted to of
selling corn by samples.[4]   Doubtless this arose as a simple economy
of carriage expense.[5]   The practice was but beginning in 1718 when
it was thus described:

---

[1] The prices set were wheat, 48*s*, barley, 28*s*, oats, 13*s* 6*d*, the quarter.   When
corn reached these prices "then it shall be lawful for all and every Person and Persons to ship, load, carry and transport any of the said Corns or Grains, from the
Havens or Places where they shall be of such Prices, unto any Ports beyond the
Seas as Merchandise."   Sec. 2.

[2] The prices were the same as above.   When corn reached these, "then it shall
be lawful for all and every Person and Persons (not forestalling nor selling the same
in the Market within three Months after buying thereof) to buy in open Market,
and to lay up   .   .   .   and sell again, such Corn   .   .   .   without incurring any
Penalty."   Sec. 2.

[3] Smith, Corn Trade, 8–9, presents this view.

[4] Sales of corn *by sample* are mentioned in the regulations of the London markets
as early as 1420; see Lib. Alb., III, 79.   Its practice must have been limited, and
was prohibited by ordinance.

[5] Gent. Mag., 1756: 623; Pitt, Staffordshire, 231.

Others (farmers) bring only Parcels of Corn in a Bag or Handkerchief, which are called Samples; and these are expos'd, perhaps, in private Houses, to a few Jobbers or Engrossers.[1]

Carrying grain to a market where buyers were contingent and sales unsure or even forced by the expense of carrying it home again, and carrying it to a market and past possibly the very man's door who might buy it, were foolish operations, viewed in the light of ease and savings accruing by the device of sales by samples. Farmers having grain to sell needed only to carry a small sample of the grain to market and make known the quantity they had to sell like the sample; when buyers had been found, the delivery was done with less expenditure of effort and time.

The method naturally lent itself to large buying. Defoe describes the tendency about 1740 thus:

The factor looks on the sample, asks his price, bids and then buys; and away they go together to the next inn, to adjust the bargain, the manner of delivery, the payment, etc.; thus the whole barn, or stack, or mow of corn, is sold at once.[2]

Large buyers thus had a vast advantage after 'sample' sales were devised: heretofore a load or two, which the farmer could bring up to market, constituted the maximum sale, and most buyers were able to buy; but now the farmer would prefer a buyer who could take all he had to sell rather than bargain with many small buyers; and if a small buyer wanted to buy he had to pay more than the larger.[3]

Selling by samples was chiefly carried on in those market-towns which were at a small distance from London, or at least from the river Thames, such as Romford, Dartford, Grayes, Rochester, Maidstone, Chelmsford, Malden, Colchester, Ipswich, Morgate and Whitstable. By 1750 it was quite the general practice and even very "small markets" like Lamborne and Kingscleer sold "a large quantity of corn by sample."[4] Each of these markets presented an appearance at odds with the accustomed corn-market. Instead of the vast number of horses and wagons of corn on market day, there were crowds of farmers, with their samples, and buyers such as mealmen, millers, bakers, corn-buyers, brewers, etc., thronging the market; and on the days between markets the farmers carried their corn to the hoys and

[1] "Essay against Forestallers," 20.
[2] Defoe, Com. Eng. Tr., II, 181. The practice is well described by one Lechmere in the House of Commons; see Parl. Hist., Vol. 32, 237.
[3] V. C. H., Oxford, II, 203.
[4] Pococke, II, 50, 58.

received their pay.[1]   The effects of sales by sample were noted in Oxford market for instance, where it was said a load of corn was rarely seen, whereas fifteen years earlier it was difficult to find room for the corn wagons.[2]   Thus there was arising a differentiation in the market between the place of selling and the place of handling and shipping.

But this device at once became a means of forestalling and speculation.[3]   The actual corn was kept from the market, and the volume of corn ready to come to the market or by sample already on the market could only be guessed by a view of the samples and the amount represented by each.   But if the display of samples were intrusted to agents or representatives at the market, the way was open to manipulation, for the agents needed only to display what samples and as many samples as they cared to.   The apparent volume of corn on the market was subject to the varying touch of manipulators whose deceptions brought them profits.   The actual working of this speculation will be treated later, but it is here mentioned to show it an active principle in disintegrating the market system.

Another weakness in this system of licensed buyers was in the execution of the law.   The license was issued by the Justices of the Peace, and they were also the ones who cared for the punishments of its violations.   But these Justices were burdened with a variety of other affairs and could not question and supervise every sale or contract made in their jurisdictions.   Unless information was lodged against a buyer, a thing not at all likely since it was only known to two persons both of whom profited by the sale and purchase, many an unlawful purchase passed uncaught.   Besides, the Justices themselves were very likely the wealthier men of the districts and the most likely buyers.   As a critic said:

Because the information and prosecution upon those laws have been left at large, and to every one's discretion it must follow, that unless a particular set of men be especially enabled and empowered to enquire into, detect, pursue, and effectually suppress the offenders in every one of these kinds, the remedy must fall short of the distemper.[4]

During the seventeenth century the economic function of corn-buyers found occasional recognition.   In the clothing districts of

---

[1] Defoe, Com. Eng. Tr., II, 181.
[2] V. C. H., Oxford, II, 203.
[3] Defoe, Com. Eng. Tr., II, 182.
[4] "Essay against Forestallers," 30-1.

Somerset some of the hundreds were losing their rural character and there was a "great neglect of tillage upon many great farms." Frome Hundred, for instance, became dependent upon Wiltshire for its chief supply of corn. Such hundreds defended the presence of badgers as necessary for their food supply. Six were admitted in Hartfliffe and Bedminster to provision Bristol in 1623.[1] It was reported in this district "that the constant viewing and searching for corn caused an imminent dearth" and thus defeated its very purpose. Gradually the assize of corn was abandoned and badgers more freely licensed, with the hope and opinion that their freer operations would equalize prices better.[2] About the same time the Justices of the Peace sometimes employed badgers in the parishes to buy corn and sell it to the poor "12*d* in every bushel better cheaper than it did cost."[3]

In 1718 a critic and most virulent pamphleteer and ardent defender of the old system gave ample testimony that the old system was decadent and that trade was breaking the shackles of non-speculating market methods. The badger, lader, kidder, and carrier acquired bad reputations and became contemned on the charge of regrating, etc. The dictionaries hereafter defined the terms badger, etc., as "an ingrosser, a fore-buyer, or forestaller of the market, one that buyeth corn and other provisions beforehand,"[4] and anyone who had the ability to "get an acquaintance, or make an interest, or find credit, at once set up . . . to buy and sell" as he pleased.[5] There thus arose a more general set of corn-buyers and the old nomenclature of badgers, laders, kidders, and carriers gave place to the new of buyer, ingrosser, jobber, and hawker. Their functions were essentially the same except that their freedom gave them greater opportunity to perform them better; they bought, stored, carried, sold, and speculated more freely and extensively than heretofore. Growing capital and easier means of communication furthered their operations. For these and various reasons they became a more numerous and prominent class, and their operations attracted the public attention more.

In times of famine the stores of the ingrossers of corn were especially envied and corn riots became quite the fashion by the middle of the

---

[1] S. P. Dom. Jas. 1, CXLIV, 24; V. C. H., Somers, II, 308.
[2] Somers, Rec. Soc., XXIII–XXIV passim.   Sessions R. bk. II, pt. I; V. C. H., Somers, II, 308.
[3] V. C. H. Sussex, II, 194.
[4] Robertson, Phr. Gen., 196.
[5] "Considerations on the Present," 15.

eighteenth century.[1]   In 1693 a mob at Banbury, at Chipping Norton, and at Charlburg "took away the corne by force out of the waggons, as it was carrying away by the ingrossers, saying they were resolved to put the law in execution, since the magistrates neglected it."[2] The vehemence of the corn riot was not less virulent than the vehemence of the pen that wrote:

> Every Buyer and Consumer . . . . is miserably Impos'd upon, cheated and Oppressed, by this Villainous Cabal and Confederacy of Blood Suckers, the very Pest of Societies, ar.d Vermin of the Body Politick.[3]

The policy of the government in dealing with the corn-buyers in such times of dearth shows that it sympathized to a greater or less extent with this opinion.   For instance, in the famines of 1586–87, 1619–22 and 1630–31 it dealt rigorously with the corn-men.   The Privy Council in 1587 ordered the Justices of Peace to appoint juries in each county to return the number of persons in the household of every owner of grain in barns, etc., the amount of such grain, the "badgers, kidders, broggers or carriers of corne," the "malt-makers, bakers, comen brewers or tiplers," and the "greate buyers of corne." Then whatever surplus each had above that requisite for his family's food he was ordered to bring to be sold "in open market."[4]   Sometimes they were ordered to bring definite quantities of these food supplies to the various markets.[5]   The object of these restraints was to prevent badgers and other corn-buyers from buying corn to resell at an increased price through the necessities of the starving poor.   In 1622 the sheriff of Somerset notified the Council that the "disorderly proceedings toward persons going to market with corn" had been suppressed but that the unemployed spinners and weavers tended "to mutiny."[6]   The same course of action as in Elizabeth's time was again applied.   Some corn masters sold corn at their homes to the poor on credit also.[7]   In 1630 the justices of Sussex ordered that no

[1] Gent. Mag., 1740: 3550; 1756: 608.   "The risings of the people in several places of late, and the mischief done at those times, by pulling down and demolishing mills, breaking open granaries, stopping carriages and boats laden with corn for market, or going from one part of the nation to another where it is more wanted, and violently carrying away flour and grain of all kinds, in open defiance of law   . . . ."

[2] V. C. H., Oxford, II, 199; Wood, Life and Times, III, 319–446.

[3] "Essay against Forestallers," 27.

[4] Leonard, Early Hist. Poor Relief, 85 ff.

[5] V. C. H., Oxford, II, 193; Bucks, II, 74; S. P. Dom. Eliz., 199, No. 43.

[6] Cal. S. P. Dom. Jas. I, 1622, p. 392.

[7] S. P. Dom. Jas. I, 142, No. 44; V. C. H., Bucks, II, 76.

corn should be sold in the markets to any but the poor until two hours after the market bell had been rung; they reduced the number of badgers who were suspected to be forestallers; and ordered all malt-sters who had engrossed any quantity of grain to serve the market weekly at a reasonable rate.[1] In Rutland Sir John Wingfield wrote that he had "taken order that ingrossers of corne should be carefullie seen unto and that there is no Badger licensed to carrye corn out of this countye" and had "refrayned the maullsters from excessive mak-ing of mault and . . . suppressed 20 alehouses."[2] These in-terferences of the government in the corn-markets succeeded in their purpose, namely, to reduce prices. It was an unpopular action in the larger corn-markets, of course. Wycombe, for instance, pro-tested against the low prices gotten by the corn-dealers and farmers, and showed that by reason of these forced losses the farmers ceased setting aside corn for the poor as formerly.[3]

The ingrosser, having once attained to uncommon wealth, exercised a considerable empire over the markets and fairs at which he was a buyer. His purchases were so large that he could practically fix prices at which the others had to buy or lose the chance of buying at all. This dominance would naturally stimulate an inveterate jeal-ousy on the part of the poorer buyer and provoke corn-riots and repeated efforts to revise the Edwardian legislation.[4]

The corn-buyers operated especially at markets and fairs, although, as the laws against forestalling fell into desuetude, they made farm-to-farm canvass of the districts in which they bought, buying directly from the farmers. Especially was this so after they had once estab-lished relations with the farmers by buying from them by samples at the market.[5] Thereafter they would call on the farmer and the latter troubled himself no more to come to the market. Certain markets favorably situated in good corn districts and with good water-com-munications became prominent as corn-markets, and the prices pre-

---

[1] S. P. Dom. Chas. I, 177, No. 61; V. C. H., Sussex, II, 194.

[2] Cal. S. P. Dom., 1629–31, p. 414; V. C. H., Rutland, I, 241.

[3] S. P. Dom. Chas. I, 177, No. 50; V. C. H., Bucks, II, 77.

[4] For such an effort at revival see, Edward, Bishop of Durham, Engrossing of Corn, 11; ditto, Gent. Mag., 1740: 355.

[5] Defoe, Com. Eng. Tr., II, 181. The business of the badger in 1587 is shown at South Stoke, Oxford, where an unlicensed badger had bought 40 quarters of barley at £17 the score, and had not paid; another had bought "on the grounde" four acres of winter corn, ten acres of barley, and two acres of pulse, for £20; four acres in another place for £4, and sixteen acres for £11. S. P. Dom. Eliz. CXCVIII, 56; V. C. H., Oxf., II, 194.

vailing in these bore a regular relation to those of London.[1] About 1750 the *Gentleman's Magazine* was publishing regularly the prices of corn that prevailed in the following markets: Basingstoke, Reading, Farnham, Henley, Guilford, Warminster, Devizes, Gloucester, and Crediton. These were the principal markets whence the London supply was drawn. The corn-markets of importance mentioned by Pococke in north interior of England were Cross Hall and Orms-kirk and Prescot.[2] Farnham Market, Surrey, was "the greatest Corn-Market in England, London excepted; particularly for Wheat," and in 1738 it was reported that as many as "eleven hundred Teams of Horse, all drawing Waggons, or Carts, loaden with Wheat; every Team supposed to bring a Load, . . . Forty Bushels of Wheat," might be counted on a market day.[3]

This carriage of corn to market in these districts by wagon and cart developed very early, for in 1663 a special act[4] was passed to improve the roads, since "in many of which places the road, by reason of the great and many loads which are weekly drawn in waggons through the said places, as well by reason of the great trade of barley and malt that cometh to Ware, and so is conveyed by water to the city of London, as other carriages . . . is very ruinous, and become almost impassable." The corn thus assembled at the markets was bought by the corn-buyers, carried to the milling districts, like Guilford and Hertfordshire and upper Thames towns, whence it found its way by water or land carriage to London.[5] Kingston, Henley, Great Marlow, Reading, and Abingdon were towns of great embarkation on the Thames, for the great quantities of malt and meal brought from the neighboring towns and loaded on barges for London.[6]

This long legislative contest against the rise of middlemen in the corn business was at basis a struggle between the economic interests of the locality and of the metropolis. The local public market system was designed to serve primarily the local community with a sure supply of necessities. Only after the denizens had had opportunities to buy and the real existence of a surplus was thereby known were any non-freemen permitted to buy. The consumptive wants of the home-town were to be satisfied before buyers for the metropolitan

[1] Gent. Mag., 1756: 575; 1758: 278.
[2] Pococke (1750), I, 207, 209.
[3] Defoe, Tour, I, 213–14.
[4] 15 Chas. II, Cap. 1.
[5] Defoe, Com. Eng. Tr., II, 175.
[6] Defoe, Tour, II, 54-5.

supply dare operate. The rise of the badger through the device of the license and sample sale represent therefore the growing ascendency of the metropolitan and wholesale markets over the local direct-sale public markets. This ascendency meant a centralization of the corn trade and a concentration of demand for corn in metropolitan centers. And this concentration was fraught with danger to the supply for the local communities. The price hereafter was practically determined by the London price: whereas formerly the supply and demand upon the immediate local market fixed the price there. Unless the denizens were willing to pay the London price, less the transportation charge, more than the actual surplus above the local consumptive want moved toward London. There was effected an equalization of supply and of price.

Meanwhile business methods had somewhat changed in direction. The husbandmen were formerly the active agents in getting the corn to market. They carried or caused to be carried to the market the excess of corn not needed for their own consumption; they were their own salesmen there. Some of them or the badgers bought the community's surplus and carried it to other markets. But with the rise of the wholesale and metropolitan trade the wholesale merchant became the active agent and master of the trade. This middleman, as will appear shortly, engaged factors resident and itinerary who went to the markets and the estates and bought up the grain and cared for forwarding it to their principal. Thus concentrated, the trade underwent a thorough organization, marked by the continuous movement of corn to the metropolitan wholesale markets, which corn left the husbandmen, not with the intention of satisfying the local consumption first, but of satisfying the wholesale-market demand directly.

In concluding this sketch of the corn-buyer it is proper to consider the peculiar function of the raw-material or extractive-products buyer. In the first place, he is an assembler. The exporter, the miller, the brewer, the mealman, the merchant—want their materials or wares in great quantities. It would be economically burdensome if each of these had to perform all the perambulations and dickering and carrying done by these buyers in order to procure the large volumes of materials needed. This specialization of buying and bringing together is therefore an economic advantage. He buys from many, assembles, and sells to few.[1]

[1] For a contemporary opinion to this effect with respect to the corn buyer see "Legislation and Commerce of Corn," 292.

In the second place, they are speculators. "They assume the commercial risk for the privilege of making any profit that may arise from a change of price in harmony with their predictions."[1] They pay at one market a price and the producer has an immediate return. They specialize in estimating future prices or prices elsewhere: in either case, time or places are equalized in supplies, and the prices become more stable over periods of time and more uniform among intercommunicating parts. Calculability of prices gives business confidence and increases the volume of business done.

FACTOR.

Factors are agents of their principals. They do not assume the entire commercial risk as the corn-buyers and jobbers and merchants do. Their function is not speculation. Their earnings are not the profits, the difference between a cost and a selling price, be it high or low. Their function is to effect exchanges of commodities by bringing buyer and seller together. Special training and experience put them in a position to aid both buyer and seller: they build up an acquaintance and correspondence with both classes, and ease the way for transactions between them. They are salesmen and buyers for others on the accounts of these others.

Corn-factors arose very early. As buyers of corn in local markets, they were treated under the head "Broggers."[2] A large consumer or exporter of corn, being a large buyer, would employ a brogger or factor to assist at buying. As the corn trade developed, factors set up at each considerable market or port and established a correspondence with factors at other markets and ports, and were ready to buy or sell on that market for any who might need their services. As the "New Agriculture" spread in the eighteenth century, the "Engrossing Farmer"[3]—the landed gentleman who threw together several estates and made large-capital farms, or the renter who rented several farms situate adjacent—began to employ factors to do his selling. The fact, therefore, that corn factors were quite well distributed over England, must not be overlooked while this study deals particularly with the London group.

London possessed two great corn markets, Bear Key and Queen Hithe. The latter had been the chief landing place of the upper

---

[1] "Mod. Bus.," II, 41.

[2] See treatment above.

[3] See "Considerations on the Present," 7–10; "The Prices of Provisions," 16; "Flour Trade and Dearness," 19–20; "Abuses Relative to Provisions," 4.

Thames valley corn, coming by way of the Thames barges, as early as the thirteenth century[1] and in 1722 was the chief market for malt[2] which still came by the same route and conveyance. Bear Key was the great mart to which, as was said, "comes all the vast Quantity of Corn that is brought into the City by Sea, from the Counties which lie commodious for that Carriage" and was only excelled as a corn-market by the markets in Holland at times.[3] Market was held here on Mondays, Wednesdays and Fridays. Here, on account of its nearness to the coasting vessels, the factors and dealers carried on their business exposed to the weather and other inconveniences. But about the middle of the eighteenth century the factors operating there bought a parcel of ground and erected the "Corn Exchange" in Mark Lane. Hereafter Mark Lane became the center of the corn trade of England.[4] During the next half-century the manner and conditions of conducting the corn trade did not change, except in volume.[5]

This exchange was erected as a private enterprise and property, and divided into eighty shares, which were held by factors, buyers, and Kentish hoymen. The property was given in trust to a committee who were in entire control; the committee was chosen by the proprietors. Inside the Exchange stands were erected on which samples might be displayed; the stands, 72 in number, were rented to factors and dealers; the proprietors would allow no more stands to be built, and only re-let those when vacant. The Exchange was nominally open to all who cared to buy and sell, but since sample-selling was the vogue and stands were necessary and the number of stands was limited, it was practically impossible for anyone not a member of the exchange to carry on the trade of factor to any material extent. There were a few instances of persons attending the market, who brought samples in their pockets, and sold thus to a limited degree. Every opportunity and inclination were open to the factors to favor those of their calling and be partial in the manner of transferring and leasing the stands. They could restrain the increase in number of factors by refusing to lease to a would-be factor and giving the preference to a person who would only operate as jobber. The number of

[1] Wheatley and Cunningham, London, III, 142.
[2] Defoe. Tour, II, 174.
[3] Ibid., 174; Hatton, New View, II, 784.
[4] Rep. from Com. H. C., IX, 144, 153.
[5] Ibid., IX, 148, testimony of Joseph Stonard, a Corn Factor during this period, given 1801.

factors having stands decreased, therefore, and by the end of the century the Exchange was practically in the control of fourteen factors. They thus monopolized the advantages of being factor on the Corn Exchange.[1]

The factors were employed on the consignment plan. Farmers or buyers of corn would consign it to their factors at Bear Key or the Corn Exchange at their own risk and empower the factors to sell it at the best market price they could, on commission.[2] They sold the wheat to millers and exporting factors; the barley to maltsters and distillers; the oats and beans to jobbers and dealers; and the tick-beans to shipping factors for the West Indies.[3]

Occasionally factors dealt on their own account on the side; of course, to the extent they did this they passed from the field of factor to that of jobber or merchant. For example, they employed agents to buy where corn was most plentiful and most conveniently shipped and received it into granaries hired for the purpose; thus turning from factor to jobber.[4] Others imported corn on their own account. But generally the factors abstained from such dealings considering "that the business of a Corn Factor is perfectly distinct from that of a Corn Merchant, because a person who receives consignments, and deals at the same time on his own account, may not always be inclined to serve his employers with that impartiality he otherwise would do."[5]

The coast parts of Kent marketed their corn in a manner differing from other parts of England. Their corn was sent up about once every fortnight by the farmers for the most part, and was sold on the Exchange by Kentish hoymen, a particular class who had stands on the Exchange. When their corn was disposed of, they would make out an account of sales for the inspector of the Exchange and return home.[6] These hoymen combined the several functions of ship-master, super-cargo, and factor on the Exchange.

Some practices of the factors are interesting. Mention has been made of "stands" for "samples." The factor was not obliged to display all his samples at the same time. On each sample displayed the volume of like kind for sale was indicated by placard attached;

---

[1] The validity of the facts of this paragraph rests upon testimonies given before a Parliamentary Inquiry Commission. See Rep. from H. C., IX, 144, 145, 148, 154.

[2] Rep. from H. C., IX, 146; Gent. Mag., 1751: 510.

[3] Ibid., 146.

[4] Gent. Mag., 1751: 510; "Abuses Relative to Provisions," 27–28.

[5] Rep. from Com. H. C., IX, 144.

[6] Ibid., 146–147.

hence, if all the samples were shown the total supply of the market would be known. But the factors concealed part of their samples at times, and by varying the ostensible supply in this manner they could manipulate prices to a limited degree.[1] Factors doing an exte sive business and having broad correspondence could keep good care of the probabilities of the supply of the market, and could adjust their display of samples accordingly. And since the supply was so dependent upon the accidents of weather and sea, and was so very fluctuating, it is a fair inference that this practice of withholding samples from display actually steadied the volume on the market and the prices accordingly.

Another practice was "selling in runs;" which is thus described: "There is scarce any instance where a vessel bringing corn from the Farmers has a cargo consigned to one Factor—it generally happens that such cargoes are consigned to four, five, or six Factors. What is consigned to each Factor of the same species of Corn in general is sold to one buyer, and the Factor, respectively settles the value of each person's consignment, according to the quantity, so as in the whole to render as near the aggregate amount as he can. Corn sold in this manner is called 'being sold in runs.' "[2] This practice served several purposes: it economized labor and time and effort by rendering so many small sales into one large one; it made possible a greater dispatch of the vessel, which otherwise might be hung up by some unsold parcel of corn; it was more desirable likewise to the buyer to buy in bulk and not have so many factors to deal with.

A final consideration is the factors' influence on prices. Charges and denials were very common as to factors fixing prices on the Exchange.[3] It was to the interest of all factors who were selling for farmers, corn-buyers, etc., to keep up and increase the prices of corn, for in this way they recommended themselves to their principals and also reaped a higher commission. This was especially true also of those factors who did jobbing or exporting and importing on the side. Coupled with these incentives they had the means and facilities for advancing the price. Their manipulations of their monopoly of the Exchange and of their samples might readily effect increase of price. Given the power, means and incentive, were there not other considerations, it would be a tenable presumption that the factors did raise

[1] Rep. from Com. H. C., IX, 144, 149, 151.

[2] Ibid., 149, 155.

[3] For examples, see "Considerations on the Present," 12, 27; "Sentiments of a Corn Factor," 13–14.

the general price level and that there was some justice in the public clamor against them. There were counter incentives, however. The rise in price reacts on the volume and ease of sales, and in the long run the increase in price might reduce the total commissions and elicit disgust from the farmer because of delayed sales. The factor, most probably, weighed such considerations and according to his foresight, skill, craft, financial standing, etc., moderated his actions so as to reap the greatest good from his monopoly privileges.

JOBBER.

Jobbers are essentially speculators. They "are those who, conceiving there is a probability of the markets rising, will make very large purchases for the sake of selling again at an advanced price, or retailing it out,"—"who attend the Market for the express purpose of buying Grain to resell on the same market day, or within a day or two afterwards."[1] They had stands on the Exchange.[2] They were favored by the factors (a) because they were not competitors, (b) because the factors did the buying and selling for the jobbers and this buying and selling brought them good commissions; and (c) because oftentimes the large-buying jobber would advance prices and make the small buyer pay higher out of a sense of fear lest he be not able to buy at all.[3]

The function of the jobbing speculator is to steady the supply and prices. Fullness of knowledge would annihilate speculation. Speculators are a specialized class who try to use every means available for gathering information that will help determine the future. The speculator tends to eliminate the possibility of speculation by eliminating uncertainty. And to the extent he does reduce uncertainty our general economic welfare is advanced. Trade and commerce become more certain, regular and sensitive and there is a vast economy of waste.

The jobbers of corn sometimes operated over longer periods, as six months; in which case they owned or hired granaries and stored their purchases, and brought them out onto the market at opportune times. The size of their stores might be so large as to determine the price on the market. In times of plenty, speculators tended to keep the market supply and price constant; whereas in times of scarcity they had it in their power to influence the market to their advantage,

[1] Rep. Com. H. C., IX, 154, 156.
[2] Ibid., 154.
[3] Ibid., 154.

since then their warehouse stores constituted them monopolists of the market. This circumstance is well illustrated in the report of the Mayor of Hull to the Privy Council in 1622. Derbyshire had been supplied for some time with foreign grain sent from Holland. He reported thus during the dearth; "We . . . have at this present in the hands of divers merchants and others, within this town, by them brought from beyond the seas, reasonable store of rye and other grain to the quantity of two thousand quarters and above for the service of the . . . country . . . of which their is daily some parts sold and delivered out of such reasonable rates as they may be afforded, . . ."[1]

It was possible for them to create an artificial scarcity by keeping the port of London closed against importation. By the acts of 1663 and 1685,[2] the port of London and the outports might be opened to the importation of corn when the prices of corn had reached a scale of prices set by the laws. The prices at each port were to be determined by the Justices of the Peace, and in London also by the Mayor and Aldermen. Oaths were to be taken by "two or more honest and substantial Persons of the respective Counties, being neither Merchants nor Factors for the importing of Corn, nor anyways concerned nor interested in the Corn so imported," and the Justices were to use "such other Ways and Means as to them shall seem fit, to examine and determine the common Market prices of middling English Corn." These prices were to be determined twice a year, in October and April. At these times it was possible for the jobbers to flush the market, actually throwing vast quantities into trade or spreading rumors of great quantities en-route thither by ship or barge, and depress the prices below the schedules that permitted the port to be opened. During the next six months they recouped themselves by monopolistic prices.[3] It is probable, however, that the possible use of the foreign corn supply tended on the whole to equalize rather than disturb the market price of corn. It did, in particular, before the acts of 1663 and 1685. During the extreme dearth of 1619–22, for instance, the imports of corn kept the price down in Derbyshire.[4]

Few commodities of commerce have been the basis of so much

[1] V. C. H., Derby, II, 180.

[2] 15 Chas. II, Cap. 7, Sec. 3; 1 Jas. II, Cap. 19, Secs. 3, 5.

[3] Allegations to this effect are given in "Abuses Relative to Provisions," 28; Gent. Mag., 1751: 474, 510; J. H. C., 30: 763.

[4] S. P. Dom. Chas. I, Vol. 113, No. 17; V. C. H., Derby II, 180.

speculation as corn, nor has any a more widely organized market. These facts result from peculiar qualities of the ware (as pointed out above), viz. it allows bulk-handling, can be stored for long periods without deterioration, can be graded into different classes in accordance with the demand for certain standard qualities, and there is an extensive, inelastic demand for it.   These qualities made possible the jobber and his practices: he bought in bulk, he stored in his granaries, he sold by sample, and he was sure of a market. He could contract for future delivery because he was sure he could get the same kind and quality for which he bargained. The grades of the ware were recognized on the market as having certain specific qualities respectively, and contracts could be made for "English Middling" or other grade though the contractor did not then have it on hand. Thus grading made possible a special form of speculation, i. e. dealing in "futures." Sample-sales were the intermediate step between bulk-sales of ungraded corn and the modern sales on the basis of tariff-classification or standardization.[1] They were also a means of separating the place of sale and the place of handling the ware, i. e. of dividing the market into two distinct economic parts for the convenience and advantage of both.   The Corn Exchange and the elevator, granary or ship were related to each other by the sample of grain and transfer slip, and no essential economic disadvantage was caused by the greater or less distance between them.

MERCHANT.

It is impossible to distinguish with any precision the corn merchant from the corn jobber. Their operations overlap and fuse into each other.   Both are speculators, though the jobber limits himself to one market more than the merchant. The jobber speculates more in time-relations, the merchant in place-relations: the jobber buys and sells according to his estimates of the future prices on the particular market with which he is concerned; the merchant buys and sells on many markets—home and foreign—according to the prices prevailing or likely to prevail on each of these markets.   In other words, the merchant is a dealer in bulk doing an import and export business. It is these foreign relations which especially characterize the *merchant* class.   Dealers doing a domestic business only are in strict nomenclature *tradesmen*. The businesses of the two are generally combined.

Until the close of the fifteenth century England produced a surplus of corn for export; between 1500 and 1660 imports possibly exceeded

[1] Schmoller, Grundriss, II, 35.

exports; the period of the Restoration was one of rapid transition and was followed by a century of unparalleled exportation. It has been elsewhere shown that due to the excessive growth of London the metropolitan consumption overtaxed the producing parts of the Kingdom in the period 1500–1660; again the Industrial Revolution so industrialized the English population that not even the "New Agriculture" could keep the island as well supplied with corn after 1760. These changes are registered by the changes in government policy with respect to the corn trade and by changes in the mercantile organization which performed that trade.

In the days of the manor tolls were levied on corn in the internal trade as it passed the town lines. There was a tax (lastage), levied for fiscal purposes, on corn exports, and frequently licenses to export corn were issued to merchants, especially in time of war. Since the import trade in corn was negligible the state refrained from legislation with respect to it. By the beginning of the fourteenth century the non-producing but consuming population in the towns, particularly London, became an important factor in corn legislation. This section of the people was naturally. in favor of large home supplies at low prices, looked with disfavor upon exportation abroad or carriage to other parts of England and upon middlemen handling corn and apparently raising prices. The policy with regard to the export of corn thereafter fluctuated much according as the producing or consuming classes gained the ascendancy in Parliament or had better access to the royal ear. Discriminating taxes were imposed upon alien exporters and importers in 1303; four decades later the tax was extended to denizens. During most of the fourteenth century exportation was prohibited except under special license; this policy of prohibition became more popular as the century waned.[1] The first half of the fifteenth century was reactionary and compromising[2] and indicates that the surplus for export was becoming larger and the need of foreign corn or all the domestic corn was less feared. During the latter half of the century it was the normal thing to be exporting corn. Except in years of dearth this was freely done on payment of the export duty, provided prices were lower than prescribed moderate schedules; in case prices were higher importation was allowed.

---

[1] Cf. 34 Ed. III, Cap. 20.

[2] 17 Rich. II, Cap. 7; 15 Hen. VI, Cap. 2; 20 Hen. VI, Cap. 6; 23 Hen. VI, Cap. 5; 3 Ed. IV, Cap. 2.

During this period the first English corn merchants arose. Mention was made of some during the twelfth century.[1] The Cambridge district was the seat of many early exporters; many notices of them are scattered through the Patent Rolls of the fourteenth century.[2] They shipped to the countries bordering the North Sea. Although they dealt mostly in corn other wares are mentioned as fish, wool, ale, cloth, etc. They appear to have had close connection with the government and filled many royal posts. In the minor towns of the region they engaged corn factors who bought up and dispatched corn to the seaports; for this purpose they had ships and boats, and handled other goods for exchange. Whether these merchants did any retailing in the port towns is uncertain; most probably they did.

The Tudor corn policy in the sixteenth century was dictated by the needs of London. The producing powers of England were not competent to guarantee the metropolis an adequate supply of corn. Hence the city favored the prohibition of corn exportations, except as it was found from time to time that exports could be comfortably spared. It does not seem that the statutory policy was more than the expression of an ideal of the producing parts. When, according to the act of 1554,[3] the price of corn reached 6s. 8d. the quarter, exportation was prohibited except as permitted by special royal licenses specifying in detail what amount might be exported by the licensed; at any and all times when the price was less than this any Englishman might export freely. In 1563 and 1593 these price limits were raised to 10s. and 20s. respectively. But since these limits were so low the free exportations of corn was really only permitted a very few years of the century. During the first half of the seventeenth century the limits were further raised[4] but not enough at any time to permit much exportation. The period, therefore, from 1500 to the Restoration was one of importation rather than exportation; though some exports were made they were occasional or under special license; and the statutory corn policy favored the consuming classes, while parading the ideal of the producers.[5]

During this period the import trade was in the hands of Dutch merchants. They procured corn in the Baltic regions and carried it

[1] Madox, I, 558.

[2] Cal. Pat. Rolls. Ed. III, Vol. II, 415; III, 80; VII, 388; IX, 363; Rich. II, Vol. III, 281. See also Cart. Mon. de Ram., III, 141–151.

[3] 1–2, Ph. & M., Cap. 5, sec. 7.

[4] 1603–04 to 26s.8d., 1623–24 to 32s, and 1656 to 40s.

[5] For other views of this policy see such writers as Hasbach, 32–33, Schanz, I, 479, Faber, 87–89, and Cunningham, Growth, II, pt. I, 87.

to England. In years of dearth large quantities were imported. In the State Papers numerous references are made to these Dutch importers[1] during the reigns of the first two Stuarts. They came to a somewhat sudden end about 1660. When London ceased to need foreign corn their business was gone; they could not become exporters of English corn because of the discriminations laid against aliens in the Navigation Acts, in the bounty system, and in the customs duties. Consequently the way was open for the rise of denizen corn-export merchants.

The Restoration era was one of important transactions. Denizen export merchants supplanted the Dutch import merchants. England and Poland became the granaries of Europe. Commerce became freer; the state really repealed the laws against regrating and ingrossing, ceased its system of municipal provision of corn, and left the export trade unhampered or fostered it by export bounties. The English merchants seized upon their opportunities and developed a big export trade. The period between 1660 and 1780 covers the time of England's greatest exportation of corn. During this century and a score of years her agriculture was revolutionized and extended, and an extensive corn surplus resulted. Meanwhile war and pestilence were ruining agriculture in parts of the continent. England and the Baltic countries became the source from which Europe drew its corn. The increase in exports was sudden and prodigious. For the two years 1662 and 1663 the exports of corn were valued at £4315, and for 1668 and 1669 a smaller amount, £2011. But the yearly average for the period 1699 to 1710 was £274,141, or nearly 150 times as much as in an average year three decades before.[2] During the period of Walpole's peace the exportation continued to increase, until for the five years 1744–48 the average yearly exportation was estimated by Anderson at above £1,600,000.[3] It was during the decade 1780–90 that England changed from a grain-exporting to a grain-importing state, the chief cause being the rapid rise of the manufacturing population under the Industrial Revolution.[4]

The accompanying table[5] gives the average exportations of wheat, barley and malt for the two years 1734–36, years of peace and even trade. During these years London exported more wheat than the eight next largest ports combined, and Portsmouth, her strongest

[1] Cal. St. P. Dom. Jas., I, Vol. X, 607; Chas. I, Vol. III, 594; IV, 203; XVI, 4, 240; Rep. LVII, pt. II, 123 b.

[2] Davenant, Rep. Public Accounts, Part II, Works, V, 424.

[3] Anderson, Origin, IV, 158.

[4] Busching, Entwickelung, 118–119, contains statistical statements.

[5] Table of Exports of Corn (Data based on Gent. Mag., 1736: 559; 1743: 35):

competitor, was doing less than one-third the business of London. But, on the contrary, London's exportations of malt were insignificant, whereas Yarmouth, Wells and Lynne Regis did an immense business in this ware. Estimating the relative importance of the several ports by the export duties paid by the ports respectively on corn exported, London and Yarmouth were very close competitors for first place, Wells third, and Hull ninth.

PORTS	WHEAT QRS.	MALT QRS.	BARLEY QRS.	BOUNTIES POUNDS
London..................	53,777	1,837	5,099	14,387
Yarmouth................	6,982	93,876	5,869	13,892
Wells....................	333	58,441	316	7,566
Portsmouth..............	15,351	4,122	1,095	4,489
Lynn Regis..............	4,074	18,300	3,000	3,654
Chichester..............	7,818	6,895	300	3,000
Southampton.............	5,722	1,914	1,506	1,915
Berwick.................	7,782	1,084	1,268	2,256
Hull....................	2,778	6,113	215	1,709

The business of the corn merchant was facilitated and increased by the bounties paid on exports. By a statute[1] of 1688 trade and tillage were stimulated by allowing bounties on corn exported while prices were low.[2] The fact that the burden of taxes was imposed upon the landed interests and that the Whigs desired to placate these interests indicates, no doubt, the political aim of this legislation; it stimulated agriculture and England's export of corn increased rapidly.[3] It was, however, in line with Continental policy and early writers had urged

[1] 1 Wm. & Mary, Cap. 12. When malt or barley was 24s, rye, 32s., and wheat 48s., or lower, per quarter, any exporter was allowed by the government bounties of 2s. 6d. per quarter for malt or barley, 3s. 6d. for rye, and 5s. for wheat exported beyond seas.

[2] According to Prothero, Eng. Farm., 452, the total of bounties paid were:

1697–1705..	£289,670	14s.	0d.
1706–1725..	1,371,032	4	0
1726–1745..	1,769,756	4	2
1746–1765..	2,628,503	4	7
1697–1765 Total..	6,058,962	6	9

The effect on the exportation of corn (other causes, of course, contributing) is indicated by the following averages of the excesses of exports over imports of corn, flour, and meal:

	Quarters		Quarters
1697–1701........................	140,000	1730–1734........................	469,000
1702–1707........................	289,000	1735–1739........................	597,000
1708–1711........................	299,000	1740–1744........................	446,000
1712–1715........................	454,000	1745–1749........................	933,000
1716–1719........................	486,000	1750–1754........................	1,080,000
1720–1724........................	533,000	1755–1759........................	274,000
1725–1729........................	217,000	1760–1764........................	696,000

[3] Cunningham, Growth, II, 541; Craik, Hist. Br. Com. II, 145; Anderson, Origin, II, 583.

the state to follow the example of Venice or other such ports in regulating the export. Malynes in 1603 proposed that the authorities of the ports be furnished with information from the justices of the counties as to the "quantity of corne in all places" and "consider what the realme may spare, having a regard to the season of the yeare, and making the price accordingly . . . knowne in certaine publike places" once a week; thus what would be "by license transported" would be "done upon due knowledge."[1] It was the common Elizabethan policy to put the provision of corn for the poor as a duty upon the town officials and to allow them to import corn if necessary from abroad in times of dearth.[2] Charles II permitted, 1670,[3] the importation of corn subject to import duties which decreased as the home market price increased. He also permitted the exportation of corn whenever the market price was above prescribed minimum prices and export duties were required.[4] These export duties were removed practically in 1689 and expressly in 1700.[5] So the application of the sliding scale of prices as the determining element as to importation and exportation was not an altogether new principle of commercial policy; but the payment of export bounties under the 1689 act was new. This body of regulation which discouraged importation and encouraged exportation continued till 1765, when the exportation of corn was prohibited and importation was made duty free. This lasted till 1773. The acts of 1765 and 1773 reversed the former policy—encouraged importation and discouraged exportation.

The corn-bounties had a very peculiar effect on the commerce of corn. Throughout this period the rate of interest was lower in Holland than in England by 2 or 3 per cent.[6] To speculate heavily in corn required large capital or credit, but money could be had more cheaply in Holland. Hence in Holland larger stores of corn could be carried in warehouses for the same outlay of capital and interest charge. It was preferable to store corn in Holland's granaries. The export bounty on corn more than paid the difference of transportation charge. The merchants of London, accordingly, were in the practice of hiring storehouses in Holland, Hamburgh, Dantzig, and other

[1] Malynes, England's View, 90–93; somewhat similar recommendations are given by E. Lamond, Discourse on Com. Weal, 163.

[2] Leonard, 123–24; Faber, 97.

[3] 22 Chas. II, Cap. 13.

[4] 12 Chas. II, Cap. 4; the minimum prices were raised in the fifteenth and twenty-second years of his reign.

[5] 1 Wm. & M. st. I, Cap. 12; 12 Wm. III, Cap. 20.

[6] Hatton, Comes, Supp., 3; "Abstract of Grievances," 9; etc. See Chapter VII.

continental towns, and shipping their corn thither.[1] Here it was kept
for a year or so, until the prices in London and the outports rose above
the schedule whereat the ports were opened and importation allowed.
The above-paid exportation bounty was more than sufficient to pay
also this transportation charge. Thus a profit was realized from the
bounties in addition to the profits of the speculation or difference
between cost and selling price.[2] This sort of trade was possibly extensive. Of the £274,141 average yearly export of corn from 1699
to 1710, £151,934 was shipped to Holland.[3] About 1728 it was
said that "the Quantity of Corn, which in plentiful Years they (the
Dutch) import from England, is scarce to be computed . . . ;
in one Year there was shipt off mostly for Holland, in the Port of
Hull and the River Humber, above 200000 quarters of all Sorts of
Grain, and not much less the same year out of the County of Norfolk."[4] However, the importations of corn from 1697 to 1765 were
relatively negligible, averaging for the 69 years about 20,000 quarters
a year,[5] only a part of which may be considered as having been stored
in Holland by English merchants according to the scheme of trade.
But in considering the volume of this trade it is to be remembered
that it was occasional with regard to re-importation into England,
and that re-exportation from Holland was more often to other than
English ports.

The bounties thus increased the profits and the trade of the
merchant, but nevertheless very likely tended to defeat one of the
functions of service which the merchant ought to perform for society.
Undoubtedly the city of London was less evenly and steadily supplied
and at higher prices by this very roundabout route of supply. Prices
would have to rise a fixed amount before the port could be opened.

[1] "Way for Enriching," 4; Coke, Discourse of Trade, 62; Dobbs, Essay on Trade,
II, 68–69.

[2] Middleton, Middlesex, 560–61; "Thoughts on Pub. Reg. Gran.," 35 note.

[3] Davenant, Works, V, 424.

[4] Atlas Mar. et. Com., 115.

[5] Nicholson, Corn Laws, 31–32. The following table is made from data taken
from Prothero, Eng. Farm., 452:

KIND OF GRAIN	QUARTERS 1697-1731	EXPORTED 1731-1766	QUARTERS 1697-1731	IMPORTED 1732-1766
Wheat, Flour, etc..........	3,592,163	11,540,163	124,417	291,773
Barley, Malt, etc...........	7,467,129	10,259,675	35,340	49,270
Oats, Oatmeal, etc	217,490	364,779	432,514	1,050,320
Rye, Ryemeal, etc..........	1,098,885	1,437,727	178,224	22,205
Peas, Beans...............	690	25,274	185	9,569
Totals..................	12,367,357	23,627,671	770,680	1,423,137

The jobbers strove to keep the port closed by depressing prices in April and October. Hence wide fluctuations surely resulted and the service which the merchant would have otherwise rendered was destroyed or held in abeyance. Were it not for the bounties, some contemporaries held, granaries would have been erected in the near vicinity of the metropolis and the service of supply been improved.[1] Under the head "Corn Buyers," above, the Tudor granary system was briefly outlined. The aim of this system was purely to *supply* the consumption of London. The method of provision by voluntary money contributions from individuals and the method of forced corn contributions by the Liveries Companies were tried out during the sixteenth and seventeenth centuries and abandoned. The supply of corn was intrusted to private initiative thereafter. At various times, usually times of dearth, projects were published for establishing a system of granaries for *trade* purposes. King James had proposed, and proclaimed the liberty to set up a system in 1623 "For the Well-Storing and furnishing of the Realme with Corne."[2] At the next period of dearth 1631–1633 similar projects were announced.[3] Yarranton in 1677 wrote and worked for the establishment of public granaries for the corn collected in Oxford and Northants and brought to London by river.[4] He would have combined with his granaries a sort of banking and credit business. None of these schemes found practical realization either at the hands of town or state; what granaries existed were the private properties of corn dealers and big farmers; but the bounties on export tended to reduce the number of these.

The corn merchant had to be a capitalist of some strength and have control of considerable credit. Necessarily the rate of turnover of his wares was slow, not more than three or four times a year.[5] Besides, if he was to avail much as a merchant he had to buy heavily when markets prices were low; his outlay was thus spasmodic and for long periods. He usually sought independence of the carriers by buying up a controlling interest in the vehicles of the commerce in which he engaged, even to monopolizing them. For instance, at Ware every barge that carried corn to London belonged to the corn

---

[1] Middleton, Middlesex, 561, for example.

[2] Oddy, II, 248; Cunningham, Growth, II, 318; Council, Reg., Jas. I, Vol. VI, 63; Rymer, VII, Pt. IV, 86–87. See also S. P. Dom., Jas. I, Vol. X, 124, 129, 130, 140; Council Reg., Vol. IV, 372, 294–95.

[3] Council Reg., Chas. I, Vols. VI, 477–78; VII, 131–32; VIII, 249–50; IX, 506; Cal. S. P. Dom., Chas. I, Vol. V, 428.

[4] Yarranton, Eng. Imp., 114–38.

[5] Smith, on Corn Trade, 17.

men of the metropolis about 1760.[1] The great corn merchants of
the first half of the eighteenth century effected very broad and extensive organizations, establishing resident buyers in the chief corn districts, and resident factors to do their selling in the chief markets;
besides doing a banking and exchange business to facilitate their
mercantile pursuits. During the Restoration period the export corn
business of London tended to concentrate in the hands of a few
merchants. The records show that Moore, Sturt and Buckle must
have done a considerable proportion of the trade.[2]

The most celebrated corn merchants of the later period were the
Coutts firm of Edinburgh and London. They had private resident
agents in Northumberland, in the various grain-raising counties of
Scotland, in all parts of England and Wales, in Ireland, and sometimes they bought from Dantzig and Königsberg. The ports they
used in particular as shipping points were Yarne, Stockton, Lynn
Regis, Fakenham, Yarmouth, Haverford-west, Hilton, Belfast and
Drogheda.[3] They developed a very extensive system of correspondence for gathering intelligence respecting the prices of corn in the
various markets, and for doing their banking and exchange operations. Without these broad connections it would have been impossible to join successfully so risky a business as dealing in corn with
that of banking, which requires special and consistent caution. The
combination of country banking and mercantile pursuits was the
order of the day about 1750.[4]

If the testimony of hostile contemporary pamphleteers may be
trusted, the corn merchants were not altogether passive, equalizing
differences of prices between markets. It was granted they did a
great service in equalizing prices from season to season, and from place
to place. Oftentimes they bought up the grain at the beginning of
the year or just after harvest when the price was low, and sold it back
again at a later season possibly to the same individuals. When the
poorer farmers were pressed for money to pay their rents, they sold
to the export factors, who thus advanced the needed capital,[5] and such
purchases and sales amounted to a loan and its collection. But it
seems that the merchants sought wilfully to raise and lower the price

---

[1] "Considerations on the Present," II.

[2] Rep. XVI, 138.

[3] Bourne, Eng. Mer., 336, contains a quotation, source not specified, from which
these statements are drawn.

[4] See Chapter VII.

[5] Weldon, Hints, 16–17; Smith, on Corn Trade, 11–13.

of corn; by filling the newspapers with false reports as to the abundance of the harvest at home or abroad, or as to the likelihood of the export bounty being removed, or as to the destruction of crops by storm, etc., prices of corn were depressed soon after harvest or other times and the corn bought up cheaply.[1] Such operations were more easily performed then than they would be today, when the means of communication are well perfected. But whenever they be executed, they are economically harmful, even though they may for the time swell the merchant's profits, for they create public distrust and lessen production.

CORN CHANDLER.

The corn chandler was the retailer of corn in the towns and cities. He bought corn and meal in the country or on markets and sold it in the city in the public markets or in shops. He usually kept a shop with a supply of corn, flour, and meal, which he retailed to the public. Not until the repeal of the law against regrating in 1673[2] was such shop-keeping wholly free from public interference. The city and state did not observe a consistent policy with respect to his business; at times he was treated as regrator and ingrosser and his dealings were done outside the pale of the law in "shopps and other obscure places within this Cittie;"[3] but gradually about the middle of the seventeenth century he was more leniently treated and his shop became the real prototype of our present-day flour-, meal-, and feed-store.[4] Later statutes[5] specifically excepted such retailers from the list of ingrossers and allowed them to buy in the markets and sell the same again in the city. The chandler sometimes combined with his retail business a wholesale or merchant business or bought on commission for stable keepers.[6]

MILLER.

Among the middlemen who handled corn-products, the millers, maltsters, mealmen, brewers and distillers were the most prominent. The prime function of the miller was the conversion of corn into meal and flour. As such he was essentially a manufacturer who served the

---

[1] "Considerations on the Present," 10.
[2] 15 Chas. II, Cap. 7, Sec. 3.
[3] See Rep. XXXII, 364, and LVIII, pt. II, 54–55.
[4] Rep. LVIII, pt. II, 54–55; LXV, 59b; LXVI, 143b.
[5] For example, 31 Geo. II, Cap. 25, Sec. 21.
[6] Rep. Com. H. C., IX, 157.

corn owners by grinding their corn when brought to his mill.[1]   The right to have mills for grinding corn was limited to particular persons. The mills were worked by horsepower.   In the time of Edward I the miller paid in kind and in money certain legal amounts per quarter ground.   The grain was publicly weighed before it was entrusted to the miller.   He had a bad reputation for peculation.[2]   But many opportunities were thrown in his way for enlarging his business and combining other parts of the corn trade with this grinding.   In the middle of the seventeenth century a special class of "cadgers" were employed by the millers of Yorkshire to collect the grain from the vicinity, carry it to the mill, and deliver again the ground product.[3]

There was, about the same time, a refinement of this business wherein the miller became merchant.   In 1630 complaint was laid as follows: "Where in some Parts of the Realme divers Millers, who ought only to serve for grinding of Corne that shall be brought to their Mills, have begunne lately a very corrupt trade to be common Buyers of Corne, both in Markets and out of Markets, and the same doe grind into Meale, and do use as Badgers, or otherwise to sell the same at Markets and in other Places, seeking thereby an inordinate gaine, besides the Misusing of other Mens Corne brought thither to be ground, by delaying grinding, or that worse is, by changing and altering their good Corne to the worse."[4]   In accordance with these allegations millers were prohibited from buying grain on purpose to sell it again as grain or meal.

It appears that this prohibitive legislation was quite successful while the laws against ingrossing and other laws regulatory of the trade were enforced.   But during the first half of the eighteenth century the old practices were begun again, the millers combining with their milling the occupations of mealman, flour-factor and corn merchant.   The economic dependence of a pure miller on the corn owners was undesirable and hazardous to him, and in seasons of poor crops he lived a miserable existence.   By buying up stores of grain he could employ himself steadily and reduce the accident of crops. Consequently all who could raise sufficient capital engaged in the meal and flour trade.[5]   And usually the corn riots of the middle of the

---

[1] Gent. Mag., 1758: 424.

[2] Lib. Alb. I, LXXIII, 354–55; 691.

[3] Surtees, 33: 103.   At this time the millers paid these cadgers about 5*d*. a day, and they carried from 8 to 10 bushels on a horse.

[4] Massie, "Orders . . . . for Preventing," 20.

[5] Defoe, Com. Eng. Tr., II, 178; Smith, on Corn Trade, 17; "View of real grievances," 228–29.

century were violently directed against the mills of the millers as ingrossers of corn.[1] The combination of these several trades into one integrated whole also gave the miller a much better control of the flour and meal market and consequently of prices.[2] Besides, this innovation wrought great changes in the economic position of the miller. From the mean dependent employment as miller for others he became a man of vast business and owner of huge mills and accessory business organizations.[3] As the country progressed these tendencies on the part of the millers developed. They began to employ factors as buyers of corn on the Corn Exchange, as well as in the country markets in the vicinity of their mills, and otherwise extend their business.[4]

MALSTER, MEALMAN, AND FLOURMAN.

The great milling districts were in Hertfordshire, Surrey, and the upper Thames.[5] As flour and meal were more difficult to handle, especially at sea, and more apt to spoil, foreign commerce was mostly restricted to raw corn and malt; but the internal commerce of flour was immense, particularly by way of the Thames and its affluents, upon which special flour and malt barges plied. The immensity of this Thames trade can be realized from the consumption of meal by the city of London, which was computed by Maitland to amount to 369,635 quarters annually in the period about 1730.[6] The great Farnham-Market corn sales were carried by land to the River Wey about seven miles distant, on whose banks there were many mills; having been ground and dressed, the meal was carried by barges to London.[7] From Reading, Henley, Maidenhead, Abingdon and Farrington, large barges, carrying meal and malt, were dispatched to London. By the records of the Berkshire County Sessions of the date 1726 is shown that the maltsters were rebated for losses of malt due to wrecking of the barges on the Thames. "Thus on 11 April, 1726, Benjamin and Joseph Tomkins exhibited complaint alleging that . . . 130 quarters of malt was greatly damaged by . . . the coasting away or sinking of a certain barge . . . transporting

---

[1] Gent. Mag., 1756: 408–09; Frame, County of Lanark, 67.
[2] Owens, Weekly Chronicle, 196; Gent. Mag., 1758: 425.
[3] Defoe, Com. Eng. Tr., II, 179.
[4] Rep. from Com. H. C., IX, 146.
[5] Defoe, Com. Eng. Tr., II, 175.
[6] Maitland, London, I, 756.
[7] Defoe, Tour, I, 217.

malt from Abingdon to London."[1]   The cost of carriage by water
was much lower than by road, and the roads were not used when
river navigation was possible.   In 1800 it was said that the water
rates were only one-third as high as the land rates, and the roads had
been improved much by that date.[2]   The Thames barges were the
largest in use in the inland trade of England.   Down stream from
Reading, Abingdon and other river-ports they carried the corn, malt,
and meal; up stream from London they brought to these same towns
as distributing points, coal, salt, groceries, tobacco, oils, and heavy
goods.[3]   "They were remarkable for the length of Vessel and the
Burden they" carried "and yet the little water they" drew.   Some
carried a thousand quarters of malt at a time, and yet drew but two
feet of water.   This burden was at least a hundred tons.   The Thames
was navigable a hundred and fifty miles for such barges.[4]   As early
as 1637 there had become established a regular system of water-
carriers on the Thames.   Twice-a-week such barges plied between
Queenhite and the upper Thames towns; and once a week one went
as far as Reading.   A weekly hoy sailed between London and Colchester.   These had regular schedules, termini, and docks.[5]

The malt was assembled at the river marts in wagons by the larger
farmers; for example, in 1745 Defoe said that "at Abingdon   .   .   .
they have a barley market, where you see every market-day four or
five hundred carts and wagons of barley to be sold at a time, standing
in rows in the market-place, besides the vast quantities carried directly
to the maltsters' houses;"[6]   while the "malting trade at Ware,
Hertford, Royston, Hetchin, and other towns on that side of Hertfordshire, fetch their barley twenty, thirty, or forty miles."[2]   The
southern coast towns sent their meal "about by long sea," as they
called it.   In the first decades of the century the Chichester merchants
diverted part of the Farnham business to their port by building
elevators and storing up the corn of the vicinity until ground in their
mills and shipped to London by sea.   Other coast towns followed this
example.[7]

All this malt and meal came to Queenhithe, London, making it

---

[1] V. C. H., Berks, I, 407.
[2] Ibid., II, 214.
[3] Defoe, Tour, II, 47.
[4] Ibid., 175.
[5] Taylor, Car. Cos.
[6] Defoe, Com. Eng. Tr., II, 180.
[7] Defoe, Tour, I, 204.

the greatest meal and malt market in England.[1]   Here at Queenhithe or other smaller markets of London these meal merchants of Chichester, Arundel and the coast of Sussex and Hampshire had factors to sell their meal for them.[2]

About 1735 there was an elimination of the mealman's business going on, which is described by Defoe as follows: "these Mealmen generally live either in London, or within thirty miles of it, that employment chiefly relating to the markets of London; they formerly were the general buyers of corn—in all the great markets about London, or within, thirty or forty miles of London, which corn they used to bring to the nearest mills they could find to the market, and there have it ground, and then sell the meal to the shop-keepers, called mealmen, in London.   But a few years past have given a new turn to this trade; for now the bakers in London, and the parts adjacent, go to the markets themselves and have cut out the shopkeeping mealmen;[3] so the bakers are the mealmen and sell the fine flour to private families, as the mealmen used to do. And as the bakers have cut out the meal shops in London, so the millers have cut out the mealmen in the country; and whereas they formerly only ground the corn for the mealmen, they now scorn that trade, buy the corn, and grind it for themselves; so the baker goes to the miller for his meal, and the miller goes to the market for the corn . . . . It is certain the mealmen are, in a manner, cut out of the trade, both in London and in the country, except it be those country mealmen who send meal to London by barges, from all the counties bordering on the Thames, or on any navigable river running into the Thames west; and some about Chichester, Arundel, and the coast of Sussex, and Hampshire, who send meal by sea."[4]

The various functions of the mealmen are apparent.   He was a dealer wholesale and retail in flour and meal.   In London he kept shop and sold to private families.   In the upper Thames district he was a wholesale shipper and dealer in meal.   In the south coast region he did an elevator business, caused corn to be ground and dressed, shipped it to London, and sold it by means of his factors.   Flour

[1] Defoe, Tour, II, 174.

[2] Defoe, Com. Eng. Tr., II, 179.

[3] That this elimination was not very complete or permanent, is evident from the following statement from Smith, Essay on Corn Trade, 22: "Whilst others (bakers) buy all they Use, in London, more particularly, in Flour of the Mealmen, or Meal Factors."   Smith may have had in mind as mealmen the combined miller-mealman.

[4] Defoe, Com. Eng. Tr., II, 178–79.

bought from the mealmen was regarded superior to that bought from the farmer directly; because the mealmen bought a variety of flours and meals and mixed the same; this composite flour made better bread in the long run than unmixed flour did.[1] But this mixing gave opportunity for adulteration of good flour with poor and making the latter marketable: a practice that caused no little criticism by the user.[2]

Originally the malting business was a domestic affair, each farmer malting for his own use. The more considerable farmers malted a surplus which was carried to the towns and cities. But the increase of drinking in England was prodigious in the eighteenth century, and the supplying of London with malt gave rise to a large business and special tradesmen. The maltster farmers began to buy up the barley of their neighborhood, convert it to malt, and market it in London. Some gave up farming and did a pure maltster business. Outsiders, attracted by the apparent advantage of the malting trade, set it up by itself. Thus arose the maltster. This process is illustrated in Oxford in the latter part of the sixteenth century. The malsters were included in the census taken in 1587 of the dealers in corn. At Thame the three "malsters" reported were respectively a bricklayer, a shoemaker, and a butcher. The malting business was combined also with brewing and baking and victualling.[3] Charles I contemplated the reform of abuses in the Berks malting business by the formation of an Incorporated Company of Malsters. One of the provisions of the proposed charter was "that noe brewer or other person useing any other traide mistery or occupacion shall conuerte any graine to maulte to sell the same to theire use or with theire stock by breweing of beere or ale."[4] This proposed clause was most likely aimed at a tendency of the day.

Other clauses of this charter aimed to demark the malster from the middleman class. "Noe person" was to "buy any corne to conuerte to maulte butt in the open markitts to sell agayne;" and "noe person that conuerteth any sorte of Graine into maulte to sell" was to "buy any maulte to sell againe." The former clause was a market regulation common enough in that day and meant to protect the consuming public against forestalling corn; the latter meant to prevent the manufacturing maltster from becoming simply a dealer in

[1] Smith, on the Corn Trade, 23.
[2] Gent. Mag., 1758: 425.
[3] V. C. H., Oxford, II, 194.
[4] V. C. H., Berks, I, 404.

malt. Taken in conjunction with the other clauses it would work the elimination of the malt dealer. Due to the business of the Civil War Charles never effected this incorporation.

The malsters sold mostly to the brewers. About 1500 an Enfield (Middlesex) malster named John Hunnesdon sought to recover a debt from a Southwark brewer named Robert Trott, who had "used wekely to bye malt by the space of many yeres of" him, and on a running account whereon there had "remayned unpayed for 2 or 3 quarters of malt, at some tyme 4 or 5, at som tyme mor."[1] This case likely represents the accustomed method of business—i.e. a malster sold his produce to regular customers. In other parts, however, local ordinances required all non-freemen malsters to sell in the public market and not in shops and houses.[2]

The malsters were subject to many regulations. At Abingdon in 1591 they were compelled to use officially sealed measures.[3] Variances among the markets in the size of the weights and measures caused to "ensue many inconveniences." In Cornwall, for instance, "some Ingrossers" bought "Wheat of the husbandmen, after 18 gallons the bushell, and deliver(ed) it to the transporting Merchant, for the same summe, at 16."[4] Thus, although the system of public markets protected the buyer on a particular market against false measures and bad bargains the want of uniformity as among the markets allowed other abuses. The period of making malt was also limited. Charles had proposed to prevent malting during the three summer months.[5] In Warwick the time of malt-making was not to be less than seventeen days in summer and twenty-one in winter.[6]

Some of these traders operated on a large scale. Already in the reign of Elizabeth the Berks malsters were among the most prominent citizens.[7] The consumption of wood in the maltkilns was complained of during the Tudor régime.[8] This indicates a considerable malting business. The great volumes of malt shipped down the Thames have been shown above. The trade of the London malsters was great enough to enable them to employ resident factors in the corn regions,

---

[1] V. C. H., Middlesex, II, 127; Surrey, II, 381.

[2] For illustration, Shrewsbury in 1621; V. C. H., Shrops, I, 423; Shrops, Arch. Soc. Trans. III, 283.

[3] V. C. H., Berks, I, 406–07.

[4] Carew, Cornwall, 54.

[5] V. C. H., Berks, I, 405.

[6] V. C. H., Warwick, II, 267; book of John Fisher, ed. Kemp, 146.

[7] V. C. H., Berks, I, 406.

[8] V. C. H., Worc. II, 254.

who bought up malt and forwarded it to their London principals.[1]
Competition among the big malsters appears to have been very rife,
and destructive in some cases.   The historian of Chichester ascribes
the decline of the malting houses to the greed of the malsters.[2]

BAKER.

Bakers were manufacturers and only incidentally middlemen.   It
was a very old industry and trade peculiar to the cities and larger
towns.   London's supply of bread was made partly within her walls
and partly without.   In the fifteenth century part of it came in horse-
packs or carts from Stratford in Essex, Bremble near Stratford,
Stevenhethe (Stepney) and Saint Albans.[3]   Both in London and in
provincial parts the bakers were subject to considerable regulation.
Strange bread was sometimes prohibited from being brought to the
city, usually on the ground of adulteration.   The prices of loaves
were fixed by public law.   Each loaf was sealed.   It could only be
sold in public market and not in the baker's shop "before his oven."
Cornhill and Cheap were popular bread markets; each baker had
assigned to him his own particular market.   It was brought to the
market in "panyers" and boxes or hutches.   Regratresses, female
retailers, carried it from house to house for sale; they bought it from
the bakers and made a profit of every thirteenth loaf; they dared not
buy in markets outside London, nor from foreign bakers before these
had brought their bread to the market at Cheap; they bought on
credit sometimes from the bakers.   The foreign bakers undersold the
city bakers by two ounces per loaf.   The bakers were forbidden to
buy corn for the purpose of resale.   Nor were they to set up in business with less chattels than 40s; accompanying this prohibition was
one against sharing their profits with their landlords who might supply them with bakehouse, oven, or materials.   Their products were
inspected by a public inspector and made to conform to the standard
of the assize.[4]

In Beverley, illustrating the rural town, the danger of the large
buying by the bakers was lessened by restraining them from buying
before one o'clock, i.e. after the other denizens had bought for their
own use.   Similar regulations were laid in 1401, 1418, and 1555; so

[1] Defoe, Com. Eng. Tr., II, 181.
[2] Hay, Hist. of Chichester, 330, 336.
[3] Lib. Alb. I, LXVI.
[4] See detailed regulations in Lib. Alb. I, LXVIII–LXX; 264–65.

that it is likely very little change of organization took place during the fifteenth and sixteenth centuries.[1] They were also, among other regulations, restrained from hiring "any mill for any term."[2]

This prohibition suggests the tendency of the baker to take up other trades than simple baking. Four centuries later the same tendency existed and it was common for bakers in country places to buy corn and have it ground on hire or at mills of their own, thus combining the functions of corn buyer, miller, mealman, and baker.[3] As was noted in the last section, the bakers assumed to eliminate the mealman and deal directly with the miller. Some such direct dealing was made possible by their large purchases and by the improved means of communication. In Dublin a like integration of mealman and baker functions was going on and in 1746 an ordinance reëxpressed the oldtime policy to differentiate the two and keep them distinct.[4] But the regulation was not effective, for the two trades thereafter had "secret trusts" and pooled their interests. The bakers illustrate, therefore, a common feature of all middlemen in the corn trade, viz., to function in several capacities and break down the ordinary demarkations that in public estimation and policy were supposed to put and keep each man in one trade only.

The government during the eighteenth century tried out the policy of regulating the price of bread by making the size of the loaf conform to the price of wheat, by a sliding scale. Such an act was passed in 1709.[5] In 1757[6] it was made to apply to other grains than wheat.[7] This act only extended to the places where the assizes of bread were held, and another statute[8] shortly afterwards applied it to the other markets. The execution of this legislation resulted in great uncertainty among possessors of corn, meal, and flour. These merchants had to incur the expense sometimes of withdrawing their stocks from one market for sale in another. If the assize fixed too high a price larger profits than necessary were made by the bakers; while, on the other hand, if too low, the corn- and mealmen would not bring their wares to town or market. In either case the trade suffered disadvantage.[9]

[1] Selden, XIV, p. 38.
[2] Ibid., 37.
[3] Smith, On the Corn Trade, 22–23.
[4] "Case of the Bakers," 3.
[5] 8 Anne, Cap. 18.
[6] 31 Geo. II, Cap. 29.
[7] For its working see Rept. 1772, Parl. Hist. XVII, 555.
[8] 3 Geo. III, Cap. 11.
[9] See C. Smith, Three Tracts on Corn, 28.

BREWER, DISTILLER, TAVERNER.

Again, the brewer and distiller are properly manufacturers, but the combinations of certain middlemen's functions with their business warrant some study of their marketing methods.

Before the French War, beginning 1689, the excise duties on the brown ale and small beer then made were low, and prices accordingly low. These liquors "were mostly fetched from the brewhouse by the customers themselves, and paid for with ready money; so that the brewer entertained but few servants, fewer horses, and had no stock of ales or beers by him, but a trifling quantity of casks, and his money returned before he paid either his duty or his malt."[1] The local regulations of the preceding centuries had varied considerably in this respect. In fifteenth century London the brewers sold ale by retail to the public directly as well as by wholesale to such dealers as were not brewers themselves but privileged to sell it. Brewers and hostelers were sometimes made the exclusive salesmen of ale.[2] At Abingdon the brewers must have done their own retailing for an opinion was expressed that they "ought not to put out their signe or Alestake untill their Ale be assayed by the Aletaster and then to sell and not before."[3] At High Wycombe, in the next century severe orders were levied against brewers retailing, or "tippling" as it was called, at their own houses. They were required to send it to town to be sold by the "tipplers" at prices fixed by the Mayor.[4] On the other hand, inn-keepers, vinters, victuallers, and alehouse-keepers were forbidden to brew and infringe upon the brewer's trade. For instance, at Abingdon in 1579 a heavy fine was imposed on any such if he should presume to "brue in his House any Beere or Ale to be sold offerid or drunke in his Howse, either by the pinte potte, quarte pottell, or gallon potte."[5] Similar ordinances prevailed in Berks in the seventeenth century.[6] This sort of regulation was designed to stop evasions of the assize prices of liquors as laid by the corporation council.[7] But this regulation was not existent everywhere. The poet laureate, John Shelton, has rendered classical the "tunnying"

[1] Gent. Mag., 1760: 527.
[2] Lib. Alb. I, LXI.
[3] V. C. H., Berks, I, 406.
[4] V. C. H., Bucks, II, 105.
[5] V. C. H., Berks, I, 407.
[6] Ibid., 405.
[7] Ibid., 406; Sussex, II, 261.

of Elynour Rummynge who kept an alehouse "in Sothray."[1] The towns prescribed officially stamped measures, appointed ale-tasters or conners, to test the quality, and fixed the prices: these things were done in behalf of the consumer. Sometimes they went further and suppressed the alehouses and appointed common brewers and tipplers who were to sell at fixed prices. For example, in Croscombe 1617–1618 all the tippling houses except Thomas Delton's were suppressed; and in Taunton 1615 the innkeepers were constrained to buy from the common brewers appointed by the court at fixed prices.[2]

Another line of regulations concerned the maintenance of the public peace. In London all ale-house doors in the fifteenth century were closed at curfew.[3] The license system was sometimes applied locally. Abingdon licensed her retailers of ale and fined the brewers who put it into the cellars of unlicensed retailers.[4] During Elizabeth's time Sir Walter Raleigh was given a patent for licensing wine taverns, and he appears to have made free use of his franchise.[5] But this license system was of great service to the police power of the state, centralizing, as it did, authority and giving the innkeeper a social importance and public responsibility. It also became a frequent and considerable means of raising money for the exigencies of the government.[6] During the Puritan régime alehouses were expropriated of their licenses for many minor offenses, especially gambling and drinking on Sunday.[7]

In 1577 a census of the inns, alehouses and taverns through England was taken. York had 3941, 3679 of which were tippling houses; Nottingham had 1028; Lincoln 766; Kent 702; Cumberland 656; Devon 560; etc. The numbers seem prodigious considering the number of the population; and the counties which were relatively poorest in wealth seem to have had an undue number of alehouses. In the counties nearest the metropolis the ratio of inns and taverns to alehouses was greater than in the more remote counties. In Berks one-eighth, in Herts one-fourth, in Bucks one-fifth, and in Suffolk more than one-third were inns and taverns. The inns served the more intinerant classes and their reported numbers may be some rough index

[1] V. C. H., Surrey, II, 378–79.
[2] V. C. H., Somers, II, 402; see also Hants, V, 427.
[3] Lib. Alb. I, LXII.
[4] V. C. H., Berks, I, 406.
[5] Cf. Hall, Eliz. Soc., 79.
[6] Ibid., 80.
[7] V. C. H., Berks, I, 406; Hants, V, 427.

of relative travel. The towns, Boston and St. Albans had 33 and 55 drinking places, respectively.[1] These inordinate numbers give evidence that the scale of business per retailer must have been quite limited and not enough to support him wholly. The inference is supported by statistical data of 1587, when in Nottingham town there were 115 traders who combined the manufacture or sale of ale or spirits with other occupations.[2] Agriculture, brewing and retailing ale were a frequent combination. Much of the ale was retailed directly at a "tap" or "brasserie" in the brewery.[3] It is very probable that the brewers did a custom trade, in whole or part, as the above-quoted 1760 authority affirmed to be the practice before 1689.

But the wars from 1689 to 1713 brought excessive taxation, especially excises on malt, hops and coal. Since the duty on hops was less than that on malt, the brewers devised the drink "beer" which would use more hops and less malt. The prohibition of French wines also gave added stimulus to brewing "the finest malt liquors in the kingdom."[4] Beer-drinking became the fashion, and brewers began to produce large quantities. This larger production went hand in hand with the development of a special moneyed class of beer-traders, who bought up large stocks of beer from the brewers, stored them for some time, and sold it as "stale beer." Stale beer gradually gave place after 1722 to "porter," the period of storage of which, in the maxim of trade, became four to five months.[5] The beers of certain counties and towns became famous throughout the Island. Pococke found, for instance, Cerne Abbas in 'Dorset "more famous for beer than in any other place in this country;" Dorchester also had "incomparable" beer; great quantities were sold in London and some was sent to various parts of the world.[6] The trade was therefore taking on proportions and ramifications that necessitated and employed bigger middlemen. Three factors were coöperating to develop a separation of employments in the liquor trade: (a) the rise of travelling and communication caused an increase in the number of taverns, inns, and places of drinking, which became retailing places for brewery products; (b) the increasing consumption made a larger trade possible and certain parts of the trade able to sustain a specialized middle-

---

[1] Statistics reported in Hall, Eliz. Soc., 163.

[2] S. P. Dom. Eliz., CXCVIII, 57; V. C. H., Nott. II, 289.

[3] Hazlitt, Liv. Cos., 384.

[4] Cox, Mag., 1720, p. 67.

[5] Gent! Mag. 1760: 527–28.

[6] Pococke, Travels; "Eng. Displayed," 1769, p. 67; "Deser. of Eng. & Wales," 1769, 229; V. C. H., Dorset, II, 368.

man; and (c) the change in kinds of liquor drunk, viz., to beer and porter, required storage for a period of time.

This tendency toward differentiation of employments in the liquor trade continued, but in the third quarter of the century an integration resembling the modern method of conducting the trade was well on its way. This was the ownership and establishment of retail shops over the Kingdom by the brewers and distillers themselves. It was described by a contemporary as follows: "the common Brewers and Distillers, who, not contented with such Trade and Gain as might fairly and spontaneously arise, are known to buy up paltry Houses and settle Retailes in every little Parish, as well as in every Town and City, and for fear there should be a Place in the Kingdom, exempt from their Advantage, we have scarce a Village without some of their Cottages and Huts . . . "[1] This practice indicates that the malt-distillers and brewers had become powerful capitalists. Their rapidly increasing business and their limited number made possible profits that outran the profits of other trades. And the control of the retailing of their goods, by ownership of the shops, aggrandized their power over the corn, malt and liquor markets.[2]

Their purchases of corn were so large that in 1756 and later years during periods of dearth, prohibitions were laid by law[3] against making low wines and spirits from wheat, barley, malt, or any other sort of grain, or from meal or flour. These acts were passed for two reasons, first, that the consumption of so necessary an article of food in the form of liquor was harmful because it lessened the food supply, and, secondly, because it increased the number of buyers of corn and, therefore, the price of corn beyond what the poor and needy were able to pay. The distillers usually bought through factors on the Corn Exchange and other markets, and in such large bulks that their purchases had a considerable effect on the prices prevailing there.[4]

From the sixteenth century onward the brewers were considered among the big buyers on the corn markets. In Coventry in 1520 some 68 brewers were consuming weekly in their trade 146 quarters of corn, i.e. about 16 bushels each a week.[5] Various ones of them were charged with forestalling and regrating barley in 1544. The

---

[1] "View of real grievances," 33.

[2] "Considerations on the Present," 10.

[3] 30 Geo. II, Caps. 10 and 15; 31 Geo. II, Cap. 1; 32 Geo. II, Cap. 2; 33 Geo. II, Cap. 4.

[4] Gent. Mag., 1759: 631.

[5] Coventry Leet Bk. ed. Dormer-Harris, I, 160; V. C. H., Warw., II, 267.

brewers were usually given a monopoly of the borough market as against "foreign beer" for instance in Weymouth and Southampton.[1] Sometimes it was conferred upon one or two particular brewers for a limited period of time or until undone by ill-rule; in such cases prices were prescribed and sales forced. Some brewers rose to considerable affluence and repute. About the middle of the seventeenth century Thomas Harrison of Reading was the chief brewer. He was mayor several times but lost his fortune during the Civil War. Here as at Abingdon the brewers were the chief men of the town.[2] William Hucks, member of Parliament for Wallingford, was a well-known brewer of the eighteenth century. He was brewer to George I; and took an active part in the local civic life of his community.[3] The lists of mayors and bailiffs of Oxford during the seventeenth century shows that brewing and malting were the most popular trades of their time. Henley brewers were very well-known. Many very prominent families were associated with the trade. Some extant breweries date from this and the next centuries;[4] for example, Hall's Brewery was in existence before 1718.

Some estimate of the volume of the liquor trade may be surmised from the total consumption of liquors in England. Defoe undertook to estimate the consumption on the basis of the malt produced in 1728: he concluded that there were no less than forty million bushels of malt brewed and distilled in England yearly exclusive of what was exported abroad, and that this was the means of making 10,000,000 barrels of strong beer, consumed in England, and valued at £10,-000,000. Of this £3,200,000 per annum represented the value of the beer sold to the retailer. His estimates in 1745 were slightly more conservative, but to the same general tenor.[5] This liquor was retailed through 200,000 alehouses, inns and taverns throughout England. The quotient of the purchases by the number of shops gives £16 each as the average business per annum of these shops, surely a very small business. Yet there was scarcely an inn, alehouse or coffee-house in the Kingdom that did not derive a goodly share of its profits from the retailing of liquors.[6]

---

[1] V. C. H., Dorset, II, 368; Hants, V, 473.

[2] V. C. H., Berks, I, 406.

[3] V. C. H., Midd, II, 168.

[4] V. C. H., Oxford, II, 262–63.

[5] Defoe, Plan, 197, 198, 202, 204; Com. Eng. Tr., II, 218. For wines see Com. Eng. Tr., II, 214.

[6] Gent. Mag., 1736: 576.

Besides the keepers of the ale-houses and taverns there were also hucksters who retailed ale. They, like the taverners, bought from the brewers or brewed themselves. Edward I forbade brewers to sell any manner of ale to hucksters, and forbade hucksters to buy from brewers for resale.[1] Such "hukkesters" appeared elsewhere in the Kingdom. They were common in Sussex in the fifteenth century. "At Appledram, 1422–1432, Henry Cobehay, one of several 'hukkesters,' or ale-sellers (as opposed to brewers) who kept 'cappelboothes,' was presented for breaking the assize, selling by false measure, and commonly selling food and drink by retail."[2] In the same county a few years later the "hukkesters" were reported to be buying from the brewers and evading the maltode, a tax.[3]

A substitute organization for the huckster and tavern systems was that of the itinerant brewer, who traveled about and worked at private beer houses. The squires and others of big estates maintained their private breweries. The itinerant brewer's services were in great request. This was a very common method in the eighteenth century.[4]

In 1736 was commenced as a national system a practice which has attached to the retailing of liquor to a greater or less degree ever since, and in most countries; viz., that of licensing retail liquor shops. The purpose and nature of the license are amply shown in the resolutions drawn up in the House of Commons pursuant to the act. " 1. That the low Price of spirituous Liquors was the principal Inducement to the excessive and pernicious Use thereof. 2. That in order to prevent the excessive and pernicious Use of Spirituous Liquors, a Discouragement should be given thereto by a Duty to be laid on all such Liquors by retail. 3. That the vending, bartering, or uttering the said liquors should be restrained to Persons keeping publick Brandy Shops, Victualling Houses, Coffee-Houses, Ale-Houses and Innholders, and to such Apothecaries and Surgeons, as should make use of the same by way of Medicine only. 4. That no Persons keeping a publick Brandy Shop, a publick Victualling House, Coffee-house or Ale-house, or being an Innholder, should be permitted to vend, barter, or utter the said liquors, but by a Licence, with a Duty payable thereupon."[5] These resolutions were incorporated into a bill and passed after a long and spirited debate, being opposed chiefly

---

[1] Lib. Alb. I, LXIII, 360–61; III, 141.

[2] V. C. H., Sussex, II, 261.

[3] Hist. MSS. Com. Rep., V, 49a; V. C. H., Sussex, II, 261.

[4] V. C. H., Berks, I, 407.

[5] Gent. Mag., 1736: 575; J. H. C., 22: 638.

by the West India sugar interests. The economic and social effects of such license system are subjects in the arena of present-day disputation and politics. The result, so far as the middleman was concerned, was to reduce the number of shop-keepers, eliminating the smaller shops, and to concentrate the trade in the hands of the fewer larger retailers.

ACCESSORY TRADES.

(a) Wines.

Wines were an imported commodity. France, Portugal and Spain supplied England with the greater part. The Liber Albus enumerates Malvesie, Vernage, Crete, Provence, Romaney, Rhenish and Red wines, as sold in the London taverns at the opening of the fifteenth century. They were sold only in draught.[1] At this time it appears that the keepers of the ale-houses were distinct from the wine-taverners and they were quite likely prohibited from selling each other's commodity.[2] In the city there were a body of "wine-drawers" whose business was limited to the loading, carriage and unloading of tuns and pipes of wine from the Quay sellers to other parts of the city. There were ordinances prescribing their charges according to weight and distance.[3] In the time of Sir Walter Raleigh, according to the wine licenses he was empowered to issue, maximum prices were fixed at which French and other wines might be retailed; while others as muscatel a taverner might sell "at his .   .   . moste profite and commoditie." The wines of Spain, Italy and Greece were permitted to be sold at higher prices than the French. It appears that some Spanish wines were received through Holland where they were adulterated.[4]

International policy interfered much with the wine trade. Prohibition of the wine-trade was a military weapon. During wars with France encouragement was given to the Spanish and Flemish wines and impositions were put on the French.[5] The shifts in the volume of trade occasioned by the English-French tariff war between 1664 and 1713 were most marked, Portugal's trade increasing or decreasing with every change upward or downward of the French tariffs.[6] The

[1] Lib. Alb. I, LXIV.
[2] Ibid., LXI.
[3] Ibid., LXV, 526.
[4] Hall, Eliz. Soc., 77.
[5] Ibid., 78.
[6] See statistics, British Merchant, I, 302; 307, 319.

Methuen treaty was heralded as a wonderful achievement and as giving England the Portugese wine trade.[1]

The importing merchants appear to have sold their wines to the taverners who retailed them. The distributing carriers were the "wine-drawers."[2] The enforced distinction between wine taverner and ale-house-keeper no longer obtained after gild-control declined in the city and travel increased; both kinds of beverages were sold by each class. It was the custom for the wine-merchants to send coopers over to Portugal as agent wine-buyers; they mixed the wine there in rented cellars before they shipped it to England.[3] A custom house regulation prevented the merchant importers from doing a retail business in connection; the duty on wines for retailers was 8 per cent higher than on those for wholesalers and if a merchant sold any at all by retail he was charged the higher rate on all.[4] There appear to have been many evasions of the regulation, however. The Vintners' Company was essentially mercantile in its early days and the vintners evaded the law limiting them to the wholesale trade by assigning their ware to taverners for sale as agents.[5]

(b) Cider and Perry.

The juice of the apple and pear provided a considerable industry in several counties, chiefly Hereford and Hants. One John Beale, in 1656, entitled a publication of his, "Herefordshire Orchards a Pattern for all England." In Hants during the same period one John Delamere was the manufacturer of cider-mills on a considerable scale.[6] The organization of the Hereford cider industry in the last quarter of the eighteenth century was described by a writer on agriculture. Much of the cider was sent to external markets, the principal one being London, whence it was exported, in part, to the West and East Indies and other foreign markets in bottles. Bristol also exported. The home consumption, however, was greater than the foreign; "not only London and Bristol, but 'every town in this Island' as well as Ireland were supplied by Herefordshire. The immediate purchasers, termed 'cidermen,' for these markets were dealers who lived in the

---

[1] See discussion of the commercial aspect of drinking as given in Lecky, I, 517, et seq.

[2] Cf. Hazlitt, Liv. Cos. 1, 322.

[3] Atlas Mar. et Com., 154.

[4] Case of Messieurs Brooke and Hellier, ca 1700.

[5] Hazlitt, Liv. Cos., 317.

[6] J. Worlidge, Vinetum Brittoricum, 1676 ed. 160; V. C. H., Hants, V, 475.

district, chiefly at Upton and Ledbury, but Bristol, too, sent buyers, and of late years London dealers had bought large quantities. The liquor was sold either immediately from the press, or after the first racking, or ready for market in casks, or occasionally in bottles. The growers generally objected to selling the fruit, as thereby they lost the washing of the 'must' for family liquor, and most of the liquor was sold straight from the press, the dealers preferring to have the fermenting of it and an opportunity of suiting the taste of their customers. The London and Bristol dealers had places in or near the county, chiefly at Upton and Hereford, where they worked the liquor they had bought."[1] There were some public grinding mills. The decline of the Hereford cider business about 1800 was ascribed to the adulteration of the liquor by the middlemen who thereby brought it into discredit.[2]

(c) Hops.

Hops were introduced into the English brewing industry during the reign of Henry VIII. Beer-brewers, in contradistinction to ale-brewers, arose during the reign of Elizabeth.[3] Hop plantations were started about Reading in 1552 and about Colchester in 1571. In 1607 it was said that "Suffolke, Essex, and Surrie, and other places doe find to their profit" to raise hops on their "lowe and spungie grounde."[4] In these counties the cultivation of hops became a leading industry and continued so for two centuries. Chelmsford and vicinity dispatched their hops to Stourbridge and marketed them there at the great annual fair.[5] Hedingham was the chief center of cultivation. Worcestershire became a hop-producing region during the seventeenth century. Worcester had one of the greatest hop-markets.[6] It grew particularly during the eighteenth century.[7] Bewdley had a weekly hop market.[8] At these markets the hops were bought up by the brewers or their agents and carried, as packed by the growers,[9] to the brewing districts and houses. As has been shown

[1] Marshall, Rur. Ec. of Glouc. II, 206, 364; V. C. H., Hereford, I, 427.
[2] Cooke, Cider and Perry, 9, 10.
[3] V. C. H., Berks, I, 405; Essex, II, 366; Worces. II, 254.
[4] Norden, Jno., The Surveyor's Dialogue, 206.
[5] Defoe, Tour, I, 125.
[6] 2–3 Anne, Cap. 8; 3 Geo. II, Cap. 23; 4 Geo. II, Cap. 25.
[7] Univ. Mag., June, 1763.
[8] Postlethwayte, Dict. II, 846.
[9] See description of package, V. C. H., Essex, 366.

above, the excises on hops, etc., effected a change of fashion, from the consumption of ale to that of beer, after 1689, and this made larger the use of hops. The hop industry declined after the opening of the nineteenth century.

CONCLUSION.

The most prominent phenomena of the history of the middlemen in the corn and corn products trade, during the period 1660 to 1760 in particular, were movements toward the following ends: (*a*) freedom from governmental control, the only important exception being the license system imposed on the retail liquor trade; (*b*) speculative activity, wherein the jobber and merchant were much engaged; (*c*) extension over a broader geographical market; (*d*) dominance of the capitalistic class, especially the bigger dealers; (*e*) separation of functions and divisions of the middlemen's occupations; and a counter-movement toward integration of businesses wherein there was a fusion of functions and a fuller control of the successive processes of the industry.

The first feature was evident in the disintegration and abandonment of the license system relative to corn buyers; in the reduced importance of the public corn market and the rise of unrestrained ingrossing and regrating on the same, and in the greater freedom of internal commerce that complemented the decline of the town's control. Private elevators, large mills, corn-merchant-bankers, big business, and the ownership of vehicles of commerce fully attest the rising importance of capital in the corn trade. Great speculations in corn, bought in one time or place and sold in another time or place respectively, bespeak a wide control of capital; while the new practices of selling by sample, of dealing in futures, of bears and bulls, etc., on the newly-separated Corn Exchange indicate that the corn trade had become distinctly speculative. The broad system of agency for buying and selling, exemplified in such a firm as the Couttses, as well as the improved ways of transporting corn, show that the territory drained by particular markets was extending into broader zones. And the spread of the miller's activity into the corn-buying and meal-selling and into speculations in corn, and of the distiller's incorporating the retail liquor shops into his domain, are demonstrations of a tendency counter to the movement whereby the factor ceased being merchant or jobber, and the merchant left retailing to the chandler.

All these tendencies were means to a greater commerce as they were realized. The stimulus the corn trade gave to agriculture and the wonderful increase that resulted in that surplus of corn to be marketed at home and abroad were interactions of first magnitude. And it is particularly appropriate to note how the organization of the trade led the way or conformed itself to the increasing volume of business it had to perform.

CHAPTER III.

Middlemen in the Animal and Animal Products Trades.

DISTRIBUTION.

Corn excepted, cattle were the most general product of English agriculture. Not only were the grass lands, as the moors, fens, and mountainous parts, devoted to cattle and sheep raising, but these animals engaged a part of the economy of every farm wherever situated. The wide distribution of cattle raising is indicated in the tabular display of the various counties' products appended to the previous chapter. In nearly every county the reporters in these several years found cattle a leading product. The distribution of sheep was the same as that of wool described in another chapter.[1] The total yearly breed and the total stock in England and Wales about 1700 is shown by the following table:[2]

Animal	Yearly breed	Total stock
Beeves, etc...........................	80,000	4,500,000
Sheep, lambs, etc.....................	3,600,000	12,000,000
Swine, pigs, etc......................	1,300,000	2,000,000

In consequence of this wide dispersion and the plenty of each farm, the movement of cattle, sheep and meat, effected by the dealers' organization, was toward the town and city consumer, and toward the exporter. Of the former, London was the grand objective; every part of the isle of Great Britain contributed to the supply of this city, even the distant parts of Scotland.[3] England did not export meats especially. Bristol and Liverpool in their West India trade sent out small quantities; but on the whole England was in need of the importation rather than the exportation of her animal products. Much agitation arose in times of dearth and high prices for the repeal of the laws prohibiting the importation of Irish meat cattle. The English graziers bought many cattle in Wales. Pococke notes the great cattle-markets, for example, at Cadvestone.[4]

[1] See Chapter V.

[2] Davenant, on Trade, Works, II, 219.

[3] Anderson, Origin, III, 468; Defoe, Tour, I, 69; Postlethwaite, s. v. British Empire.

[4] Pococke, II, 200.

GRAZIER.

A grazier was a fattener of animals, whether their food was grass, turnips, oil-cake, or other provender.[1] As such, he might more properly be classed as a producer than as a middleman. But since he usually bought his stock and did not breed them, and since he kept in close touch with the market and operated as other middlemen did in order to affect the prices reigning there, he had some middleman quality.

In the period of high prices in the middle of the eighteenth century much complaint was manifest against the grazier for his at least alleged control of the cattle market.[2] At this time it was said that whenever a farmer had any cattle which he proposed to drive to London, the grazier or his agent became a purchaser on the spot; the farmer thus saved himself the trouble, expense and risk of driving them to a distant sale; but the grazier thus monopolized the cattle fit for slaughter, and by sending to or keeping from the market could influence prices at will, the relatively small number of graziers making the act easy. The charges were denied by the graziers. The question cannot be determined, and is only mentioned to show that the grazier had middleman possibilities.

Attention is called to two instances illustrating the business of the grazier. The first concerns the marketing of Scotch cattle, by the graziers of Norfolk.[3] There was a little village, St. Faith's, in Norfolk to which the Scots brought the most of their export cattle; and at this place they were bought up by the Norfolk graziers. They owned a vast tract of meadowland and fed these "Runts" from the cold and barren highlands into the fattest beef in England. In these marshes 40,000 were being pastured in 1722, sufficient for the supply of Norwich, Yarmouth and the other towns of the county, besides a great number dispatched to London weekly throughout the winter season.

The other instance concerns sheep.[4] This traffic centered in Weyhill, the greatest fair for sheep in the Isle, where 500,000 were sold in one fair; the graziers out of Berks, Oxford, Bucks, Bedford, Hertford, Middlesex, Kent, Surrey, and Sussex were the buyers, but not for immediate killing. The farmers of these several counties clubbed in

---

[1] W. Marshall, Norfolk, II, 380 (1787); cf. R. L'Estranger, Seneca's Morals (1678) 47; Gent. Mag., 1755: 365.

[2] For example, see Gent. Mag., 1755: 294.

[3] The data are taken from Defoe, Tour, I, 69.

[4] Ibid., II, 45.

groups of ten or twenty and sent one of their members to do the buying for the whole, and a division was made upon his return. This is a particularly interesting case showing the need of a middleman, but where none arises due, likely, to the spasmodic nature of the traffic he would serve. These "store" sheep were sold at the local or London market when fattened.

The practices of the graziers had been the subject of legislation from an early date. In the Edwardian statute[1] against ingrossers, regrators, and forestallers, 1552, sheep, lambs, and calves were by name included in the list of victuals, none of which were to be regrated, etc., and it seems cattle were included in the more general terms. But in addition to this prohibition, a further one was laid to the effect that no one was permitted to buy cattle or sheep and sell them again alive unless he had kept and fed them for the space of five weeks on his own land or common. It has been shown that these statutes fell into decay after 1660 and were not executed.[2]

DROVER.

In 1552 drovers had "been wont" to perform the double function of dealing in cattle and of driving them to market. The same concept attaches to the name in the statute of 1670 and the acts to continue the same in 1692, 1699, and 1706. But during the eighteenth century, as the license system (to be treated later) waned, the two functions were differentiated and the jobber assumed the buying and selling part of the business. According to the testimony of different drovers before a committee of the House of Commons in 1796 the drovers had become hirelings of the carcass butchers and the Smithfield salesmen, and drove their cattle and sheep from the markets in the country, such as Hayes, Rumford, Southall, Mile-end, etc., to the city markets.[3] It seems that he made regular calls or solicitations from the breeders and owners of cattle to do their driving.[4] During the eighteenth century, therefore, the drover lost the middleman quality.

[1] 55–56 Ed. VI, Cap. 14.

[2] See Chap. II.

[3] J. H. C., 51: 639. About this time, the drover's salary and the salesman's commission on Somersetshire cattle amounted to 12*s.* per head at London, 5*s.* at Salisbury, and 3*s.* at Bristol. Billingsley, View of Somersetshire, 241. About 1760, cattle were driven from Suffolk one hundred miles to London and sold, the total expense for the driving, selling, keep, and turnpikes, amounting to only 5*s.* per head. Moore, Considerations, 16. These rates appear very reasonable.

[4] J. H. C., 51: 636.

The degree of importance of the drover can scarcely be realized now when the method of driving cattle to market hundreds of miles has been superseded by cattle-trains and ships. In the days when the black cattle from Ross, Scotland, and the neat-cattle of Brechnoch, Denbigh and Somerset met the Surrey cattle at Smithfield after tramps of months' duration and by pathless country, there was an essential need for a competent drover. And in performing the act of driving for one or more remote cattle-raisers every opportunity was offered him enroute to buy and add to his herd from the farms he passed. A priori, it seems plausible that the first drovers were cattle-raisers or their servants, and that their middleman business was adventitious in the above manner; and that with the accumulation of capital they entered more fully into the business of buying cattle to sell at a distant market.

Edward VI inaugurated a license system for the control of the drovers. This was part of his general scheme for protecting the consumers against the malpractices of the middleman in the necessaries of life. Every drover was required to procure a written license from three justices of peace of his district, which entitled him to buy cattle at his "free Liberty, and Pleasure, and to sell the same again at a reasonable Price, in common Fairs and Markets distant from the Place or Places where he shall buy the same forty Miles at least."[1] Ten years later certain qualifications were laid which the licensed had to meet, viz., to have had a three-year residence in the district, and to be a married householder at least thirty years of age.[2] By another act a century later (1670) no drovers were to be licensed within eighty miles of London, and each drover was required to enter bond. This was passed to correct abuses on the Smithfield market.[3] But like the badger's license, after commerce broke the regulatory shackles and entered a freer course, the drover's license was evaded and neglected.[4] At the same time the middleman element in this business was passing from the drover to the jobber.

JOBBER.

The jobbers bought cattle and sheep either at Smithfield market or at the nearby towns along the roads by which the animals were

---

[1] 5–6 Ed. VI, Cap. 14, Sec. 16.

[2] 5 Eliz., Cap. 12, Sec. 4.

[3] See treatment below under the caption "Salesmen at Smithfield."

[4] For the process of decay, see "Essay against Forestallers," 14.

being driven to market. They bought from the graziers, drovers, and farmers and from one another. They sold at Smithfield and occasionally at country markets. The buyers were the carcass and cutting butchers, the graziers who bought lean cattle, and other jobbers.

Before 1750 the jobbers had gained a monopoly of the live-stock market. Their practice of buying in the country stock which was coming to market was a most glaring violation of the laws against "forestalling;"[1] it is likely that this course of business was delayed in its emergence by this opposing legislation, and the free and extensive practice of forestalling the Smithfield Market is the most salient evidence of the degree to which trade had freed itself from governmental restraint and interference.

As buyers from the farmers and graziers, the jobbers made their purchases at the several farms by personal canvass. They higgled over the price to be paid; the prevailing market price was not then so well known as now, for the metropolitan newspapers scarcely reached the rural parts with their statements of the market's course. This circumstance favored the jobber who was more in touch with the conditions at Smithfield. If any grazier was persistently disinclined to sell to the jobber, the latter sometimes endeavored to tempt the grazier by offering a price higher than he intended to give or than prevailed at Smithfield. If afterwards the grazier tried to market the animals he would fail to realize the price offered by the jobber. As a consequence the next drove the grazier had to sell he was inclined to sell to the jobber lest he lose as he did before.[2] By divers devices merely suggested by this one, the graziers and farmers were brought into more or less dependence upon the jobber.

But the greater part of the purchases were made en route to London.

---

[1] The practice had gotten well in operation by 1718. "Bargains of this sort are frequently struck by the Jobbers and Forestallers at the Town's-end, or perhaps within a Stone's cast of the Market; and they have their Inns and Yards, which are a kind of Half-way Houses for this purpose, where they meet and cabal and there openly carry on the Forestalling Trade, as if some Fair or Market were actually settled in those places by Patent or Prescription." "Essay against Forestallers," 14.

[2] J. H. C., 51:637. According to the testimony of one Adams, who had been a salesman in Smithfield for fifty years, the practices of jobbing had been common at that market ever since he could remember; he noticed nothing new in the practice at the time he gave the testimony (1796). It may be assumed that the data furnished by the hearings in 1796 need be discounted in value but little for the period before 1760.

The jobbers met the herds and flocks along the roads or at the towns, the "resting places." Such towns were Islington, Mile-end, Knightsbridge, Romford, Southall, Hayes, etc. They also were the most prominent buyers at the fairs and markets.[1] The monopoly they developed was sweeping. Various estimates of its extent were given.[2] In the North it was asserted that they bought up more than half the lean cattle; others said that of all that came to Smithfield both of cattle and sheep three-fourths were jobbed; the maximum estimate was that not one in ten escaped the jobber's hands. At the Newgate Market one jobber was known to have bought up two-thirds of the animals alone.[3] But even this does not represent the total business because they were re-sold several times from jobber to jobber, as they moved along, so that before they reached Smithfield they had been jobbed four or five times.[4] As early as 1718 a pamphleteer declared that "in the Space of 10 or 12 Days, the several kinds of Cattle designed for Provisions, do commonly pass through Seven or Eight Hands before they come to the Butcher."[5]

Having a monopoly of cattle and sheep the jobbers were able to exercise a dominating influence over the market. They, like all ingrossers in this period, were the object of violent invective and attack for that alleged baneful influence which ingrossers were supposed to exert on prices. The butchers claimed that they were defrauded from a free market for buying fat cattle and the graziers likewise for buying lean; and that prices were arbitrarily raised "Twenty Shillings in Ten Pounds," or "20 or 30s." per bullock, or "3 or 4s." per sheep, etc.[6]

Early in the eighteenth century the jobbers had developed a sort of "Stock Yards." They owned tracts of grass lands in the vicinity of the cities where they marketed.[7] In these they kept a "Reserve" for two purposes: the first was that they might at short notice be able to supply a thin market; the second was that they might at will be able to flood the market, reduce prices, and buy up at bargain rates the cattle and sheep which farmers or graziers might try to market themselves. The first of these had a good economic effect: it tended

---

[1] J. H. C., 51: 636, 638.

[2] Ibid., 30: 787; 51: 637; 51: 636; 30: 787, respectively.

[3] Ibid., 30: 787.

[4] Ibid., 30: 788; 51: 637.

[5] "Essay against Forestallers," 14.

[6] Ibid., 14; J. H. C., 30: 787; 51: 638.

[7] "Essay against Forestallers," 15, 25; Rep. from Com. H. C.. II. 382; J. H. C., 51: 638.

to equalize the supply of the market and likewise equalize prices. The second was a means of maintaining their monopoly and was in itself harmless unless the monopoly was abused by introducing speculation and artificial variations of prices. In the long run no benefit could be derived from creating a dearth of cattle and sheep, or high prices, on the market.

The practice of "regrating" was common in Smithfield. Cattle were bought in one part of the market, driven to the other side, consigned to another salesman, and sold; but the salesman was informed as to the minimum price he should sell for and unless they brought this they were driven out of the market and held for another day. This sort of gambling in live stock was sometimes done with the same cattle three days successively or even more, until prices were realized.[1]

In order to avoid holding much land and flocks or herds on their own land, the jobbers bought on time-delivery. They contracted with the breeder to take their purchased cattle away at the next fair or market day. The live stock was in this way kept on the breeder's rather than the jobber's land till needed on the market.[2]

It was the opinion of many that jobbers were not necessary in the live stock trade. Marketing could be done as easily and well, in their opinion, without the jobber. The grazier and farmer could consign their cattle to the Smithfield salesman and by letter inform him at once how many were to be sent on such a day. When jobbers did not intervene it was the custom for the salesmen to send around their drovers to the different farmers and graziers for their cattle and to write them when they found the market was likely to want a supply.[3] The fact of their existence and long continuance sustains the presumption, however, that the jobber served a needed function to the trade. He was comparable to the wool-stapler and the corn-jobber or merchant; he performed the capitalistic, speculative part whereby an unequal distribution of the supply, both in time and place, was made to fit the steady demand of the consumers. Defoe noticed in 1722 that the improvement of the roads in the vicinity of London made it possible for the farmers and graziers themselves to market their live stock summer and winter at about the same price, where formerly they had to sell off their stock in early autumn when the roads began to get bad; he maintained that this was reducing the jobber's business as done by the farmers and butchers near London.[4]

---

[1] J. H. C., 51: 638–639.
[2] Rep. from Com. H. C., II, 382; J. H. C., 30: 787.
[3] See testimonies, J. H. C., 51: 636–7, 696–7.
[4] Defoe, Tour, II, 370.

The suggestion is that the periodic changes in the conditions of the roads disturbed the regular supply of the market and gave occasion to the jobbing business. The legislation of the day tried to abolish jobbing within eight miles of London,[1] but failed miserably, a fact which attests that some natural conditions existed such as the above mentioned roads, which gave a continuing opportunity and need for the jobber in connection with the great market. His function was, in short, to steady the market and equalize the distribution among markets.

SALESMAN AT SMITHFIELD.

Smithfield Market for several centuries was the great cattle, sheep and horse market of London, the greatest in the British Isles. In 1603, Stow showed that the once large field had been encroached upon and inclosed; only a small portion remained of the field which had served formerly as a market for horses and cattle, and as a field for military exercises, jousts, tournaments and great pageants and triumphs, "before the princes and nobility both of this realm and foreign countries.[2] In the early eighteenth century Smithfield had specialized in certain grades of animals. Calves and sucking pigs were sold in Newgate and Leadenhall.[3] Middling stock found poor sale at Smithfield, but it was the best sort of market for the largest and fattest animals, and for the small and lean.[4] In 1725 Smithfield was supplying a little less than one-half the meat consumed in the city. The carcass butchers bought stock in all the towns in the counties about London, and at the fairs in Northampton, Cambridge and Norfolk, and these animals were not sent through Smithfield. The farmers also slaughtered their animals outside London and brought in the carcasses. By these sources the other half of the London consumption was supplied. Altogether in this year the city was consuming 98,244 cattle, 711,125 sheep and lambs, 194,760 calves, 186,932 hogs and 52,000 pigs.[5] In 1800 the total annual consumption was about 110,000 head of neat cattle and 770,000 sheep.[6] The progress of these immense herds towards London must have been a sight comparable to the Union Stock Yards in the American markets today!

---

[1] 22–3 Chas. II, Cap. 19.
[2] Stow, Survey, 351.
[3] Maitland, II, 757.
[4] Gent. Mag., 1743: 538.
[5] The data for this year are taken from Maitland, London, II, 757.
[6] Middleton, View of Middlesex, 541.

"By an authentic list—there passed through Islington turnpike for Smithfield in 1754–5, oxen 28,692, sheep, 267,565; and in 1757–8, oxen 30,952, sheep 200,180."[1] The total annual sales at Smithfield in quinennial averages during the last quarter of the century 1660–1760 were as follows:

Year	Sheep	Black Cattle
1731–5	568,000	94,000
1736–0	599,000	98,000
1741–5	531,000	86,000
1746–0	656,000	81,000
1751–5	681,000	81,000
1756–0	617,000	92,000

Two corrections, among others, should be given to these statistics.[2] The first is the increase[3] in the size and weight of the animals during the century through breeding: in the years 1700–1800:

	1700 lbs.	1800 lbs.
Bullocks, at an average, weighed.........................370		800
Calves, at an average, weighed......................... 50		140
Sheep, at an average, weighed......................... 28		80
Lambs, at an average, weighed......................... 18		50

It is obvious that the weight of the animals had nearly trebled and a part of this increase came before 1760. The second correction relates to the double counting resulting from tolls paid twice on the same animals.[4] The statistics are based on the tolls' register. The marshmen bought sheep and took them away from the market and fed them again for sale, paying tolls again. But this reduction was more than balanced by others that escaped being registered. Tabular displays[5] of the animals sold at Smithfield on each market day indicate that the Monday business was much larger than the Friday business, these being the two days of the market.

The Smithfield salesmen were commission factors at this market. They bought and sold for the small commission of 1 s. 6 d. per bullock or 3 d. per sheep.[6] The cattle and sheep were consigned to the

[1] Gent. Mag., 1758: 92.

[2] The table is taken from Moore, Considerations on Price, 12; like statistics for each year, 1732–67, are given in Middleton, View of Middlesex, 538–9; and in Anderson, Origin, IV, 156 (1732–72).

[3] Middleton, View of Middlesex, 541.

[4] Gent. Mag., 1743: 259.

[5] Ibid., 1741: 86, for the years 1735, 1738; Maitland, II, 756–7 for the year 1725.

[6] Moore, Considerations on Price, 16.

salesmen by the breeder, grazier or jobber, and were considered as actually delivered to them as soon as they arrived at their "resting places" around the city, after which the salesmen became responsible for any lost. The salesman employed his own drovers to bring them on into the market and had the sole direction as to when they should be brought.[1] This expense and trouble was often saved by disposing of the animals at different resting places to the jobbers; the salesmen charged the grazier the same commission whether sold in Smithfield Market or twenty miles away.[2]

The salesman studied the market and tried in every way to inform himself of what stock was coming by each road and to estimate the relative supply of the market. Some of the salesmen did not stay continuously at Smithfield but attended, say once a fortnight; in their absence, however, they kept in close communication and had continued intelligence how the market went. By means of this information they were enabled to steady the supply and prices prevailing at Smithfield, to their own and the city's advantage.[3]

The salesmen sold to and for the jobbers. When graziers consigned stock to the salesmen they usually put no price on them, but the jobbers set a minimum on their consignments.[4] By letting the salesman know what the cattle cost them the jobbers threw the responsibility on the salesman to hold up the price, whereas with the grazier's cattle the salesman used more his discretion.

Conflicting motives existed in the salesman's mind with respect to the jobber. The jobber sold and resold on the market and at each sale employed the salesman on commission: this was an incentive toward association. But the jobber disturbed the relations between the salesman and the grazier or farmer. Mention has been made of the tempting prices sometimes made to the grazier or farmer for cattle which the grazier was determined to market without the intervention of the jobber, prices which the salesman could not meet. The grazier then became dissatisfied with the salesman. When the graziers sent their cattle to market after the jobbers had been with them, it was impossible for the salesman to give satisfaction, because the jobbers had bid more for the cattle than they knew they were worth.[5] Under these opposing motives it is likely the salesman's

[1] J. H. C., 51: 638.
[2] Ibid., 638.
[3] Gent. Mag., 1743: 538.
[4] J. H. C., 51: 638.
[5] For this opinion see J. H. C., 51: 636.

attitude toward the jobber was determined by the relative importance of the business he did for the graziers and the jobbers: self-interest would incline him to attach himself to the one furnishing him the more business.

The salesman sometimes performed all the activities peculiar to the jobbers. They owned or leased great areas of pasture land and were thus enabled to withhold cattle from the market as best suited their purposes. They made excursions out twenty or thirty miles on the different roads to purchase for themselves or others cattle en route to the market. The residue of the proceeds of the sales made for others amounted to no small sum remaining in their hands for a certain time, according to the distance at which their principals lived from London or to the intentions of these principals of coming into town. By the use of this money they could do a considerable business as jobbers on their own accounts and yet be men of but small property.[1]

The practices of jobbing, both by the jobbers and salesman, were the subject of legislation as early as 1670,[2] when a special act was passed to "prevent frauds in buying and selling of Cattle at Smithfield." No jobber, salesman, or other broker or factor was to buy any cattle, except pigs and calves within eighty miles of London. But two years' experience proved this prohibition "to be very prejudicial to the sale of Cattle of this Realm, and a great Inconvenience and Discouragement to those that feed the said Cattle in their respective Counties, who by reason thereof are forced to make Journies up in their own Persons to London, or to send others purposely for that Imployment, which commonly taketh up and wasteth all or the greatest Part of the Profit or Gain that they make on their said Cattle." For these reasons the prohibition was repealed in so far as it concerned salesmen employed by the butchers or jobbers.[3] The legislation, with this exception, was re-enacted under William III and Anne,[4] but lost its effectiveness and passed into complete decay in the first half of the eighteenth century.

The same statute of 1670 forbade the reselling of fat cattle in Smithfield; provided for marketing cattle sold there; and removed the customs of "foreign bought and foreign sold" from the Market.[5] This

---

[1] Practices of this nature were listed among the "Abuses relative to provisions," 6.

[2] 22 and 23 Chas. II, Cap. 19.

[3] 25 Chas. II, Cap. 4.

[4] 4 and 5 Wm. & Mary, 24; 11 and 12 Wm. III, Cap. 13; 5 Anne, Cap. 34.

[5] The custom of "foreign bought and foreign sold" was one used by the medieval towns in their protective policy and practice; it required non-freeman to buy from and to sell to freemen only.

last provision encouraged internal trade in live stock; the first provision was unavailing; and the second was evaded occasionally when self-interest was advanced by the evasion.

The actual service and function performed by the salesman is indicated above in the enacting clause of the statute of 1672 when the privilege was restored to the salesman to act as factor for the breeders and graziers. They effected an economy for these latter and thus justified their existence. Their service to the jobbers, though less essential, was quite important. They were prepared and skilled to accomplish sales. They were well versed in the technique of the market, could anticipate dearths and gluts in the supply, and reduce the variations of prices. They made it practicable for the jobber to act over a wider domain and increase his business untrammeled. The jobber studied the buying end of the live-stock market and trade and the salesman specialized in the selling. The two specialists working together facilitated the satisfaction of both the breeder and the consumer by reducing the difference between cost at the farm and selling price in London, i.e. raising the selling price for the breeder and lowering the cost price for the consumer.

CARCASS BUTCHER.

The carcass butchers were the wholesale butchers and meat dealers of London.[1] They bought their live stock at Smithfield, and in the country, and in the other markets of London. They sold to the cutting butchers, i.e. the retail butchers.

The chief meat markets of London were Leadenhall, Newgate, Honey Lane, St. James, Clare and Borough,[2] and the market at White Chapel which dealt wholesale only.[3] At these markets live hogs, sucking pigs and calves were sold. One of the most noticeable things about the dealings in these animals and meats was the degree to which the business was concentrated in the hands of a relatively few. Certain dealers stood out preëminently for the large fraction of the total business of the market which they did. In 1730 and thereabouts one Prescott, a wholesale mutton-butcher, killed on an average more

[1] Defoe, Com. Eng. Tr., II, 211–12.

[2] For a description of Newgate Market, see Maitland, London, II, 925; of Leadenhall, Defoe, Tour, II, 173–4. These descriptions were for the first half of the eighteenth century. Descriptions for the end of the century may be found in Middleton, View of Middlesex, 542.

[3] Maitland, London, II, 757.

than twelve thousand sheep yearly. One White sold nearly eleven thousand calves on Newgate Market, about one fifth of the total business. Two salesmen of hogs, Odell and Roberts, sold 80 per cent of the 147,000 hogs sold on the London markets, and no others sold much above one-tenth as many as either of these. These dealers specialized in one kind of animal and meat handled—one dealt in cattle and beef, another in sucking pigs, another in mutton, etc., and their operations were centered more or less on certain markets, for instance, those dealing in calves dealt mostly at Newgate, those in pigs at Leadenhall, etc. Their business was somewhat seasonal, doing a minimum in the hot summer months and a maximum in winter.[1]

The wholesale butchers were of two classes, one of which might be denominated grazing butchers, for they lived near London, owned stock lands, bought stock at Smithfield in the autumn and, having fed it a few months, sold the meat in carcass in winter at a better price.[2] The representative of the other class was more exclusively a middleman: he bought at Smithfield or scoured the country like the jobbers and bought on the roads and farms; he slaughtered his animals and sold them to the cutting butchers.[3] Butchers of this latter class, throughout the eighteenth century were regarded as forestallers of the meat market,[4] through their buying, like jobbers, live stock enroute to the market. The cutting butchers fell into an economic dependence upon the carcass butchers and complained continuously of not being able to get live stock or meat except through them.

It was the policy of Parliament to restrain the butcher from jobbing either animals or meat. In the middle of the sixteenth century the butchers were forbidden to buy fat cattle or sheep with the intention of selling them again alive.[5] A century later it was reported that this prohibition had failed to effect the intended reformation "by Reason of the Difficulty in the Proof of such buying and selling, being for the most part at Places far distant, if not in several Counties, by Means whereof the Parties so offending have escaped unpunished." Another act was therefore passed giving the informant a half of the fine imposed upon the violator of the prohibition.[6] The same idea was put into

---

[1] The above data are gleaned mostly from Maitland, London, II, 757.

[2] Defoe, Tour, 1, 7.

[3] "Abuses relative to provisions," 7.

[4] Compare Defoe, Tour, II, 171 (1722), and J. H. C., 29: 1046 (1764), J. H. C., 51: 640 (1796).

[5] 3 and 4 Edward VI, Cap. 19, Sec. 3.

[6] 15 Chas. II, Cap. 3.

the 1670 statute.[1] Under Anne the butcher was further restrained by being forbidden to sell in any market within ten miles of London to another butcher any fat cattle or sheep, either dead or alive,[2] but calves, sheep, and lambs dead were excepted from this prohibition by act of Parliament two years later.[3] The purpose of this legislation was to prevent, as was said, "a pernicious Practice, now in Use, for one Butcher to buy a greater Quantity of fat Cattle and Sheep than he can vend, unless by selling them again to other Butchers, which reduces the number of Buyers in Smithfield, and may be a very great inconvenience both to the Graziers and Housekeepers, by subjecting them both—to such Price as they shall think fit to give or demand." From which it appears that the carcass butcher was viewed in an invidious light because he bought in large volume and because he had uncommon power at making market prices. All this legislation failed primarily because it sought to eradicate a very useful agent in the meat business. The wholesaler of meats was probably more necessary than the wholesaler of more durable goods: expedition and dispatch were prime essentials in the distribution of the carcass. The cutting butcher needed a source from which he could buy at short notice what his customers required; this source was the carcass butcher. He, by having a large wholesale custom, could equally serve his retailer customers and at the same time reduce the risk of having meats spoil on his hands. He saved the cutting butcher from the necessity, but without removing the possibility, of doing his own buying and slaughtering.

CUTTING BUTCHER.

The cutting butchers were the retailers of meat in London and vicinity. They procured their supplies from the carcass butchers or purchased and slaughtered for themselves. The greatest part of the business was done at the stalls in the public markets like Leadenhall. Fleet Market, etc.[4] These stalls were eight, ten, or twelve feet long, and four, five or six feet broad, with racks, blocks, hooks, and all other conveniences for the sale of their meat, and were sheltered from the weather by roofs or by the ware houses above them; walks led between the rows of stalls. Fees were charged for the stalls, stand-

[1] 22 and 23 Chas. II, Cap. 19.
[2] 5 Anne, Cap. 34.
[3] 7 Anne, Cap. 6.
[4] See descriptions of these markets as given in Maitland, II, 989, 1002–3.

ings, and other accommodations. Public beams, scales and weights were provided. The city of London passed Acts of Common Council for settling and well ordering these markets.[1]

Another type of retailers were the hucksters who cried out their meats through the city.

The city of London and the provincial towns regulated the retail butcher business extensively even in very early times. The protection of the denizen dealers against "foreign" dealers, and the assurance of having the consumer's wants supplied directly before middlemen could buy, were the policies behind the legislation. The fifteenth century meat markets of London were at the Flesh Shambles of St. Nicholas, near Newgate, and at the stalls under the covered place or market house "Le Stokkes," the Stock Market. The shops were closed at night and sales began at six o'clock. Maximum prices were set on meats; any dealer who refused to sell at the publicly assessed price or withdrew from trade by reason of it, lost his citizenship. Foreign butchers were required to sell in the forenoon by retail; after that until vespers they sold by wholesale; they were to sell out their entire stock within this time. All carcasses brought to market had to have their hide or woolfel with them.[2] Taking Beverley's as illustrative of the fourteenth century provincial meat market regulations, one finds that every butcher was required to sell the meat killed by himself in his own shop, and not to send it to another butcher to sell; he was given four days from the time of killing to sell his meat, or on the fourth day to put it in salt. These arrangements eliminated the wholesale butcher. The denizen and foreign butchers sold in different markets: the former elected one end of the lord's market and the strange butcher took the other end; the fish market occupied the center. This division was followed each market day.[3] In the contrast between the London and Beverley market the absence of the carcass butcher in the latter is the most striking fact, and, apart from the prohibitive legislation, was likely due to the smallness of the market itself. Wholesaling cannot subsist on small business.

On the whole, the business of the cutting butcher differed little from that of all retailers. They cut up and sold in parcels the carcasses which they had bought, to somewhat regular customers.

[1] Maitland I, 460 et seq.
[2] See regulations in Lib. Alb. I, LXXX, 263.
[3] Selden, XIV, 29.

OTHER ANIMAL AND ANIMAL PRODUCTS TRADES.

(a) Horses.

Smithfield was the great market for horses in the days of Henry II. An excellent contemporary description of the business and pleasures of this market at that date exists. It was the scene of tournaments and jousts at arms between mounted knights. The horsebuyers came here. Their ways of trying out the paces of the horses attracted the public as spectators.[1] In later centuries horsefairs attained some prominence in provincial parts. At Towcester and Northampton fairs horses were the most important thing sold.[2] Worcestershire had "three yearly fairs . . . particularly famous for the sale of strong black horses."[3] Defoe emphasizes the large number of horses produced by Leicester and York.[4] The former produced a big part of those entering into the horse trade. According to him, in 1722 and thereabouts, Northampton was "counted the Centre of all the Horse-Markets, and Horse-fairs in England, there being no less than four Fairs in a Year;" here they bought "Horses of all Sorts, as well for the Saddle as for the Coach and Cart."[5] Horses in this region were brought up by "copers" (or "kopers"). To Penkridge in Staffordshire "not less than an hundred" of these "Horse-Kopers . . . from London" came "to buy Horses for Sale." Some gentlemen came also "attended with their Grooms to buy Gallopers, or Race-Horses, for the Newmarket Sport." These Penkridge horses were assembled from York, Durham and "all the Horse-Breeding Counties in England."[6] Somerset bred colts and sold them "into the Northern Counties, where the Horse-Copers . . . in Staffordshire and Leicestershire" bought them and sold them "to London for Car and Coach Horses,"[7] the horse-dealers in London were called "Corsors."[8]

(b) Poultry.

The poulterers were a prominent class of tradesmen in early London markets. The markets for denizen poulterers were at Cornhill and St. Nicholas Flesh Shambles; those of the foreign poulterers were at Leadenhall and Friars Minors. The division of the market was "so they meddle not with the . . . . foreigners in sale or in purchase."

[1] See Lib. Cus. II. pt. I, 7–8.
[2] Pococke, I, 166.
[3] Nash, I, 411.
[4] Defoe, Tour, II, 333; III, 113–4.
[5] Ibid., II, 328.
[6] Ibid., II, 317.
[7] Defoe, Tour, II, 24.
[8] Hazlitt, Liv. Cos., 155.

Before nine o'clock the foreigners could sell only by retail to consumers and not to denizen poulterers. The foreigners dared not lodge with the denizen and had "to bring their poultry into full market, without selling any poultry out of the market, or in secret." The prices of poultry were set by public ordinance.[1] Forestalling was prohibited. The poulterers dealt in rabbits, game, eggs, and poultry. In the fifteenth century these were carried to market in baskets on men's and horses' backs.[2] They bought fowl in the country villages and advanced them to London for sale. It was sometimes quite impossible to pay high prices in the country and sell within the assizes' prices in the city.[3]

Lincolnshire and the "fens" were the great source of the poulterers' supplies. Suffolk also contributed much. Rabbits were marketed from Suffolk, where during the seventeenth century there were "so many warrens . . . in every place which . . . furnish(ed) the next markets and (they were) carried to London with no little reckoning."[4] Young reports a warren in Brandon, Suffolk, that yielded more than 40,000 rabbits a year, valued at 10 to 12*d*. each.[5] This industry afforded a by-product, viz., rabbit-skins, in large enough quantity to give rise to a tradesman or pedlar who hawked them about the country and from whom they were gathered up by the "tawyers."[6]

But poultry was the chief ware handled by the poulterers. The ruffs and rees were caught in the Lincoln fens and fattened at Wentworth for market.[7] During the eighteenth century special carriers of poultry between Lincoln and London arose. They employed a new sort of vehicle built with four stories one above another. These wagons were drawn by horses, two to twelve in number, day and night, and made as much as a hundred miles in two days and one night.[8] These wagons would carry a great number. This method was used "in particular for carrying young Turkeys or Turkey-poults in their season . . . also for live Chicks in the dear Seasons." From Peterborough such wagons were despatched to London twice a week, loaded so heavily that twelve horses were needed.

---

[1] Lib. Alb. I, 465–6; III, 186–7; Lib. Cus., II, CV.
[2] Ibid., I, LXXXI–LXXXIV.
[3] For a case, see Lib. Cus., II, pt. I, XCI–XCIII.
[4] Reyce, Breviary of Suffolk, 35; V. C. H., Suff. II, 247.
[5] Young, Gen. View of Agric. of Suff., 220.
[6] V. C. H., Lincoln, II, 387.
[7] Pococke, I, 67.
[8] Defoe, Tour, I, 62–3, 91.

From Surrey and Suffolk the turkeys and geese were driven on foot to the London market. The Dorking market was the most famous poultry market of all England. It was known for "the largest Capons" and "the fattest Geese." Sussex also sent up poultry.[1] Suffolk and Norfolk turkeys were driven in droves of 300 to 1000; over Stratford Bridge on the Stour Defoe declared 150,000 turkeys passed on their way from Ipswich to London yearly; "and yet this (was) one of the least Passages, the numbers which traveled by New Market-Heath, and the open Country, and the Forest, and also the Numbers that came by Sudbury and Clare, being many more." The geese were marshalled in droves between 1000 and 2000. They started after harvest and travelled through the stubble fields a hundred and more miles, and arrived in London by the end of October in fattened condition.[2]

(c) Cheese and Butter.

London drew its butter mostly from the east of England. In 1730, according to Maitland, there came by sea carriage from York, Hull, Scarborough and Stockton 115,000 firkins, from Newcastle-upon-Tyne 16,000, and from the County Suffolk 57,000 firkins. Of the 105,000 firkins that came by land carriage one Abraham Daking received 75,000. Altogether London was consuming 292,000 firkins of imported butter.[3] Four decades later it was reported that Suffolk and Cambridge were sending up great quantities of salted butter, and also York was beginning to contribute "no inconsiderate quantity . . . though not so good in quality."[4] Carmarthen in Wales had "a great trade in butter for London."[5]

More than half the cheese consumed in London came from Cheshire. This county sent up about 6000 tons; Hull and Gainsborough 1400 tons; Suffolk 1000 tons; and Newbury and Abingdon sent by Thames barges 2400 tons. The total consumption by the city in 1730 was thus 10,500 tons or more than 21,000,000 pounds.[6] The Cheshire and Suffolk cheese came by sea; the Oxford and Wilts cheese came by the Thames; the other chiefly by wagon.[7] Essex produced con-

---

[1] Defoe, Tour, I, 226.
[2] Ibid., I, 61–3.
[3] Maitland, II, 758.
[4] Postlethwayt, Dic. s. v. British Empire.
[5] Pococke, II, 193.
[6] Maitland, II, 759.
[7] Postlethwayt, op. cit.; Defoe, Tour, II, 38.

siderable cheese through four or five centuries.[1]   A fair was held at
Ipswich, "a very considerable one for Butter and Cheese, to which
the whole Country round resort(ed), to furnish themselves with
Winter Stores" and "also many of the London Dealers in those
Commodities."[2]

The Cheshire cheese was delivered by the farmers at Chester, where
it was shipped directly to London, or at Frodsham, from which place
it was conveyed by way of Liverpool to the London market.[3]   In 1722
London was consuming, according to Defoe, 14,000 tons; this is more
than twice as much as Maitland reported: the figures are rough
estimates by these writers, and can only be thought of as indicative
of a large trade.   Defoe also stated that 8000 tons more were distributed by way of the Severn and Trent, the former to Bristol, and
the latter to York, and the towns enroute.   Considerable quantities
also went to Ireland and Scotland.[4]   Shropshire, Staffordshire and
Lancashire also produced a surplus of cheese for market.   The Cheshire
men carried the London cheese either "by long sea" around southern
England and up the Thames, or else "by land to Burton upon Trent,
and so down that River to Gainesborough and Hull, and so by Sea
to London."   This divided route will in part explain the disparity of
Defoe's and Maitland's statistics.   About 4000 tons went by this
way of Hull; during the wars when the sea-route by the English
Channel was dangerous the part going by the north and east route
was much larger.[5]

Gloucester cheese came by land-carriage to Lechdale and Crickdale
on the Thames and down this river.[6] A big proportion of this county's
cheese was consumed in Bristol and Bath; these two cities also exported much to the West Indies.[7]   On the London market Wiltshire
cheese was known as Gloucestershire cheese.   It was carried by
wagon to the Thames and by barge to the metropolis.   Its spring
cheeses were very popular in the city during May and June.   War-
wichshire had no water carriage nearer than by way of Oxford on the
Thames.   So they carried it by land a hundred miles to London; the
London cheesemongers then distributed it by sea and river navigation
into Essex, Suffolk, Norfolk, Kent, Sussex, and Surrey.   Or else they
carried it by land once a year to Stourbridge Fair, whence the shopkeepers of all the inland counties bought it.[8]   Banbury in Oxford

---

[1] V. C. H., Essex, II, 370.
[2] Defoe, Tour, I, 36.
[3] Holland, Survey of Cheshire, 315–6.
[4] Defoe, Tour, II, 308–9.
[5] Defoe, Tour, II, 371; III, 9.
[6] Ibid., II, 38.
[7] Ibid., II, 38.
[8] Ibid., II, 371–2.

was famous for its cheese from the sixteenth to the eighteenth century.[1]

Somersetshire produced the famous Cheddar cheese.[2] It was manufactured at a coöperative dairy among the farmers at Cheddar. It brought a very high price, three or four times as much as the Cheshire cheese. A large part of the surplus came to London.

Factor. The cheese in these various districts was bought up by factors resident operating for the London cheesemongers. The factors in Cheshire visited the farmers and contracted with them to deliver their product at Chester or Frodsham.[3] At Uttoxeter Market in Staffordshire the cheesemongers of London maintained a factorage.[4] At Woodbridge and at Dunwich in Suffolk some very considerable merchants were engaged as butter factors for Londoners.[5] On the other hand, some provincial cheesemongers engaged London factors who sold their product for them. It was thought that the interposition of these factors was one cause of the high prices of butter that ruled in London as compared with the Bedford market in 1741, the former being three times as high as the latter.[6] In Warwich the factors were really regrators. Atherstone in Warwich had a famous cheese fair, where the cheese-factors bought up vast quantities and sold it again at the Stourbridge fair which began about the same time but lasted much longer. The buyers at Stourbridge sold again for the supply of Essex, Suffolk and Norfolk.[7]

Cheesemonger. This tradesman is described in 1714 as "a Retailer of Cheese, Butter, Eggs, Bacon, and Hams." His business was "pretty precarious" by reason of the perishability of his goods.[8] Edward VI had forbidden anyone to "buy to sell again any Butter or Cheese, unless he . . . sell . . . by Retail in open Shop, Fair or Market, and not in Gross;" inn-holders and victuallers were excepted for what they sold in their houses by retail. Retail was here defined to appertain "only where a Waye of Cheese or a Barrel of Butter, or of less Quantity and not above" was "sold at any one Time to anyone Person in open Shop, Fair or Market."[9] By a statute two

---

[1] V. C. H., Oxford, II, 277.

[2] Defoe, Tour, II, 30–1; V. C. H., Somers., II, 538–9.

[3] Holland, Ches., 315–6.

[4] Plott, Nat. Hist. of Staff., 122.

[5] Defoe, Eastern Tour, 110–2.

[6] "Considerations on the present," 13–4.

[7] Defoe, Tour, II, 331.

[8] Campbell, 281.

[9] 3–4 Ed. VI, Cap. 21.

years later the licensed badgers were permitted to buy butter and cheese; as were also victuallers to the extent of one-month's supply for their house.[1] But this act made no provision at all for retailers of cheese and butter; they fell under the prohibition of ingrossing. In 1623 the government recognized the services of the cheesemongers in fetching butter and cheese from the "divers Counties, upon their great Travel, Charge and Adventure, for Provision of the . . . City" and relieved them from troublesome informers and litigation about retailing done by them; the remedy consisted in allowing all regularly apprenticed denizen cheesemongers and tallow-chandlers to retail "in open shop, Fair, or Market by any Quantities at one Time, and to one Person, not exceeding four Wey of Cheese, or four Barrels of Butter."[2] Charles II in 1662 standardized the butter firkin for the whole Kingdom and issued regulations to prevent the fraudulent packing of butter.[3]

Besides this retail business on a small scale some of the cheesemongers became wholesalers and did a big business. In 1733 Abraham Daking was the greatest dealer in butter and cheese in the Kingdom and probably in the world. In that year he sold 40,566 firkins of butter and about the same value of cheese; and of the butter that came up by land he handled 30 per cent.[4] As early as 1662 it was necessary to regulate the transactions of the wholesale cheesemongers; penalties were prescribed for short-weighing to the retailers and the cheesemongers were forbidden to repack butter.[5] A few years later the importation of butter and cheese from Ireland was stopped.[6] Much of these products was brought to London to "the great Loss and Prejudice of this Kingdom"—such was the justification offered for the statute. The cheesemongers of London through their factors appointed in almost every butter-and-cheese-shipping seaport an officer called "weigher" whose office it was to search and weigh the butter which came to port to be shipped. The factors bought in the country places and markets and contracted to have it delivered at the port towns. Complaint was laid against these weighers for the deductions which they ordered for defective butter; the country sellers were at the weigher's mercy under the

[1] 5–6 Ed. VI, Cap. 14, Sec. 7.
[2] 21 Jas. I, Cap. 22.
[3] 13–14 Chas. II, Cap. 26.
[4] Maitland, II, 758.
[5] 13–14 Chas. II, Cap. 26.
[6] 32 Chas. II, Cap. 2, Sec. 9.

statute of 1662. This handicap was removed in 1692. The weighers were required to leave off personal discriminations among the shippers who brought butter to the port for shipment; butter was to be shipped in the order in which it was received; and their fees were prescribed. They were to keep a book of receipts and shipments which was open for inspection by the shippers. The masters of the ships had likewise to observe the rules of impartiality among the shippers. The cheese-mongers of London who had vessels of their own might send their own vessels for "their own proper and respective Goods."[1]

This 1692 law did not apply to the Chester and Lancashire ports and trade and ships. In the Cheshire cheese trade the London cheese-mongers operated a line of vessels of their own.[2] During the last decade of the eighteenth century they waged a long fight against the freemen of Liverpool who levied dues on Cheshire cheese shipped by that port.[3] By 1670 they had totally engrossed the carrying of cheese between Chester, Liverpool and London, and were striving to monop-olize all the carrying "trade to those Places, by carrying Goods at a lower Price than others afford to do, and laying it on the Freight of Cheese."[4] This is a case of "charging what the traffic will bear" and giving cutthroat rates on goods for the back-freight cargo to save going in ballast. A complainant averred in 1772 that they were associated in a club; owned sixteen vessels; had warehouses in Cheshire; settled at their weekly meetings what quantity they each would have brought up to London; and intimidated the outsider cheesemongers from engaging any other vessels to bring up cheese.[5] Along with the petitions against the bill limiting the number of horses drawing car-riages on the turnpike roads in 1751 "The Cheesemongers' Reasons for Support of their Petition" gave evidence of the large volume of their overland business.

(d) Fish.

The trade in fish was, from medieval times, subject to much regula-tion. It formed a most important item of food, and one which re-quired rapid dispatch between catcher and consumer. The fisher could scarcely organize a sales business. The middleman was quite irrepressible under these circumstances; yet the state and local author-

[1] 4 Wm. & Mary, Cap. 7.
[2] Picton, II, 48; 4 Wm. & M., Cap. 7, Sec. 8–9.
[3] Picton, I, 300–5.
[4] "View of Real Grievances," 276.
[5] Ibid., 275.

ities tried to repress or prohibit him.[1] In London the first fish market
was founded in 1283, "Stocks Market."[2] There were fish stalls here,
and at Woolchurchhaw and other markets in the fourteenth century.[3]
Ordinances during this century prohibited forestalling, and forbade
the fishmongers from being partners of the fishermen. The dealers
dared not buy until the nobler citizens and the populace had their
needs supplied. The prices were fixed by assizes.[4] In the time of
Edward I the chief fishmongers came to an agreement with the mayor
to hold two hallmotes annually. This was continued for centuries.
One form of forestalling that was particularized was that of going on
board vessels in the Poole and buying the cargo. This was prohibited
in London, and practically all river ports and seaports.[5] The regulations in provincial parts were to the same tenor as at the metropolis.
"Beyond the memory of man," it was the custom at Poole in Dorsetshire that all fish be exposed for sale on the public market before
being carried elsewhere for sale; this assured the public consumption
against the monopoly and extortion of dealers in fish.[6] Beverley
required the "basketmen," i.e. fishermen, to serve the citizens first
before they carried fish out of the town for sale; the place of sale was
the public market and not their private houses.[7] In addition to
regulations like all the above Southampton provided against a sort
of speculation in fish wrought by fishers offering their cargoes by parcels and thus maintaining a price.[8]

In 1552 it was provided by Edward VI, "That it shall be lawful to
all . . . the King's . . . Subjects now dwelling or inhabit-
ing . . . within one Mile of the main Sea, to buy all manner of
Fish, fresh or salted (not forestalling the same) and to sell the same
again at reasonable Prices."[9] That is, the offense of regrating was
not applicable to coast dealers in fish. Billingsgate early became the
leading London fish-market. In 1699 it was made "a free and open
Market for all Sorts of Fish" wherein it was "lawful for any Person
to buy or sell any Sort of Fish without Disturbance."[10] New markets

[1] Cf. Mrs. Green, Town Life, II, 36.
[2] Lib. Cus. I, CIV.
[3] Lib. Alb. I, LXXIV–V.
[4] Lib. Cus. II, pt. I, 117–120; Lib. Alb. I, 380–1.
[5] Lib. Alb. I, 377; I, LXXVIII, 373–376, 289; Gardner, Hist. Dunwich, 120;
V. C. H., Suff. II, 290.
[6] V. C. H., Dorset, II, 355.
[7] Selden, XIV, p. 58.
[8] V. C. H., Hants, V, 467.
[9] 5–6 Ed. VI, Cap. 14–15.
[10] 10–11 Wm. III, Cap.; Maitland, II, 791.

were from time to time set up and express permission was given to the buyers of fish at these markets to sell them again elsewhere "without any Lett or Disturbance from any Person . . . whatsoever for so doing."[1]   It was common practice for the Yarmouth and other fishermen to moor their loaded fish vessels in the lower Thames ports and send up only small quantities to market at a time "with a View to keep up the Price of . . . Fish." In 1749 and afterward the fishermen on their arrival on the coast between Yarmouth and Dover were given eight days within which they must dispose of their fish.[2]

In the latter part of the eighteenth century the market at Billingsgate served the dealers first: "those who kept shops in the various parts of the town" and the "hawkers, who during the forenoon cried them through every street."[3]   The fish were first sold by the wholesale "Salesmen." The wholesale market opened early in the morning and each "Salesman" continued to sell until he had disposed of all his fish. His place was then taken by the retailer. Usually the wholesalers were done by eight or nine o'clock and the retail market was then begun.[4]   The fishmongers had divided into two distinct and opposed classes—the "salesmen," or fishmongers proper, and the retailers. Another line of cleavage was between the salt-fish trade and the fresh-fish trade.

The transportation of fish offered a very serious problem in marketing. In medieval times they were brought mostly by boat and a few by horse and wagon, likely from the lower Thames ports.[5]   Besides the poorness of the roads, the perishability of the fish was the chief difficulty. Packing in ice was first resorted to about 1785.[6]   Town hucksters of fish were common at an early date; in London they were called "Birlsters."[7]   As early as 1380 "ripiers" were listed in the Sussex poll-tax list.[8]   They were carriers of fish from this county to London. The turnpike act of 1709 exempted these ripiers from paying tolls on the Tunbridge Wells-London Road. "Grimsby codchests" were a Lincolnshire tradition and were used in transporting

---

[1] 22 Geo. II, Cap. 49; this is illustrative and refers to the Westminster market. This market was a failure: Gent. Mag., 1760: 256.

[2] 22 Geo. II, Cap. 49, Sec. 12; Rep. Com. H. C. X, 364.

[3] Middleton, Middlesex, 543.

[4] Rep. from Com. H. C. X, 364, 366.

[5] Lib. Alb. I, LXXV.

[6] Rep. from Com. H. C. X, 369.

[7] Lib. Alb. I, LXXV.

[8] V. C. H., Sussex, II, 266.

cod from these parts.[1]   Colchester had "a peculiar art in barrelling"
oysters "by which means they   .   .   .   (were) so well preserved
that great quantities of them   .   .   .   (were) sent to London and
other parts."[2]   These barrels were shipped by land.[3]   A new sort of
vehicle was devised by the Lincolnshire fishmen for carriage of live
fish to London.   It consisted of "great Butts filled with Water in
Waggons;" the butts were filled with fresh water repeatedly enroute
at the inns; tench, pike, perch, and eels were thus carried; the carriers
took other goods along in their wagons besides fish.[4]   A similar device
was used for carrying live-fish to London by sea—a specially designed
sloop called "fish-pool."[5]

(*a*) *Fishmongers*.   The fishmongers' business took several. lines of
differentiation and specialization.   It divided on the basis of kind of
fish handled—salt fish, fresh fish, and oysters.   It divided between
wholesale and retail.   And between the wholesaler and the fisherman
the "salesman" or factor interposed himself.   There appear to have
been wholesale fishmongers in the fourteenth century in London at
"Fysshwharfe"[6] and they had to wage a long contest for the right to
do retailing.[7]   William III set up a body of regulations for the Billingsgate market in 1699 which included the prohibition of the practice
of fishmongers buying large quantities of fish which were divided up
by lot among them with the intent to sell them afterwards by retail.
This method was evidently an evasion of the common market regulation against ingrossing and indicates the function of the jobbing
wholesaler.[8]   The term "fishmonger" came to be more and more applied to the wholesaler.   He was described in 1747 as "a Tradesman
calculated for the Great and Wealthy: His Profits" being "without
Bounds, and" bearing "no Proportion to his Out-layings."[9]   The
monopolizing fishmonger was much complained against as the cause
of high prices of fish in 1755.[10]   Their practice was to contract with
fishermen for their whole cargoes and stop the vessels at Gravesend,
whence the fish were "brought up to market only, by boatloads at a

[1] V. C. H., Lincoln, II, 392.
[2] Cox, Mag. Brit. I, 707.
[3] Defoe, Tour (1724), I, 12–13.
[4] Ibid., (1738), II, 346.
[5] Ibid., I, 5.
[6] Lib. Cus. II, CXIII.
[7] Ibid., 384, ff.
[8] Maitland, II, 791.
[9] Campbell, 279.
[10] Gent. Mag. 1755: 129.

time, the remainder of the cargo being shifted into a wellboat, or storeboat under the care of some servant, who sent it up by degrees as the fishmonger directed."[1] Besides raising prices under their alleged monopoly they were charged with adulterating their fish and selling stale for fresh, coarse for fine, etc. at former prices.[2] The fishmongers sold to retailer fishmongers; they were either themselves "salesmen" or engaged "salesmen" to do their selling. They either bought their fish from the masters of fishing boats, or owned fishing boats themselves in whole or part and hired fishermen to go as masters; the apprentices of these fishermen were, for the purpose of better control, bound directly to the fishmonger.[3] According to his testimony one London fishmonger had part interests, averaging one-eight part, in thirty-two vessels; he had usually three or four partners who were not fishermen or fishmongers.[4]

In Yarmouth, the center of the North Sea and herring fisheries, the fishmonger was called the "oast" or "host." The immemorial custom had been for the master of every "foreign" boat, who came to fish off Norfolk, at his first coming into Yarmouth port to voluntarily "hoast" himself to some freeman of the town. In later centuries the host had become the fish-merchant to whom the incoming fisherman sold his entire cargo, at the tide or market price of that day. This price was the price agreed upon between the fisherman who came first that tide and his host or merchant. When the price was agreed to the host had to pay for all the herrings brought into port by the fisherman that season. The fisherman could sell to this one host only, and at the tide price, which reigned for twelve hours. The host was necessarily a freeman of the town.[5]

At Yarmouth a peculiar system of auction was in operation at the opening of the eighteenth century; it broke down in 1728 but was continued long afterward in the coast towns. A bill was drawn up by the host summing the tide price paid for a cargo and an allowance for provisions for the ship's crew. This bill was brought by him into the Free Chamber of the town and delivered to the Chamberlain. One-half of the cargo was then sold at public auction to the highest bidder among the freemen of the chamber, above the price set in the bill. All freemen except the host were competent to bid. Upon the

---

[1] Gent. Mag., 1760: 255–6.

[2] Morant, Hist. of Colchester, 87; V. C. H., Essex, II, 433.

[3] Gent. Mag., 1760: 255.

[4] Rep. from Com. H. C. X, 365.

[5] Surtees, 105: XXVI–XXVII.

sale thus by auction the herrings were divided between the host and other freeman buyer in equal proportions. This system was a very ingenious device for the prevention of monopoly prices at the will of a fortunate host.

Sometimes the hosts engaged in fishing directly, and were the owners or employers of boats.[1] Instance of the operations of an early fish merchant is found in the will of one William Godell of Southwold in Suffolk. He owned many ships, some of which were engaged in Iceland, some at home.[2] During the famous Fish Fair at Yarmouth the merchant hosts hired great numbers of "Cobles" which came from the coast towns to the north—Scarborough, Whitby, etc., and "Barks" which came from the coasts of Kent and Sussex.[3] At Rye in Sussex, "in the winter season every particular fyssherman" had "his shoppe unto hymselfe" and did his retailing. But during "the somer tyme" many of the shops were closed up while the fishermen were at sea fishing; the hosts then had both wholesaling and retailing to do.[4]

Salesman. It was the policy and practice of the government to prohibit agency on the fishmarket at Billingsgate. For instance in 1699 a statute forbade any "Fishmonger to engross . . . any Quantity of Fish, but what shall be for his own Sale or Use, and not on the Behalf of any other Fishmongers exposed to Sale."[5] On the other hand it was considered undesirable that "oastes" act as factors for the London fishmongers in the Sussex ports.[6] These efforts to enforce personal sale by the owners appear to have been actuated by fear that the factor by acting for several principals or by other ways would foster monopoly. But since a big portion of the fisherman's time was spent at sea and the times of sale were spasmodic and the establishment of a dependable and dependent body of customers was out of the question, the need of a system of factorage was great and inevitable. There arose during the eighteenth century a class of "salesmen" factors who bought and sold on commission; they did not buy on their own account to sell again.[7]

---

[1] V. C. H., Sussex, II, 266.

[2] Gardner, Hist. of Dunwich; V. C. H., Suff. II, 292.

[3] Defoe, Tour, I, 71n.

[4] Hist. MSS. Com. Rep. V, 140; V. C. H., Sussex, 266.

[5] Maitland, II, 791.

[6] V. C. H., Sussex, II, 266.

[7] The following data on the business of this class are gleaned from Rep. from Com. H. C. X, 364 ff, which contains much testimony of salesmen as to the conduct of their business.

The selling "salesmen" were employed by fishermen or fish-merchants living in the north coast ports. These merchants employed between one and five factors each, depending on the quantity of fish they sold. They sometines specialized in the sale of a particular kind of fish. They did not do all the selling at Billingsgate; some fishermen and some fishmongers continued to sell wholesale there. In 1760 there were between twenty and thirty factors and they simply sold for others; but in the decades following, they became part owners of fishing boats and exercised some control over their fishermen principals.

The salesmen occupied stalls for which they paid the owners some rental. The fish were placed on forms about eight feet long in baskets; some were in open air, some were covered. Lists detailing the numbers of fish and their qualities, according to the bills of lading in the hands of the salesmen, were posted, in conformity with the law, so that the buyers might be apprized of the quantity in the market. A system of higgling or auction was used in the sale; it was highly competitive; the fish were sold in parcels of different sizes so as to accommodate various customers; large lots were sold first, and the salesmen aimed at keeping the price about the same all morning. The buyers were the retailers and wholesalers, both of London and nearby towns, and consumers. Some bought from the salesmen and, at the close of the salesmen's sales, retailed them out in the same market. The salesmen sometimes bought for the retailer and wholesaler. It was alleged in 1760 that several fishmongers agreed upon one factor and had him buy a large quantity of fish for them in conjunction; they then divided up this bulk by lot among themselves or in parcels as they thought best. In this way they reduced competition and were able to realize better returns. It also gave them the economies and advantages of large buying.[1]

The merchants who exported fish to the Mediterranean and other foreign parts were prominent citizens in some fishing towns.[2] Another class bought catches on the Flanders and Callise coasts, and brought them to England for sale.[3] Their operations differed little from those of other more general merchants.

---

[1] Gent. Mag. 1760: 255.

[2] Instance Bridport in Dorset, V. C. H., Dorset, II, 348, 356; cf. V. C. H., Cornwall, I, 583.

[3] Hist. MSS. Com. Rep. XIII, App. IV, 18; V. C. H., Sussex, II, 267.

(e) Leather.

Southwark became the greatest leather market in England at an early date. The leather industry got well seated there during the fourteenth century. London, like all other towns of the medieval period, was jealous enough of her markets; and it was only because of the offensiveness of the slaughtering and tanning and leather business that she tolerated the rise of this market in a suburb. The Thames afforded the Londoners immunity from these offensive occupations on the Surrey side.[1] Bermondsey was also an early seat of the industry. It was promoted by the settlement of religious refugees here, by its oak-woods, and by its tidal-streams which afforded water power.[2] In Oxford the towns Witney and Bampton were great manufacturers of blankets. These were made from fel-wool, bought in great part with the fells at Southwark. The leather industry grew up in Witney as a by-industry of the blanket; "the Fell-mongers' sheepskins . . . being here made into wares, viz., Jackets, Breeches, Leather Linings, etc., which they chiefly vent(ed) into Berkshire, Wiltshire and Dorsetshire, no town in England having a trade like it in that sort of ware."[3] During the seventeenth century there was considerable tanning done in the Thames ports Reading, Wallingford and Abingdon.[4] The plentifulness of oak trees was the primary cause for the location of this industry in this county. It appears that there were shoemarkets in the small towns. In Beverley, for instance, in 1364 stalls were assigned for this purpose, called the Shoemarket, during market and fair days. It was then an old practice.[5]

The leather business was conducted under much restraint from the town and state governments. One line of legislation aimed at the demarkation of processes in the manufacture and distribution of leather; each operative was required to specialize in some one process and devote himself to that only.[6] During the fifteenth century the Worcester barkers, curriers, corcesors and saddlers were forbidden to act as leather middlemen—"to buy or sell leather either from butchers or from foreign hide or leather merchants, except in open markets."

[1] V. C. H., Surrey, II, 249.

[2] Ibid., 330.

[3] Plot, Nat. Hist. Oxford, 279; V. C. H., Oxf. II, 255.

[4] V. C. H., Berks I, 397.

[5] Selden, 14, p. 30.

[6] 25 Ed. III st. II, Cap. 4; 1 Hen. VII, Cap. 5; 19 Hen. VII, Cap. 19; 2–3 Ed. VI, Cap. 11.

The object here was to prevent the "grete custom of hids belongyng to the baill's offis for the tyme beyng (from) be(ing) loste . . . (through) byeing of hids of persons strangers owte of open market."[1] Nottingham had similar regulations requiring tanners and others to buy and sell only at the public market.[2] A system of searching and sealing leather was used at Leadenhall which persisted until 1803.[3] The laws against engrossing applied to leather: purchasers dared not buy any tanned hides with the object of reselling them.[4] All sales within three miles of London were confined to Leadenhall,[5] Southwark was exempted.[6] This act was enforced against several Surrey leathermen.[7] It was understood that if hides or leather were bought to be sold again they were to be improved while in the hands of the buyer.   None were allowed to buy raw hides and sell them untanned.[8] Elizabeth allowed to tanners only the right to buy raw hides, and to leather artificers only the right to buy red tanned leather from the tanners.[9] These regulations are enough to illustrate the straitened course of the leather business.   During the first half of the eighteenth century there was a general breakdown of the regulated market system.[10]

There was, therefore, very little purely middleman business in leather.   The Southwark and Bermondsey hide dealers bought sheepskins, tore off the wool and sold the unwrought skin; or else they sold fel and felwood together to the Witney blanketers.[11] The tanners had regular customers among the cordyners, and the butchers likewise among the tanners; in most towns the trades were controlled by gilds; and it was common practice to boycott debtor customers until debts had been paid.[12] The biggest tanners and dealers were found at Southwark; as early as 1606 it was common for some to deal in thousands of oxhides and sheepskins per year.[13] The volume of busi-

[1] Green, Hist. Worc., App. LXV; J. T. Smith, Eng. Gilds, 384; V. C. H., Worces. II, 302.
[2] V. C. H., Notting, II, 338.
[3] V. C. H., Surrey, II, 337.
[4] V. C. H., Sussex, II, 260.
[5] 24 Hen. VIII, Cap. 23.
[6] 5 Eliz. Cap. 8, Sec. 23.
[7] V. C. H., Surrey, II, 331.
[8] 3–4 Ed. VI, Cap. 9; 5–6 Edw. VI, Cap. 15.
[9] 5 Eliz., Cap. 6.
[10] V. C. H., Northants II, 312–3.
[11] V. C. H., Surrey, II, 333.
[12] Selden, XIV, p. 120, 122.
[13] V. C. H., Surrey, II, 335.

ness increased with the growth of Smithfield and the other London markets for live stock.

The tanned leather was disposed of to the "leather-dressers at Leaden Hall." The dressers sold their product to the "leather sellers." These latter were shopkeepers, and in some measure wholesalers, requiring considerable capital. During the first half of the eighteenth century a new middleman arose called "leather-cutter." Formerly the shoemaker "bought his Leather in Skins or half Hides from the Dresser, and cut out his Work himself; but the Number of poor Shoe Makers, who (were) . . . not able to lay out more money at once than the Price of Materials for a Pair of Shoes (gave) Rise to this Branch. They cut out their Leather in Soals and Upper-Leathers . . . according to the several sizes, and (sold) . . . it to the necessitous Shoe-Maker."[1] The rise of this middleman illustrates both the function of the jobber and the advantage a system of credit in a trade may effect.

Conclusion.

In summary, the most important economic movements in the live-stock and meat trade during the century under particular study were in the direction of greater intricacy of technique and in the direction of greater freedom of operation. The jobber differentiated from the drover; the salesman from the jobber; and the carcass from the cutting butcher. Business flowed more fully through the hands of the salesman. The complete failure of all legislation restraining the trade was most pronounced; the drover's license system, the prohibition of salesmen acting as factors for jobbers, and of carcass butchers acting as jobbers of live stock and meats, the prohibitions against the jobbers' forestalling and regrating, the abolition of drovers in the vicinity of London—one and all failed miserably: freedom was only realized by over-riding such restraining legislation.

[1] Campbell, 216–7.

CHAPTER IV.

MIDDLEMEN IN THE MINERAL TRADES.

COAL.

Divisions of the Trade.

The mines of Northumberland and Durham discharged their output through the Tyne and Wear rivers, the ports of exportation being Newcastle and Sunderland respectively. The Derwent carried the product of the Cumberland mines to the coast and it was exported from Whitehaven. South Wales dispersed its coal from Swansea Bay and port. In the first quarter of the eighteenth century there arose a river trade in coal from the mines of Lancashire and Yorkshire sufficient to supply the cities of the interior. The trade in coal on the Severn, particularly in Salop, increased very fast as the iron industry developed during the eighteenth century. The whole coal trade, therefore, considered with reference to the supply, is distinguishable into five parts, three of which are sea-borne traffic and two river-borne traffic.

The Whitehaven[1] coal trade was a growth, for the most part, of the eighteenth century. The destination of this course was the Irish capital and coastal towns, some parts of West Scotland, and the Isle of Man. There were (ca 1750) engaged about two hundred ships and two thousand seamen. Whitehaven ranked next to Newcastle as a coal exporting point, and Ireland was almost entirely dependent upon this city. This trade originated during the sixteenth century but made no rapid progress until the latter half of the seventeenth century; under the genius of Sirs John and James Lowther Whitehaven rose rapidly to prominence in the coal export business. Sir John developed a system of staithing coal, like that used on the Tyne, so as to steady the supply of coal for Dublin. The inventions of steam-pumping engines gave a great impetus to the mines and shipping. A system of carriage by wagons bearing 4400 pounds and rolling on iron-

---

[1] Refer to Defoe, Tour, III, 100: "Essai sur l'état," 110, 122; Galloway, Chapter X; Postlethwayt, Dic., s. v. *Coal*, for descriptions of this trade.

strapped tracks was introduced, also about 1700. For these various reasons Whitehaven came to rank second among the coal regions of the kingdom.[1]

The counties of Devon, Somerset, Dorset, and others burned only coal from Carmarthen, Pembroke, and other parts of South Wales, most of which was shipped from Swansea and Milford Haven.[2]

The Humber River coal trade was also a growth of the eighteenth century, and it furthered and was furthered by the rise of the manufacturing cities in the Northern district,[3] by the opening of the Trent, Calder and other rivers to navigation, and by the export tax[4] laid on sea-coal but not on river-borne coal in 1713. Derbyshire and Nottingham had considerable coal areas but the difficulties of carriage confined their product to local markets[5] i.e., in the midland counties. Attempts were made to market Derbyshire coal in London via Hull but they were unsuccessful until roads' improvements had come.[6] Nottingham coal was distributed by loaded asses and coal carts.[7] Every summer coal carts came from the neighboring counties bringing corn and carried back in exchange coal from the mines of Wollaton and Selston.[8] Coal became the most important item of export from this county during the eighteenth century.[9] The towns on the Humber, Ouse, Trent, Aire, Calder and Hull were supplied by boats from the inland counties of Derby and Nottingham, by the Trent, and from Wakefield, by the Calder. These boats went as far as York on the Ouse and this city acted as distributor to the others not passed. The cost of this down-river traffic from the pit to York caused the difference of about seven pence per bushel in the price of coal at the two places. Besides what came by these boats the towns were supplied with coal from Durham brought by "paniermen." They carried it in "paniers" on horseback.[10] Pococke states that a horse-

---

[1] See V. C. H., Cumberland, II, 359–62, for fuller description.

[2] "Essai sur l'état," 110, 122; Postlethwayt, Dict., s. v. Coal.

[3] Descriptions of this traffic are given in Postlethwayt, Dict. s. v. *Coal;* Defoe, Com. Eng. Tr., II, 171–2; Tour, III, 93–4.

[4] 12 Anne, Stat. 2, Cap. 9, Sec. 9; 6 Geo. I, Cap. 4, Sec. 1.

[5] V. C. H., Derby, II, 352–3.

[6] Gent. Mag. 1766, Feb.

[7] V. C. H., Nott. II, 296; Add. MSS. 18,552.

[8] Cal. S. P. Dom. 1619–23, p. 130; 1631–3, p. 18; S. P. Dom. Chas. I, CLXXXIX, 12; Jas. I, CXL, 10; V. C. H., Nott. II, 283.

[9] Deering, Vetus Nottinghamia, 92.

[10] V. C. H., York II, 340.

load weighed about 320 pounds.[1] The coal in the upper Severn counties was carried down to the river in "small carriages, with four wheels of above a foot diameter, thrust by men;" it was dumped into "boats which lye in the Severn ready to receive" it.[2] These were the first railways in the Isles and were first used between 1620 and 1650.[3] About 1750 such railways were introduced at the great Derby furnaces and handled about 20,000 tons yearly; these cars were drawn by horses and oxen.[4] During the last half of the seventeenth century "the most common freight upon the Severn" came to be "pit coal from Broseley, very famous for the collieries;" it was carried to Bridgnorth, Worcester, and other river towns.[5] In this river in 1758 were plying 376 vessels in inland navigation.[6] 297 of these were owned in Shropshire, principally at Broseley, Bridgnorth and Madeleywood; 61 were owned in Worcestershire, Worcester and Tewksbury standing highest in point of ownership. These 376 vessels were owned by 210 proprietors, an average of about two vessels each. The vessels were of two sorts: the smaller were called "barges" and "frigates," were from forty to sixty feet long, had a single mast and square sail, and carried from twenty to forty tons; the larger were called "trows," were of forty to eighty tons burden, had a main and top-mast about eighty feet high, with square sails and mizzen masts, were from sixteen to twenty feet wide and sixty long, and cost completely rigged about 300 pounds sterling. They were navigated by three or four men. During the Tudor period the Severn traffic was handicapped by tolls levied at Worcester, Gloucester, and other places along the stream.[7] The character of the Severn carriers was none too commendable.[8]

But the great termini of the coal trade from the remote days of Henry V till the nineteenth century were Newcastle and London. Newcastle and Sunderland supplied the whole eastern and southern coast of England from Portsmouth to Whitby, as well as all the parts of the interior which had river connections with these ports, with the

---

[1] Pococke, I, 49; see also V. C. H., Shrops. I, 465.

[2] Galloway, Annals, 202.

[3] V. C. H., Shrop. I, 465. For further data on the use of railways see Galloway, 64–6.

[4] Ibid., 463.

[5] Shrop. Arch. Soc. Trans. IX, 197; V. C. H., Shrop. I, 454.

[6] See Gent. Mag. 1758: 271–8, for the data from which the facts are drawn and computations made.

[7] V. C. H., Worces. II, 250–1; Nash, Worces. II, 46.

[8] V. C. H., Shrop. I, 426.

single exception of the Humber valley. Newcastle,[1] Sunderland and Blith engaged a prodigious fleet of colliers,[2] and this trade was regarded by the mercantilist statesmen of the day as the most effectual nursery of English seamen. These ports exported considerable quantities to Holland and France, also.[3] The harbor at Sunderland was poor and shallow; the colliers had to load in open road—a dangerous task for the keelmen; but it had the advantage of being on the open sea and the ships could put off with every wind, whereas at Newcastle they were constrained to await favorable winds.[4]

The relative importance of the ports with respect to the import of Newcastle coal is indicated by the total duties paid[5] in some year. Passing London which paid ten times as much as any other port, the rank of the ports in this regard was Lynn, Yarmouth, Rochester, Boston, Southampton, Portsmouth, Whitby, Ipswich, Exeter, Wisbeach, Plymouth, Truro, etc., Lynn paying about four times as much as Truro.[6] Lynn distributed her receipts by way of the Ouse, Nen, and Witham into the Isle of Ely, and the counties of Lincoln, Northampton, Leicester, Buckingham, Bedford, Cambridge and Norfolk. Essex and Suffolk were supplied through Colchester and Harwich; Kent and Sussex through the Medway, Cray, Aran, and Stour.[7]

London far exceeded all other ports in the receipt of coal. Petty estimated that in the interval between 1636 and 1676 the imports of this article had quadrupled and were, at the latter date, 80,000 tons.[8]

---

[1] The amount of coal shipped from the Tyne coastwise from 1661 to 1723, and coastwise and oversea from 1723 to 1766 were in decennial yearly averages (based on Surtees, 105: 206–1):

	Tons		Tons
1661–1670	336,000	1723–1730	710,000
1671–1680	424,000	1731–1740	764,000
1681–1690	512,000	1741–1750	747,000
1691–1700	479,000	1751–1760	785,000
1701–1710	482,000	1761–1766	860,000

[2] Sometimes there were five or six hundred of these colliers in the port of London at one time. See Postlethwayt. Dict., s. v. British Empire; Galloway, 34.

[3] The earliest mention of the foreign coal trade was during the reign of Edward II. During the sixteenth century Newcastle coal became "that thinge that France can lyve no more withowte than the fyshe without water." See Galloway, 12, 20–1.

[4] Postlethwayt, Dict., s. v. England.

[5] The duties were payable at the port of importation; 9 and 10 Wm. III, Cap. 13.

[6] Anderson, Origin, IV, 691.

[7] "Essai sur l'état," 121; Postlethwayt, Dict., s. v. British Empire.

[8] If any dependence can be placed on Petty's estimate, this 80,000 was about one-fifth of the total Newcastle coastwise traffic, considering it an average year of

He ascribed the increase to the doubling of the population and to the new uses of coal, such as for fuel in chambers and in brickmaking.[1] A century later, 1776, the importation was 700,000 chaldrons.[2] A large part of this coal was consumed in the city of London and the rest was distributed into the interior by way of the Thames and its affluents. In this manner were reached the counties of Middlesex, Hertford, Buckingham, Oxford, Gloucester, Berks, Hampshire, Surrey and Essex.[3] In the conduct of this trade there were many loadings and unloadings. In the Pool the coal was discharged from the sea-going colliers into coal lighters; from these lighters into the great west-country barges for Oxford or Abingdon; from these barges into carts and wagons to be carried to the country towns and the consumer. The total cost of carriage from Newcastle to the final destination, plus the tax on sea-borne coal, raised the price to five times the original cost at the mine.[4]

Coal-Owner.

Coal-owner was the technical name given to the person who sunk the shaft and had the expense of raising the coal.[5] He was the mine owner or lessee, the capitalist employer, mine organizer, and coal-producer. In the larger mines he employed thousands of miners and surfacemen.[6] At the mine's mouth the coal was loaded into wagons which were dragged down an artificial inclined wagon-way with two chaldrons of coal three or four miles to the river's edge and

the decade; cf. table supra. According to the Hostmen's books the average yearly shipments about 1616 were from 250,000 to 270,000 tons, and about 1627, 300,720 tons; comparing this with Petty's estimate for the '30's it is suggested that London received above one-tenth of the total Newcastle shipments. See Surtees, 105·73, 71.

[1] Petty, Pol. Ar., 99 (I, 204 in Hull). Anderson, Origin, II, 536. The increase in consumption of coal was noticeable a century earlier. Harrison noted the increase in the number of chimneys and observed that "theyr greatest trade beginneth nowe to growe from the forge into the kitchin and hall." Harrison, Description, in Hollinshed, Chron. 85, 115. The London ladies opposed the substitution of sea-coal for wood in the fireplaces. Galloway, 24, quoting Howes, 1631.

[2] Anderson, Origin, IV, 321; it was 600,000 chaldrons in 1755; "Essai sur l'etat," 120.

[3] Postlethwayt, Dict., s. v. British Empire; "Essai sur l'état," 121.

[4] Defoe traces the progress of the coal from pit to Western consumer; see Defoe, Com. Eng. Tr., II, 172–3.

[5] Rep. from Com. H. C., X, 541.

[6] In 1649 the capitalistic nature of coal-mining had become very evident, for it was said, "one coal-merchant imployeth five hundred or a thousand in his works of

dumped into a storehouse called a staith. The staith projected in part over the water so that keels could be loaded by opening traps. The keels carried it to the ships.[1]

The coal-owners were not middlemen. Their relations to the fitters will be discussed later. They disposed of their coal either to, or through the agency of, the fitters. In the middle of the seventeenth century they were constrained to sell to the magistrates of the city of Newcastle.[2] They made various efforts to reduce competition and secure special advantages in the disposal of their coal: (*a*) led by one Gardiner they fought the monopoly of the coal trade held by the Hostmen;[3] (*b*) they procured part ownership in the ships so as to have a preference in carrying their coal instead of others';[4] (*c*) they made contracts, containing discriminations in their favor, with certain of the middlemen of the trade[5] and resorted to other devices.[6] But they always continued quite distinctly in the sphere of producer rather than middleman.

Keelman.

The keelmen were the managers of the keels or lighters in which the coal was carried from the staiths to the ships. They formed a separate and distinct part of the population of Newcastle.[7] As early as 1655 there were at Newcastle 320 keels, with a capacity of 800 Newcastle chaldrons each.[8] The vessels used were built especially to

coals." Grey, Chorographia, Harl. Mis., III, 279. In this respect the miners of the forest of Dean in Gloucestershire stood in contrast. Here the principle of "free mining" dominated. Restrictions of numerous sorts were laid for perpetuating the small miner. Large-scale capitalistic mining was retarded in its development. Nicholls, Forest of Dean, 45–47; V. C. H., Glouces. II, 223–4.

[1] See description in Defoe, Com. Eng. Tr., II, 172–3.

[2] "England's Grievance Discovered in Relation to the Coal Trade," 1655, quoted in Anderson, Origin, II, 431.

[3] Social England, IV, 447–8.

[4] Rep. from Com. H. C., X, 551.

[5] 9 Anne, Cap. 28, Sec. 1.

[6] The colliers in Dean Forest, Gloucestershire instituted a system of "bargainers" who fixed the prices at which the colliers would deliver coal to outsiders at the various towns. This was a case of simple joint agreement to maintain prices—a joint sales agency. The mine law court appointed these bargainers and the colliers did not underbid one another. The system was set in operation in 1668. After 1680 the mine law court itself fixed the prices. Nichols, Forest of Dean, 45, 52; V. C. H., Glouces. II, 223–4, 227.

[7] Surtees, 105: L.

[8] 136 Newcastle chaldrons were equivalent in capacity to 217 London chaldrons; the former held 53 cwt., the latter 36 bu.

accomodate the handling of coal.[1] They were carvel-built vessels with square sails; were described as "strong, clumsy, and oval" and carrying twenty tons apiece. Besides the use of the square sail for propulsion, the keelmen, three in number, used long pole-like oars called "puys," with which they, walking along the sides, pushed the keel along, the distal end based on the river bed; while a fourth worked his in the rear both as puy and rudder, or "swape." Special commissioners were provided by the government to attend the admeasurement and marking of these keels, with the purpose of preventing frauds.[2] The keelmen received a compensation for their services which was paid them by the ship owner or master.[3]

The Hostmen of Newcastle opposed the keelmen's assuming any middleman's function. The keelmen were, in the earlier centuries, servants of the Hostmen. Any Hostman buying of a keelman was dismissed from the Hostman's Company and the keelman dismissed from the service. The books of the Hostman's Company contain many references to orders and fines for keelmen selling coal, and the practice continued into the second quarter of the eighteenth century, if not farther.[4] However, it seems the keelmen never attained to much eminence as middlemen in the coal business.

Fitter.

The fitters since the seventeenth century formed an important part of the Hostmen's Company. The term fitter does not appear until 1634, but in the charter of 1600 "factors" appear along with "servants and apprentices" of the "governor, stewards, and brethren of the same fraternities; at this date they had "their officer and businesses."[5] In 1604 the Governor, Stewards, and thirty-seven other Hostmen agreed to appoint eight men as "factors and bookekeepers generall, to deale indifferentlie for the loadinge of all Coles to be vented in shipps and other vessels for and to the use of the persons ymmediatlie followinge," and the list of twenty-eight included merchants, widows, knights, sheriffs, aldermen, etc.[6] This appointment appears to be the origin of the coal-factors, or fitters, as intermediaries between the coal-owners and the ship-owners in

[1] Descriptions and historical sketches are given in Brand, II, 261–2; Surtees, 105: L; Galloway, 15–6.

[2] 9 Hen. V, Cap. 10; 30 Chas. II, st. I, Cap. 8; 6 and 7 Wm. III, Cap. 10.

[3] Rep. from Com. H. C., X, 563.

[4] For examples see Surtees, 105: 41, 57, 190.

[5] Surtees, 105: 14.

[6] Ibid., 52. Cf. 79, where a fitter to a particular man is mentioned.

the coal trade. In 1634 the employees of the Hostmen are designated under the four appellations, "Fitters, Servants, Agents, or Factors;"[1] and in 1651 the "Fitters" are the same as the "Factors;"[2] During the first half-century of their existence, therefore, the fitters were paid employees of the coal-owners (who at this time were Hostmen) and were appointed severally or by a group of coal-owners. The function of the fitter was "to fix the cargoes for the coal-owner with buyers from a distance, and to get the coals delivered by keels from the colliery staiths to the ship."[3]

By the admission of apprentices and others there arose in the Hostmen's Company a group of Hostmen who were not coal-owners, and who by the right of their admission had the right to engage in the coal business. These became agents for coal-owners who were not members of the Hostmen's Company, and acted as fitters for them. In the progress of the century the Company thus lost its character as being a company of coal-owners and became one of chartered fitters. The Hostmen tried to check the tendency, but in vain, and by 1700 the terms Hostmen and fitters were equivalent concepts.[4] At this date their business was to care for the loading of coals, brought in keels from the collieries, into the ships, and they had taken on themselves "to buy coals at certain prices of the owner of collieries, and to carry them in keels and sell them to the ship-masters," and sometimes to act as agents "paid at certain rates for their negociations between the owners of the . . . collieries and the ship-masters."[5]

In 1711 an act[6] was passed by Parliament requiring the fitter to give a certificate to the ship-master, for every voyage, containing the date of the loading, the name of the ship and ship-master, the quantity, the colliery, and the price of every sort. The course of this certificate will be traced in the hands of the ship-owner or master.[7] The purpose of the certificate was to reduce and prevent frauds, combinations and discriminations.

The functions of the fitter in the latter half of the eighteenth century were those of a *del-credere* factor. He had a stipulated allowance called fittage, at Newcastle 1s., at Sunderland, 2 s 6 d, per chaldron.

[1] Surtees, 75.

[2] Ibid., 92.

[3] Ibid., XLVIII.

[4] Ibid., 119, 162.

[5] Ibid., 162.

[6] 9 Anne, Cap. 28, Sec. 2.

[7] This requirement was effective in 1774, see Surtees, 105: XLIX. 211; and in 1800, see Rep. from Com. H. C., X, 541.

Several fitters contracted with the coal-owner for the whole output of
the colliery during the year, at a certain price, and each took such a
share as he thought he could sell.   They accounted severally to the
coal-owner at that stated regular price, and were understood to guarantee that price to him.   If the fitter was on a salary basis no such
guarantee was understood.[1]   The fitter was the agent for selling and
for furnishing keels for conveying the coals from staith to ship, and
for making out the required certificate; these things done, his concern
ceased.[2]

Hostmen.

The Hostmen of Newcastle early gained a monopoly of this town's
trade in coal and grindstones.   It appears that the Company was a
branch of the Newcastle Merchant Adventurers Company, in the
sixteenth century at least.[3]   But owing to the paramount place which
coal acquired among Newcastle's exports, the Hostmen's Company
attained a like prominence, and controlled the magistracy of the
town.[4]

In the medieval town economy a foreign merchant was required to
go to "Host" with a freeman of the town during his stay.   The host
jealously watched his actions, his buying and selling, and protected
the freemen against illegal dealings.   Few towns of England had a
coal trade, and as the gilds in Newcastle arose on lines somewhat
similar to those in other towns no special place was found among
them for the coal trade.   The host naturally had the earliest opportunity of furnishing his guest with the coals and came naturally into
this sphere.   The Hostmen's Company strengthened itself by admit-
ting to membership such freemen of the town as owned coal-mines
and thus anticipated all opposition to their assumption of exclusive
rights.[5]

Another common artifice of gaining and maintaining a monopoly
used by the medieval towns was the custom of "foreign bought and
foreign sold."   By it, goods brought into a town by a foreigner, i.e.,
non-freemen, could be sold only to a freeman; likewise goods bought

---

[1] See the testimonies as reported in Rep. from Com. H. C., X, 541, 543.

[2] In 1799 there were 29 firms or individuals who acted as fitters at Newcastle
and 48 at Sunderland.   Rep. from Com. H. C., X, 63, 1–2.

[3] Brand, II, 270.

[4] "England's Grievance discovered, etc.," 1655, quoted in Anderson, Origin,
II, 431.

[5] For this theory see Surtees, 105: XXXI, XXXII.

in a town by a foreigner could be sold to him only by a freeman. In every purchase or sale a freeman was one of the contracting parties.

This principle, in conjunction with a statute[1] of the sixteenth century, threw the whole coal trade into the hands of the Hostmen. Henry VIII, for the purpose of making the collection of customs duties easier, required that all traffic within the tidal limits of the Tyne was to embark and disembark at Newcastle, the head of the port of the Tyne. Hereafter all produce from the interior had to be brought to Newcastle, and by the custom of "foreign bought and foreign sold" had to be sold to the freemen of Newcastle. The coal-owners who were not freemen of the town and members of the Hostmen's Company and who had mines in the vicinity of the Tyne had to employ the Hostmen as intermediaries between themselves and the foreign buyers.[2] It was for these reasons that the discoverer of "England's Grievance . . . in Relation to the Coal Trade," in 1655 complained that "now the owners of the collieries must first sell their coals to the magistrates of Newcastle, . . . (and) the magistrates to the masters of ships."[3] And likewise for these reasons the coal-owners who were not free of the Hostmen's Company found little profit in operating mines in competition with the freemen and disposed of their mines to the latter, thus strengthening the Hostmen's monopoly. One Sutton in 1569 obtained a long lease on the mines of Whickham and Gateshead. This was the famous "Grand Lease" and worked into a monopoly in the hands of the Newcastle merchants. Liddell and Ravensworth and other notable men were active in maintaining and perfecting monopolistic combinations of the mines of these parts.[4]

The dissolution of this Hostmen's monopoly was gradual, but hastened after 1726 when the custom of "foreign bought and foreign sold" was forfeited.[5] Under the head "Fitters" it is shown above that a change had contemporaneously occurred in the composition and character of the Hostmen's Company and that the Hostmen had ceased being coal-owners and became a company of licensed fitters.

The regulation of the vend of coal by the Hostmen while they were in control and of the coal-owners generally thereafter was one of the

[1] 21 Hen. VIII, Cap. 18.

[2] See general treatment in Surtees, 105: XXX–XXXII.

[3] Anderson, Origin, II, 431.

[4] See history in Galloway, 93 et seq.

[5] The process of decay is traced through several suits at law in Surtees, 105: XXXV–XXXVII. See also V. C. H., Durham, II, 327.

most conspicuous phenomena connected with the coal trade. For two centuries and a half after the chartering of the Company in 1600 combinations for limiting the vend and regulating prices were effected intermittently and dissolved as often as formed. The consumers in London were the chief complainants. During this whole period the combinations were much alike in details and character.

In 1630 the Hostmen entered into a "proiectt or experyment for the utterance" of all their "severall parts and porcions of Coles" agreeing to vend their coal in partnership. They divided themselves into four groups whose total vend averaged about 2500 tens[1] per group. Each group had a special bookkeeper who kept book for the whole party. Each member of the group, composed of six or eight members, was limited to a fixed vend; if any could not have his share ready within the specified time, he bought from his partners at a reasonable price; the group also made collective purchases and distributed them proportionally. The groups were to keep nearly even in the total delivered from time to time. Special provisions were laid so that no scarcity of coal and high prices would result, and that buyers be not delayed. Penalties were affixed for breaking any conditions of this agreement. It was limited to one year.[2]

The minutes of January 1, 1616–17, contain the plan of another combination for regulating the vend. Eight persons were nominated to pass upon the quantity of the coals and to attend to the clearing of all ships. Each of these eight took unto him such a number of partners that their coals combined would equal one-eighth of the total vend for the year: the group sold in partnership. The proceeds of the sale were divided within the group upon some prearranged ratio. The groups kept their vends as nearly equally distributed as possible in time. The vend of each group averaged about 1700 tens, and the number of partners ranged from three to eight; the vend of each partner was determined. This agreement was to terminate in one year.[3]

Similarly arranged group-partnerships were agreed to in 1622 and 1627.[4] In 1666 it was agreed to limit the output of the mines by ceasing to operate them for three months.[5] In 1738 the ships were

[1] A ten equalled about 21 tons, i.e., a keel-load.
[2] Surtees, 105: 43–47.
[3] Ibid., 105: 63–7.
[4] Ibid., 105: 67–71; 72–74.
[5] Ibid., 105: 131.

required to take turns at loading and to lie at anchor at least ten days.[1] To effect this latter arrangement there was also an agreement to the same effect with the coal-owners and Hostmen of Sunderland.

Similar devices for limiting the vend were in use in 1794 and 1800 as those described in the years 1603 and 1616.[2]

Neglecting the opportunity that the monopoly of the Hostmen and coal-owners gave for effecting combinations of the sort described, an economic cause must be recognized for their formation in the fact that collieries had to be kept in regular operation or abandoned. The operation of the mines had to be continuous and all fluctuations in the supply reduced to a minimum. Cutthroat competition was particularly damaging. The limitation of the vend by these various combinations undoubtedly effected an economic good to the trade and the commonwealth.

Ship-Owner and Ship-Master.

Until Charles II's Dutch Wars, Ipswich was the great center of collier-shipbuilding. It built colliers that would "reign" for forty or fifty years, as employed in the Newcastle-London coal trade. It was also the town where most of the masters of these ships dwelt. But during the War of 1668 so many Dutch flyboats were captured and entered in the English register and in the coal trade, for the interests of the Yarmouth and London merchants, that Ipswich lost its pre-eminence.[3]

In 1702–4 nine ports had more ships than Ipswich and three had greater tonnage.[4] Yarmouth and London owned the larger number,

[1] Surtees, 105: 196, 197.

[2] See very ample description in Surtees, 105: XLIII–XLIV; and in the testimony, Rep. from Com. H. C., X, 552; on page 572 is a tabular view of the vend of coals in use in 1800.

[3] Defoe, Tour., I, 32.

[4] The following table is made from data in Brand, II, 677:

City	Ships	Chaldrons	Average Tonnage	City	Ships	Chaldrons	Average Tonnage
London	168	11,230	67	Haystings	33	1,112	33
Yarmouth	211	13,272	63	Hull	28	987	35
Whitby	98	6,385	65	Lynn	74	3,397	46
Ipswich	40	5,774	144	Margett	24	1,001	41
Ramsgate	42	2,147	51	Scarborough	54	2,613	48
Newcastle	71	5,567	78	Stockton	27	708	41
Bridlington	48	1,374	28	Sunderland	32	1,855	58
Brighton	56	1,527	29	Wells	34	820	24
Colchester	25	1,227	48	Other Ports	..	.....	..
					1,277	68,219	

but the distribution was well proportioned among the ports. Newcastle owned fewer than one would expect. The ships of the various ports differed much in their respective tonnage: those of London, Yarmouth, Whitby and Newcastle being about one size but less than half the size of those of Ipswich. The ships of Sunderland were used in the Newcastle trade in winter when the weather was bad. It is noticeable that ships of the south and west coasts were employed in this coal trade.[1]

While the Hostmen, as merchants, controlled the trade and held the magistracy of the town Newcastle, the owners of the collieries had to sell to the magistrates of the town, and the magistrates sold to the masters of the ships.[2] When the Hostmen, as fitters, controlled the trade, they were the privileged agents who effected sales between the coal-owners and ship-masters. The Hostmen and coal-owners do not appear at any time to have striven for ownership of the ships, except occasionally to own a fractional share of a ship with the purpose, not of getting profits as ship-owners, but of encouraging that ship to carry their coals in preference to others'.[3] This want of integration in the trade is remarkable: the Newcastle dealers remained comparatively passive so far as the real "adventures" of sea-traffic were concerned and allowed the ship-owners and-masters of Ipswich and Yarmouth to run the risks: the most likely explanation lies in the small amount of capital the Hostmen controlled, not sufficient to perform both the large mining operations and the shipping.

The ship-master might or might not be the ship-owner in whole or part. It was generally desirable that he own a small share at least so as to fix a greater sense of responsibility, but too large a share might shift the interests of the master against the owner. It was customary for the ship-builder to make out the "grand bill of sale" to the ship-master in his own name, for the whole ship, however small the part the master owned; and this bill gave the master the sole management of the vessel, to use it at his discretion. It was always difficult for the ship-owner to control the master with the grand bill of sale in the latter's hands.[4] To correct abuses of this nature an

---

[1] In the first half of the seventeenth century, at least, the ships of France and of the North Sea countries were much engaged in carrying coal abroad from Newcastle. Galloway, 34, quoting a writer of that period.

[2] Anderson, Origin, II, 431.

[3] See testimony in Rep. from Com. H. C., X, 551–2.

[4] These various relations of owner and master are presented in "A Letter on the Coal Trade," 33–5.

act[1] was passed in 1703 requiring the master to "keep, and once a Year render to such Owner or Owners, if required, a true, plain, just and perfect Account in Writing of the Produce and Expence of every respective Voyage . . . made within such Year in such Ship." As a matter of insurance by division of risks the ownership was usually cut up into eighths, sixteenths, or thirty-seconds parts, and the ship-owner held interests in several ships.

The ship-master was a sea-faring merchant, shipping to and fro between Newcastle and London, buying from the Hostmen or fitters at the former and selling through crimps at the latter. As has been shown, the fitter made out a certificate and cocquet of the loading and sale at Newcastle and gave them to the ship-master. The master carried them to London, turned them over to a crimp whose clerk carried them to the Custom-house, paid the duty, brought the proper papers from the Custom-house to the Coal Exchange, and then the crimp was at liberty to sell the coal. Any person had free recourse to the register of these certificates at the Custom-house.[2] The owners soon devised means through the delivery of the cocquets of effecting "turns" in the discharge of their coals. The masters delivered the papers into the hands of particular agents employed by the owners, and were disabled from delivering their coals until permitted by such agents. The agents held up the cocquets and turned them in in order. The statute of 1730[3] sought to correct the evils of "turns" by requiring that the cocquets be delivered within four days after the arrival of the ship, and penalized the owner for ordering the master to do anything that would relate to keeping "turns" in selling or delivering in the Thames. At Newcastle, also, it was the practice among the masters to take "turns" at loading and to hold up large numbers of ships so as to regulate the supply at London. In 1710 prohibition was laid on holding up more than fifty ships for more than seven days.[4]

Besides carrying the fitter's certificate to London, the ship-master was also required to carry away from London a copy of the contract between the buyer and the master, attested by the crimp, by whom the cargo was sold. This copy was delivered to the ship-owner or owners (when required) after every respective voyage.[5] This was a further means used by the ship-owner for the control of the ship-master.

---

[1] 3 Geo. II, Cap. 26, Sec. 9.
[2] 9 Anne, Cap. 28, Sec. 2; Rep. from Com. H. C., X, 541.
[3] 4 Geo. II, Cap. 30, Sec. 2.
[4] 9 Anne, Cap. 28; Sec. 5.
[5] 11 Geo. II, Cap. 15, Sec. 7.

Watermen.

The Watermen, including the lightermen before 1700, were an un-chartered Company at London whose business it was to care for the unloading of the ships in the Pool.[1] They used lighters to carry the cargoes from ship to wharf or barge. But to this manual occupation the watermen were prone to annex the business of coal dealer or crimp. Until 1730 the dealers were forbidden to use lighters of their own,[2] and the watermen enjoyed a monopoly of this business. The charges for their services were prescribed by the officiary of London; however, the business was competitive and the masters or owners of ships allowed secret salaries, gratuities and rewards to certain of them for prefer-ences in unloading their coals and dispatch in doing it. An ineffectual prohibition on such practices was laid in 1710.[3]

The lightermen effected combinations with the coal dealers of London to the end that they favored certain ones, with whom they were in partnership, in the delivery of coals. The last mentioned statute also failed to break up these amalgamations and discrimina-tions. In the first quarter of the eighteenth century they frequently acted as crimps; they unloaded and sold the coal to buyers, likely their own partners. This practice was forbidden in 1730.[4] A further step was made by the middle of the century when many had become ship-owners.[5] There was, therefore, at the London end of the trade a tendency toward integration of the various parts of the business, in contradistinction to the Newcastle end; but adverse legislation checked the development.

Crimp or Coal Factor.

Crimps were, before 1700, persons who undertook and agreed to unload cargoes of coal; by 1800, this function had passed to persons called "coal undertakers." Meanwhile crimps had become coal factors, in the sense of doing the selling for the ship-masters and owners. The crimps were sprung from the wharfingers and water-men.[6] The ship-masters were permitted in 1730 to employ as crimps

[1] For descriptions of the process of unloading ships on the Thames see Defoe, Com. Eng. Tr., II, 171–3; Rep. from Com. H. C., X, 563.

[2] 3 Geo. I, Cap. 26, Sec. 1.

[3] 9 Anne, Cap. 8, Sec. 3; "Considerations on the present high prices," 15.

[4] 3 Geo. II, Cap. 26, Sec. 3.

[5] "Considerations on the present high prices," 15.

[6] Compare Rep. Com. H. C., X, 563; B. E. Dict. Cant. Crew, s. v. Crimp; Defoe Tour, II, 176; Campbell, 318; Anderson, Origin, II, 421.

any persons not being lightermen.[1] This was an exception to the general tenor of the law which aimed at making ship-masters sell directly to the London dealers; the intervention of the factors was intended to prevent the proprietors of coal from imposing on the dealers; the coal factors or crimps were supposed to be influenced by no private motive since they were prohibited from buying or selling coals on their own accounts, and to do justice between buyer and seller.[2] But the intent of the law was not realized. Besides doing the commission business of selling cargoes for owners, they dealt in a wholesale way in coals on their own accounts.[3] The part of their business which characterized them, however, and to which they gave most attention, was that which the law proposed—the commission business.

The coal was consigned to them by cargo; they engaged sales of it by cargoes, halves, or quarters. The first few purchases on each market day were effected only after considerable higgling as to price. but, this price once determined by the sale of two or three cargoes, the mass of the factors and buyers followed the same price during the rest of that market.[4] All bargains or contracts for the sale of coals by the factor were required to be entered in the factor's book, subscribed by both buyer and seller and attested by the factor. The factor gave a copy of the contract so signed and witnessed to the ship-master.[5]

The crimps worked frauds in several ways. The most common was to vend their consignments to their servants in trust, or to their partners who were wholesalers.[6] They also became ship-owners and sold their own coal to the prejudice of their principals' consignments.[7]

During the most of the period here studied, the London market for coal was at the head of Billingsgate Dock, on a place called Room-Land.[8] The coalmen and woodmongers assembled here every morning and the place was a real Exchange for the coal trade. It was very inconvenient in the winter-time since there was no protection from the weather.[9] The market was transferred in 1768 to a new building in Thames Street and took the name Coal Exchange.

[1] 3 Geo. II, Cap. 26, Sec. 5.

[2] "Considerations on the present high prices," 15.

[3] Campbell, 318.

[4] The determination of price is described in Rep. from Com. H. C., X, 551.

[5] 3 Geo. II, Cap. 26, Sec. 6; 11 Geo. II, Cap. 15, Sec. 6. See a copy of agreement of sale, in Rep. from Com., H. C., X, 577.

[6] 9 Anne, Cap. 28, Sec. 7.

[7] Rep. from H. C., II, 561.

[8] Defoe, Tour, II, 175; Maitland, London, II, 791.

[9] Rep. from Com. H. C., X. 566, 571, 598.

The Coal Exchange was a freehold divided into sixty-four shares and owned by ship owners, coal factors, and coal buyers.[1]   The building at first contained an open quadrangle where buyers and sellers met freely and did their business.   A part of this quadrangle was later inclosed into what was known as the "Subscription Room;" herein the great volume of sales were executed, away from public observation.[2]   And the consumers of coal were practically excluded from buying here,[3] although the terms of admission were not exorbitant.   Any one could become a subscriber without being proposed or ballotted for; the dues were £3, 18s. per year, or 6d. for each market day.   This was charged, at least ostensibly, to cover up-keep of the Hall.   There was received here "The Public Letter"[4] daily from Newcastle stating the number of ships loaded and the number of ships waiting for cargoes.   This Letter gave the subscribers the advantage of the earliest information as to the probable supply of the market, a matter of first importance in their dealings with the uninformed public.[5]

Coal Merchant or First Buyer.

Apart from Newcastle and Sunderland themselves in their foreign trade there were few exportations of coal.   When duties were levied on coastwise importations drawbacks of duties were usually allowed upon re-exportation; but the difference of cost made direct commerce the better.   After 1713 export duties were laid on coal which favored the English shipping: the rates were 5s. per chaldron on coal carried in foreign bottoms, and 3s. in English bottoms.   The coal merchants, in the sense of exporters abroad, were the ship-owners and masters, heretofore discussed, who shipped to Holland and France rather than to the English ports.   No statistics are available for determining the proportion carried abroad.[6]

But the coal merchant, in the sense of wholesaler of coals, was very prominent in London and known as "first buyer."

The Edwardian policy had been with respect to coals as it was with respect to corn, meat, and live stock, that none should buy fuel except

---

[1] Rep. from Com. H. C., X, 566.

[2] Ibid., 598.

[3] Middleton, View of Middlesex, 545.

[4] For the data see testimonies in Rep. from Com. H. C., X, 546–7.

[5] A copy is given in Rep. from Com. H. C., X, 571.

[6] Statistics of foreign exportation, 1790–9, are given in Rep. Com. H. C., X, 612–5, when about 12 per cent went abroad.

such as either burned it themselves or retailed it at a reasonable price.[1] An irregular supply, however, coupled with a seasonable demand which came from the poor and needy of London, made the execution of this policy impossible and undesirable. There was a larger consumption of coal in winter than summer, especially after it had become the custom to burn it in fireplaces. On the contrary, the supply came to the City altogether in the summer: the Ipswich colliers, though built with remarkable strength, did not hazard themselves in winter seas, and not until about 1760 did coal begin to arrive by winter shipping.[2] This contrariety of supply and demand was the most essential condition occasioning the wholesale man, the coal merchant or first buyer. The City had to depend on accumulated supplies; the consumers became dependent on a middleman class from whom they bought as exigencies of consumption required and as their financial ability made it possible. By the most natural process of differentiation, the larger and more competent of these middlemen began to supply their less able colleagues with coal for retail selling: the larger became wholesalers, the smaller remained retailers dependent upon them; the former were called "first buyers," the latter "dealers" or "small coal men."

The "first buyer" bought entire cargoes upon the Coal Exchange from the factors, and sold in broken bulk to several sorts of customers, such as "loaders-on-account," "second buyers," i.e., subwholesalers, and retailers, and those whose business had not become highly specialized sometimes sold directly to consumers and housekeepers. The first buyers, after they were permitted in 1730, acquired craft of their own for unloading the ships.[3] They bought usually on 28 or 30 days' credit.[4] After 1730 all time payments were required to be evidenced by promissory notes given by the first buyer and containing the specific words, "Value received in Coals."[5] When a

---

[1] 7 Ed. VI, Cap. 7, Sec. 5. The ingrosser or forestaller of coal is met with in various parts of the Kingdom and at various times. Instance Nottingham in 1480. One Thomas Marshall of Sandcliffe "forestalled 4 wainloads of sea-coals, not allowing those coals to be led and carried to the king's market in the town." Stevenson, Rec. Boro. Nott., II, 421; V. C. H., Nott. II, 325, 328. Or again towards the close of the seventeenth century, when it was alleged that the dealers accumulated such large stocks as to hinder and forestall the market. Stevenson, op. cit., V.

[2] The change may be determined by comparing Defoe, Tour, I, 33, and Rep. from Com. H. C., X, 571.

[3] For the ownership of lighters in the latter part of the century see Rep. from Com. H. C., X, 552.

[4] Ibid., 548.

[5] 3 Geo. II, Cap. 26, Sec. 7.

cargo was bought, it was agreed to deliver the ship emptied in so many days and in case of default to pay demurrage.[1] It became the fixed practice of first buyers to aim at making 1s. per chaldron clear profit. In addition they had the profits of lighterage, metage, cartage, surplus measure, and from the credit allowed to their customers.[2] They extended credit to their customers for periods ranging from three months to one year, and the profits on the longer credit sales were often double those on cash or short term sales. Their capital was on the whole turned over three or four times a year.[2]

The first buyers had several means of controlling somewhat the market. They gained control of the lighters and restricted their number and use in such a way as to make them practical regulators of the rate of discharge from the ships. They bought more cargoes than they could immediately discharge with their unloading facilities, and thus gained a speculator quality. Until forbidden in 1788, they combined in groups for purchasing coal and resisting the demands of the crimps which might seem exorbitant.[3] They acquired shares in the ownership of ships which gave them self-interest in high prices paid for coals.[4]

The "Land Coal-Meters Office" had special connection with the first buyers who as sellers had to pay the metage, 4s. per chaldron. This Office was established in 1746[5] and consisted of two managers called "Principal Land Coal-Meters" and deputies appointed by them called "Labouring Coal-Meters." They were to measure every sale above eight bushels and issue tickets containing the names of the seller and consumer, the quantity, the price, the dates of sale, delivery and admeasurement, the metage charge, and the names of the carmen. Dealers and those interested in any way in the coal business were not to be appointed to this office; a good many of the appointees were shopkeepers and tradesmen. These meters measured the coal brought by land; another meters' office in connection with the Custom House measured the coal in the ships before being unloaded. The purpose of the Land Office was to prevent frauds in the admeasurement of coals as sold by the wholesalers and retailers.[6]

[1] Rep. from Com. H. C., X, 560.

[2] See testimony in Rep. from Com. H. C., X, 548–9, 570.

[3] The act of 1788 forbade any number greater than five from uniting to purchase coal; 28 Geo. III, Cap. 53.

[4] These various ideas are brought out in testimonies in Rep. from Com. H. C., X, 551, 560, 561.

[5] 19 Geo. II, Cap. 35; 22 Geo. II, Cap. 37; 32 Geo. II, Cap. 27.

[6] A long list illustrating these various frauds may be found in Rep. from Com. H. C., X, 600–4.

Dealer and Retailer.

The dealer and retailer were the final distributors, into the hands of the consumers. The two differed slightly. The dealer owned craft for unloading ships but was wanting capital enough to buy at Billingsgate, where the practice was to buy whole cargoes and allow credit for 28 or 30 days. He accordingly bought from the first buyers, did his own unloading, and retailed principally to housekeepers. But the retailer kept a shed and sold coal by the bushel, i.e., in very small lots.[1] He was called in early times "Small Coal Man."[2] The retailers were likely descendants of the woodmongers, who took to selling coal as wood became scarce. In 1664 they are mentioned with the woodmongers as engaged in the coal business.[3] They distributed the coal in sacks which had been measured, sealed and marked as having the lawful dimensions; the bushels used were likewise measured and approved by government agents.[4] They delivered their coal in cars, carts or wagons, and had, as woodmongers, control of the carmen within the city's bounds.[5] The total expense of distributing 100 chaldrons of coal yearly to nearly 300 familes averaged annually during the nine years, 1734–43, about £29.[6]

The earliest market in the city for coal was Seacoal Lane in the vicinity of Fleet Ditch. Seacoal was brought here and stored as early as the beginning of the thirteenth century. At the same time some seacoal came to Billingsgate. The more common fuel was wood and charcoal brought by cart and sold from cart at Smithfield and Cornhill. The seacoal was sold in sacks and measured by inspectors called "meters."[7] Another set of "meters" inspected the charcoal brought by land. The colliers of Croyden in Surrey supplied much of London's consumption and they sometimes became men of no mean distinction. One Grimme or Grimes, collier from this town was a noted personage in reign of Edward VI. It appears that the inspection at London was very severe on these "foreign" colliers.[8]

In 1379 an Order of Common Council shows that the policy and practice were to forbid the operations of middlemen in the fuel busi-

---

[1] Rep. from Com. H. C., X, 548.
[2] Gent. Mag., 1734: 666; Besant, Eighteenth Cen. Lon., 134.
[3] 6 and 7 Chas. II, Cap. 2, Sec. 1.
[4] 3 Geo. II, Cap. 26, Secs. 11, 13.
[5] Hazlitt, Lon. Com., 151–2.
[6] Rep. from Com. H. C., X, 588.
[7] Lib. Alb. I, XXXV.
[8] V. C. H., Surrey II, 245

ness; consumers were required to buy directly from the wharves; forestalling and engrossing were prohibited under pain of forfeiture.[1] But it appears that by 1553 "Fuel, Coels and Wood" ran "many Times through four or five several Hands or more, before it" came "to the Hands of them that for their Necessity" did "burn or retail the same." Accordingly, in conjunction with the Assize of Fuel fixed that year, it was enacted that none should buy fuel except those who expected to burn or retail it to those who were to burn it.[2] A century later Charles II revived this sort of legislation and empowered the officiary of London and the justices of the counties to set prices on all such coals as were sold by retail, as they from time to time judged reasonable, allowing a competent profit to the retailer. In case the retailer refused to sell at the prescribed prices the coals could be seized and sold by the officers.[3] This policy was made perpetual and extended by statutes under William III and George II.[4] They were never effectually executed.

Conclusions.

The coal trade differed from the other trades in having both the production and consumption of its ware localized. It was produced in one place and consumed in one place far distant. Consequently the trade took one direction and the organization was simple, being a direct series of sequences and agents. There was no process of manufacturing; the ware passed with no transformation in form or composition from producer to consumer. For this reason all accessory and adventitious middlemen were eliminated, and the complexity of relations that affected the organization of some other trades was entirely absent.

The simplicity of this business technique consisted in its straightforward succession of independent middlemen. In the home trade coal passed from producer through fitter to the travelling merchant shipmaster; he disposed of it through crimp to first buyer, and first buyer to retailer. Each business was unusually clear-cut and differentiated. Indeed this almost total lack of integration is easily the most salient characteristic of the trade. Only at the London end did there appear any tendency to integrate businesses, and this never attained a degree

[1] Hazlitt, Lon. Com., 151–2.
[2] 7 Edw. VI, Cap. 7.
[3] 6 and 7 Chas. II, Cap. 2, Sec. 1.
[4] 7 and 8 Wm. III, Cap. 36; Sec. 2; 17 Geo. II, Cap. 35.

worthy of mention. The first buyer sometimes dispensed with the factor and competed with him at buying cargoes from the ship master. Some few first buyers and factors acquired interests in the ships. But these developments were unimportant in their effect upon the trade.

Another feature peculiar to the coal trade was the ship-owner and ship-master acting as travelling merchant and resident in towns where perhaps he did no business whatever. He had no place of business at either terminus: his ship was his store, his home was his office, his cargo was his stock of vendables. He often combined the functions of ship-owner, merchant, supercargo, and ship-master. His market was determined—except against the dangers of sea and the shifts of price he was no venturer; he visited no new climes, made no long voyages, stayed in coastwise pursuits, and dealt with known fitters and factors. His seas were comparatively free from pirates and dangers from the enemy. The home government encouraged him and supported his colliers with the largest convoy fleet of its navy. He was comparatively secure, and not like the general merchant in this degree of risk.

A fourth peculiarity of the coal trade was the prevalence of combinations and associations for the control of vend, price and agents. Unrestrained competition was a positive detriment to producer and consumer and middleman: the operation of mines could not be occasional, had to be continuous: regularity was the first essential. Pools were the means of lessening the evils of competition; it does not appear that they lessened the whole volume of trade in the long run. At the London end the combinations effected among the watermen and the factors and buyers, and the Subscription Room monopoly were developments of the same general character. Since the several businesses were so distinct, association within the groups was the means of defensive and aggressive action in maintaining or acquiring privileges as against another group; while intergroup association was the means of amicable adjustment of differences as between groups. The Subscription Room in the Coal Exchange illustrates the former, the combination of lightermen and first buyers illustrates the latter associations: the subscribers with their Public Letter were able to deprive the uninformed outsiders of business; since both first buyers and lightermen owned lighters competition between them was allayed by partnerships and sharing of profits mutually. Lastly, the association of ship-owners and ship-masters by partnerships in the ownership of the ship was a means of control over the master as agent of the owner.

OTHER MINERALS.

(a) *Iron.*

The iron mining and manufacturing districts of the Isles were, of course, determined by the presence of iron and fuel—charcoal or pit-coal. They were more widely distributed in earlier times, when charcoal was the most used fuel. The rapid deforestation of some counties was the cause of no slight anxiety to the inhabitants during the sixteenth and seventeenth centuries. The iron industry in Surrey and other counties suffered from the increasing costs of production.[1] Henry VIII commenced the policy of conserving the forests in 1543[2] by requiring the leaving of so many standils per acre cleared. Elizabeth forbade the use of timber for iron smelting within twenty-two miles of London[3] and detailed what trees and in what places timber might be cut in England for this purpose.[4] Special precautions were taken for preserving the forests of Surrey, Sussex and Kent.[5] The conservation policy took other lines during the next century: the importation of pig iron from Sweden and, later, its production in the American colonies were encouraged. The old policy of Edward III of prohibiting the export of iron was in vogue until 1693 and probably had some slight effect on iron-production.[6] The Iron-Mongers' and the Blacksmiths' Companies of London in 1668 petitioned for protective duties on Swedish iron[7] lest the domestic industry be wiped out by competition. The domestic producers were very much handicapped by this free importation.[8] As the forests became exhausted and as smelting by coal was invented the iron industry tended to concentrate in more defined districts.

One reason of its wide dispersion in the early period was, therefore, the wide source of fuel; another was the freedom that characterized mining operations in early times. The "free miner" was one of the freest personages known to medieval law. The high risks attached to mining adventures and the high need of iron for military and other purposes probably inclined the state to a most generous policy with respect to the miner. For instance, in Gloucestershire every free

[1] Cf. V. C. H., Derby, II, 359; Glouces. II, 230.
[2] 35 Hen. VIII, Cap. 17.
[3] 23 Eliz., Cap. 5.
[4] 1 Eliz., Cap. 15.
[5] 27 Eliz., Cap. 19.
[6] 28 Ed. III, Cap. 5 (1354) to 5 Wm. & M., Cap. 17 (1693).
[7] S. P. Dom. Chas. II, Vol. 238, No. 20; V. C. H., Derby, 359–60.
[8] "Dialogue," 120–1.

miner might with the consent of the king's gaveller dig for iron ore or coal where he pleased within the bounds of the forest Dean whether on the royal demesne or on the lands of private persons.[1]   The result of this freedom was small-scale, individualistic production and the dispersion of the industry.   The result of the dispersion was to make each section quite selfsufficing, to prevent any well-defined directions in the trade, and to check the rise of middlemen since trade was direct from producer to consumer.

Two lines of public policy also restrained the rise of middlemen dealing in iron.   One is illustrated by an ordinance of York, 1417, which was meant to keep the girdlers' trade within that town.   "Na man of the gyrdeler-crafte (was to) passe oute of this cite unto na market but alanely unto cried opyn faires to sell any girdeles by retaile or holesale within the space of xxxii mile."[2]   The effect of this enactment was to limit the points of the market and to make the out-of-town sales periodic; both of which facts made it more easy for the manufacturer to do his own marketing.   The other policy was that very common one which required every handler of a ware to transform that ware before selling it again.   In this case smiths were forbidden to buy unwrought iron and sell it again "in lyke manner and fourme, not altered, converted, wrought and made in manner and fourme accordinge to theire scyence."[3]   The smiths were rather manufacturers than middlemen.

The "iron age" was really born of the eighteenth and nineteenth century inventions for mining, smelting and transporting iron and coal.[4]   The volume of the trade in iron did not generally require middlemen before the Industrial Revolution.   During the seventeenth century the iron miners either had small furnaces of their own for smelting or else disposed of their ore to proprietors of furnaces.   "The proprietors of the furnaces chiefly disposed of their pig-iron to the owners of forges which were settled at several places where water power, as well as charcoal was abundant."[5]   In Gloucester a miner was forbidden to own a smithy.[6]   The miners had a monopoly of the carriage of ore and coal but the number of their horses was limited to four and wagons were forbidden.[7]   The miners' and smiths' operations were limited by the poor credit facilities that existed.   The mining and manufacturing were seasonal and credit was needed during the

[1] V. C. H.. Glouces. II, 221.
[2] V. C. H., York, II, 390.
[3] Selden, XIV, 93.
[4] Galloway, 101–3.

[5] V. C. H., Shrop. I, 460.
[6] V. C. H., Glouces. II, 224.
[7] Ibid., 223, 228, 229.

dull seasons.[1] This indicates the opportunity for the capitalistic mine operator and manufacturer[2] who arose in the next century, but during the early seventeenth century the man of small means was distinctly favored.

A common method of doing a larger business than usual was to lease others' furnaces and forges. One George Sitwell of Renishaw in Derbyshire controlled considerable interests in this way.[3] He sold his products to a wide market, even to the sugar planters of the Barbadoes; they were marketed by way of Bantry and Hull to London. One of the most celebrated London Ironmongers was Ambrose Crowley. In 1682 he set "a Factory . . . in Sunderland in the county of Durham for making Iron ware." He became a large employer and imported into Sunderland a large element of foreign workmen.[4] They were engaged at his works, forges, slitting mills, etc. in Winlaton, Swalwell, and Winlaton Mill. Some idea of the variety of goods made may be had from Crowley's advertisement, 1699, in the *Post Boy* which enumerated "Augers, Bedscrews, Box and Sad Irons, . '. . Chains, Edge-Tools, Tiles, Hammers, Hinges, Hows for the Plantations, Locks . . . Nails, Patten Rings, and almost all other sorts of smiths ware."[5] He also sold faggots of steel, hoops, bundles of rod steel, bars of blistered steel, bars of iron, bundles of rod iron and casks.[6] He conducted these manufactures under a highly paternalistic system.[7] It was a domestic system, also: the workman entered into bond for a considerable sum to cover advances of tools and iron; the worker took these to his own shop and engaged apprentices and his family at manufacturing products which were sold to Crowley and the cost of tools and materials was deducted from the selling price. He established an old age pension system and a pawn-shop arrangement in London whereby he facilitated the migration of London workmen to Durham.[8] His goods reached the whole island and distant parts of the world. His London connections put him in contact with the braziers of that metropolis who retailed his goods, along with others which they made themselves or bought to sell again.

[1] "Dialogue," 126.
[2] Ibid., 120.
[3] V. C. H., Derby, II, 359.
[4] P. C. Reg. 1687–8, fcl. 702.
[5] "The Post Boy," No. 510, 1699; V. C. H., Durham, II, 282.
[6] Ibid., 283.
[7] Ibid., 283–5.
[8] Ibid., 286.

In conclusion, it is noticeable that the iron trade is peculiarly characterized by its want of definite middlemen.

(b) Salt.

Saltmaking was to some extent a coastal occupation. Some parts of the coast for different reasons specialized at the business. One such was Limington and Portsea in Hants. The sea water was drawn into trenches and ponds and allowed to concentrate by evaporation by the sun's heat and later in large pans by furnace heat.[1] This industry of Hants declined before the growing competition of the rock salt of Cheshire and Worcestershire.[2]

The Droitwich salt springs in Worcester have been continuously worked for salt manufacture since the eighth century. In 1539 there were 360 furnaces used for evaporating the saltwater from three springs. Wood was used for fuel. The output of salt was voluntarily limited so as to maintain prices and to retard the deforestation of the district.[3] Monopoly and scarcity of fuel, therefore, at this date prevented the development of the industry. The industry had made little progress by the reign of James I. At this time Habington described the salt industry and detailed the method of ownership and manufacture.[4] The inhabitants divided the spring's water among themselves on strict proportions according to the number of "phates" or parts of phates owned by each person in fee simple. A phate consisted of 215 large vessels of saltwater; it was made up of twelve "wickburdens" of eighteen gallons; six gallons being drawn from the top, middle, and bottom of the well, respectively, to insure that each got water of like concentration. Certain "tyesmen" supervised this admeasurement. The saltwater after this inspection by the tyesmen was carried to the "seates" where it was evaporated. The ownership of a phate was the basis of citizenship and of wealth. The industry was handicapped by poor transportation facilities. In 1680 a salter Gardiner was encouraged to sell salt in Gloucestershire: this was a greater distance than had as yet been attempted at marketing.[5] The monopoly of the salters was broken in 1690 by one Steynor. The trade greatly increased and the price of salt fell very precipitately.[6]

[1] See descriptions by Celia Fiennes, 38.
[2] V. C. H., Hants, V, 471.
[3] Leland, Itinerary, IV, 110.
[4] Habington, Survey of Worces., 296–7.
[5] Nash, Worces., I, 306.
[6] Ibid., 298.

The introduction of coal as fuel and of iron-pans instead of lead was contemporaneous with the breaking of this monopoly.[1] In 1725 deep-boring was found to yield a heavier brine and in greater abundance. This resulted in cheaper cost of production and consequent lower price. By 1769 the product amounted to 480,000 bushels. From very early times the salt was carried by pack-horses by the "Salt Ways;" after 1771 a canal into the Droitwich stimulated the trade.[2] The salters or owners of phates appear to have done their own marketing.

The greatest center of salt production was in Durham and Northumberland. It dates from the thirteenth century. Cowpen was the chief salt town; Hart, Ross, Sunderland, and Gretham, also, were prominent. The trade finally settled in South Shields. The church had control of the trade in the early part of the sixteenth century. About 1600 there were produced about 7,650 weys of salt; and there were engaged about 430 panmen. Coal was used as fuel; it was brought by keelmen, cadgers and wainmen. The owner of the pans also supplied the panman with coal and kept keels for this purpose. The panman delivered forty weys of salt to the owner for this provision. The manors at the mouth of the Wear and Tyne appointed official "measurers" to supervise the measuring of salt. There was much complaint against the interference of these measurers and their office was maintained with difficulty; the southern buyers were constant complainants against the short measurements of the salters. The smaller salters disposed of their salt "usually to the cuntry and in the markets thereaboutes by small quantities as they (could) win it; . . . their markets (were) within the land at Durham, Newcastle, Alnewick, Barwick, Morepath, Hexham and such places."[3] Besides these markets, the larger salters shipped salt to the coast towns to the south. The large lumps of salt were sent to Colchester and were used there as a basis of crystallizing more salt.[4] Charles I chartered a monopolistic salt company, headed by the Shields salt-pan owners, in 1630, but it failed in 1639.[5] The failure was due in part to a rival scheme headed by the London Fishmongers. After the Restoration the product of the Durham salt pans increased very fast. The pan-owners perfected no intricate sales system. They either dispatched

[1] Camden, Brit., 362; Nash, I, 300.
[2] V. C. H., Worces., II, 250, 262.
[3] V. C. H., Durham, II, 296.
[4] Brereton, Notes.
[5] V. C. H., Durham, II, 297.

vessels of salt to the southern ports where it was bought by the fish-mongers and others; or else were passive and let the latters' ships come to Shields and sold the salt at their pans. The pan owners were essentially middlemen in a domestic system of manufacture.

(c) *Lead.*

This mineral was produced in Somerset, York, and Derby. Bristol was the exporting point for Somerset lead. The largest portion of this came from the Mendips. The chief foreign customer was Spain. For military reasons a prohibition was laid by England upon the export of lead to Spain but constant allusions were made to the infractions of the prohibition.[1] The York mines were centered at Richmond, Nidderdale and its market town Kirkby Malzeard. The lead from Richmond was often carried to York and Newcastle; that of Nidderdale came to Hull. These were the markets in the thirteenth century.[2] The industry increased in volume throughout the centuries following until about 1870 and much the same ports were used. In medieval times Derbyshire lead centered in Derby and Chesterfield and Winster. It was despatched chiefly to London. In the seventeenth century Chesterfield became the most important lead market in the Kingdom. The lead was carried by pack-horse to Bawtry and Chesterfield, then by river to Hull, and thence by sea to London. In 1723 the relative rates for carriage over these sections of the route were 14s., 4s., and 2s. 6d., respectively. Much of the product was exported to the Continent. In 1607 the relative rank of the ports in export of lead to the Continent was London, Bristol, and Hull; of course the Bristol lead came from Somerset.

"Free-mining" predominated in the Mendip. "Yeff any man whatsoever . . . intend(ed) to venture hys lyfe and to be a workman of the occupasyon he" had to "fyrst of all requere lycence of the lord of the soyll where he" purposed to work and "by the ould custm of the occupasyon" the lord could not deny him license. He was then free "to pyche wythyn the seyd forest of Mendyp and to brecke ground where and yn what place he . . . shaull thynk best hymself for hys oune byhouff and proffyt, . . . so that he doe paye the tenth of that in lede or wore to the lorde of the soyll where hyt was dyged."[3] These claims were called "grooves" or

---

[1] V. C. H., Somerset, II, 374.

[2] V. C. H., York, II, 352–3.

[3] S. P. Dom. Eliz., CCLXXXVII, 97; V. C. H., Somerset, II, 367.

"pitches" and were the property of the miner as long as he actually used them.[1] Likewise in Derbyshire, the tenure of the working miners was absolutely free; immemorial custom gave the right of mining to each and every comer; not even were unions formed among the miners to close the trade. In the vicinity of the peak they set their claims and the barmaster measured off their "meers" which became their property as against all other miners.[2] Free-mining resulted in a wide ownership of mines by miners of small means. The partnership system was very prevalent and dispersed the ownership still more. "In general as small shares as forty-eights, ninety-sixths, or even 384ths and 768ths, were held in Derbyshire mines and the very smallest mines have often many partners concerned in them."[3]

The product of these small mining properties, operated by the owners, was sold to a wealthier class who functioned both as smelters and merchants. They sometimes financed the poor miners. Their smelters were near the mines. They carried the lead to Derby and Chesterfield and sold it. It proved a very lucrative business, was the means of many fortunes, and was engaged in by many yeomen.[4] In 1581 at Duffield it was reported that "the most lords and owners of manors within the said county of late years" had been "disposed to buy ore or make it themselves;" they were given the first option on the lead taken from their manors and paid cash for it at the prevailing price. These smelter-merchants were known as "brenners." Some of them had agents in London; the younger sons of the country gentry acted in this capacity.[5] In Somerset also the miners sold to merchants and, occasionally, to the wealthier miners. If sold to a wealthier miner he paid the same prices as the other merchants.[6] In York lead-merchants were mentioned as early as the thirteenth century, coming from Richmond, Arkengrathdale, Redmire, Preston-under-Scar, and Leyburn, to Newcastle and York to sell their lead.[7] During the eighteenth century the miners came more and more to sell their ore and lead to regular customers who had their headquarters at Hull. The price of lead at Hull determined the price at the mines. The

[1] Cf. S. P. Dom. Eliz., CCLXXXVII. 369, for proceedings by which such claims could be lost.

[2] See the transcriptions which outline the customs at various dates, in V. C. H., Derby, II, 326, 335, 340.

[3] Farey, Agric. of Derby, I, 370; see Houghton, Compleat Miner, for tables for computing shares.

[4] V. C. H., Derby, II, 331.

[5] Ibid., 346.

[6] V. C. H., Somerset, II, 375.

[7] V. C. H., York, II, 351.

merchants became accustomed to pay on the basis of a sliding scale, the price paid to the miner at the mine for ore being one-half the Hull price for the lead. This more direct system of marketing occasioned the decline of Chesterfield and the other lead-markets in Derbyshire after 1750.[1]

During the seventeenth century many large owners of lead mines arose. The share system, among other things, made it easy for capitalists to acquire large holdings. These "adventurers" subscribed agreed shares which entitled them to their proportionate share in profits and management; but liability was limited to the subscription. It was easy for the richer to buy up controlling interests in many mines, in addition to those they owned wholly. One method of acquisition smacked of champerty—for a mining regulation laid at this time forbade a miner to sell to a "gentleman who found money for him to maintain a suit."[2] The rich owners of mines sometimes owned and worked their own smelters, but this was not usual.[3] When the poor miners disposed of their mines to the rich they usually sank to the status of wage-workers for the latter. They were usually paid a price-rate which varied with the amount of ore that they got. They worked in gangs and were paid on settling days a sum which they divided among themselves, somewhat after the custom of artels to-day.[4] Though lead-mining thus tended to become a more capitalistic system of production, the organization of sales appears not to have been changed. The large mine owner like the small mine owner continued to dispose of his ore to the brenners or smelter-merchants who smelted and marketed it.

The lead trade in Derbyshire was regulated by a "bar-master" and "bar-mote." The former was appointed before 1665 by the miners and merchants[5] and thereafter by the Crown. He measured the meers and the ore, summoned the barmotes and presided over them, and acted as coroner. He was assisted by deputy-barmasters. The barmotes were special mine-courts—the small barmotes assembled tri-weekly and adjudicated petty cases—the great barmotes were held twice a year and their decisions accumulated over several centuries into a body of mine law.[6] In Somerset the barmaster functions were

---

[1] Farey, Agric. of Derby, I, 379.
[2] V. C. H., Derby, 332; see V. C. H., Somerset, II, 374, for other methods.
[3] Ibid., 346.
[4] Ibid., 332.
[5] Houghton, Compleat Miner, 2.
[6] See Houghton, Compleat Miner, and Steer, Complete Mining Laws of Derby.

performed by an officer known as "lede-reeve;" there were also "Grand Jury" decrees which constituted the mining code.[1] One of these regulations appointed Tuesdays and Fridays as weigh-days. No man dared buy or sell a piece of lead unweighed and unstamped with the minery mark. This system facilitated trade by attesting the purity and weight of the bars of lead.

(d) Tin.

Devon and Cornwall have been the seats of tin production throughout the Christian Era. The activity of mining in these parts has moved in cycles. Pestilence, war, discoveries, and government interference, and more recently, inventions have caused alternating periods of depression and boom. Tin production was very active, for instance, from 1305, until the Black Death 1348–9; this devastation was followed by a depression, which continued through the reigns of Elizabeth and the early Stuarts with but two temporary revivals about 1400 and 1508, respectively. After the Restoration there was a rapid increase and capitalistic production on a large scale made headway. The center of the mines moved westward: until the thirteenth century Devon led Cornwall in output; Devon was displaced by Cornwall, and then East Cornwall by West Cornwall, in relative importance. The Devon coinage towns Chagford, Tavistock, Plympton, and Ashburton were relatively superseded by the Cornish towns Bodmin, Liskeard, Lostwithiel, Helston and Truro. In Cornwall Lostwithiel declined as Penzance arose in importance.

Like the iron and coal mines of the Forest Dean, and the lead works of Alston Moor in Cumberland, and of the Peak of Derbyshire, and of the Mendips of Somerset, the Cornwall and Devon tin mines were characterized by the prevalence of free-mining. Before any royal decrees or parliamentary legislation had been promulgated for the administration of the tin industry and districts the tinners[2] of Devon and Cornwall had evolved a system of customary laws which were permeated by the principles of free-mining. The national legislation

[1] The revised customary code and later orders of the minery at Bath and Wells is contained in a 17-century MS. known as Browne's Book; excerpts of which are given in V. C. H., Somerset, II, 369–72.

[2] The term "tinners" had a varying connotation: see the definitions cited by Lewis, pp. 96–103, for the years 1198, 1305, 1376, 1507, 1524, 1588, 1608, 1627, 1631, 1641, and 1752. It appears to have undergone a broader inclusion of content at the later dates and came to embrace all engaged directly in the production, ownership and distribution of tin.

and charters were usually but codifications of these existing customs. The tinner was naturally induced to free-mining by the very inexpensive outlay required to set up a mine: the tin was, at least in the earlier times, mostly taken from "streams" of alluvial deposits with the simplest tools and washed in trenches of running water.[1] The burden of this initial outlay was further reduced by a system of partnership. The small tinner predominated in medieval times over the larger;[2] some of them were engaged at other occupations at the same time and drew part of their sustenance from husbandry.

The freedom of "free-mining" as it existed at the close of the medieval period is thus described by the surveyor of Cornwall in 1602: "Their workes, both Streame and Load, lie either in severall, or in wastrell, that is, in enclosed grounds, or in commons." "In Seuerall, no man can search for Tynne, without leave first obtained from the Lord of the soile; who, when any Myne is found, may worke it wholly himselfe, or associate partners, or set it out at a farme certaine, or leave it vnwrought at his pleasure. In Wastrell, it is lawful for any man to make triall of his fortune that way, provided, that hee acknowledge the Lordes right, by sharing out vnto him a certaine part, which the call toll. . . . the Tynners constitutions in Devon . . . enable them to digge for Tynne in any mans ground, inclosed or vnclosed, without licence, tribute or satisfaction. . . . The worke thus found and bounded, looke how many men doe labour therein, so many Doales or shares they make thereof, and proportionable divide the gaine and charges."[3]

The "Manner of setting on worke adventurers" was described as follows: "When the new found worke intiseth with probabilitie of profit, the discouerer doth commonly associate himselfe with some more partners, because the charge amounteth mostly verie high for one mans purse, except lined beyond ordinarie, to reach vnto: and if the worke doe faile, many shoulders will more easily support the burden. These partners consist either of such Tinners as worke to their owne behoofe, or of such adventurers as put in hired labourers. The hirelings stand at a certaine wages, either by the day . . . or for the yeere."

In the Cornish mines there are illustrated three systems of organization.[4] First, the discovering tinner may operate the mine independ-

---

[1] See description of tools and methods of mining in V. C. H., Cornwall, I, 541–6.
[2] See statistical indica in Lewis, 186–7.
[3] Carew, Survey of Cornwall, 12–13.
[4] Cf. Lewis, 198–9.

ently or associate with him working tinners and all work together;
the output and the charges are then divided into as many "Doales"
or shares as there are laborers. This becomes what is known in mining organization as the "cost agreement" system whenever any of the
partners, instead of working personally, hire substitutes to do their
share. This system's chief virtue is that it offers a way for "sleeping
partners" who contribute capital but are exempt from management
of the venture; by this means the working capital of the community is
conserved and little lies idle. It was an opening for capitalistic production. The second method of mining organization is called the
"tribute" system. The mine association set out the tributers with
mine and tools and supplies; the tributers divided the ore with the
associates in some predetermined proportion. This method leant
itself to the independence of the tributer and to the exploitation of
the mines, but was always transitionary and ended in a wage system
because the tributers were weak as bargainers with the tributee and
as sellers of their ore to the merchants. The third system was
the lease. If any mine associates lacked the means of operating
their mines or any mine it was farmed out to a lessee for a fixed
money rental; the lessee was a man of some capital; he took all the
risks and the profits; and operated it mostly by hired labor. Roughly
stated, the above order of treatment indicates the historical order
in which the cost agreement, tribute, and lease systems acquired
prominence over each other. It is noticeable that they each opened
the way for capitalism.

During the eighteenth and nineteenth centuries capitalistic organization was increasingly evident. The original "doals" system of
partnership evolved into the "cost-book" system.[1] The doals were
transferable rights and the tinner-partners sold them sometimes to
Cornish merchants; laws were repeatedly enacted against the disposition of tin doals to the more wealthy and powerful.[2] Many persons
of various occupations, as goldsmiths, pewterers, clerks, nobles,
churchmen, widows, merchants, etc., were contributors to the town
coinage; they evidently did not work themselves in the mines and
were "sleeping partners" under the "cost agreement" plan. Such
was the condition during the later medieval period. By 1765 the
tribute system, somewhat more capitalistic, seems to have prevailed.

---

[1] James, Pseudo-Cost-Book Companies, 22, 45; Bartlett, Treatise on British
Mining, 24; "Cornish Mining," 11; Report on Stannary Amendment Bill, 1887;
Watson, Compendium of Brit. Mining, 11; Pike, Britain's Metal Mines, 52.
[2] Lewis, 189.

One Gabriel Jars' statement at that time was that "the usage established in all the mines" was "to give out the extraction of the metal to entrepreneurs" who "employ(ed) workmen at wages" to "work according to their orders," and for some entrepreneurs to work themselves. The entrepreneurs bought the contracts at auction; the adventures were sold by the "pitch." The workmen provided their own tools, light and powder; the adventurers provided machinery and ropes. Seven, eight or nine workmen were engaged for six months per pitch. The contractors received a third, fourth, or fifth, or other fraction of the output.[1] There was in this system a division of risk between adventurer and entrepreneur; the former was a capitalistic owner, the latter a capitalistic employer.

The distribution of the ore and bar-tin derived its peculiarities from the mining organization, the collection of the government excise on tin, and the control of the trade by the London pewterers. At no time did the miners form gilds or unions; they, also, preferred the independence afforded by the tribute system, to the wage-system pure and simple: both these facts made them poor bargainers with the tin-buyers. They lacked unity of action as well as the means of supporting themselves till the best market. As a result the merchants acquired considerable control of the tin business by making advances of capital to them and by acquiring doals. The Cornish miner stated the necessity under which his class labored in 1677 with respect to the regrating and ingrossing tin-merchants as follows: "We cannot sell, or dispose of any Tinn until it be Coin'd, and we have not above two Coinages a year; and there is such shuffling and dealing betwixt some men that have been late in Great power and others of our Country, with some Merchants in London, that it makes our Commodity of no value, and we the poor labourers very miserable, and the Mine lye unwrought for want of Monies or Credits . . . to pay Workmen and maintain our Families, . . . they (merchants) have so linkt themselves together, that if I should offend one of them, all the rest will be my Enemies, and then I and my family may starve."[2]

Certain towns were "specially priviledged for the Coynages;" in 1602, for instance, they were Helston, Truro, Lostwithiel, and Liskerd. The two coinages were held about Midsummer and Michaelmas. The "coynage" was in the hands of special officers who maintained a special room, assayed the tin, weighed and stamped it, and collected

[1] Jars, III, 202; cf. Pryce, 173–90.
[2] "Dialogue," 128.

the royal excise.[1] The owner of the tin and the merchant higgled for the price per thousand.[2] It was the opinion of the above cited complainant that the bargaining power of the miner-owner might be strengthened by a system of credit based upon pawns of tin in a public ware house.[3] But it does not appear that this would have brought much relief, for under the existing system the owner received a certificate of deposit from the coinage officers which was negotiable and which he generally disposed of immediately to the merchants at a discount.[4] By 1750 the smelters appear to have inaugurated a personal credit for the tin left with them by the mine-owners, which bills circulated freely "at the market price as well as bank bills."[5]

The merchants acquired an economic duress over the miners by making advances of money to them on pledge of delivery of their tin at the next coinage. "When any Western Gent. or person of accompt, wanteth money to defray his expences at London, he resorteth to one of the Tynne Marchants of his acquaintance, to borrow some; . . . they give bond for euerie twentie pounds so taken in lone, to deliver a thousand pound waight of Tyn at the next Coynage, which shal be within two or three months . . . "[6] Since the price of tin was usually about £25 per thousand these advances were made at high usury; "reaping thereby a double commoditie, both of excessive gaine for his lone, and of assurance to bee serued with Tynne for his money." In the opinion of this outsider this was "cutthroate and abominable dealing." The advances were sometimes made in commodities, such as cloth and provisions, and a profit was made on these.

The merchants about 1600 were mostly Londoners—the haberdashers of London.[7] Their profits appear to have been exorbitant.[8] As a relief against the exploitation waged by the merchants against the tinners Elizabeth and the first two Stuarts tried their method of privileged monopoly, establishing fixed preëmption prices at which the tin would be bought, and providing loan funds out of which loans were made at low interest to the miners between coinages.[9] These

---

[1] See descriptions in Carew, 13–14; V. C. H., Cornwall, I, 537–9; Pococke, I, 123.

[2] See description of this action by Carew, 13–14.

[3] "Dialogue," 128–9.

[4] V. C. H., Cornwall, I, 537; Lewis, 211–212.

[5] Pococke, I, 122.

[6] Carew, 14–15.

[7] S. P. Dom. Eliz. CCLIII, 46; Welch, I, 268; II, 10; Lewis, 216.

[8] Ibid., CCXLIII, 13; Jas. I, VI, 138.

[9] Ibid., CCLXXIII, 74; CCLXXXVI, 26; Chas. I, CCCXXII, 1–2; CCCXXVI, 2, 8, 60; Lewis, 219.

measures relieved but indifferently the oppression.[1] The monopoly method was abandoned between 1650 and 1660 with good results.[2] It was spasmodically used by Charles II and Anne and in the interims the tin dealers reëstablished themselves.[3]

After the Restoration the local Cornish shopkeepers and men of means gained an increasing part of the business of dealing in tin, both as factors for the Londoners as in the past, and also as independent dealers and exporters. The smelters, particularly, increased in power and supplanted the Londoners as financiers of the tin trade. In medieval times the miner had smelted his own tin ores. But the establishment of blowing-houses came to be an independent capitalistic venture; the owner of a smelter hired blowers or leased parts of his smelter to smelters; he smelted tin for owners of tin and took a percentage of the product. The owner of the tin received a note from the smelter when the ore was delivered by which the smelter agreed to deliver a certain quantity of tin at the next coinage. These notes were negotiable and were formerly sold at once to the merchant dealers.[4] The smelters about 1700 began to buy back their notes at a discount and thus indirectly purchase the tin without incurring as high risks as would attach to outright purchase of the tin which could be sold only at periodical coinages. This system continued till the abolition of the coinage system.[5]

The greater portion of the tin of this district was used in the manufacture of pewter. The London pewterers established themselves into a gild during the fourteenth century and during the following century acquired a practical monopoly of the pewter industry of England. Chapmen of tin were restrained from business in 1504 by a statute[6] which forbade all sales of pewter except at fairs or pewterers' shops. This statute constituted the pewterers in monopolistic power. They also gained control of the foreign exportation of tin. They fought the monopolies conferred by Elizabeth and her successors and gained some concessions. After the Restoration they declined rapidly.[7]

---

[1] V. C. H., Cornwall, I, 558.

[2] Ibid.

[3] "Aggravii Venetiani."

[4] Borlase, Nat. Hist. Cornwall, 181; see above Pryce, Mineralogia Cornubiènsis, 292–3.

[5] V. C. H., Cornwall, I, 562; Lewis, 223–4.

[6] 19 Hen. VII, Cap. 6; 4 Hen. VIII, Cap. 7; 25 Hen. VIII, Cap. 9; 33 Hen. VIII, Cap. 4.

[7] See Lewis, 45–54.

The pewterers bought their tin from the merchants usually, although they sometimes sent factors to Cornwall to buy directly from the miners.[1] The Pewterers' Company sometimes bought quantities of tin by collective bargaining and parceled it out among its members.[2] The tin was either manufactured into pewter instruments and sold to alehouse-keepers and others, or was exported in certified bars abroad.[3]

[1] S. P. Dom. Eliz., CCLIII, 46.

[2] Welch, I, 217, 268; II, 10.

[3] See discussion of the medieval and sixteenth century export trade in Lewis, 55–64.

CHAPTER V.

MIDDLEMEN IN THE TEXTILES AND TEXTILE MATERIALS TRADES.

WOOL AND WOOLENS.

Introduction.

The boast of Englishmen for centuries was their wool and woolens. Eulogies were profusely sounded, setting forth their paramount importance in the English trade and industry. And not without reason. It was in fact the "Master Wheel of their Trade." Misselden was not amiss when he pronounced cloth "to bee a Flower of the Kings Crowne, the Dowry of the Kingdome, the chiefe Revenue of the King. This," he said, "is a bound to fortifie and a Bond to knit the subjects to their societies. This is the Gold of our Ophir, the Milke and Hony of our Canaan, the Indies of England; and therefore Desire's and Deserves to be had in an everlasting remembrance."[1] A century later Defoe declared that "the woolen manufactures of Great Britain are the general wear in all the countries in Europe—go where you will you find it: 'tis in every country, in every market, in every trading place; all the world wears it, all the world desires it, and all the world almost envies us the glory and advantage of it."[2] About 1700 King and Davenant made some calculations to the following effect: that the annual income of England was £43,000,000; the yearly rent of the land was £10,000,000; the value of the annual wool clip was £2,000,000; the value of the woolen manufactures was £8,000,000; the value of the woolens exported was £2,000,000. From which it appeared that one-fifth of the rent was paid by wool, one-fifth of the national income was by the woolen manufactures, one-fourth of the woolens was exported and brought in one-twentieth of the national income.[3] No other product was so important or did so much for the common weal. In wool and woolens the English were in boast and fact the "Nonpareils of the World."

Corresponding to this predominance accorded wool and woolens was the degree of organization of the trade in these wares. The

[1] Misselden, Free Trade, 40.
[2] Defoe, Plan of Eng. Com., 181, 183.
[3] Smith, Memoirs, I, 222.

255

trade was highly organized and centralized in spite of the fact that the production was so broadly distributed over most of England. London played a most conspicuous rôle in the collection and distribution both of the raw and manufactured product. These two processes occasioned a complex set of middlemen, and the great volume of trade made possible a higher degree of specialization of its various branches than was to be had in the other trades.[1]

Distribution.

Roughly considered, the woolen industry was divided into three districts, first, the Eastern division centering in Norwich, Colchester, Sandwich, Canterbury and Maidstone; secondly, the Western centering in Taunton, Devises, Bradford, Frome, Trowbridge, Stroud, and Exeter; and lastly, the Northern or West Riding division.[2]   But no section was without some woolen manufacture, and household production for family use was universal.   The one fact of all others to be noted is that these several districts and parts within these districts specialized in particular kinds of cloth, and each became famous for its brand.[3]   This differentiation in kind of cloth produced made each section dependent somewhat on the other for those sorts of cloth which it did not produce itself.   Thus a trade in cloth had arisen and was very extensive although no part of the Kingdom was without its cloth manufacture.   The Yorkshire district drew the finer cloths from Wiltshire and Gloucestershire; the Norwich and Exeter manufacturers had their coarser cloths from the North; while the people of the Southwest were supplied from the North and East in exchange for their serges.   This reciprocal interchange of cloth was in part direct from district to district, but the greater part was centered in

[1] The writer is very much indebted to the writings of Unwin, Ashley, Cunningham, and others for generalizations and valuable suggestions as to the organization of the cloth industry and wishes to make due acknowledgment of their help in developing this chapter.

[2] Hobson, Mod. Cap., 26.

[3] The Eastern division produced worsteds, stuffs, serges, camlets, crapes, bays, sayes and perpetuanos; the Western turned out duroys, druggets, shalloons, broadcloths, medley cloths, dyed cloths, etc.; the Northern furnished the market with coarse cloths, kerseys, stockings, and cotton-weft goods.   Colchester had long been famous for its bays and sayes, Norwich for its druggets, duroys and serges, Wiltshire for its dyed cloths, Nottingham for its stockings, etc. See the "Atlas Mar. et Com.," 109, for a more extensive treatment. Defoe, Com. Eng. Tr., 194–5, gives a very complete tabular display of the cloths produced in each county in 1745.

London, to which each sent its surplus and from which each drew its supply. It was in this respect that the organization of the cloth trade was so permeating, the tentacles of the London factor touching every cloth-producing or -trading center of Great Britain.

But the particular interest at hand is not the woolen manufactures, but the raw wool—where it was produced and whither distributed. A glance at the Table[1] suggests at once that the raising of sheep and wool was widely dispersed. However, certain parts of England were more particularly devoted to this industry and were known for either quantity or quality, or both, of their wool. Four districts may be roughly distinguished. One district centered about Wilts and embraced Sussex, Hants and Somerset on the south, the highlands of Wales on the West, and Berks, Buckingham and Hertford on the East. From very early times the central market for this broad district was Cirencester, in Gloucestershire, near the Wilts border. Winchcombe, Gloucester, Stroud, and, in fact, practically all the towns of Gloucestershire owed their early prominence to the Cotswolds.[2] This county was paying in revenue to the crown as early as the thirteenth century 30,000 sacks of Cotswold wool;[3] after the introduction of the turnip, about 1750, the flocks increased and it was reported that the county had 400,000 sheep.[4] The other counties were nearly as productive. Camden described the Isle of Wight as maintaining many sheep "whose wool is reckoned the best after that of Leicester and Cotswold, and is 'in great request among woolen manufacturers."[5] Dorset was reported in the eighteenth century to be sending to Smithfield Market, London, some of the largest and finest sheep "both for flesh and wool" and to be producing "surprising quantities of wool." This wool was more and more sent into Somerset and Devon for consumption.[6] Worcestershire was exporting wool in the thirteenth century; its markets were Worcester, Kidderminster and Evasham; sales were made to the Flemish and Florentine merchants by the monasteries and abbeys. It appears that it did not produce as much wool as Norfolk, Gloucester or Lincoln, when in 1341 Edward III levied upon the several counties.[7] But its export

[1] See Chapter on Corn, Appendix.
[2] V. C. H., Gloucester, II, 154.
[3] "The Cotswold Flock Book," Vol. 1.
[4] "County Curiosities," 25.
[5] Camden, Britt., 1587; V. C. H., Hamp. V, 426.
[6] V. C. H., Dorset, II, 361,
[7] Cf. Parl. R. (Rec. Com.) II, 131b.

surplus grew in the succeeding centuries,[1] until by 1550, the woolen manufacturing had so developed as to use up all the domestic supply and even necessitate imports of wool.[2] Worcestershire drew upon Herefordshire and Shropshire for this supply.[3] In the latter part of the eighteenth century the Worcestershire manufactures declined and this county began to supply Oxfordshire[4] manufacturers. Surrey must have stood high in the wool output, for the borough arms of Guilford represented a wool sack and in 1574 every alehousekeeper was obliged by town ordinance to hang up a signboard with a wool-sack: these facts testify that wool-stapling was once a most important trade of this county.[5] Sussex produced a poor quality of wool[6] as evidenced by prices of wool from the various counties in 1337, 1343, and 1454[7] but were improved in the eighteenth century[8] and contributed to the consumption of the Wilts district what was not needed at its local center of manufacture Chichester.

There was a general tendency for the wool of the central southern counties, Wilts, Hants and Dorset, whose downs were prolific with sheep, to move westward (a) into Somerset, where it was mixed with Lincoln and Spanish long-staple wool and made into medley cloths,[9] and (b) into Devon, where it was mixed with Irish wool imported by way of Biddeford and Minehead, and made into serges, druggets and stuffs. Like this Irish wool the Welsh wool tended to move eastward. The Somerset clothiers bought the wools of Pembroke and Carmarthen and carried them home over the Severn; Milford was the chief exporting point, became very dependent upon it, and suffered "great distress" when the port officer tried to prohibit the exportation.[10] Brecknoch also was a considerable market for Welsh wool.

---

[1] Early Chan. Proc. (P. R. O.) bdle 66, No. 462; Cal. Pat. 1476–85, p. 519; V. C. H., Worc. II,282 n. The export went, apparently, by way of London and was sold to London exporters. For instance, in 1476, a case is recorded of one Thomas White, husbandman, who brought an action of debt against one Thomas Synnam, "a man of power and might dwelling in a foreign shire in London," for twelve sacks of Cotswold he had ordered and kept for six years.

[2] V. C. H., Worc. II, 282–3.

[3] Ibid., 289.

[4] V. C. H., Oxford, II, 251.

[5] V. C. H., Surrey, II, 345.

[6] V. C. H., Sussex, II, 255–6.

[7] Close, 11 Edw. III, m. 32; Cunningham, Growth, 628; Suss. Arch. Coll. X, 77.

[8] Young, Agric. of Suss. 359.

[9] Pocock, II, 37.

[10] Cal. S. P. Dom. 1619–23, p. 290; V. C. H., Somer. II, 411.

As was said, the greatest market for this district was Cirencester.[1] It was the distributing point for wool over the Western district of manufacture. The manufacturers came thither from Tedbury, Malmesbury and other towns of Gloucester and Wilts and Devon to buy their wool. The wool-merchants of Leicester, and the fel-wool-men from Southwark, and the Sussex and the Welsh and Irish wool-men, all brought vast stores of wool to this market for the Tuesday and Friday sales. Even Spain contributed.[2] Defoe said, "The quantities sold here are incredible."[3] It was handling at least five hundred packs of wool per week about 1700.

Another prominent class of wool that poured into Cirencester was fel-wool. As has been noted elsewhere, many thousands of sheep were brought yearly to Smithfield and other London markets and slaughtered by the carcass butchers. Much fel-wool thus came to the London market. It was bought up by two sets of buyers; the one bought for the Eastern district, for the makers of bays and sayes; the other bought for the Western district, where, with the other wools above mentioned, it was manufactured into medley or white cloths; these, when dyed, were called Spanish cloth; this wool was bought of the wool-staplers of Barnaby Street, Southwark, and carried westward by the same carriers as brought up the West country cloths to Black-well Hall. The blanket makers of Whitney, Oxon, were probably the greatest consumers of this fel-wool. A writer in 1677 said, "this place has engrossed the whole trade of the nation for this commodity (blankets) in so much that the wool for their use, which is chiefly fell wool (off from sheepskins) centers here from some of the further-most parts of the kingdom, viz. Rumneymarsh, Canterbury, Colches-ter, Norwich, Exeter, Leicester, Northampton, Coventry, Hunting-don, etc., of which the Blanketers . . . do work out above a hundred packs of wool per week. . .. . They send all sorts of Duffields and Blankets weekly in waggons up to London, which return laded with fell-wool from Leaden-hall and Barnaby Street in South-wark, whither 'tis brought for this purpose from most places above mentioned; Oxfordshire and the adjacent counties being not able to supply them."[4]

---

[1] "Essai sur L'Etat," 29–30; V. C. H., Glouc. II, 154–5, 162–3.

[2] Exch. Q. R. bdle 457, No. 35; V. C. H., Glouc. II, 159. In 1567 125.5 cwt. of Spanish wool were imported.

[3] Defoe, Tour, II, 268.

[4] Plot. Nat. Hist. Oxf., 278–80.

A second wool district, which suffers rough demarkation and which produced the best wool and with the longest staple and taken from the largest sheep in England, was centered in Leicester. It embraced Leicester, Northants, Nottingham, Rutland and Lincoln. Defoe calls Leicester the "vast Magazine of Wool for the rest of the Nation."[1] This district, bounded by the Anker, Humber, Trent and Ouse, about sixty miles in breadth, was celebrated for its mutton and long staple wool; and the manufacturing districts competed for them. In 1291 the staple for the wools of "Lincolnshire, Northampton, Leicestre, and Notingham shires was at Lincoln, and there stapulled, custumyde, and poysed, wyth other tolles thereto belongyng, to the behoffe and releve of the payment off the fee ferme of the seyd cite."[2] But in 1369 Boston was made staple for these counties and all wool was dispatched abroad from this port for the staples of Antwerp, Calais, etc.[3] Hull, Yarmouth, and Newcastle also exported wool in considerable quantities, but Boston ranked second in England, after London. The introduction of the stocking and worsted manufacture provided these counties with a larger home market for wool in the latter centuries and the foreign trade gave place to the domestic.

Part of the wool was "used within the county, being comb'd and weav'd into Serges, Tammies, and Shalloons, at Kettering and other towns."[4] The fallow or shorter wool was usually sent into York and into the Western district to Cirencester and Taunton. A spirited competition existed between the York or Northern district and the Western district for the Lincoln wool: "the records of the Yorkshire woollen trade are full of complaints of the way in which the south country clothiers bought up all the best Cotswold, Lincolnshire and Norfolk wools."[5] That to Cirencester was carried by packhorse; here it was made up into yarn and then bought up by the yarn-merchants and distributed among the clothiers of Wilts and Gloucester. They mixed it with Spanish wool and manufactured it into those famous West England medley and white cloths. Part of that which was carried into the North, into the remoter parts of York, Westmoreland

[1] Defoe, Tour, II, 332.

[2] Hist. MSS. Com. Rep. XIV, App. VII, 263; Ross, Civitas Lincolnia, 12; see petition for the re-establishment of the staple at Lincoln by the counties of Leicester, Nottingham, Lincoln and Derby, in Parl. R. (Rec. Com.) II, 332; ditto, in 1376, Rot. Parl. II, 322 f. and Cunningham, Growth, 316.

[3] V. C. H., Lincoln, II, 302; this requirement was evaded: cf. statute 14 Ed. IV, Cap. 3.

[4] Morton, Nat. Hist. of Northants, 16 ff.; V. C. H., Northants, II, 33.

[5] V. C. H., York, II, 415–6, III, 460.

and Cumberland, was spun into fine yarn, and in this form was then carried by horse-pack, averaging a hundred packs a week, down to London and manufactured into various sorts of cloth at Spitalfields.[1] A third portion of the Leicester district wool was bought up by broggers and taken to Stourbridge Fair, "and thence to Norwich and to Braintrey, Bocking and Colchester, where 'tis wrought into stuffs and bays."[2] The Stourbridge Fair was the greatest and most famous wool market of England.[3] Particularly did the wool from Lincoln find its way through Stourbridge into Norfolk and Suffolk, proximity likely accounting for the fact.

The third wool-producing region embraced York and Lancaster and the counties on the north. The poorest wool of all came from this district: it is one reason why this district never competed in the better classes of cloths. Besides the wool was not produced in great enough quantity to provide much for export while England was exporting wool, nor enough to provide the Lancashire clothmakers as early as 1654.[4] Consequently, Lancashire began at this time to import this raw material. Roberts in 1641 said "The town of Manchester . . . buys the yarn of the Irish in great quantity, and weaving it, return the same again into Ireland to sell; . . . buys cotton wool in London that comes first from Cyprus and Smyrna and at home work the same, and perfect it into fustians, vermillions, dimities, and such other stuffs and then return it to London, whence it is vented and sold, and not seldom sent into foreign parts."[5] The Lancashire clothmakers preferred to buy Lincoln wool but were usually overbid by the Norfolk and Wilts clothiers; the Irish wool was of poor quality: one buyer declared, "Irish wool is the best at first show, and the more a man deals with it he shall fynd it to be worse and generally worse."[6]

[1] For contemporary authority on the distribution of Leicestershire wool, see "Atlas Mar. et Com." 109 (1728); "Essai sur L'Etat," 29–30 (1765); it will be noted that in this interval the northern manufactures were being established, and that at the later date the wool was mixed with the coarser wool of the North and manufactured more into kerseys, etc., at Halifax, Bury, etc., and less was sent to London in the form of yarn. See also Defoe, Com. Eng. Tr., 189–193 (1745); Defoe, Tour, II, 36–7 (1745); St. P. Dom., Jas. I, LXXX, 13 (quoted in Unwin, Ind. Org. 188–9). Comparatively little change had taken place in the distribution of the wool from 1616 to 1755.

[2] Morton, Nat. Hist. of Northants, 16.

[3] Defoe, Com. Eng. Tr., II, 188.

[4] S. P. Dom., 1654, LXIX, 7; V. C. H., Lancas., II, 377.

[5] Lewis Roberts, quoted in V. C. H., Lancas. II, 301.

[6] Exch. Dep. by Com. Tiin. 28, ch. II, No. 29; V. C. H., York, II, 415–6. For further discussion of the sources of Lancashire raw materials see Ure, Cotton Mfg. I, 185.

The fourth district was Norfolk and Suffolk. It was the earliest manufacturing district and seat of the Flemish and French immigrants. As has been shown above, this region's demand for wool exceeded the local production and its manufacturing towns, Colchester, Norwich, Braintree, Coggeshall, and others drew fel-wool from Southwark, long-staple wool through Stourbridge, and Irish wool through London. Further notice of this district's supply will be taken under the head of "Yarn Merchant."

Besides Stourbridge and Cirencester, the other great wool-market was at Blackwell Hall, London, and Barnaby Street, Southwark.[1] One district marketed its wool at London because of the prohibitive legislation against "owling" wool to France; the law, though much evaded along the Kentish coast, was very severe, and forbade the graziers to sell their wool within a certain number of miles from the sea; so for want of other market the wool-growers sent it to London whence it found its way to Wilts as Kentish wool.[2]

The English woolens manufacturers drew their wool from four sources: (a) the least important source was the African and Turkey coasts of the Mediterranean, known respectively as Barbary and Caramania wool.[3] Both were good, had long staple and fine fiber; but the quantity imported was insignificant. (b) Irish wool reached England by way of Liverpool into the Northern district, by way of Biddeford, Barnstaple and Minehead into the Western district, and by way of London whence it was carried to Norfolk and Essex.[4] As it became the settled policy of the English to suppress the wool and woolens industry in Ireland and to encourage the linen industry, the importations from Ireland were limited to a certain few ports and times and never reached the volume the island could have supplied.[5] (c) Spanish wool was imported in large quantities from Bilbao. It was a fine, short-fiber wool, and was mixed with the coarser native wool, and made into the finest cloths. The great part (d) of the wool consumed was native wool, which with the exception of the Spanish was superior to the wools of the Continental states or their colonies. Before the immigration of the Hugenots and the Flemish cloth-workers England had exported her fleeces to Flanders, whence she received back in turn her cloth. This exportation gave employment to the

---

[1] See treatment under "Factor," below; Defoe, Tour, II, 36–7.

[2] Ibid., II, 36–7.

[3] Defoe, Com. Eng. Tr., II, 187, 189, 192.

[4] Ibid., 187.

[5] See dissertation on the policy in Postlethwayt, Dict., s. v. British Empire.

Merchants of the Staple for centuries. But the rise of the exotic manufactures in the Isle curtailed this traffic, and England began importing rather than exporting wool, except the clandestine smuggling to France from the Romney Marsh and the Kentish coast.

Wool Buyers.

The protectionist policy prevailing in the Tudor period found one expression, among innumerable others, in a statute,[1] 1552, for the suppression of middleman-buyers of wool, specifying in detail what persons might buy and sell wool, and what persons were forbidden, and at what times. The intent of this act was to force growers of wool to sell their wool directly to the manufacturers and eliminate the wool dealer. The view-point of the day is expressed by a later writer in the following manner: "Here are a considerable Party of Men that flourish like Solomon's Lilies, that neither toyle nor spin, that only get a Profit out of the Wool, and no way encourage the Woolen-Manufacture; but on the contrary, a pack of wool carried forty Miles backwards and forwards, will not make the more Cloth at the Journies end, I wish I could say it would not make less."[2] In other words, the middleman was quite often regarded as an unproductive being preying upon the public.

The state and people found other objections to the woolmen's business. The one complaint which has been perennial through the centuries to the present time has been that middlemen raise prices. It is supposed that each successive handler adds to the otherwise low price the amount of his profit. Many direct complaints to this effect might be cited. For one instance, in 1585, "a petition of the clothiers, mostly of Suffolk, was presented to the government against the activities of the licensed brokers, complaining that as their own capital was not great they had to buy at second, third and fourth hand in the latter end of the year at excessive prices."[3] Another complaint was to the effect that they bought wool, not only to sell to the clothier but also for export, and the English clothier held that he had a first claim or exclusive right to English raw material.[4] As late as 1697 the Kidderminster clothiers were aggrieved by the wool-broggers who were taking

---

[1] 5 and 6 Ed. VI, Cap. 7. For earlier statute 1464, see Stat. Realm (rec. Com.) II, 410. See also IV, 141, and 22 Hen. VIII, Cap. 1.

[2] "Clothiers Complaint," 26.

[3] Lansd. MS. 48 fol. 67; V. C. H., Suff. II, 258.

[4] S. P. Dom., Eliz. CXV, 41; V. C. H., Suff. II, 258.

"a general Liberty" to "wind and mix Wool of divers Countries together;" which occasioned "faulty Cloth to be made."[1] In these early days when markets were so limited by the various obstacles natural and artificial and when the people as a whole had so small a capital store laid by for bad years, there was sound reason in the general fear of the possible extortions by the engrosser.

Provoked by such evils the paternal government interfered freely with the broggers' operations. The act of 1552 aimed at controlling them by the system of license. It made some effort to enforce the act. In 1577 the Justices were ordered to bind over in £100 apiece the "Broggers and buyers of wooll," that "neither they nor their heirs shall at any time hereafter buy or bargain any manner of wools that grow or hath grown within the county of Buckingham, but only such quantity of wools as they buy themselves or their apprentices shall yearly make in his own mansion house."[2] This was more stringent than the license system and was occasioned by the failure of the license through constant evasion. One common method of evasion was for a brogger who could not get a license to pursue that vocation as nominal agent of the larger wool-growers.[3]

Fortunately for the economic good of the Kingdom the execution of this statute had fallen into abeyance by the time the Stuarts ascended the throne. But James I was urged to revive the force of the act, by the manufacturing interests, and he acceded to their demands in 1616, not in total suppression of the wool-dealer, but licensing certain middlemen and carriers who were to fill the stated orders of certain poor and needy clothiers.[4] But seven years later the Parliament showed its disapproval of the King's policy by repealing[5] the Edwardian statute and nullifying the King's orders. This repeal reopened the way for the developing organization of trade.

During the hard years 1619 to 1623 the government interfered in a different way, by ordering "the wooldealers not to store up wools, thereby to enhance the price, but to sell them on moderate terms," and offering as the justification of the order, that "those who have saived in profitable times must now be content to lose for the public good till the decay of the trade be remedied."[6] This pointed to the

---

[1] Jour. H. Com., XII, 150.

[2] S. P. Dom., Eliz. CXV, 8; V. C. H., Bucks, II, 75, 128.

[3] S. P. Dom., Eliz. CXV, 14, 40; V. C. H., Suff. II, 258.

[4] Privy Council Register, 6/23, 1616, p. 321–2; 4/26, 5/12, 6/2.

[5] 21 Jas. I., Cap. 28, Sec. 11.

[6] Cal. S. P. Dom., 1619–23, 343.

evil of ingrossing. The court records of the English counties contain many a case where wool-ingrossers were tried.[1] In spite of all interference the woolman's business continued, grew, and won its legitimate place in business, law and public opinion. Woolmen were the first middlemen in the trade. During the centuries before England took to manufacturing woolens she supplied Flanders with wool.[2] This export trade necessitated the wool-buyer and the wool merchant. Both are commonly mentioned in the thirteenth and fourteenth centuries in the records of the various counties. For instance, in Sussex, Chichester in 1353 and Lewes in 1363 were appointed ports for shipping wool;[3] there were reported shortly afterward in this latter town five wool-broggers, six cloth-merchants, one wool-merchant, and one wool-packer.[4] In Essex "woolmen," Thomas Roos and William Prentys, were mentioned in 1491[5] as connected with the export trade at Billericay. The letter books of the Cely family are the best possible data showing the operations of the wool-merchant and wool-buyer. The Celys bought most of their wool from a great woolman named Midwinter, in Northleach, Gloucestershire; they also bought from one John Busshe of Northleach. The wool was carried to London by horse-pack and dispatched to Calais. Cely cared for packing it at Northleach. Midwinter allowed Cely credit for nearly a year's length.[6] Cely sometimes rode out in person to buy from Midwinter and sometimes sent agents to buy for him. When woolen manufacturing gained the ascendancy over the wool export business the capitalistic services of the wool-buyer became increasingly indispensable to the clothier and the wool-buyers therefore grew apace.[7]

Broggers.

The operations of the various wool-buyers were so little differentiated, each one performing at different times the same business as the others, that a rigid classification is quite impossible. And it is to be understood in the following treatment that clear-cut distinctions did not exist among the various buyers of wool.

[1] See V. C. H., Worces. II, 283, 289, and the citations there given.
[2] V. C. H., Essex, II, 381, gives the state of this trade and the effects of Edward III's policy.
[3] Sussex, Arch. Coll. X, 70–1.
[4] V. C. H., Sussex, II, 256.
[5] Benham, 97–8; V. C. H., Essex, II, 381–2.
[6] Cely Papers, pp. 11, 21, 27, 28, 32, etc.
[7] Cf. V. C. H., Suffolk, II, 257.

The buyer who was most specialized was the brogger. The brogger was an agent or broker of a manufacturer or exporter or big wool-merchant or jobber.[1] He made a farm-to-farm canvas, established regular customers from whom he bought from year to year, and picked up what wool he could outside this regular custom. As appears from some business accounts of a wool-buyer in Yorkshire early in the eighteenth century the whole number of persons from whom he bought ranged from ten to twenty-nine, and his purchases averaged £1 5s. per person per year.[2] The brogger bought the wool, weighed it, and paid for it. It appears that the brogger was a hard bargainer or dishonest, for the clothiers petitioned that "the Brogger of Woolle may not buy any Woolle but what shall be first weyed by a man that shall be sworne to deale truly betweene the buyer and the seller."[3] He either packed it up himself or employed a specialized class of wool-winders or wool-packers, which arose in the wool-producing sections or the markets,[4] as, for example, in London, where the wool-staplers, packers, winders and combers together made up the wool-men's livery company. After it was wound and packed the brogger arranged to have it fetched away.

Jobber and Merchant.

The wool-jobber and merchant was closely allied with the wool-brogger on the one hand and the wool-stapler on the other. All were buyers of wool, either direct from the wool-grower or from the first buyer. The brogger has been distinguished as a buyer on another's account, but sometimes the name was applied indiscriminately to the buyers of wool, whether in agency or not. Wool-jobbers embraced "all those who buy and sell wool in the fleece" and deserved "the Name of Wool-merchant."[5] In a strict sense, the fleeces were not sorted by the jobber: he sold them in the same pack in which he bought them.

Two facts gave occasion to this occupation. In the first place, the wool harvest was quickly made: in less than a month the whole year's clip was ready for sale. It at once became dead capital in the grower's

[1] "Reasons for a Limited Exportation," 22.

[2] Smith, Memoirs, II, 465–6.

[3] S. P. Dom., Jas. I, CXXVII, 76; CXXVIII, 20, 51; V. C. H., Oxford, II, 196.

[4] Compare Surtees, 33:30–1; "Clothiers Compliant," 26; and Hazlitt, Liv. Com., 670–1.

[5] Smith, Complaints, 25, 26, 28, 29, 31. The general function of the wool-jobber has been gleaned from these references.

hands, and to carry the stock was an economic loss, due to the interest charge against it. But, on the contrary, the needs of the manufacturers were nearly constant throughout the year: and it was an economic loss to them to buy up in advance large provisions for their consumption during the year. They sought a seller who would sell them small lots as they needed them; whereas the wool-growers sought a buyer who would take at once their whole clip. These two functions were combined in the wool-jobber.

He was a capitalist. He bought for cash large volumes of wool seasonally; he owned warehouses for the storage of his purchases; he sold to clothiers and manufacturers on credit and in such parcels as they needed. In performing these capitalistic acts he incidentally did others that promoted the wool trade. He acted as collector and forwarder of the wool from the grower to the manufacturer. As a buyer of wool and a seller of wool he developed a clientele of buyers and sellers, both of whom he cared to preserve by fair and honest dealings; and consequently reduced the frauds of the false winding graziers, so much complained of where manufacturers bought directly from the grazier. He conducted a wider correspondence and effected broader connections than would be possible or profitable to a grazier and in this way broadened the market of wool, more equally distributed it according to needs, and at a steadier price. By these labors, the manufacturer was enabled to specialize in making cloth and free himself from the tasks of buying wool from the scattered farms.

The earlier members of this class were exporters. Their history is that of the merchant staplers. Before the sixteenth century wool constituted the chief commodity exported by the Merchants Adventurers and Merchants of the Staple. The rise of cloth manufacturers caused their decline or necessitated their becoming importers of wool rather than exporters.[1] The monasteries took an active part in the exportation of wool, but by reasons of their relations to the Holy See they sold mostly to visiting Italian merchants; oftentimes the monastery wool was pledged years in advance for loans made to the monasteries by these alien merchants.[2] Another source of this class was the sons of the gentry of the provincial counties who acted as wool and lead

---

[1] This is illustrated in the history of the Bristol merchant staplers in the sixteenth century; V. C. H., Glouces., II, 158–9.

[2] Instance, Furness monastery, Lancashire, in the fourteenth century, V. C. H., Lancas. II, 270.

merchants in London in the seventeenth and eighteenth centuries.[1] A further group were the Flemish merchants resident in England.[2]

Many of these wool-merchants became local or even national celebrities. John Keyser was one of a great group of Newark, Nottingham, merchants; he had frequent financial relations with Edward III, and "combined with his traffic in wool the office of purveyor of wines to the royal household.[3] The Cely family were merchants of the staple at London in time of Edward IV. They bought wool from the woolmen of Northleach, Camden, and Chipping Norton and of Gloucestershire; they dispatched agents, sometimes, to these districts to buy up the wool. At London they packed it up and dispatched it to Calais to their agents there for sale. Their hardest competitors in the Cotswold districts were the Italian merchants.[4] It was the common practice of these merchants to have agents abroad and resident there; the closer contact gave a more effectual control of the trade at the staples. In 1332 we find James Keyser, of Newark, Nottingham, dwelling in Bruges and with him many other English merchants.[5]

The wool-merchant often combined wool-buying with other lines. Instance has been given of Keyser who bought wine, and of Derbyshire men who bought and sold lead. One Andrew Weyman of Southwark, a wool-merchant of large business, also did a considerable leather business. In fact most of the Southwark fel-wool merchants dealt in leather also.[6]

Wool Stapler.

Staple, in connection with the textile materials, means the fiber of any material used for spinning and is expressive of the character of the material. A stapler was one who was employed in assorting wool according to its staple. In connection with this assorting, the stapler performed all the functions attaching to the jobber and merchant. He had large warehouses and required a great capital.[7] But his special and distinctive function consisted in *breaking* and *assorting* wool, making it up into sortments fit for the manufacturer.[8] With-

[1] V. C. H., Derby, II, 346.

[2] V. C. H., Nott. II, 342.

[3] Ibid., 342–3.

[4] The Cely Papers, Camden Society, 3rd series, Vol. I, contains much interesting material relative to their operations.

[5] V. C. H., Nott., II, 342.

[6] V. C. H., Surrey, II, 335.

[7] Campbell, 199–200.

[8] Ibid., 199–200; Smith, Complaints, 25.

out the stapler the clothier was under the necessity of buying his wool in the fleece, and unless he could work up all sorts of wool, a thing no clothier could do to any advantage, he suffered a loss of those parts not used. This was the condition in Scotland as late as 1738, and with this handicap, due in turn to the smallness of the Scotch manufacture, the Scots found great difficulty in competing with the English stapler-supplied clothier.[1] Campbell was so impressed with the importance of the wool-stapler that he pronounced him "the Sheet Anchor of Great Britain."[2] The staplers resided in chief wool-raising and manufacturing districts and markets of wool. They were numerous in Barnaby Street, in Southwark and in Bradford of Dorsetshire, and in Norwich, Lincoln and Leicester.[3]

Cirencester was the seat of the wool-staplers of the West of England. Its great market for wool was conducted by broggers, merchants and staplers, particularly the staplers. A writer in 1800 said "There are numerous vestiges of the combers' wool-lofts still to be seen in some of their old houses, distinguished by doors in the garret walls, for the conveniency of taking in wool-packs."[4] They bought up wool, assorted it, combed it, and got it spun in the cottages roundabout this market.[5]

The value of the assorting of wool done by the staplers is well presented in a description, 1677, of the fel-wool men of Southwark. "This Fell wool they separate into five or six sorts, viz. long fell wooll, head wooll, bay wool, ordinary, middle and tail wooll: Long fell wooll they send to Wells, Taunton, Tiverton, etc., for making worsted stockings; of head wool and bay wool, they make the blankets of 12, 11, 10 quarters broad, and sometimes send it, if it bear a good price to Kederminster for making their stuffs, and to Evesham, Parshore, etc. for making yarn stockings; or into Essex for making Bays, whence one sort of them, I suppose, is called bay wool; of the ordinary and middle they make blankets of 8 and 7 quarters broad; and of these mixed with the courser locks of fleece wooll a sort of stuff they call Duffields . . . of which Duffields and blankets consists the chief trade of Witney."[6]

---

[1] For the advantages of staplers in wool, see Smith, Memoirs of Wool, II, 267–8; "Interest of Scotland considered," 109; "Appeal to Scotsmen," 56.

[2] Campbell, 199.

[3] Defoe, Com. Eng. Tr., II, 188.

[4] Hist. of Ciren. & Tewksbury, 175.

[5] V. C. H., Glouces., II, 162.

[6] Plot, Nat. Hist. of Oxf., 279.

Yarn Merchant.

The yarn merchants were a class of merchants who owed their existence to the localization of spinning and weaving. This localization increased the interdependence of the different parts of the Kingdom. The clothmaking districts were forced for want of spinners to draw part of their yarn from quarters near and remote. The operations of getting the wool from the wool-buyers, and into the hands of the spinners in their localized districts, and of collecting again and selling the yarn to the clothiers were performed by this specialized class. Sometimes they simply bought up the surplus yarn spun by the country spinners and carried it and distributed it among the clothiers. They commonly combined the functions of the wool-stapler (viz., assorter, kember, washer, scourer, and trimmer) with that of yarn-merchant proper.[1]

The demand for yarn of the Eastern manufacturing district, centered in Essex and Suffolk, was greater than the spinners of the clothing towns could provide. As early as 1575 it was reported that "The custom of our country (Suffolk) is to carry our wool out to carding and spinning and put it to divers and sundry spinners who have in their houses divers and sundry children and servants that do card and spin the same wool."[2] The outlying parts of this district also contributed yarn to London. In 1618 Reyce's Breviary reported that the spun yarn was divided between the Norwich manufacturers and those of London, whither it was carried weekly and "readily sold to those who make thereof all sorts of fringes, stuffs, and many other things which at this day are used and worn."[3] A century later, according to Cox (1720) Essex was still engaged "partly in Spinning of great quantities of yarn, which is sent to London for the fringe-makers and Spitalfield weavers."[4] In 1748 Morant, the historian of Colchester, found that over the greater part of the country "the poorer sort are almost universally employed in spinning the wool" for the weavers[5] and in 1770 thirty-two parishes were specially mentioned, in or adjacent to the cloth-making portion of the county, as devoted to this work.[6] The same parts are enumerated in statutes of

[1] Reyce, Breviary of Suffolk, 26.
[2] S. P. Dom., Eliz. CXIV, 32; V. H. Suff. II, 258.
[3] Op. cit., 26.
[4] Cox, I, Mag. Brit. I, 722.
[5] Morant, Hist. of Colch., 75.
[6] "Gentleman," II, 49; V. C. H., Essex, II, 401.

the realm[1] of 1606 and 1609 which were enacted to reduce the frauds of the "spinners of wool within the Countie of Essex that shall receive any wooll to be spun into yarne" for clothiers "dwelling in the townes of Cogshall, Bocking, Braintree, Halstead, Wittam, or Colchester."[2] It therefore appears that for two centuries Essex and Suffolk were a spinning district for local and distant clothiers and that opportunity existed for the rise of middlemen handling yarn.

Round about the Wiltshire clothing district was situated another spinning district. Elsewhere it has been remarked that the wool-staplers of Cirencester put out their wool in the environs of their town and county. To the north, Evasham was described by Pococke as having "a great manufacture of yarn,"[3] Camden "a manufacture of spinning thread,"[4] Shipton, "a manufacture in combing wool."[5] This spinning district extended as far north as Derbyshire where "the number of spinners must have greatly exceeded that of the weavers."[6] Early in the fifteenth century the women of this county were accustomed to "take wool to spynne of clothe makers and by that meanes . . . have a convenyente lyvynge."[7] To the west of Wales, Somerset and Devon produced an excess of yarn. Irish yarn could be imported (about 1700) more cheaply than the local yarn makers could produce it by 1*d*. per pound and the importation was extensively carried on.[8] Defoe reported that these western clothiers imported twenty-five thousand packs of yarn ready spun from Ireland.[9] Cerne and Wine Caunton in Dorset had "a manufacture of spinning thread and woolen yarn."[10] Further to the southwest and west, Porlock yarn had a great reputation among the Wilts clothiers and was eagerly sought after by them through their agents or the yarn-merchants.[11] This yarn was marketed at Dunster in Somerset from the sixteenth

[1] 4 Jas. I, Cap. 2 and 7 Jas. I, Cap. 7.

[2] This occupation was one used to employ the poor by the executors of the poor law and so received the coöperation of the local governments. Leonard, Early Eng. Poor Relief; Hist. MSS. Com. Rep. XIV, App. VIII, 139.

[3] Pococke, II, 277.

[4] Ibid., II, 280.

[5] Ibid., II, 280.

[6] V. C. H., Derby, II, 371.

[7] Fitzherbert, Boke of Husbandrie, XIII, 97.

[8] J. C. H., 1697: 37.

[9] Defoe, Com. Eng. Tr., II, 189, 192.

[10] Pococke, II, 143, 150.

[11] Lewis, Topog. Dict. III, 556.

century onwards.[1] Carhampton also produced much yarn for sale.[2] This yarn-spinning was a household industry[3] and the spinners were reported to be "very necessary members of the commonwealth."[4] The clothiers' wives and children and women servants performed much spinning—"spullars of yarn," "forcers and cisters of wool."[5] On the eastern side of Wilts the spinners divided their output of yarn between Wilts and London. Cricklade manufactured woolen yarn, as did Auburn and other parts of Berks; in 1750 Pococke found that the people "spin cotton for candles, for cotten cloths and stockins; and the carriers go with cotton backward and forward through this place to and from London."[6]

Far up in the north was another spinning district. Great quantities of the wool bought in the Leicester district were carried north, even into remote Westmoreland, to be spun into yarn and be carried back to Norwich and London.[7]

It is evident from the data at hand that the trade of spinning was, to a considerable degree, localized. Although some spinning was done in nearly every home, in some districts it was made a specialty and a surplus of yarn was prepared for the market. The yarn merchant made a living by buying wool, distributing it among the spinners, collecting the yarn, and selling it to the clothiers; more commonly, he simply bought and sold yarn.

Repeated complaints were made to the government against the yarnmen and spinners of yarn. The most familiar was that they made up reels of yarn that were of defective length and were wanting in the proper number of threads.[8] The weavers, for example, of Norfolk proposed to hold the yarnmen responsible for such defects and secured an order of the Privy Council specifying the proper length and number of threads and penalizing any defaults by confiscation. This order of 1617 was supplemented in 1621 by efforts to procure an act of Parliament to the same end.[9]

---

[1] Somers. Arch. Soc. Proc., XXXV, 238; V. C. H., Somers. II, 407.

[2] Savage, Hist. of Carhampton, 86.

[3] Young, Annals of Agric., IX, 308.

[4] Cal. S. P. Dom. 1634–5, 472.

[5] Unwin, 85; V. C. H., Worces. II, 289.

[6] Pococke, II, 248, 251.

[7] See note on pages 260–61.

[8] See statutory regulation of the delivery of wool to spinners and its return, 1512, 3 Hen. VIII, Cap. 6.

[9] S. P. Dom., Jas. I, CXL, 82; S. P. Dom., Ch. I, CLIII, 53.

Clothier.

The clothier was the central figure in the Domestic System of manufacture which characterized increasingly the productions of cloth from the middle of the fifteenth century till the Industrial Revolution. His business was a composite of the middleman's business and the manufacturer's business, but must be regarded in larger measure that of middlemen. In a restricted sense, he was not a manufacturer since he had ceased to exercise the craft of clothworker; nor was he a pure middleman, for all the wares he handled underwent transformation while under his control and assumed a very different aspect from the time he purchased the raw wool till he sold the finished product. He was an organizer of the manufacture, of the labor and of the distribution of the materials. His shop was a neighborhood, a village and its environs. Not until the closing decades of the period covered by this study did he assume the ownership of the tools of manufacture, and even then they were leased out to the artisans under his employ. Nevertheless, since he did not directly manufacture the materials which he bought and engaged himself exclusively (a) in the buying of materials and of labor used upon them and outside his supervision and (b) in the selling of the cloth, his middlemen characteristics are very obvious, and on the basis of these features his relations to trade are studied here.

(*a*) *West District.* It is deemed best for the purpose of comparative analysis and definite statement to treat successively the clothing organization of the three manufacturing districts. That of the West of England reached the highest degree of organization and approached the factory system most closely before the Industrial Revolution. It was dominated by the capitalist manufacturer middleman—the clothier.[1] Here the clothier's function as organizer was the most striking phase of the industry. He was a man of capital and credit. Cunningham has shown the rise of capitalistic employers and the division of labor in the clothing industry between 1461 and 1485.[2] During the sixteenth and seventeenth centuries these clothiers rose to a prominent place in Gloucester life.[3] And they appear to

[1] It is suggested that the reader compare Defoe, Tour, II, 33 (1722); Tucker Instructions, 36 (1758); and the Report from the Committee on the Woolen Manufacture of England (1806), and note the small degree of change in organization during the eighteenth century.

[2] Cunningham, Growth, I, 437–8; V. C. H., Glouces. II, 154.

[3] V. C. H., Glouces. II, 159; Ibid., 523–4; Somerset, II, 313; Nashs. Worces. II, app. CXIV.

have reached the acme of their renown and importance between 1690 and 1760,[1] after which they declined rapidly under the throes of the Industrial Revolution 'and the migration of industry to the north. The family fortunes were usually indigenous to the trade; the clothiers began as poor masters and attained to wealth.   Richard Baxter said, "My People were not Rich   . . .   there were none of the Tradesmen very rich   . . .   The Magistrates of the Town were few of them worth 40 l. per An. and most not half so much.   Three or four of the Richest thriving Masters of the Trade, got about 500 l. or 600 l. in twenty years, and it may be lose 100 l. of it at once by an ill Debtor."[2]

Defoe found that about Bradford in Wiltshire it was no extraordinary thing in 1722 to find clothiers worth from £10,000 to £40,000 and that many of the great families of gentry had risen to wealth and rank in the capacity of clothier.[3]   These accumulations of wealth are evidence of large profits at least in the earlier decades of the industry.   But if the public declarations of the clothiers themselves may be trusted the rate of profits declined very much in the second quarter of the eighteenth century.   One states that during the '30's four-fifths of the Western woolens had been manufactured on a 3 per cent basis upon the capital invested.   Intense local competition, the north district's growing competition, the decline in the foreign demand for Spanish cloth, and the custom of carrying larger stocks of finished cloth were the causes ascribed for the decline.[4]

At various times and places the more adventurous, able and wealthy clothiers attempted to set up production on a large scale.   The ventures were not always successful.   William Stumpe clothier of Malmesbury in 1546 rented Osney Abbey and engaged "himself to fynd work for ii (2,000) persons from tyme to tyme, if they may be gotten, that wyll do their worke well contynually in clothemaking, for the succour of the cytye of Oxenford and the country about yt, for the which intent the mylles were made."[5]   This charitable attempt failed; but the success of some others was so great that traditions have gathered about certain clothiers' names much as they have about the semimythical military heroes of primitive Britain.   Berks prides herself

[1] V. C. H. Glouces. II, 160.

[2] "Baxterianae Reliquiae," pt. I, 94.

[3] Defoe, Tour, II, 35.

[4] Gent. Mag., 1739: 125, 135, 236–7, 479.   "Public Register," 24 Jan. 1741. Cf. Nash, Worces. II, app. CXIV; V. C. H., Berks, I, 391–2.

[5] Gough, MS. Oxon., 70; Records of City of Oxf., 184–6; Cunningham and Mac-Arthur, Outlines, 204–5; V. C. H., Oxf. II, 244.

on the names of Jack of Newberry, Thomas Dolman, and John Kendrick; Oxford had the great Sylvester family; Somerset produced the Cogan family of Chard, the Sharlands of Mells, the Mandelyns of Croscombe, the Norths, Chorleys and Featherstones of Wiveliscombe, the Styles, Kents and Chapmans of Bath; and so forth.[1]

The clothier was a resident of one of the larger towns of this district,—Cirencester, Tedbury, Gillingham, Malmesbury, Devizes, Bradford, Frome, Banbury, Burford, Horseley, Stroud, and others. The region stretched along the great western highways toward Bristol and Bath. Stroud was "a sort of capital to the clothing villages."[2] Apart from this immediate center were many great clothing towns in Worcester, Devon, and Hants. Being employers of labor the clothiers thrived best in towns where laborers were concentrated. Those who lived in the country raised their own wool in whole or part.[3] The contest that long prevailed between the craft gilds of the towns and the country craftsmen, and the severe town protectionist policy that led the city masters to migrate to the country were concomitant causes for this self-sufficiency of the country clothiers as to raw material. Those who lived in the towns usually bought their wool from the wool "embroggers."[4] As the business increased in volume the population became more and more engrossed in the cloth making; there was a "great neglect of tillage upon many great farms,"[5] much arable land was converted into pasture, and the population was "mostly clothiers, weavers, and spinners."[6]

Having, then, raised his wool, or bought it at the Cirencester or London or other markets, or having dispatched broggers into the country to buy, the clothier delivered it out weekly among the spinners who lived in the vicinity of these clothing towns, in the country and the hamlets. The spinners were paid for their work and the yarn was then carried to a weaver, who was likewise paid by the clothier. The yarn dealer sometimes intervened and relieved the clothier of these earlier parts of the business. And so successively through the remaining processes of the manufacture—milling, dyeing, shearing,

---

[1] V. C. H., Berks, I, 388–9, 91; Oxford, II, 244–5; Somerset, II, 413.

[2] Pococke, II, 269.

[3] V. C. H., Worces. II, 290.

[4] For example, in the Prattinton MS. there were named in 1589 more than a score of the clothier citizens of Worcester town who depended on the wool-buyers; V. C. H., Worces. II, 290.

[5] S. P. Dom., Jas. I, CXLIV, 24.

[6] S. P. Dom., Chas. I, CLXXVI, 29–40; CLXXXV, 40; CCIV, 112; CLXXVI, 29; V. C. H., Somers, II, 308.

dressing, etc.,—the clothier carried his ware and paid the artisans. He thus employed many distinct classes of artisans and each performed only one operation upon the wool or cloth. The excellence of this system consisted in the concentrated direction of all the process by the clothier under a well-defined division of labor. Its greatest defect was the wastes caused by repeated carriage over considerable distances between successive artisans, and the cause of this decentralization was fundamentally the fact that power machinery needful to concentrated factory production had not yet been invented. But the clothier's business at this early time required considerable capitalists and men of broad correspondence who could undertake the risks involved.

The clothier occupied a very responsible and prominent place in the local community. He was the moneyed man, the paymaster and the employer to the whole vicinity. The neighborhood's activity and prosperity rested in his hands. One admirer exclaimed, "what an Advantage it is to the Poor to be born under the Influence of a Clothier, who, like the Sun, scatters Life and its Support to every one round him."[1] How responsible the clothier felt for the welfare of his community is illustrated in Gloucester during the hard times 1619–22 when it was reported to the government's inquirers that "One Will Bennett, a very ancient and good clothier, doth offer to live by brown bread and water, rather than his great number of poore people should want work, if he had means to keep them in work." Many clothiers declared they were compelled to pawn their clothes to keep their people at work.[2] When a clothier set up in a town it was an earnest of prosperity. For instance, during Mary's reign, one Edward Gascogne was heralded at Winchester, Hants, as one who "hath planted himselfe in that your cittie and hathe there takin in hande the makinge of cloth to the releiffe and setting on worke of a multitude of poore folkes."[3]

From very early date they became employers of labor outside their immediate journeymen and apprentices. They seem to have supervised directly the spinning of the finer yarns and to have sent the coarser woof wool into the country to be spun.[4] In 1467 "spynners, websters, dyers, shermen" are named as employees of the "maisters

[1] Gent. Mag., 1739: 205.

[2] S. P. Dom., Jas. I, CXXVIII, 49.

[3] Stowe MS. 846, fol. 180d; V. C. H., Hants, V, 484.

[4] In 1623, for instance, at Reading, Berks; Reading Rec., II, 159; V. C. H., Berks, I, 391.

and makers of cloth" of Worcester.[1] In Southampton the employees consisted, 1616, of "serge weavers and woolkemmers" and "cloth-workers" such as "doe . . . rowinge, burlinge, fullinge, dressinge and pressinge."[2]

Those clothiers who stand out with the greatest halo of tradition tried the concentration of these employments in large halls.   Deloney in 1632 in his introduction to "Thomas of Reading" said in retrospect that "Every one of these (nine clothiers of the West) kept a great Number of Servants at Worke, Spinners, Carders, Weavers, Fullers, Dyers, Sheeremen, and Rowers, to the great Admiration of all those that came into their Houses to behold them."   The same author in a poetical dissertation on John Winchcombe, the celebrated "Jack of Newbery," gave the following statistics of his employees; at 200 looms, 200 men and 200 boys, 100 women carding, 200 "maydens" spinning, 150 children picking wool, 50 "shearemen," 80 rowers, 40 men in the dyehouse, 20 men in the fulling mill, a butcher, brewer, baker, 5 cooks, 6 scullions, and children "to turne the broaches every day."[3] This traditional clothier lived about 1500.   Fuller says "he was the most considerable clothier, without fancy or fiction, England ever beheld."   Thomas Dolman succeeded Winchcombe as the leading clothier of Newbery.[4]

Wages were paid in truck or money.   A schedule of wages paid by a Gloucester clothier to his numerous employees in 1737 shows that one pack of wool would give employment to 58 persons for one week at a total combined wage of £19 8s.   The list contained one sorter, one dyer and cleaner, four men and two boys, 'scribblers," thirty women carders and spinners, four spoolers and winders, four "burlers," five weavers.   The spinning and weaving were the most costly.[5] The evils of the truck system caused much complaint: one disgusted employee at Worcester in the sixteenth century was receiving "soup, candels, rotten cloth, stinking fish, and such like baggage."[6] Even in the previous century this city was forbidding truck payments by

---

[1] See regulations laid by the town, 1467, V. C. H., Worces. II, 286.

[2] Hist. MSS. Com. Rep. XI, App. III, 95; V. C. H., Hants, V, 486.

[3] Deloney, Jno. Winch, 37.   The existence of this celebrated clothier has been called in question by historical critics in recent years; and of course these statistics are but poetical statements and not at all likely to be true.   It is not likely however that the position of the clothier as employer was fabricated by the poet, but that he described the organization which was familiar to him in his day.

[4] Henry, Hist. of Gt. Br., 424.

[5] "The Golden Fleece," 1737.

[6] Pollard, The Protector Somerset, 214; V. C. H., Worces. II, 288.

clothiers; artisans were being "payde in mercery vitelle or by other meanes and not in sylver" and the practice had "grown to grete hurte;" it was legislated, therefore, that the workmen should be compelled to "ressyve no thinge in chaffre, but in gold or sylver of eny makers, chapmen, or syllers of cloth."[1]

Lest there be undue emphasis given in the above description to the capitalistic nature of the clothing business, it must be remembered that there existed alongside these capitalistic clothiers others of less means. In every region the small master seems to have continued despite the tendency to large scale production. In 1615 one class of clothier was described as "one that seldome or never travells into the woolle country to buy his woolle, but borrowes the most part of it att the markett, and setts many poore on worke, clothes it presently, and sells his cloath in some countries upon the bare thred—and then comes to the woolle markett and payes th' old debte and borrowes more."[2] Another class was described as too poor to buy up stocks of wool but able to buy parcels of yarn which they wove into unfinished cloth and sold weekly at the market. The poverty and limited scale of business done by these classes of clothiers favored the business of cloth merchants on the one hand and wool staplers on the other. Since the poor clothier sold the cloth in an unfinished state and others completed the processes of manufacture and distribution his control over the industry was very limited and he was the first to suffer in periods of dearth or of dull business. This system was more comparable to the Yorkshire system.

The clothiers of the West of England marketed their cloths in various directions. Bristol and Lyme Regis were the leading exporting points after London. Very much Somerset cloth went out by way of the the latter port from the sixteenth century onwards.[3] When the Americas became of commercial importance the cloth exports thither from this district increased somewhat, but the cheap cloths of the north and the Whitney blankets found a readier sale in those foreign parts.[4] The Welsh cloths moved northward and eastward to Shrewsbury; the Welsh clothiers carried their "webbings," as they were called, being a thick sort of flannel for military uniforms, to market at Oswestre in north Salop, and they were "loaded here on wagons and carried to Shrewsbury"[5] as a Severn port. About 1600 the Gloucester clothiers

[1] V. C. H., Worc. II, 286.
[2] S. P. Dom., LXXX, 13.
[3] See shipments per boat listed in V. C. H., Somers, II, 411, for the year 1586.
[4] Plot, Nat. Hist. Oxford, 278–80.
[5] Pococke, II, 15.

carried unfinished cloths to Coventry in Warwick where they were sold and finished.[1]

But the total volume of cloths marketed at the above points was insignificant in comparison with that carried to London. The clothiers of all England sold mostly through London. Mention has been made of the practice of interchanging sorts of cloth among the various sections of England by way of London, and the centralized organization of trade that resulted. The great London market for cloth had been for many centuries at Blackwell Hall.[2] The non-resident clothiers were constrained to bring their woolens for display and sale to this market, and an elaborate set of rules were adhered to in the business transacted. The market did not open until Thursday so as to give the clothiers from remote parts ample time to come to London after Sunday. It was open from 8.00 to 11.00 a.m. and from 2.00 till 4.00 p.m. on Thursday, Friday and Saturday. A slight charge was made for entering the goods. What goods were not sold by the clothier during these market days were stored away in the Hall till some future market when he could return or were instrusted to some other clothier who sold them for him. Non-resident clothiers could sell only to the freemen of the City and these freemen were prohibited from selling any goods there; and this was to be the common place where clothiers met the drapers and merchants, their buyers.[3] Such were the rules and methods of marketing prevailing about 1660.

The management and rules were changed somewhat in 1678.[4] By this date a class of factors had arisen at the Hall and the regulations laid recognized them. The supervision of the Hall was bestowed upon a hallkeeper, clerks and master porters, who were in turn sub-

[1] Cal. S. P. Dom., 1619–23, 413; Ibid., 1627–8, 203; V. C. H., Warw. II, 255.

[2] For the early history of the Hall, see Stow, A Survey of London, 277–9; Maitland, London, II, 789; Hazlitt, Liv. Com., 204; Wheatley and Cunningham, London, I, 92; Hatton, New View, 599. It had a traditional history from the time of the Norman conquest, but its peculiai relation to the wool and woolens trade dated from the twentieth year of Richard II. At this time it was transferred from private hands and became the property of the city and henceforth was chiefly "employed as a weekly Market Place for Woolen Clothes broad and narrow, brought from all Parts of this Realm to be sold there." It was early under the control of the Drapers' Company who held the right (since 1405) of appointing the Keeper and of warehousing their cloths there. By an Act of Common Council, 1516, it was made the exclusive market for woolens and none were to be sold except in this Hall. It was rebuilt in 1588, destroyed in the Great Fire, 1666, and re-erected in 1672, and this building lasted until 1820.

[3] "Clothiers Complaint," 3, 13.

[4] Act of Common Council, June 20, 1678. The text is given in Maitland, I, 462–7; the description given below is drawn from this Act.

ject to the president, treasurer and governors of Christ's Hospital. These officers kept a register of the factors, of the owners and of the buyers and sellers of the cloths that were sold from time to time. This was done so that the clothiers would be satisfied how their cloth was disposed of. Special care was required of them to prevent any non-resident from buying in the Hall. A monthly report was made to the Hospital of the factors dealing in the Hall and of any offenses they might have committed. Besides the Hospital appointed a Board of six members whose office it was to inquire into offenses thus committed and to report them to its general court, and all fines levied were paid into its treasury.

It was required of all non-freemen to bring all cloth of specified kinds to this and the Welch Hall, and other specified kinds to Leaden Hall. Those to Blackwell Hall included twenty specified kinds "and all other commodities and manufactures made or mixed with Wool, Worsted, Jersey, or Cruel or with Cotton-Wool, or either or any of them." These were to be pitched in the Hall and not removed for sale into any other place out of the City till after three market days, allowing certain exceptions such as that they were sold meanwhile, during the three days, or that they had been bought by a merchant or draper by pre-contract with the clothier before they were brought to the Hall, or that they were small parcels contracted for in the country for private use and not for resale, or that they had received damage upon the road and needed redressing to fit them for sale.

The clothiers or factors paid for "pitching" and "hallage" certain rates per piece of cloth, varying with the kind of cloth. After the first week they had also to pay a charge for "resting." For convenience each factor had a "Rest," or certain number for which he paid regularly, whether his quota was pitched in full or not. All these charges went to the benefit of Christ's Hospital and amounted to a considerable sum, for instance in 1708 they were reckoned at £1100.[1]

Connected with the Hall was a special company of Porters to whom was given a monopoly of carrying the cloths out of these Halls or adjoining rooms; a schedule of prices for the porterage of each kind of cloth was publicly posted in each Hall and no higher charges were allowed.

Blackwell Hall was, therefore, the receiving and distributing point for the cloth of the Kingdom. Thither the clothier brought his cloths in person, and sold them in person, or by factors after 1660. Deloney

[1] Wheatley and Cunningham, London, I, 92.

described the arrival of the west country clothiers in London, about 1630, as follows: "they were saluted by the Merchants, who awaited their coming thither (to the London Inns), and always prepared for them a costly Supper, where they commonly made their Bargaine . . . The next Morning they went to the Hall, where they met the Northerne clothiers."[1]

Each clothier adopted a certain mark, trademark by which his cloths were distinguished; certain clothiers' cloths attained to a reputation for special good qualities and met with readier sale than those less reputed.[2] But two counter-tendencies were in operation whereby the clothiers' mark became less important. One was the clandestine foreign trade in woolens by which cloth of poorer quality in material and workmanship could be exported at inviting prices and no insistence or attention was put upon the marks of the maker; to meet this competition abroad poorer qualities of cloth found market through Blackwell Hall and trademarks were deemed less important by the generality of clothiers and buyers.[3] The other counter-tendency came by way of the separation of the selling clothier and the buying merchant or draper by the rise about 1660 of a new class of salesmen at Blackwell Hall known as factors. Heretofore the direct contact between the maker and the merchant forced the maker to pay close attention to the workmanship, for the responsibility for fraudulent or defective cloth could be unmistakably placed. But the interpolation of the factor removed in part this sense of responsibility; when once the factor recommended a certain kind or design of cloth, dispatch to the factor became the chief objective and less emphasis was given to workmanship and trademarks.[4]

One phase of the business at Blackwell Hall was the dealings in domestic and foreign wool. Not only was it a place where cloth was bought and sold, but the clothier here also bought and carried away a goodly part of the wool he used. Leaden Hall had likewise been a considerable wool market from early days.[5] By means of this double market, i.e., for wool and woolens, the carrier or clothier had a ware to carry each way and in this way economized time and costs in his

---

[1] Deloney, Thomas, Ch. II.

[2] Defoe, Com. with Fr., 43. See V. C. H., Somers, II, 409 for regulation of such seals and marks in 1591; Acts of P. C., 1591, 97–9.

[3] See this opinion in a pamphlet, J. B., Interest of Great Br. Considered, 21.

[4] This complaint formed part of the "Clothiers Complaint" (1692), q. v. 7–8.

[5] According to Stow, Survey, 176, much of the Hall was given over to stowage of woolsacks and to wool-winders and packers at the time he wrote, i.e. 1600.

trade.   The wool was brought to this market by the buyers, jobbers and merchants (previously discussed) and by merchant importers from Spain and the Mediterranean and from Ireland.   Besides woolen cloths and wool, "Oyl and dying stuffs" and "all goods belonging to the Clothing trade" were handled here.[1]   When factors developed they were engaged by the wool broggers to sell their wool; as was said, "they come to this agreement with the Factor or Packer that if either of these can help them to a Clothier that will take off their Wool and afterwards sell the Cloth for him, and secure him their Money for the Wool, that they shall have such a constant Salary, out of every pack of Wool, sent him down."[2]

From very early times the cloths of this whole west district found readiest market in London.   Even the port towns and counties dispatched their product to the metropolis.[3]   Deloney described the manner of carriage of west England cloth to London in the days of his early hero Thomas by saying that "he met with a great Number of Waines loaden with Cloth, comming to London" that "drive one after another," and that he stood aside "whilest the Carts passed by, the which at that Time being in Number aboue Two Hundred," so many that he "thought Old Cole had got a Commission for all the Carts in the Country to carry his cloth."[4]   Pack-horse trains and wagon trains composed the transportation facilities of the day.

The pack-horse antedated the wagon and cart, and the supercession of the former by the latter was contingent on the improvement of the roads.   Packs or panniers were strapped to the back of the horse;[5] the horses were tethered one behind another; the lead-horse carried a bell; and the train moved in single solid file by sinuous narrow pack-horse roads or bridle-paths.   The whole picture is curtly put in the line, "pile the pack on the long tinkling train of slow-pac'd steeds," from Dyer's ' *The Fleece.*'   They were in charge of a "pack-horse man."   Forty or fifty of these in single file, under one man's control, were frequently to be met with in the seventeenth century in the west-country clothmaking districts, laden with the products

[1] See petition of the Somerset clothiers in "A Treatise of Wool" (1685), 28–9.

[2] "Clothiers Complaint," 6.

[3] Hampshire is a good example; during a lull in the trade in 1630–1 the Hants clothiers complained that the regular amount was "not bought of them by the merchants of London."   Stevens, Hist. of St. Mary Bourne, 249; V. C. H., Hants, V, 427.

[4] Deloney, Thomas, Ch. I.

[5] See description in Owen and Blakeway, Hist. Shrews. I, 511.

of the spinning wheel and loom.[1] Pococke found that Cornwall and Devon as late as 1750 had "few wheel carriages by reason of the steep hills, but everything is carried either on hooks on each side of the horses" or by "drags for drawing up the steep fields."[2] Likewise Kynder in 1663 found "noe highwaies or postwaies" in Derbyshire and "the roads which existed were fit only for horses, not for carriages, and for these they were impassable during the winter months."[3]

The roads were improved during the seventeenth and eighteenth centuries and wagon trains became more general. Market days were characterized by the "whole array of packhorses and wagons just starting from or returning to the yard."[4] Late in the eighteenth century the west country train was described as follows: "Seven wagons at a time would leave Frome . . . for London . . . laden with bales. The clothiers of Mells and other adjacent villages brought their goods to this centre, whence they were despatched to town. Each wagon carried 140 pieces of cloth each valued at £14."[5] Such a train carrying about $70,000 worth of cloth was no inconsiderable traffic.

Common carriers arose pari passu with the clothing trade. The earliest records of common carriers are of the last decade of the fourteenth century. They carried cloth between Oxford and London, Winchester, and even distant Newcastle. The rate of charge for carrying a pannier of about twenty-four pounds weight from Winchester to Oxford at this time was 4.25*d*.[6] By the opening of the eighteenth century a distinct class of public carriers had arisen. In 1637 the "Water Poet" described the conditions of carriage to and from London. The carriers from very many and distant parts of England had regular schedules of coming to London and leaving; some had coaches and wagons. They lodged at regular places.[7] In the cloth trade they had become differentiated from the clothiers.[8] Common carriers were defined in 1706 as "such as travel constantly from their respective Counties to London and so back; who are gener-

---

[1] V. C. H., Somers. II, 413; Hants, V, 429; Stevens, St. Mary Bourne, 11–12.

[2] Pococke, I, 135.

[3] V. C. H., Derby, II, 185.

[4] As at Tonedale, Wellington, Somerset; Humphreys, Hist. Wellington, 213; V. C. H., Somers., II, 413.

[5] Univ. Brit. Dir. (1793), III, 133.

[6] Roger, Agr. and Pr., I, 660; II, 605, I.

[7] The whole system is related in Taylor's Carriers Cosmography, 1637.

[8] Inference from an Act of Common Council, 1678, given in Maitland, II, 463.

ally Men of Credit, and capable of giving security for their regular Carriage."[1] This definition suggests not only that a carrier class had arisen but that they had become a responsible class. In towns situate on the greater highways carriers formed an important class of citizens and had a close connection with the local and metropolitan traders.[2] In such parts they had become a self-conscious class—for "divers waggoners and other carriers, by combination amongst themselves, have raised the prices of carriage of goods in many places to excessive rates, to the great injury of trade."[3] Comment was made in 1728 on the "infinite Number of Carriers, Waggoners, Pedlars, and Travelling Chapmen . . . as well on Foot as on Horseback" and on the "proportion'd Number of Publick Houses, as Victuallers, Inns, Alehouses on the Roads."[4] A specialized class of common carriers was, therefore, arising, running schedule lines of vehicles, at reduced rates and greater speed, for the transport of travellers and merchandise and information.

Conditions ripened in the last half of the seventeenth century for the use of an agency system by the clothiers. Common carriers had developed. The post and roads were being improved. Communication eased trade. Correspondence was more easily carried. "Bank Post Bills" made the transmission of money safe.[5] Mercantile and commercial papers were carried by post.[6] The clothier could send patterns and samples of cloth by mail to agents at London and receive orders likewise.[7] In general, the way was now open for the introduction of the Blackwell Hall "factor" as middleman between clothier and draper or merchant.

But before passing to the business of the Blackwell Hall "factors" the organization of the clothiers' business in the north and east districts must be described.

(b) *North District.* The north cloth manufacture was more tardy in reaching prominence than that of the east or west. It is characterized by many peculiarities of organization. The north country was poorest: it suffered extraordinarily from the ravages of war,

---

[1] Haynes, View of Present, 91.

[2] For example, see Morton, Nat. Hist. of Northants, 18, 25, for Towcester on the Chester road in 1712.

[3] Northants N. and Q. I, 260; V. C. H., Northants, II, 291.

[4] "Atlas Mar. et Com.," 108; Defoe made the same sort of remark in 1745, in his Com. Eng. Tr., II, 174.

[5] Bisschop, Rise, 141–2; Gilbart, I, 41, 138.

[6] 12 Chas. II, Cap. 35.

[7] J. H. C., 1745–50: 751–2; 26 Geo. II, Cap. 13, Sec. 7–8.

famine and pestilence; there was a chronic dearth of raw materials except the poor-quality far-north wool. It was distinctly the producer of cheap cloth—the well known kerseys—hybrid kinds of cloth, made with linen or woolen woof and cotton or short-wool weft. It was dominated by the foreign Eastland trade and the metropolitan trade; foreign and London merchants were resident in these parts or had agents resident there; and these merchants were the centralizing force in the clothing organization. There was also a rank opposition to the immigration of fine skilled workmen into the north: the Flemish and Huguenot immigrants brought no such profit to this region as they did to Norwich; and this is one reason why the region stuck to cheap kerseys.[1]

The originals of the kerseys were household products of very early centuries. They reached little importance before the sixteenth century.[2] The towns of these parts encouraged clothmaking in numerous ways at different times; for example, Lincoln allowed all persons who came to buy cloth, or bring wool, woad, madder, oil, alum, or other necessaries for clothmaking to be free of toll for seven years.[3] The manufacture of "fustians," later called "cottons," a mixture of wool and linen, had been begun in Salford Hundred before 1600[4] and established itself during Tudor times. This manufacture was stimulated by the organization of the cloth-export trade by the Merchants Adventurers and the Eastland Merchants and their facilitation of transportation to the Baltic region, where these coarse durable fabrics were used by the Pomeranian and Polish nobles to clothe their retainers.[5] This increase of trade to the East reacted favorably on the manufacturing organization by breaking down the gild municipal control and freeing independent producers from restrictions.[6] During the seventeenth century the expansion was very rapid. The gild control during the previous century had been so repressive as to cause a migration of clothmakers from the towns to the country.[7] Towards the end of the seventeenth century a new phase was entered upon by the woolen manufactures of the north, for the worsted trade then began to be transferred thither, at a phenomenal rate, from Norfolk

---

[1] See discussion of the immigration problem in V. C. H., York, III, 458–61.
[2] V. C. H., Lancas., II, 295.
[3] Hist. MSS. Com. Rep. 14, App. VIII, 26; V. C. H., Lincoln, II, 381.
[4] V. C. H., Lancas., II, 296.
[5] V. C. H., York, III, 460; B. M., Reasons, 816 m (100).
[6] Ibid., 451–2.
[7] Ibid., II, 411–2; III, 450.

where it had been monopolized for centuries.[1] This increase in the north's trade during the eighteenth century was, contrarily to what had happened in the sixteenth, promoted by the practical extinction of the two great trading companies that had exported its cloth and the substitution of independent merchants.[2]

The water carriage in the north was facilitated by its many rivers and harbors. The roads were poor. The cloth trade tended to concentrate in the river and sea ports. The trade on the Trent, for instance, from Nottingham, and on the Ouse from York, and on the Aire from Leeds, to Hull on the Humber, was large.[3] In 1627 York sent cloth by way of Hull, Newcastle, West Chester, London, and other ports;[4] in 1676 it despatched 30,000 cloths from Hull yearly, chiefly to Stoad in Germany, and of 80,000 cloths made in West Riding 60,000 went abroad through the ports of Hull, London, Westchester and Stockton.[5]

Before coming to these seaports the cloth was assembled in interior towns in great cloth markets. There was a remarkable geographical division of labor among these towns. The old accustomed market at Barnsley was dispossessed during the first half of the seventeenth century by Wakefield. In 1627 it was declared that "Wakefeilde now is the greatest markett and principall place of resorte of all sorts of Clothiers Drapers and other traffickers for cloath in all thees parts."[6] And in 1640 a petition of the Barnsley citizens prayed that the weekly cloth market at Wakefield "but lately invented may be put a stop to."[7] But by 1676 it had gained a permanent ascendancy.[8] The broad-cloth trade and manufacture were centering in Leeds about 1700 and the kersey trade in Halifax.[9] According to a description of the country about 1800, "The whole number of the broad-cloth manufacturers in the West Riding of Yorkshire was calculated in 1794 to be 3240, no one of whom is to be found more than one mile east, nor two miles north of Leeds, nor are there many in the town, and those only in the outskirts."[10] During the sixteenth century the shoddy trade

[1] Bischoff, Comp. Hist. I, 185.
[2] V. C. H., York, II, 417.
[3] V. C. H., Nott., II, 278–9; York, II, 415.
[4] S. P. Dom., Ch. I, XI, 82.
[5] V. C. H., York, II, 416.
[6] S. P. Dom. Ch. I, XC, 54; V. C. H., York, II, 414.
[7] Hist. MSS. Com. Rep. IV, App. 36.
[8] V. C. H., York, II, 416.
[9] Ibid., II, 417.
[10] See description of the Leeds' market under the head "Factors at Leeds."

was focused at Batley and Dewsbury, and the ancestors of most of the West Riding woolen manufacturers were there one time engaged in "flokkyng of clothes."[1] The vicinity of Bolton and Leigh produced fustians and sold them "in the grey" at Bolton market to Manchester merchants, who finished them at Manchester and despatched them thence to other markets.[2] Manchester specialized in "cotton" goods.

The London trade was mostly overland. Early in the seventeenth century the Nottingham carriers had established themselves in the trade between these distant parts. Stage-wagons and trade carts are mentioned in the local traffic.[3] By 1750 the Nottingham tradesmen had become dependent upon London for their supplies and no longer bought their stocks at Lenton Fair; and from this town alone nine regular carriers left weekly for Manchester, Bristol, Birmingham, London, and parts of the neighboring counties.[4] The same date Pococke found that Kendall, a town of 20,000 people, had "four carriers, with several packhorses," which were "constantly going between this town and London, two of which go by Lancashire, and two by Yorkshire."[5] He mentions other towns which despatched their "woolen clothes . . . white to London."[6]

The most distinctive feature of the north country organization of the clothing industry was the dominance of the merchants, or their agents, of the largest towns and cities, local, metropolitan, and foreign. It seems the poverty of the north-country man in the early days was the chief cause of this peculiarity. A deposition, dating 1638, by a York man, described the clothworkers as "very poor people that are sore oppressed . . . who making every week a coarse kersey and being compelled to sell the same at the week end, and with the money received for the same to provide bothe stuffe wherewith to make another the week following, and also victualls to susteyne themselves and their families till another be made and sold, by which means the said poor and distressed people making hard shifts with continual labour and thereby such weekly returns to reserve themselves, their wives and their children from begging."[7] It is to be noticed that these clothworkers were not employees of the merchant

[1] V. C. H., York, II, 411.

[2] Aikin, Hist. of Manch., 158.

[3] Rastall, Hist. of Newark, 353–5; V. C. H., Nott., II, 284.

[4] Deering, Vetus Nottinghamia, Sec. 5.

[5] Pococke, I, 43.

[6] For example, Bacup; Pococke, I, 205.

[7] Exch. Dep. by Com. Mich., 14 Chas. I, No. 21, York; V. C. H., York, II, 415.

but were themselves independent producers on a very small scale and margin. "The presence in Yorkshire of highly diffused capital, the result of ceaseless denial and penurious habits" was most likely effected by these self-employed artisans—particularly weavers—using their own materials, bought for cash or long term credit.[1] These merchants were more distinctly *middlemen* than the clothiers of the west of England. From the weavers they usually simply bought the cloth,—the weavers having provided themselves with warps and weft; or else they simply warehoused the cloths received from the weavers and distributed them for export or consumption in the country.[2] They bought in the grey and had them colored and finished according to order of customers.

Poverty necessitated some sort of middleman in these parts. The merchant or agent of the merchant supplied this want by buying the unfinished cloth and bringing raw materials within reach. The Act of Edward VI forbidding middlemen's activities provoked the clothmakers of Lancashire to petition the government for relief. They alleged that they were "poore cotagers whose habilitye wyll not streche neyther to buy any substance of wolles to mayntayne work and labour, nor yet to fetche the same," and that the enforcement of the statute would drive trade into the hands of the few rich men of these parts.[3]

Most of the clothing trade was performed in the suburbs and rural parts. In part, as has been shown, this fact was due to the gilds' repressive control of town industries. In part it was due to the lower cost of production in rural parts. York suffered a transfer of clothiers to the small towns of Halifax, Leeds and Wakefield during the sixteenth century, for instance, from these two reasons. Production was cheaper there "for that not onely the commoditie of the water mylns is ther nigh hande but also the poore folke as speynners, carders, and other bysyde ther hand labor have Rye, fyre, and other releif good cheape which is in this citie very deare and wantyng."[4] Two centuries later it was a common comment of travellers and writers that farming was a bye-industry to spinning and weaving. In 1770 of the farmers of much of Lancashire fewer than one-tenth "raised their rents directly from the produce of their farms; all the rest got their rent partly in some branch of trade, such as spinning and weaving

---

[1] V. C. H., Lancas., II, 382; York, II, 417; Tuke, Agric. of N. Riding, 38.

[2] Ibid., II, 383.

[3] S. P. Dom. Eliz., CXVII, No. 38, quoted in Ec. Journ. X, 23.

[4] V. C. H., York, III, 450; York Munic. Rec. XIII, fol. 20a. 8 Jul. 1561.

woollen, linen or cotton. The cottagers were employed entirely in this manner, except for a few weeks in the harvest."[1] Pococke's horse-boy in Lancashire in 1751 said that "his father paid six pounds a year, kept a horse, three cows, and forty sheep; that his father and he wove woolen both for their clothing and to sell."[2] Rochedale in 1778 was a place "famous for manufactories of cloth, kerseys and shallon. Every considerable house is a manufactory, and is supplied with a rivulet or little stream, without which the business cannot be carried on."[3] Housman pictured Leeds as the center of the broad-cloth manufacturers, all of them living within a radius of two miles but none in the city proper, all in the suburbs. They were "generally men of small capital and often annexed a small farm to their other business." Some of them had "a field or two to support a horse and cow."[4]

These rural manufacturers brought their cloth to market themselves or sold to agents of the merchants. If they brought it to market they were generally required to sell it wholesale and in public market only. In 1551, as an instance, York constrained the "Kendaill men yt bringeth wollen clothe to this citie to sell" to "selle in grosse in the . . . Thursday Markett or Common hall and not to goe hawkynge and sell in any other place upon paine of forfaiture of their clothes;" few exceptions were allowed.[5] The dispersion of the weavers made it necessary for the merchants to buy at such markets or else employ local agents. Sometimes local piece masters, or fustian masters, independent men of business and not merely agents of merchants, assembled the local product. But usually the public markets were used as both places of sale of cloth and of purchase of raw materials. After the warping mill was invented the merchants generally furnished the warp to the weavers instead of the weaver making his own warp.[6] In any particular market town these resident merchants composed a goodly fraction of the tradesmen. In Leeds in 1798, of 309 cloth tradesmen and artisans, 148 were merchants and 35 were wool-staplers.[7]

Occasionally there are found in the north clothiers who conducted a trade organized like that of the west of England. Weavers and

[1] Radcliffe, 59; Butterworth, Oldham, 101; French, Crompton, 4, 5, 9; V. C. H., Lancas., II, 382.

[2] Pococke, I, XIV.

[3] Earwakers, Local Gleanings, II, 17; V. C. H., Lancas., II, 378.

[4] Housman; V. C. H., York, II, 422.

[5] York, Munic. Rec. XX., fol. 63a., 27 Oct., 1551; V. C. H., York, III, 451.

[6] Chapman, Lancas. Cotton Ind., 15–16.

[7] Woodcroft, Brief Biog., 2; V. C. H., York, II, 422.

others were engaged to make up in their own homes materials supplied by undertakers.[1] The Nottingham hosiery manufacturers were, on this account, called "putters-out" in the eighteenth century.[2] Men like Martin Brian of Manchester, one of the three famous clothiers of the "North Country," early in the sixteenth century conducted establishments, according to report of Deloney, like those of Jack of Newbery, with "a greate number of servants at worke, Spinners, Carders, Weavers, Fullers, Dyers and Shearmen." This form of organization must have been very uncommon, however, if it existed at all. The most striking and general form of organization was that above described; where the merchant or agent bought the grey cloth, had it dyed, dressed and finished by passing it successively through the hands of the millman, dyer, dresser, etc. frequently journeymen in their employ. The place of the western clothier was thus, in a way, supplied by this commissioner, but he did not exercise the dominant rôle over the whole industry that the clothier did and the various employees felt a greater independence of him and each other than in the west of England.[3]

A letter book of a prominent merchant of Soyland near Halifax contains data portraying the manner of his business during the first half of the eighteenth century. His name was Sam Hill, and he seems to have exported the cloth produced by himself and his relatives of the name Hill: the brands of cloth were named from the maker.[4] He seems to have despatched his cloth to Holland and the Baltic through one William Merold of Hull; he had agents in these countries through whom he, by correspondence, pushed the sales of his broad and narrow shalloons, bays and other cloths. His customers included such names as Hermanes Struys, Lucius Dorpore, Gatis, Crowle, Peter Deynooten, John D'orville, Justus Beke, Peter Blok, Michiliez, John Henry Bock, Ludovicus de Wielf, Erasmus Dariven, Andrew Perrot, Henderck and Petter Kops, John and Peter Dorvil, Abraham Van Broye, Henderck Verbeck, Paul Fisher & Co., etc.—showing a preponderance of Dutchmen. He tried to conform the texture, weight, breadth, color, etc., of his cloths to the foreign demand and studied the demand with this in view; his agents were to write him descriptions or send samples of the cloths most readily sold there. He was optimistic both as manufacturer and as merchant, and furnishes an excellent picture of Yorkshire mercantile life of his day.

[1] V. C. H., Lancas., II, 382.
[2] V. C. H., Nott. II, 354.
[3] Tucker, Instructions, 36.
[4] Many excerpts from this letterbook are given in V. C. H., York, II, 418–9.

(c) *East District.* The third manufacturing section embraced the east portion of England—the counties of Norfolk, Suffolk, Essex, Surrey and Kent. This was the oldest manufacture due primarily to its proximity to the Continent. The woolen industry arose here after Edward III in 1336 prohibited the importation of Flemish and French woolens. There had been some immigration of foreign cloth-makers before this time, but Edward accompanied his prohibition of imports with a toleration and encouragement of immigration, and his policy was very effective.[1] An act of 1468 mentions the prosperity of Essex, Norfolk and Suffolk as due to the "great profit and good utterance of the said cloths."[2] Coggeshall, Colchester, Ipswich and Norwich were the early centers of manufacture. Coggeshall stood second to Colchester during the whole clothing period, and both towns were most prosperous about 1600; between 1710 and 1760 the decline was very rapid.[3] By 1750 Surrey clothing trade was practically ended. The shift of the worsted business to the Yorkshire region spelled the end of it in the east. The "new draperies" that were introduced early in the seventeenth century found their three greatest seats in Canterbury, Colchester and Southampton,[4] but despite their rejuvenating effects the east gradually suffered its trade to decay.

In another place[5] it has been shown that possessors of wool put it out into rural local or distant parts for combing and spinning. Many an evidence might be cited with reference to this region. In 1518 Thomas Paycock, a wealthy clothier of Coggeshall willed certain portions of his estate to various of "my kembers, carders, and spynners," "that have wrought me verey moche work."[6] A statute in 1609 was passed to regulate "spinners of wool . . . that shall receave any wooll to be spune into yarn for any clothier or maker of bayes . . . dwelling in the townes of Cogshall, Bocking, Braintree, Halstead, Wittam, or Colchester."[7] This yarn spun in the immediate country districts was usually collected by riders sent out by the clothiers and delivered to the weavers.[8] Sometimes the yarn-

---

[1] Morant, Hist. of Colchester, 71; V. C. H., Essex, II, 381, 383.

[2] 8 Edward IV, Cap. 1.

[3] The origin, rise and decline of clothing manufacture in this district are very extensively described in V. C. H., Essex, II, 381–3, 391, 399–400; Suffolk, II, 257; Hants, V, 486; Surrey, II, 348.

[4] S. P. Dom., Jas. I, LXXX, 13.

[5] See "Yarn Merchant."

[6] V. C. H., Essex, II, 382.

[7] 7 Jas. I, Cap. 7; cf. 3 Henry VIII, Cap. 6.

[8] V. C. H., Suff., II, 259.

men intervened as middlemen.   These spinners appear never to have had a gild organization and were, as a class, very dependent upon the weaver and clothier.

It appears that the weaver was the earlier employer of labor.   The weavers were strongly organized in the earlier part of the period.   But the statute that forbade the migration of town clothiers to the country and the setting up of clothiers in the country exempted the Suffolk district[1] and this gave the weavers free way to set up as country clothiers.   There were, therefore, two sets of employers who undertook the capitalistic manufacture of cloth in these parts.   The larger clothiers of the towns employed the smaller weavers of the towns and the country weavers and kept a multitude of spinners preparing yarn.[2]

After it was woven and fulled the clothier could have it finished by local shearmen, or sell it to merchants who would care for the finishing of it.   It was marketed in the coast ports for shipment abroad or in London.   The part that went to London was usually finished by the purchasing merchant.[3]   The Surrey trade was almost entirely to London.   In 1630 one Samuel Vassall, a merchant in London, bought the whole produce of at least two important parishes of that county.[4] This was regarded a dangerous monopoly.   A growing portion of the Essex cloth went to London; it offered a considerable market for bays and says; the Dutch bay-makers of Halstead sent their bays here for sale about 1600;[5] in 1767 Young found that in many parts of Essex "The whole manufactory works chiefly for the London markets."[6] In 1700,—a date about mid-way between the above-cited two—the transport of Colchester cloth to London by water engaged a number of hoys sailing regularly each way once a week.   A statute of that date exempted these Colchester packets from certain tolls as they went "weekly from Wivenhoe to London with bays, says, and perpetuanos, and from London to Wivenhoe with wooll to be manufactured at Colchester."[7]

The clothiers sold their cloths to the merchants and drapers at Blackwell Hall and to the merchant exporters of Colchester, Ipswich, Norwich and Yarmouth.   They usually allowed credit to these buyers,

---

[1] 4–5 Ph. & M., Cap. 5, Sec. 25.

[2] Hist. MSS. Com. Rep. XIV, App. pt. VIII, 133–8; V. C. H., Suff., II, 256, 259.

[3] V. C. H., Suff., II, 259.

[4] S. P. Dom., Chas. I, CLXXV, 105; V. C. H., Surrey, II, 347.

[5] V. C. H., Essex, 389.

[6] Young, Six Weeks Tour, 58–65.

[7] 13 Anne, Cap. 20.

even in very early times. Some clothiers of Surrey and Hants in 1587 petitioned the Council against Andrew Marche of London, to whom they had granted credit in such great sums that his intent, so they believed, was to defraud them.[1] During the dearth of 1619–1622 the clothiers of Suffolk were reported to have lost more than £30,000 by the bankruptcies of the merchants.[2] In a petition of the justices of Suffolk to the Privy Council, 1619, they said that the failure of one Cragg a merchant beyond seas bankrupted several merchants of London and these failures in turn "overthrew the estates of divers clothiers" of Suffolk. One Gerrard Reade a merchant of London failed for £20,000 debt due the clothiers for cloths bought.[3] Much of this credit business was occasioned by the clothiers' evasions of the public (open) market and their commitment "to clothworkers to make sale of our (clothiers') cloths who many times commend us to men that are not able to pay," and "We are forced to lay our commodities to pawn upon a bill of sale to pay our poor workmen and others that we be indebted unto and to pawn £40 worth of commodities for £20 and to give £10 in the hundred."[4] The credit operations of the factors at Blackwell Hall will be discussed under that caption later.

Particular pains were taken to maintain the quality of the cloths of this east district. At Colchester was "Dutch Bay Hall;" here, both before the processes of fulling and finishing and after, the cloths were searched and sealed with leaden seals by officers specially charged with that function, before they could be removed for sale. No imperfect cloths were sealed. "Colchester Bays" gained a wide reputation for honesty and perfection; they sold readily in Colchester, London, and abroad "without the bales being even opened for measurement or examination and solely upon inspection of the seals they bore."[5] This dependability facilitated foreign trade particularly. "The Colchester and Bocking Bays" were "of great esteem among the merchants."[6] "Great quantities" . . . were "carried into Spain, not only to cloath the Nuns and Friars there, but into America for the use of their colonists on that Continent."[7] Spain, Portugal and Italy, and through them, America, were the foreign market. As

---

[1] Acts of P. C., 18 Je 1587.
[2] S. P. Dom., Jas. I, CXXVIII, 67.
[3] Ibid., CIX, 126.
[4] S. P. Dom., Eliz., CVI, 48; V. C. H., Suff., II, 259.
[5] V. C. H., Essex, II, 388–9.
[6] Cox, Mag. Brit. I, 722.
[7] Ibid., 707, 709, 711–12; Defoe, Tour, I, 20.

early as 1389 the importance of good quality of cloth in the export
trade had received legislative attention,[1] but the regulation was, for
the most part, left to the discretion of and execution by the towns'
gilds.

In the midst of the fifteenth century one expression of the growing
nationalism was the substitution of a system of national regulation
and supervision of the cloth industry for the old local gild system.[2]
This national interference was progressive, and affected the clothiers
directly.   For instance, in 1586, the poor spinners, carders and
winders of Somerset petitioned the Privy Council for relief from distress, and the Council responded by requiring the clothiers to assemble
and take immediate steps for setting the poor to work.[3]   This became
a common method of public relief in times of dearth; the hard times
1619–23 were so provided against.[4]   The London merchants were
ordered to buy up cloth as much as possible from the clothiers, so that
the clothiers could give relief to the dependent poor; it was held unfitting that the clothiers should at their pleasure dismiss their work-
people and deprive them of their livelihood and provoke public dis-
order.   The public good was to be served even at their private loss
"till the decay of the trade be remedied."[5]   On the other hand the
clothiers were active in opposition to such arbitrary interference on
the part of the government.   Jack of Newberry summoned two representatives each from fifty-six clothing towns to Blackwell Hall and
they there prepared a petition against Woolsey's foreign policy, which
was ruining the cloth manufacture and trade; this effort succeeded
and free trade with Flanders and France was maintained; the Car-
dinal's threats and efforts to force merchants and clothiers to do business at a loss were frustrated.[6]   This sort of legislation was less
common after the Restoration.

Summary and Comparisons.

Effort has been made under the caption "Clothier" to analyze the
organization of the manufacture and sale of cloth as shown in the
three somewhat distinctive cloth manufacturing sections of England.
It was found that in the west of the island the "clothier" was

---

[1] 13 Rich. II, St. I, Cap. 11.
[2] See treatment in Cunningham, Growth, I, 436.
[3] Acts of P. C., 1586–7, p. 93; V. C. H., Somers, II, 411.
[4] V. C. H., Berks, I, 391; Reading Records, I, 407; V. C. H., Somers, II, 312.
[5] Cal. S. P. Dom., 1619–23, 343.
[6] Deloney, J. Winch, 79–81; cf. V. C. H., Berks, I, 389.

the organizer and touchstone of the system: a peculiar composite of capitalist employer, captain of industry, and middleman. In the north district the local, city, metropolitan, or alien merchant, himself or through his factor, compared in some degree, with the western "clothier;" but he was not the integrating organizer that the westerner was; his business was more nearly that of pure middleman and less that of manufacturer; his manufacturing operations were only in finishing the grey cloth; his dominance in the industry was far less pronounced. In the eastern region the differentiation of the weaver and clothier and merchant had never been completed. Some weavers employed spinners, carders, dyers, etc., and sold their grey cloth. Some clothiers in addition to these operatives, employed weavers and the other craftsmen who finished the cloth; but other clothiers employed only these finishers. Some clothiers employed local finishers, others sold to the London merchants and the cloths were finished in London. Some clothiers sold to exporting merchants, others exported their own cloths. This want of distinctive differentiation seems most ascribable to the nearness of the region to the London market and to the fact that the cloth was in large part manufactured in exporting seaport towns. A weaver or small clothier did not need become so dependent upon a capitalistic clothier or merchant, respectively, for the marketing of his product, when the distance to market was so short, merely to London. The passage by water from Colchester to London was easy and quick: a smaller product could be profitably marketed directly by the producer than in case of the longer water or land carriage from York or Wilts. In the north and west the manufacture was inland: agents at the shipping seaports were necessary; likewise, agents at London or abroad; this agency would necessitate a large trade and large capital, and the specialized clothier or merchant arose for the function. In another place, it was also shown that the statutory exemption of the east section from the otherwise general prohibition of clothiers' setting up in the country made the differentiation of clothier and weaver less likely. Very much must also be ascribed to the distribution of capital: it has been shown that capital was more widely held, though there was probably less per capita, in the north than in the west; the wage-class was not so well marked off there, but the earlier processes of manufacture were done by small capitalist fee-holders or cottiers. In other words, it was much easier for a man to become more middleman and less employing manufacturer in the north than in the west; while the want of *large* capitalists in the much-devasted north gave opportunity to the alien and metropolitan merchant resident there.

Factor at Blackwell Hall.

The relations of the clothier to Blackwell Hall and to the merchant and draper underwent a decided and important change during the Puritan régime and the early years of the Restoration. Before this date, the Cloth-workers' Company had been the chief assistants of the clothiers at the Hall; they mantled, folded and put in buckram and packed the cloth sent or brought up by the clothier; if the clothier could not stay until the market served him best he left his cloths in the care of these clothworkers till some other market, possibly six to twelve months; hence sometimes they authorized the clothworkers to sell the cloths left in their charge; and lastly, if the clothier wanted credit it was either furnished to him by the clothworker or this latter advised the merchant of the clothier's financial responsibility.[1] In 1635 the clothiers of Suffolk and Essex complained to the Privy Council against an order which was designed to stop these clothworkers from acting as agents for the country clothiers for selling cloths left with them. The order had been secured by the drapers and merchants viz. "that no one should sell any woollen cloths either by wholesale or by retail but themselves."[2]

These practices and services indicate the opportunity and functions of a specialized class which established themselves in the business of Blackwell Hall about 1660.[3] They were known as factors and received public recognition in the regulations of the Hall laid by the Act of Common Council of 1678. These factors sprang from various professions, having served apprenticeships to other trades, and it was remarked that one could choose "a Factor from almost any profession, an Oyl-man, a cloth-drawer, a Tobacconist, etc."[4] In 1677 the *London Directory* reported by name thirty-eight Blackwell Hall factors, none of whom were men of title, and who lived mostly on Basinghall Street.[5] The author of the *Clothiers Complaint*

---

[1] These were the conditions prevailing in the reign of the first James; see State Papers, Dom., Jas. I, CXXXIII, No. 36, part of which is quoted in Unwin, Ind. Org., 112–13. Compare also Haynes, View of the Present State, 88–9.

[2] S. P. Dom., Chas. I, CCLXXXII, 130; Acts of P. C., 26 Nov., 17 Dec. 1634, 13 Feb. 1635.

[3] The Worcester clothiers complained against the innovation of factors at Blackwell Hall in 1663, alleging that the regulation obliged them to stay longer in London, interfered with their choice of agents, increased their hallage fees, etc. Cal. S. P. Dom., 1663–4, 535.

[4] "Clothiers Complaint," 4.

[5] Gathered from the lists given in the "London Directory," 1677.

in 1692 said there were about thirty factors.[1] It seems thàt they grew rapidly into wealth and power, for as early as 1677 instances were given where some had risen from low circumstances to be worth from £5,000 to £10,000 the man,[2] and by 1685 some of them were worth £40,000 or £50,000.[3]

The first factors were likely some clothiers or clothworkers with whom other clothiers had left their residue of cloths from one market till a later market. As stated above, the clothier sometimes authorized the keeper to sell the cloths in the interim, specifying a certain price at which he might sell. This authorization was the wedge by which the factor entered the trade and seized upon his limited function. In order to make sales the keeper would abate the price a few pence per yard below the price specified by the clothier. This difference in price was sufficient motive for the preference which the buyer thereafter showed for buying from the keeper. To secure sales the clothier was then forced to sell through the keepers, who set up as regular factors and thus "usurped the sole power of selling the clothier's cloth, both for what price, and for what time, and to whom they pleased."[4]

Several circumstances at once operated to strengthen and establish the factor in this his so-called *usurped* place. The convenience realized by both clothier as seller and by merchant or draper as buyer, through the instrumentality of this factor made them prone to a passive compliance, for they could then devote themselves to their more proper employments.[5] But this separation of clothier and merchant lessened the merchant's judgment of cloth, a judgment which his daily practice of examining cloth in the Hall had heretofore trained and maintained, and consequently the merchant became dependent upon the factor as a specialist in judging the qualities of cloth.[6] The factor used his profits sometimes to buy materials and employ woolworkers and became in part a clothier; this gave him an economic advantage by which he could undersell any clothier who persisted in selling his cloth himself and could force himself into the clothier's employ.[7] And further, the factor could make or break a

---

[1] See page 4.
[2] "A Treatise of Wool and Cattle," 16; also quoted in Smith, Memoirs, I, 316
[3] "A Treatise of Wool," 17, 26.
[4] "Ancient Trades decayed," 16, quoted in Smith, Memoirs, I, 322.
[5] "A Treatise of Wool and Cattle," 17.
[6] "Clothiers Complaint," 6–7.
[7] Ibid., 6.

clothier by partiality in the time of sales and in the longer or shorter period during which they retained the proceeds; naturally they favored the richer and larger dealers,[1] and the poorer became very subservient to their factors.

The factors developed an extensive system of business credit, which in turn furthered their dominance in the wool and woolens trade. The first occasion of this arose through the necessities of foreign trade. A six-months' credit was given to the merchant for the payment of the cloth he bought at the Hall. The merchants paid their purchases by drawing drafts on their foreign correspondents, but it was needful that the bills of lading be received abroad before the drafts could be accepted with safety. During this interim the credit was allowed.[2] But it appears the standard rule of six months' credit was not adhered to and payments to the clothiers were dilatorily made in nine, twelve, or fifteen months. The clothier was forced in turn to buy his materials on credit; and so on through a succession of buyers.[3] In case the clothier fell into such straits that he was compelled to draw upon the factor before the sales' proceeds were due or before the factor saw fit to make payment, the factor was in a position to assess extravagant rates for the advance.[4] The holding-up of these proceeds was a source of much profit. They were invested in Spanish wool; a monopoly of the purchase of this article was gained by them; the clothier was then constrained to secure his Spanish wool from the factor's warehouse and have it charged on his account; since a clothier used on an average about eighty packs a year and the factor demanded £4 per pack for service, the factorage for the foreign wool alone averaged £320 per annum per clothier; and this was really a charge paid by the clothier upon his own money.[5] On the other hand, this delay in turning over the proceeds of sales gave the factors a like economic control over the merchants "for the Factors having so great a stock of the West Country Clothiers in their hands . . . can give what credit they please, and can, and do make whomsoever they please Merchants, or turn Merchants themselves . . ."[6]

---

[1] "Ancient Trades decayed," 11, quoted in Smith, Memoirs, I, 322.

[2] J. B., Interest of Gr. Br. Considered, 22.

[3] "Clothiers Complaint," 9; "Abstract of Grievances," 6; Smith, Memoirs, II, 311.

[4] "Case of the Clothiers and Weavers," quoted in Smith, Memoirs, II, 312.

[5] For the facts see "The Case of the Clothiers and Weavers," quoted in Smith, Mem., II, 310–12.

[6] "Trade of England revived," 12.

This long credit introduced and forced by the Blackwell Hall factors had a further effect in the fact that it drew over an "abundance of Interlopers, or Foreign Factors, from Holland, the Hanse Towns of Germany, Flanders, France, Sweden, Etc." By this credit they were "enabled to make themselves Masters of Goods upon their Principals abroad, whose service they court(ed) before they desire(d) their bills for Payment."[1] An intimacy and friendship seems to have grown up between the home and these foreign factors and they worked together in the prosecution of their credit operations.

The development of these credit manipulations reached a crisis in 1695 when the clothiers applied to Parliament for relief and an act[2] was passed accordingly. The statute was effective for a few years but the factors soon found ways of evading it, and the former abuses were revived and developed. The said statute was named "An Act to restore the Market at Blackwell Hall to the Clothiers and for regulating the Factors there." The governors of the Hall were to appoint for the country clothiers "the most convenient Room in the said Hall for the Sale of their cloth, and likewise Warehouse Room for the lodging and safekeeping of any cloth of the said Clothier's unsold." A strict register of sales—including the names of buyer, seller, factor, date, cloths, and terms—was to be kept by them, to which the clothier was to have free access at his leisure. The factors were to make out a statement of the effects of the clothiers then in their hands and of the cloth sold, and money due. Hereafter all cloth held by merchant, draper or trader for eight days as bought on trust was regarded as sold, thus ending the practice by the merchant of drawing out many pieces of cloth so as to enlarge his display but with no serious intention of buying.

But the thing of interest at this point is the correction that was planned for the credit abuses. In the case of all time-sales by the factor, he was to get from the buyer within twelve days a note of the sum due and deliver it to the clothier, and a penalty of double the sum of the sale was attached for neglect in this matter, and all contracts to the contrary were void. The effect of this statute and the devices by which it was evaded and nullified are so lucidly told by one of the abused clothiers that he deserves quotation *in extenso*, as follows:

"For a little while this Act had its desired effect; these notes were immediately returned to the clothier, who carried them to market for

[1] "Abstract of Grievances of Trade," 7.
[2] 8 and 9 Wm. III, Cap. 9.

wool, etc., and by that means, made them answer in Trade almost as well as cash itself. The factors thus stripped of the most valuable part of their business, immediately concerted such measures as rendered the whole Act ineffectual—This was done, by tampering with those of the Trade whose circumstances were most precarious who, induced by the Promise of speedy Sale for their Goods, prior to those of any other Maker, were easily prevailed upon to forego the Advantage of the Notes granted them by Parliament. This fatal Precedent being once set, the Factors instantly exacted a like Compromise from all the rest; and if any refused not one Piece of their Cloth was sold. This important Point carried . . . . they again allowed the Drapers such unreasonable Credit, that it was impossible for the most substantial Clothier to carry on the Trade, while the Returns were so slow and precarious. On an universal Complaint therefore of this grievance, they graciously condescended to insure the Debt to be paid twelve Months after it was contracted; but in Return of so great a favor, insisted on two and a half per cent as a Reward; and if any was rash or stubborn enough to disrelish or oppose this new Imposition, he had the Mortification to wait six months longer for his money, that is to say, a year and a half in all."[1] Though this quotation savors of hostility it is testimony sufficient that the credit practices of the seventeenth and eighteenth centuries were akin and alike, and were in part used to press the clothier and merchant into alignment with the factor; and though subject to obvious abuses the credit system operated to the distinct advancement of the cloth and wool trade by synchronizing the times of payment.

Each of the factors in the Hall served many clothiers and merchants. They truckled to the wealthier to the end of a larger business but the exactions they could levy upon the smaller clothier made him quite as profitable a principal. Each clothier dealt regularly through one or more factors: he consigned his cloths to and drew inland bills of exchange upon his factor or factors for the proceeds; if the draft appeared before sale had been made the factor used his discretion in advancing money to his clothier.[2] The clothier might act as his own carrier; but as early as 1706 a very extensive system of common carriers had

---

[1] "Case of the Clothiers and Weavers," quoted in Smith, Memoirs, II, 310–11; this was written by one who signed himself Trowbridge and first published in a paper called "Old Common Sense" from which it was copied in the Gentleman's Magazine, q. v. 1739: 89–90, 126.

[2] For the advantages and disadvantages of this system of consignment and exchange as then operated, see Defoe, Com. Eng. Tr., I, 280 et seq.

developed, "Carriers and Waggoners" using "Horses, Carts, or other Carriage" performed "their respective and wonted Stages" and travelled "constantly from their respective counties to London and so back" and gave "security for their regular carriage."[1] The improvement in the Post Office facilitated the above method of business and in the last quarter of the seventeenth century the clothier sent up to his factor "Letters of Patterns" of the cloths he had made up and had ready for sale.[2] This practice accomplished a better accommodation of the kind and volume of cloth to the demand of the market, and saved unnecessary or ill-timed carriage thither.

At the Hall there were numerous expenses that were charged by the factor against the proceeds of sales. The factor was paid a percentage of the selling price, or so many pence per cloth, or was hired on a salary basis, the first method being most common; this was the expense called "Factorage." The charges for "pitching" and "resting" have already been mentioned, as also that of "Portridge," the payment to the master porter for service of carrying from the Hall. The use of samples coming by mail as well as the general correspondence caused a charge for "postage." There were charges for "pressing" because the cloth had to be redressed after its carriage to London and occasionally from wear of handling in the Hall.[3] Many complaints were raised against the factor, alleging abuses in the accounting of these charges and the proceeds of sales. They were usually lumped and without any particularization.[4] Accounts were very tardily rendered and were confusing.[5] The details of the terms of the contracts were not related and the exact status of credits given and moneys received was not revealed. To correct these and other connected abuses the statute[6] of 1696 required "weekly Registers" to be kept by the officers of the Hall specifying the name of the factors, the buyers and sellers, the date of sale, etc., to which registers the clothiers were to have recourse at all convenient times without fee or gratuity. The factors were also to render an account of the existing status of their trade, specifying the stock of money and cloth on hand and the credits due the clothier on past sales. This was to clear the way for the operation of the "weekly Registers" and a new start in accounting. But this act was soon evaded and its provisions neglected.

[1] Haynes, View of Present, 90–1.
[2] "Abstract of Grievances," 7.
[3] These and other charges are listed in "Abstract of grievances," 5.
[4] Smith, Memoirs, II, 312.
[5] "Treatise upon Wool and Cattell," 17; "Treatise of Wool," 17–19.
[6] 8 and 9 Wm. III, Cap. 9, Sec. 4, 7.

Since 1516 Blackwell Hall had been made the exclusive London cloth market. The ordinance of 1678 and the act of 1696 confirmed this monopoly. But the factors found clandestine ways of dealing outside the Hall when it convenienced them especially. For instance, the governors of the Hall permitted them to hire warehouses in the Hall for their own private use; thus opportunity was given for them to enter on other than market days and carry out cloths and expose them to sale in their own houses.[1] The use of patterns likewise afforded a means to evasion; along with the cloth the clothier sent up patterns of the same, which the factor took to his house or store-house or to the drapers' houses and made sales in advance of the Thursday market.[2] Another practice which amounted to a similar evasion and which was opposed by the clothiers was that of trust sales whereby large stocks of cloth of various patterns were sent out to drapers, ostensibly as sold; the draper carried them in stock for a week or two and returned what he had not sold, claiming they were in excess of the bargain, the worse for wear and handling, and the factor charged the cost of repressing to the clothier.[3] The amount of the sale was thus determined outside of the Hall, as was also the specific cloth sold.

At times, for the purposes of profit or as a weapon employed to maintain their monopoly against the clothier in the Hall, the factors engaged themselves as clothiers. During times of prosperous trade they furnished employees with wool, oil, dye-stuffs, etc., and made cloth of their own and gave it the preference of the market. They thus assumed to themselves the advantage of boom times to the detriment of their clothier principals.[4] If the poorer sort of clothiers of any particular locality offered continued and active resistance to the domination of the factors in the trade, it was claimed that the factors would join their capitals and set up the clothmaking trade in some other nearby town and force such competitive pressure as to undo the refractory town. Actual instance of such action occurred at Kidderminster in Worcestershire.[5] Efforts were made in 1678 to stop the factors' doing any other than the true agent's function; they were prohibited from dealing in cloth on their own account except for

[1] 8 and 9 Wm. III, Cap. 9, Sec. 1.

[2] This was practiced in 1692: see "Clothiers Complaint," 14–15, where it was claimed the market day had lost its signification through this practice.

[3] Haynes, View of the Present, 89 (1705); "Case of the Clothiers and Weavers" (1739), quoted in Smith, Memoirs, II, 312–13.

[4] See "Case of Clothiers and Weavers" (in Smith's Memoirs, II, 313) for the opinion the clothier had of the effect of this practice on the clothier and trade.

[5] See Smith, Memoirs, I, 318; Yarranton, Extract from a Dialogue, 1.

purpose of exporting it themselves; as to the domestic trade they were to act only as factors for clothiers.[1]   These efforts were ineffective.

The factors at Blackwell Hall did an increasing business as representatives of foreign mercantile houses.   Not till the eighteenth century had they established foreign connections to much extent.   But it became very noticeable about 1740 that the Dutch and Spanish merchants had changed their methods of buying between 1698 and that date; that they no longer bought directly from the clothier, as they had become habituated before that time, at his house in the country; but that they bought through the Blackwell Hall factors.[2] It is possible that the economic control exercised by the factor over the clothiers was a compelling force in working this transition in practice, whereby the factor attained a more complete monopoly of sales; at least the subserviency to the Hall in this matter of foreign sales was a subject of complaint by the clothier.[3]

The economic significance of the factors at the Hall is difficult of analysis.   To the clothiers who were more impressed with the abuses imposed than the services rendered, the factors were, as was said, "a public nuisance and prejudice to the clothing trade;"[4] and nowhere in the literature of the century studied are found any praises for the benefactions of the factor to the wool and woolens industry, while there is a comparative abundance of invective and complaint against him.   Unquestionably the volume of the literature is no test or criterion by which to estimate the factor's worth to trade.   The most salient abuses of his office have been analyzed at length; the general tenor of his way was so unobtrusive that his fundamental services were unrecognized except in the fact that he was constantly employed to buy and sell.   It may be concluded that if the practices of these thirty or more men had become so intolerably obnoxious as the epithetic phraseology of the pamphleteer suggests, either this paltry number of factors would have succumbed to the host of assailing clothiers and corrections have been allowed or means would have been devised whereby a set of interloper or competitive factors would have arisen.   The simple fact is that the factors were doing a real service to the wool and woolens trade, a service that was quite indispensable and that grew more so as the volume of cloth handled increased.

[1] Act of Common Council, 1678; the text of the act is given in Maitland, London, I, 463.

[2] Webber, Consequences of Trade, 14; Gent. Mag., 1740: 501; Webber is also quoted in Smith, Mem., II, 376.

[3] Gent. Mag., 1740: 501.

[4] "Treatise of Wool," 29.

The prime service of a factor is to facilitate exchanges; buyers and sellers are brought together through specialized representatives; wide correspondence and connections swell the number of buyers and sellers; there is a broader, steadier market; an economy of time, cost and effort at sale is effected; the producer, in singleness of effort, is enabled to produce more and better; the agent becomes an intelligencer to the manufacturer; and so forth. These and other functions the Blackwell Hall factors did for the clothier quite without recognition by him. The data are not at hand to determine whether the charge for factorage, etc., was so arbitrary and exorbitant as to exceed the money value of the services rendered; nor to determine, as was alleged whether English woolens came to market dearer than those of other nations.[1] Supposing the factors to have untrammeled monopoly, other things being equal, an intelligent and reasonable action would be, not to discourage the clothier upon whose product their livelihood depended, but to aim at maximum sales at good prices. If they did not have a monopoly, business principles would incline them to cultivate and befriend the clothier. In either case, on *a priori* grounds, the conclusion is that the actual abuses were far less detrimental than the allegations.

Factor at Leeds.

So far this study of the middlemen in the wool and woolens industry has been particularly devoted to the London market. The next most important cloth market of England was at Leeds, where the new West Riding district marketed its cloth in great part. Since factors played so prominent a rôle in the buying at Leeds it has been deemed fitting at this juncture to take some notice of the conduct of trade at this market. In 1750 Pococke described the trade there as follows: "a town of great trade in every branch of the woolen trade, but principally in cloths of the price of 2s. 6d. to 7s. a yard. . . . On one side of the street, where four rows of forms are placed and extending about 200 yards in length, on which they have their cloth, and great sums are contracted for in one hour with very few words, the buyer asking the price, then bidding in answer, and the other then setts his price, and the buyer, if he likes it, orders it to be sent to such a place."[2]

Defoe[3] found in his travels in 1722 that there were three sorts of

---

[1] "Case of Clothiers and Merchants," 1739, in Smith, Memoirs, II, 313.

[2] Pococke, I, 52–3.

[3] For the facts related in this exposition, see especially, Defoe, Tour, IV, 90–3.

buyers of cloth at Leeds, viz., travelling merchants, buyers to send to London, and buyers to send abroad. The first of these three will be discussed under another head.[1]

Those of the second class either bought on commission for London drapers or merchants as principals, or acted themselves as principals, and authorized factors or warehousekeepers in London to do their selling on commission. These London agents supplied London retailers and drapers for the City's use, and also supplied merchants who exported these cheaper northern goods to the Plantations and to Russia and the Baltic. The factors of the London drapers and cloth merchants were active buyers in the east and west districts, also, in the days before the Blackwell Hall factors acquired their monopoly. The London merchants in the days of Winchcombe came in person or agent to Newberry to bargain for cloth. Deloney mentions "a young, wealthie Italian merchant, comming oft from London thither to bargaine for cloth (for at that time clothiers most commonly had their cloth bespoken, and halfe paid for aforehand.)"[2] In 1605 out-of-town factors bought and sold contrary to law at Colchester; complaint was laid that "divers Factors Strangers" sojourning in Colchester were buying and selling to the great "wronge and hinderances" of the burgesses.[3] The Shropshire dealers complained against the factors of the London merchants, 1621, for buying and engrossing Welsh cloths and friezes and dispatching them, before they came to their proper market at Oswestry, to the drapers of Whitechurch, Chester, and Coventry. One William Thomas, a local clothworker, was buying as factor for John Byard of London and exporting these cloths to Rochelle, Bordeaux and St. Malo.[4]

The buyers for exportation abroad were resident commission factors employed by merchant principals who lived in Hamburg and in Holland, and, farther, in the German and Austrian cities Nuremberg, Frankfort, Leipsig, Augsburg and Vienna. It was said by the author of an atlas in 1728 that he could of his own knowledge give the names of particular merchants in Holland, who had sent commissions to Leeds for these goods for above £100,000 value in a year, and that for many successive years.[5] And in the 1760's £20,000 worth of

---

[1] See "Traveling Merchant."

[2] Deloney, Jno. Winch., 86; this was about 1500.

[3] Cal. S. P. Dom., Jas. I, 1605, 229; S. P. Dom., Jas. I, XV, 17; V. C. H., Essex, II, 392.

[4] Shrops. Arch. Soc. Trans., III, 134; V. C. H., Shrops, I, 430.

[5] Atlas Mar et. Com., 109.

cloth was often sold in an hour's time, and much of it was shipped abroad at Hull.[1] This is telling evidence of the volume of this commission business.

Draper.

The woolen drapers seem to have differentiated their employment and separated their function from the general cloth manufacture and trade during the fourteenth century. In the 37th year of Edward III's reign (1363), a sumptuary act was passed in which the dealers in cloth were enjoined to furnish certain quantities of cloth and the ones then existent were "fesours des draps et drapers;"[2] another act mentions "marchauntz nomez grossiers"[3] and restricts them to cloth alone or some other single commodity. In 1364 the first charter was granted to the Draper's Company of London, signifying that a body of clothdealers was arising.[4] They were arising in various parts of the kingdom during the fourteenth and fifteenth centuries. At Beverley in 1390 the gild merchants were called mercers, in 1446 merceri, marchaunts and marchands, mercatores, merchants, drapers, and pannarii. By 1446 the gild seems to have differentiated into three somewhat distinct classes, viz. "merchants, mercers, and drapers."[5] The Beverley middlemen were defined in 1492 as including "every one living in the town of Beverley who attends fairs and markets, buying cloth to resell and retail in the town of Beverley."[6] The "draper's crafte" existed in Worcester in 1456 and 1467 and 1497 according to extant testimony in Chancery Proceedings for those dates.[7] Deloney mentions that Jack of Newbury sold to Randoll Pert, a *draper* of London, for credit,[8] but it does not appear whether he was a retailer or wholesaler or both. About the same date a gild decree at Beverley grouped all retail dealers of the town in the brotherhood and livery of the drapers.[9]

It appears that the drapers were occasioned by the migration of industry from the towns to the country and the consequent establishment of the domestic system of cloth manufacture in the homes. The rise of the country clothier was primarily due to the arbitrary restrictions laid by the town craft gilds. Heretofore, each craftsman might have retailed his own product. Hereafter, cloth that was produced

[1] Anderson, Origin, III, 459.
[2] 37 Ed. III, Cap. XV.
[3] Ibid., V.
[4] Hazlitt, London Liv. Cos., 198–9.
[5] See Selden, XIV, pp. 33, 74, 81, 99.
[6] See Selden XIV, p. 75.
[7] V. C. H., Worces., II, 285.
[8] Deloney, Jno. Winch., 106.
[9] Selden, XIV, p. 100.

in the country was brought into towns to be sold there by the drapers. It was found in Leeds that the manufacture was suburban and the sale was urban: the dwindling of town manufacturing was compensated for by the selling of cloth by the drapers.[1] Middlemen became necessary thereafter to judge and guarantee the quality of the cloth and to study the market demand so as to equalize the quantity produced and consumed.[2]

The specialized wooldealer antedated the clothdealer for the reason that England in the early centuries produced and exported wool rather than cloth and the import trade in cloth was relatively in the hands of Dutch merchants. The clothdealers sprang from those clothworkers having the greatest degree of capitalism quality, either the wooldealers or the cloth-finishers. Stray bits of historical evidence and *a priori* considerations incline one to believe that they came mostly from the cloth-finishers. The cloth passed through their hands last: they would be tempted to buy from the weaver and finish it for the customer; an accumulation of stock on hand would induce them to pay more attention to selling and less to finishing cloth, or give themselves over to buying and selling entirely. There is little evidence that English clothdealers, to any large extent, came from the wool buyers whereas the Charter of 1364 shows that the drapers at that date were still makers of cloth; and the charter gave them a monopoly of the retail cloth trade of London and vicinity. Non-freemen could sell in gross to lords and commoners for their private use but not by retail, nor in gross to merchants. By this charter they thus became local retailers on the one hand, and middlemen between makers and merchants of cloth.[3]

The drapers continued to be makers of cloth and finishers of cloth in certain parts of the land at least till the eighteenth century was well spent. At Beverley in 1492–4 express permission was granted to the drapers to "make hose and keep apprentices and servants sewing in their shops without hindrance or any payment . . . to the Tailors' craft." They were thus artisans at that time.[4] In 1561 theirs and the tailors' work were differentiated and their shops were not to be used for tailoring.[5] In Worcester a like ordinance of the sixteenth century declared "hytt shall be lawful to the saide drapers

[1] Cf. V. C. H., Worces., II, 287.
[2] See opinion of Babbage, Mach., 164–5.
[3] See Ashley's opinions in his "Eng. Wool. Ind.," 60–8.
[4] Selden, XIV, 75, 100, 103.
[5] Ibid., 105.

and their apprentices to make woman's hoses, as they heretofore have used . . . "[1] But here some discrimination was made against the pure drapers and "lynnynmen;" they "were to sell only in guildhall, and pay . . . for their stalls," whereas any "man or woman denysyn" might "sill linen cloth of their proper makyng without contradiction of eny person."[2] The drapers of Shrewsbury were the finishers of the Welsh cottage-made grey cloths from Elizabeth's time till the midst of the eighteenth century.[3] "The cloth bought at Oswestry and the two Welsh markets of Welshpool and Montgomery was brought to Shrewsbury, and there handed over by the drapers to the shearman and clothworkers to be dressed and to the dyers (hewsters) to be coloured."[4] They made them up into bales, some of which contained 2000 yards and shipped them down the Severn. These operations were very like those of the merchants of the north manufacturing district.

But the trade of the draper underwent a progressive differentiation from the artisan class, from the retailing class, and from the merchant class. At Beverley they were given a monopoly of dealing in woolen cloth and hose; this ordinance, 1572, was to prevent "marchantes" from "buyinge and sellinge of any wollen clothe belonging to the Drapers crafte, or women's hose, . . . or any other kind of wollen clothe that might be hurtefull to the saide Drapers."[5] The Tailors in particular had been, in 1561, warned to "bye no maner of wullen clothe or clothes, to the intent to sell the same againe, by hollsaile or retaile, by yerde or otherwyse."[6] It would be a safe inference from a State Paper dated 1627 that the distinction between draper and merchant was recognized at that date in Yorkshire. A petition from Wakefield stated that the "small quantitie of cloth there made is noe sea ware but sould to Drapers onlie."[7] The Drapers Company of London furnished a goodly quota to the membership of the Merchants Adventurers, some becoming merchant exporters as England began to manufacture her wool herself. The distinction between the retailing mercer and the wholesaling draper was always relative. They were often incorporated in the same gild.[8] As will

---

[1] Quoted in Noake, Worc. in Olden Times, 37; V. C. H., Worc., II, 287-8.

[2] V. C. H., Worc., II, 286.

[3] Cf. Aikin, Tour in North Wales, 74.

[4] V. C. H., Shrop. I, 431; Add. MSS. 21202. fol. 208-9.

[5] Selden, XIV, 108.

[6] Ibid., 105.

[7] S. P. Dom., Chas. I, LXI, 84; V. C. H., York, II, 414.

[8] For example, in 1572, at Oxford; see Turner, Select. Rec. Oxford, 342.

be shown more fully under the title "Shops and Stores," the mercers tended to handle a wider variety of wares, in particular, luxuries and fineries, whereas the draper stayed by cloth more exclusively: the mercer became the typical retailer, the draper the typical wholesaler.[1]

The Drapers Company of London grew very fast in numbers, extension, and exclusive privileges. At the St. Bartholomew Cloth Fair they had the right of search and marking for three centuries and a half, i.e., till 1737. Blackwell Hall was devised by the City and Parliament as a compromise in the rising contest between the country drapers and the London monopolistic drapers. The former were conceded the privilege of display and sale in gross on certain market days in this Hall and nowhere or time else. An attempt was made in 1406 to prohibit the country draper from selling to other Londoners than the drapers; but an act of Parliament maintained for the country drapers the freedom "to sell their cloth in gross to all the king's liege people."[2]

This was the common principle of regulation of sales within any town: the outsider might sell at wholesale only and in particular markets and on particular days only. A very representative regulation was, for instance, laid at Beverley in 1561 as follows: " . . . no farranor (shall) . . . bringe any kind of clothe, in packe or paks, or otherwise, to the saide towne to thintant to sell the same or any parte thereof, shall not open or shewe the same packe or packes of clothe or clothes on any privaite house or place within the same towne upon the market daie onely; and in the weake daie, to repaire to the common hall, or place there appointed for the same to shewe there saide clothes, and to taike ther most gaine by hoolesaile onely, and not to cut by yarde but only upon the markitt daie in open faire or market . . ."[3]

The draper, as has been shown, was in the early centuries both retailer and wholesaler of woolen cloth. The retail function became less and less his and was given over to the mercers. By the middle

---

[1] In Fuller's time this difference in wares was evidently apparent, for in his Church History, VI, I, 275, is found "Thus the Draper may sooner sell forty eels of freeze and course cloth, than the Mercer four yards of cloath of gold." See the working-out of the process in York, V. C. H., York, II, 416. Some times the differentiation was somewhat based on the sex to which they respectively catered, the draper tending to handle men's cloth especially. See list of goods sold by a draper or men's mercer given in Besant, Eighteenth Century London, 240.

[2] 7 Hen. IV, Cap. 9.

[3] Selden, XIV, 106.

of the eighteenth century he was a typical wholesaler.[1] As such he had connections (a) with the clothiers or the factors, (b) with the merchant importers and exporters, (c) with the provincial wholesalers, and (d) with the retailers of London and other towns and cities. This tradesman bought his cloth from the clothier directly,[2] or from the factors of Blackwell Hall, or from the makers or factors at the Leeds or other markets.[3] Such cloth was dressed and dyed, or white; in the latter case he had them dressed and dyed in the City. The merchant disposed of his imported cloth to the draper, and bought a large part of his cargoes from him for exportation. Outside of the sales to the merchant, the draper sold in gross (a) to the retailers in London, including the tailors, mercers, and petty shopkeepers; (b) to the retailers likewise in the environs of London; (c) to the country drapers or wholesalers, living in the larger towns, who acted as sub-distributors to the country retailers;[4] and lastly (d) to travelling merchants and petty chapmen. Both the imported and the domestic cloths were in this way forwarded to even the most remote parts of the Isle.

There early arose, as above noted, a controversy between the country draper and the London draper resulting in the compromise of Blackwell Hall; but in addition to that, restrictions were laid whereby the London merchant was advantaged; for example, by a statute in 1523 it was enacted that "no Person shall sell to a Merchant Stranger any broad White Woolen Cloth made in England unless he cannot sell it to some English Merchant within Eight Days after he brought it to Blackwell Hall, except the Sale be in Fairs, Ports, or Creeks."[5] In 1635 the drapers and merchants of London acquired a monopoly of buying country cloths both by retail and wholesale directly from the clothiers.[6] By 1660 the Blackwell Hall factors had become buyers or intervening agents. Therefore, both through the London draper and the foreign merchant, the cloth business was being concentrated in London and

---

[1] His business is described by Defoe, Com. Eng. Tr., 1, 2; and by Campbell, Lon. Tr., 194; his relations to the clothier are suggested in Gent Mag., 1739: 236.

[2] See "Clothier;" see also V. C. H., York, II, 413 and S. P. Dom. Eliz. cclii. 2, that they bought up stockings and cushions; and carpet and coverlets.

[3] See "Factors at Leeds;" a State Paper of 1595 said, speaking of York products, "The chefe buyers of thes ar Mr. Kent, Mr. White Nicholas Baste of Lyncolne and John Swane of Yorke who inethe at the Bell savage in London." S. P. Dom., Eliz., CCLII, 2.

[4] As at Howden in York, Pococke, I, 185.

[5] 14–15 Hen. VIII, Cap. 1.

[6] S. P. Dom. Chas. I, cclxxxii, 130.

the country draper was to a considerable degree limited rather to sub-distribution from London, than doing an independent business.

The draper or wholesale merchant employed agents known as "bagmen"—the progenitors of our "commercial travellers." This "rider" or "bagman" carried his samples in a small box with a handle in the lid which he placed under the seat of his gig or strapped to his saddle. He drove from town to town. Some merchants did their own travelling and in their own carriages. Ruskin's father was a merchant who did this. After the stage-coach became common the bagman ceased using his own vehicle and horse and used the stage-coach. The bagman of those days was as great a boon to the inn-business as the commercial traveller of these days is.[1]

Since the woolens draper represents the typical wholesaler it is proper to consider his office in trade and commerce.[2] In the first instance, the draper was capitalist and speculator. His business required "a considerable Stock of Ready Money and Credit."[3] He bought and carried in stock a large volume of goods. Besides it was a great advantage to buy from a wholesaler rather than a manufacturer for the reason that he was freer in extending credit to his customers,[4] because the manufacturer dealt with laborers who required regularly and immediately their wages in current cash. Beginners especially found it advantageous to cultivate a credit with a wholesaler by being a regular customer, since in times of financial straits or of dearth of goods the wholesaler would support them as customers more readily than as occasional buyers.

The retailer realized further benefits in the wholesaler. Being a buyer in gross and large volume, the wholesaler's custom was of more importance to the manufacturer than the petty custom of a retailer, and greater effort would be made to retain his patronage; as a consequence, the wholesaler procured a better quality of goods than the retailer could directly.[5] The large stock of goods carried constituted a better assortment, from which the retailer could select his purchases, than any manufacturer could offer. For the most part, it was not convenient for the retailer to leave his shop to do his buying, and he did it through the agents of the wholesaler, or visited his nearby ware-

---

[1] See description in Besant, Eighteenth Century London, 114.

[2] See a seventeenth century discussion in Savary, Par. Negoc., II, 93, 352, 353.

[3] Campbell, II, 195.

[4] Savary, Par. Negoc., II, 352.

[5] Drapers were used by the government to inspect the cloth. See Statutes of the Realm (Rec. Com.), IV, 136.

houses. Such were, in part, the rôle of the wholesaler in respect to the retailer.[1]

But he dealt with others than retailers; the merchant, for instance, bought from him. In making up a cargo the merchant was obliged to procure a great variety of sortments; it profited him to buy at wholesale, but not from the clothier directly, for the packages of cloth the clothiers sent up were usually larger than he wanted; he therefore applied to the wholesale drapers for making up his motley or mixed cargoes for export.[2] Greater expedition in securing a cargo was also realized. In respect to the country draper, the London draper acted as a central store and forwarder. The clothier found advantage in the draper by way of a steady market. "The merchant" bought "generally only against shipping times; the drapers" bought "but small quantities at some special times of the year, and divers others" bought "of the clothiers when they are most surcharged." Thus these "worst and hardest paymasters" really served the clothiers at all times of the year when they were "driven to London to sell their cloths to pay the wool grower and the poor whom they set on work."[3]

Packer.

While England was exporting wool in the early centuries there existed at London a Company of Woolpackers who appear to have been an association of masters whose artisans or yeomen were engaged at packing and winding the wool for export. But this Company was abandoned in the first quarter of the seventeenth century,[4] very likely from sheer want of business.[5] They were superseded by packers of cloth for export.

"The Business of a Packer" was "to pack up all Sorts of Bale Goods into proper Parcels fit for Exportation. They" were "answerable to their Employers if any damage happened to the Goods through their Ignorance or Neglect."[6] They were employed by the exporting merchant, and had good "Profits by their Business."

---

[1] The above advantages are on the authority of Savary, Par. Neg., II, 352–3.

[2] The same reasons and practice existed in Ireland in the linen trade; see "Letter from a Merchant," 57–8.

[3] S. P. Dom., Chas. I, CCLXXXII, 130.

[4] Hazlitt, Liv. Com., 153.

[5] See details of packing wool as done by the Celys; Cely Papers, XI, 15, 21, 28, 30, 32, etc.

[6] Campbell, 201.

Of course, this proper business had no middleman quality; but as early as 1692 it was said that it had been "usual for a considerable Merchant to leave the buying of four or five hundred Cloths to a considerabe Packer, and take his account made up to his hand;"[1] that is, the packer acted as factor for the merchant and bought his cloth. At the same time complaint was laid to the effect that the cloths were no sooner entered the Blackwell Hall and pitching charges paid, than they were carried directly to the packer's house.[2] It was claimed that there was a greater business in merchants' cloth done at the packer's house than at the Hall and that since only the packer's friends were admitted opportunity existed for a damaging monopoly.[3] These allegations were likely exaggerations of occasional practices, and indicate evasions of the Blackwell Hall regulations. In another direction, the packers expanded their business assuming the office of merchant and some of them were "large Adventurers in the exportation" of English manufactures.[4] The simple craft of packing cloth, in these ways, acquired a considerable middleman characteristic.

Travelling Merchant.

It has been stated that one class of buyers at the great Cloth Fair at Leeds was the travelling merchants. These were a class peculiar to the northern manufacturing section and were often called the "Manchester Men." They were wholesale merchants (more properly, tradesmen). There was a demand all over England for the cheaper cloths—kerseys, cottons, as well as the other manufactures such as cutlery, hardware, clocks, almanacs, etc., which were made in the north, and the Manchester Men acted as distributors to the shopkeepers of the Island. Throughout the century under particular study this system was in operation. In a pamphlet dating from about 1685 it was spoken of, as a thing accustomed, that "the Manchester Men, the Sheffield-men, and many others . . . . do Travel from one Marker-Town to another; and there at some Inn do profer their Wares to sell to the Shopkeepers of the Place."[5] They sold wholesale to shops, warehousekeepers, and to country chapmen at this date.

[1] "Clothiers Complaint," 5.
[2] Ibid., 14.
[3] Ibid., 16.
[4] Campbell, 201; Yarranton, Extract from a Dialogue (quoted in Smith, Memoirs, I, 318).
[5] "Trade of England revived," 21.

The mode of conveyance was pack-trains of horses or mules, driven in single file, each horse tethered to the one in front. The lead horse carried a tinkling bell to apprise travellers of their coming. Each horse carried two packs or panniers balanced across its back. These trains moved along the narrow paths and roads, veritable caravans. They were exposed to all kinds of weather, roads, and classes of people travelling.[1] They travelled chiefly in summer because of the badness of the roads in winter.

They sold by wholesale to shopkeepers and chapmen, gave large credit, and did a large business. It was "ordinary for one of these Men to carry a thousand Pounds worth of Cloth with him at a Time, and having sold it at the Fairs or Towns" to send "his Horses back for as much more, and this very often in a Summer."[2] An estimate of the total value of goods so distributed in 1728 placed it at above £100,000 in three months' time.[3] The counties of Norfolk, Suffolk, and Essex were supplied with "prodigious Quantities" of Yorkshire kerseys by the merchants of London.[4] There was thus a competition between the Manchester Men and the London wholesalers for the custom of the retailers of cloth, and the long continuance of the former attests their economic service in the distribution of the northern cloth.

Chapman.

"Chapmen" (cheap, man) was originally an inclusive name for all dealers; by the sixteenth century the term had become restricted to the small pedlar or retail dealer.[5] The term "petty" was often prefixed. In 1639 petty chapmen were described as those who "buy up commodities of those that sell by wholesale and sell them off dearer by retaile, and parcel them out."[6] Before the rise of country stores all retailing in the country was done from temporary booths at markets and fairs, or by itinerant dealers. From the latter fact the term chapman acquired the concept of our modern pedlar or hawker. This meaning was in vogue in 1745 when the chapmen were defined

---

[1] Mantoux, 96–7, quotes a description of a personal experience given in the Francis Place, Add. MSS 27828 Br. Mus., p. 10.

[2] Defoe, Tour, III, 92; some made fortunes in this business, see Th. Walker in "The Original," No. XI, July 29, 1835. (Quoted in Mantoux, 96.)

[3] Atlas Mar et Com., 108.

[4] Defoe, Tour, III, 70–1; see also Postlethwayt, Dict. s. v. British Empire.

[5] Palgrave, I, 262.

[6] Horn & Robotham, XLV, Sec. 401; cf. Defoe, Com. Eng. Tr., II, 58, for quite the same meaning in 1745.

as "Such as carry goods from market to market, or from house to house, to sell."[1] They bought their goods from wholesale tradesmen of the cities or from the Manchester Men, and travelled on foot with packs on their shoulders, or with horse and panniers, or with horse and cart or wagon.[2]

The character of the merchandise carried around by these chapmen is illustrated by the report in 1696 of a robbery of one's wagon in Bedfordshire. The things stolen included a truss of £165 of old money, a piece of broad alamode, one of narrow alamode, two pieces of black silk crape, one half pound of fine white thread, pieces of linen cloth, a plain muslin head-dress, a striped muslin head-dress, six pairs of roll stockings and eighteen pairs of short stockings.[3]

The petty chapmen had distinct advantages over the local or city stores, and much complaint was laid against them as destructive competitors.[4] In the first place they were unrestrained by any system of apprenticeship and could set up in business at will. They escaped the payment of taxes, rents and the duty of performing public office. They lived in a lower social scale and on a lower standard of living; consequently their clothing, houses, entertainments, etc., were of less expense to them. And they were less responsible in a financial way; allegations were profuse as to their dishonorable business practices.[5] By the superlative language of the philippics against the chapmen, one would surmise that the country shops and stores were in a decadent and retrograde state, under the dire competition of these chapmen; whereas it appears they were extending themselves in number, size and importance throughout the period, especially in the larger cities and towns.

The stress and strain of the public finance under William III's reign furthered the precipitation of these complaints into legislation adverse to the chapmen. Out of consideration for the interest of the local

[1] Defoe, Com. Eng. Tr., I, 1.

[2] In 1718 a critic asserted that "most of the Commodities . . . are now job'd or hawk'd about the Country, from Parish to Parish and from Door to Door, by Vagabond and Itinerant Retailers, who carry their All in a Pair of Panniers, or upon one or two Pack-Horses." "Essay against Forestallers," 21. In 1773 they "convey waggon loads;" Moore, Consid. on Price, 76.

[3] V. C. H., Bed. II, 99.

[4] "Trade of Eng. revived," ca. 1685, 22, 36–40; "Essay against Forestallers," 1718, 21; Moore, Considerations, 1773, 76.

[5] The term "hawking" has its derivation from the spying, thievish habits of the bird and man. They also acquired a reputation for ruffianism and brigandage, Smiles, Lives, I, 307; Mantoux, 97.

shopkeepers and the immunity these itinerant traders enjoyed from taxation, but also as a source of revenue, a license system was used.[1] Hawkers having certified to the Commissioners of Transportation the manner of their trade and having paid £4 were licensed to hawk; penalties were laid for hawking without a license. Exception was made to makers of goods, who might sell their own products. This act was renewed from time to time and became the standing policy.

The act was soon evaded by the practice of "lending licenses;" those not possessing licenses pretended to have left them at home or elsewhere, and if the license was insisted upon, one was borrowed in the community for the time being. To correct this abuse, in 1704 an act made it a misdemeanor for a hawker to hawk not having the license with him, and lending licenses was specifically penalized.[2]

In 1704 travelling wholesalers of woolens and linens were exempted from the requirements of having a license, and in 1717 a like exemption was tendered the wholesalers of bone lace, but it was not till 1785 that the exemption of wholesalers was made general for all commodities.[3]

The effect of the license is so complicated with other economic phenomena that it cannot be definitely disentangled. Defoe, writing in 1745, said the number of petty chapmen was very great but that it was the opinion of some that the number was not so great as it had formerly been. By this time many of them had also become keepers of "shops, or chambers, or warehouses, in the adjacent market-towns, and sell their goods in the villages round."[4] The assumption of this sedentary retailing may have been used as a way of evading the license law, but no evidence has been found to support the suggestion. It is, however, evidence that the country store was arising into economic significance.

Despite the revulsion and the opposition against the petty chapman, he did the country populace a distinct benefit. The means of communication in the rural recesses were meager, poor, and seasonal; the

[1] 8 and 9 Wm. III, Cap. 25; 9 and 10, Cap. 27; 12 and 13, Cap. 11, Sec. 11; 3 and 4 Anne, Cap. 4; 5, Cap. 19; 6, Cap. 5; 7, Cap. 7. The license system was not an entirely new invention: it had been used in the period of town economy for the maintenance of local protection; cf. 5 and 6 Ed. VI, Cap. 21; I Jas. I, Cap. 25; 1 Phil. & Mary, Cap. 7.

[2] 3 and 4 Anne, Cap. 4, Sec. 4. The lending of licenses is sketched in Dowell, Hist. of Tax, III, 33–4.

[3] 3 and 4 Anne, Cap. 4, Sec. 4; 4 Geo. I, Cap. 7; and 25 Geo. III, Cap. 78; S. P. Treas., 1717, CCVIII, 47; V. C. H., Bucks, II, 107.

[4] Defoe, Com. Eng. Tr., III, 211.

difficulties and expense attached to a trip to market were great. ·The petty chapman specialized in the service of rural delivery.   His scale of living, tenor of life, and experience of the road made it possible for him to serve the country public more cheaply and with more economy than they could do it themselves.   He carried new ideas into the rural community and created a market which otherwise would have been latent and unknown, and at the same time was a leaven in socializing the people.   His opportunity and function declined with the rise of better means of communication and the country store served his customers thereafter.

In the cities hawking was a more common method of distribution and sale than is practiced today.   The rise of trade in shops reduced the business of the city hawker as it did that of the country hawker. Besant pictures the eighteenth century street hawking as follows: "the apple-woman, with her barrow in the summer, and in the winter her stall, pan of live charcoal, and plate of tin on which she roasts her apples.   The band-box-man carried a pole over his shoulder loaded with bandboxes neatly covered with coloured papers. . . .   Baskets were carried about in the same manner on the shoulder.   The bellows-mender carried his bag of tools over his shoulder, and did his mending on the kerb or on the doorstep.   Brick-dust was carried about in small sacks on the back of a donkey . . .   The bill of the play was sold with oranges and nuts outside Drury Lane Theatre.   Cats'-meat was vended by women.   Chairs were mended by a family, of whom one carried the cane or the rushes, another collected the chairs, and a third sat down on a doorstep and mended them.   Things to eat such as cherries, hot loaves, hot spiced gingerbread, mackerel, milk, new potatoes, rabbits, strawberries, watercresses, muffins, were hawked in the streets.   Such things as doormats, brooms, lavender, matches, were also sold in the streets; . . . the lusty Turk . . .   who offered rhubarb, the carter with the sand, . . .   (the) Corsair, who sold slippers . . .   these you will find in the picture . . ."[1]   Another common commodity so hawked was water; the "Cobbs," as they were called, carried it from the conduits, in large tankards, of about three gallons.[2]   Much of the produce that was not sold in the public markets during the day was hawked about town in the evening.[3]

[1] Besant, Eighteenth Century London, 101–2; pages 102–104 of this reference contain contemporary engravings of various trucksters.

[2] About 1600; see Besant, Tudor London, 285.

[3] Besant, Eighteenth Century London, 105.

It is very obvious that the same conditions that warranted the business of the country chapmen warranted that of the city hawker. A dispersed town population, with the poorest facilities of communication within the town, could be most cheaply and effectively reached by hawkers. As streets were improved and hackney coaches were drawn into service shopping could arise and the sedentary supplant the peripatetic method of retailing.

MINOR TEXTILES.

Brief descriptions of the organization of the several minor textile industries will serve a comparative purpose.

(a) Lace.

The lace-making trade was one of the chief occupations of Buckinghamshire from the fifteenth to the midst of the nineteenth century. The chief centers were Newport Pagnell (Olney), High Wycombe, Aylesbury, and Claydon. The trade was at its best during the eighteenth century. One of the chief of these lace-makers was Ferdinando Shrimpton of Penn. He and other men of his class kept several hundred workers employed constantly.[1] They went weekly to London, generally on a Monday, and sold their goods to the London milliners at the lace markets held at the George Inn, Aldersgate Street, or in the Bull and Mouth Inn in St. Martin's by Aldersgate. They returned with a stock of thread and silk, which they gave out to their workwomen to be made up according to their orders.[2] Olney was a sort of staple town for bone-lace.[3] It was said to excel all other towns of the country in lace.[4] At a weekly lace-market great quantities were sold. Lace-buyers also came round about once a month, meeting the lace-makers at some inn and bought their lace there.[5] The introduction of machine-made lace about 1835 killed this local industry.[6]

---

[1] Treasury Papers, CCVIII, 47.

[2] Pinnock, I, 31.

[3] Defoe, Tour, II, 173.

[4] Bull. Hist. of Newport Pagnell, 17.

[5] W. Shrimpton, Notes on a decayed Needle-land, 25.

[6] Palliser, 393. The above description of the lace trade is taken from V. C. H., Bucks, II, 106–7.

(b) Hosiery.

There are several historians of the hosiery manufacture.[1] Its early seat was Nottingham, where one Lee invented the stocking loom in 1589. Pococke found Bala in Ireland a considerable stocking market, also, in 1750.[2] Hosiery made little progress in England until the midst of the seventeenth century. Cromwell incorporated the London Company of Framework Knitters in London, and gave them a monopoly of regulating all framework knitters in England and Wales.[3] Nottingham, Leicester and Derby possessed, according to enumerations of frames in 1714, most of the midland-county frames. The knitters of these shires contested the regulation by the London Company and broke away in 1730. The Company made a spirited fight in 1740–51 for restoration of their control, but their appeals were refused by the House of Commons.[4] The petitions of the framework-knitters sent to the Commons give the location of the industry and somewhat the organization. Nottingham, and Surrey towns— as Godalming, Guilford, Whitley, etc.—were petitioners; the hosiers and manufacturers of London and Westminster also petitioned. The hosier provided the knitters with materials—silk and cotton—which they knitted on their own machines as a rule and returned the finished hose to him and received pay for their labor. But about 1720 certain "employers and shop-keepers . . . got into the hose business;" they simply bought frames and let them out to knitters and received hose back. Letting out frames to any but members of the Company was prohibited by by-law. Between 1730 and 1751 three "of the principal Hosiers" kept "100 Frames each." Sometimes persons who had no other interest in the trade bought and let frames out to the knitters.[5] The hose were carried to London and sold to the city dealers. There are named in the Commons Journal five "considerable Dealers in the aforesaid Manufactures . . . all of the City of London . . . who employ (ed) great Numbers of Manufacturers in different Parts of England" in 1730.[6] There was a gradual migration, about this date and onwards, of the industry from London to Nottingham.[7] In 1750 there were fifty manufacturers, employers

---

[1] See Thoroton, Deering, Blackner, Henson, and Felkin.

[2] Pococke, I, 235.

[3] Glover, I, 240–1. See statement of powers in J. H. C., XXVI, 779, 790–4.

[4] J. H. C., XXVI, 779–88.

[5] Felkin, 435.

[6] J. H. C., XXVI, 787.

[7] Blackner, Hist. Nott., 215.

of 1200 frames, called "putters-out" in Nottinghamshire, all trading directly to London.[1]   London exported big orders of hose to Spain and rivaled Lyons in France.[2]   The frames were rented by the week.[3]

(c) *Linen.*

The linen industry was practically confined to the Manchester region and Durham, and to Ireland and Scotland.   In 1641 Roberts wrote: "The towne of Manchester in Lancashire must be also herein remembered, and worthily, for their encouragement commended, who buy the yarne of the Irish, in great quantity, and weaving it returne the same againe in linen, into Ireland to sell."[4]   A writer in 1680 mentioned linen as "a considerable manufacture in Cheshire, Lancashire, and in the parts adjacent."[5]   The linen industry was promoted by William and Mary by incorporating three great linen companies, one each for England, Scotland and Ireland, on the joint-stock plan, to introduce the improved French methods of damask and linen weaving.[6]   Darlington in Durham was advanced much by this royal aid.[7]   It was noted for huckabacks.[8]   These were manufactured in Darlington and surrounding villages, and were carried to market at Darlington in packs on the backs of weavers or their donkeys.   Each house had at its rear a shed where the weaving was carried on.   In some cases the merchants bought the linen unbleached and had large bleaching grounds; during the eighteenth century bleaching became a separate industry[9] and Scotch linens were brought hither for bleaching.   The raw material in Durham was mostly domestic produce, but that used in Lancashire was imported from Ireland.   The Irish merchants brought their linen to Liverpool and sold it to the Manchester merchants from early times.[10]   The Irish linen industry was fostered by Stafford and made much progress during the seventeenth century, enough to provoke the English to

[1] Felkin, 83.

[2] Young, Annals of Agric., X, 447.

[3] See rates of rent and values of frames in Henson, and in Toulmin Smith, Eng. Gilds, 233.

[4] Lewis Roberts, Treasure of Traffike, 73.

[5] "Brit. Languens."

[6] Scott, Joint Stock Cos. before 1720.

[7] Thoresby, Diary, II, 430.

[8] Universal Magazine, Oct. 1749: 147.

[9] V. C. H., Durh., II, 316.

[10] Leland, Itin. VII, fol. 56, p. 47.

jealousy.[1] There was a considerable trade to England.[2] At the same time London was importing much Scotch linen.[3] The century following added much to the Scotch trade and manufacture.[4] The British Linen Company advanced the Scotch industry by making loans to the manufacturers and offering premiums on good work.[5] A part of the imports from Ireland and Scotland were re-exported, particularly to Portugal.[6] The linen trade of Europe was mostly in the hands of the Russians and Germans and what warp was produced at Darlington was mostly consumed in the manufacture of Lancashire fustians, and not pure linens.[7]

The organization of the linen business, though not so well developed and definitive, coincided closely with the woolens business. There was the yarn-merchant who gathered up yarn through the country districts and markets and exported it from Londonderry, Belfast, Newry, Drogheda, Dublin, Dundalk and Colerain, to Liverpool.[8] This was made up in hanks or dozens, of prescribed length, quality, and number of threads,[9] and was inspected at the yarn-market where most of it was bought and sold. The yarn-markets were furthered much by the erection of yarn-halls: the yarn-merchant as well as the manufacturer was advantaged by the continuous market, display, and variety of yarns.[10] The function of the merchant was described as follows by a writer in 1733: "Any Person who understands Yarn, may buy it up in small Parcels from the Spinners, and sort it: and when any Weaver, Housewife, or Clothmaker, has Occasion for Yarn, they may be served by the Yarn-Merchants, with any Quantity they want, all of the same Girst or Staple, Colour and Fineness, washed and emptied, ready to be put in the Loom. (There will be) . . .

---

[1] Cunningham, Growth, II, 369; see statistics of Irish exports of linen in Oddy, II, 309; see the following legislation: 21 Henry VIII, Ch. 12; 24 Henry VIII, Ch. 4; 5 Eliz., Ch. 5; 7–8 Wm. & M., Ch. 39.

[2] Anderson, Origin, II, 518.

[3] See statistics in Anderson, Origin, 498. The linen stamped for sale in Scotland about 1730 and the bounties paid for its production are given statistically in Oddy, II, 312.

[4] Anderson, Origin, IV, 149, 173–4; Macpherson, Annals, IV, 64.

[5] Ibid., III, 287; cf. 302, 312, 321.

[6] Ibid., IV, 394–5.

[7] Smith, Memoirs, II, 270.

[8] Rep. from Com. II, 310, contains statistics for the period 1731–1750.

[9] Gent. Mag., 1746: 656.

[10] "Some Reasons for Establishing," 1736.

no more bad Cloth, nor any Cloth disliked by Bars, Strips, or Pirns, occasioned by putting different Kinds of Flax, in the same Piece."[1]

There arose a class of "hawkers" or "jobbers" between the manufacturers of linens and the linen-drapers. They bought up the cloth in the country and disposed of it to the drapers. A contemporary ascribed their rise to the abuses which the drapers practiced against the manufacturers; the hawkers were more competent to deal with the manufacturers. But the jobbers soon abused their position by ingrossing and forestalling.[2]

Another party who operated on the markets was the factor. He bought and sold on commission for the merchants, drapers and manufacturers. There was a board of trustees who had the power of appointing factors at the Dublin and other Irish markets.[3] While the factors never attained a prominent position in the linen trade, in conjunction with the merchants and importers they were the centralizing feature of it.[4] Some acted as agents for continental merchants.

The linen-draper was a tradesman of considerable capital, employees, profits, and connection. Those of London sold by retail and wholesale the linens of Scotland, Ireland, Germany, France and Holland. They became capable judges of cloth.[5] The wholesalers appear to have opposed the rise of domestic manufacture in England lest their business be, in part, superseded by a more direct exchange between manufacturer and consumer.[6] Those of Ireland likewise favored the consumption in Ireland of foreign linens since their business was intermediary between importers and retailers.[7] They exercised considerable control over the method of manufacture. The drapers of Lisburn, Belfast and other parts of Ireland formed associations agreeing not to buy linens unless in "open folds."[8] This represented a general movement toward enforcing the law of sealing all linens. The number of drapers appears to have been quite large in Ireland, for 195 drapers from four towns are reported to have joined these associations.

---

[1] "Interest of Scotland," 165.
[2] "Review of Evils in Linen" (1762), I, 29–30; II, 16.
[3] Gent. Mag., 1746: 557.
[4] "Letter from Merchant," 57.
[5] Campbell, 282.
[6] "Letter from Merchant," 30.
[7] Ibid., 56–7.
[8] "Review of Evils," 21, 23, 30–2.

The function of the draper who did a wholesale business arose from the fact that the foreign linens were imported in very large packages, each containing a variety of assortments; the importer kept a warehouse and not a shop and sold these packages as a whole. But the variety and quantity in such a package was greater than any retailer wished; the importer therefore sold to the wholesale linen-draper who sold, in convenient packages, to the retailers. In case of export, he likewise assembled and packed the large bulks of various linens and sold to the exporter.[1] In connection with the Irish markets a class of "packers" were appointed to serve drapers and others there.[2]

The linen-merchants were importers and exporters of cloth. They operated in London, Liverpool, and other large ports of the Isles and Continent. Goods were carried by land and sea; the costs by sea from Dublin were less than by land from Liverpool.[3] In the rural parts the linen which the drapers procured from the merchants was disposed of to the "countrey-pedlers."[4] Such travelling merchants also carried Scotch linen into northern England. The merchants sometimes conducted a clandestine trade with the colonies of other nations.[5] The export trade from England was not usually conducted by the same merchants that imported the linen.[6]

[1] "Letter from Merchant," 57–8.
[2] Gent. Mag., 1746: 657.
[3] Rep. from Com. H. C., II, 291.
[4] Surtees, 33: 106.
[5] "Letter from Merchant," 70, 72.
[6] "Reflections and Considerations," 1738, p. 8.

CHAPTER VI.

CONTRASTS AND COMPARISONS.

The technique of the organization of four leading trades has now been considered in detail, tracing the progress of the wares from producers to final consumers. There existed a rough resemblance among them all. Neglecting the complexity introduced into the wool and woolens organization by the transformation of the ware in the hands of the clothier and by the marketing methods of the northern district, there appeared a comparable five-fold succession of middlemen—(a) a group of buyers of the raw materials, (b) a group of jobbers and merchants of these materials, (c) a group of factors, (d) a group of wholesalers and manufacturing merchants, and (e) the retailers.

In technique the coal trade had a somewhat wide divergence from this general scheme; the reason was that the ware was produced in one vicinity by comparatively few producers and the collector of the ware was unnecessary. Had it not been for the monopoly of the Hostmen the ship-master merchant could have bought directly from the producer without the intervention of the collector or other agency; and while the Hostmen were coal-owners this was the practice; when they became fitters direct dealings were broken off. In the coal trade also the merchant was separated from the wholesaler by the intervention of the crimp. In the woolens trade there was a like differentiation between the merchant and wholesaling draper, but in this case the factor was seller to both and not, as in the coal trade, buyer from one and seller to the other.

The relative degree of complexity and the nature of it in the four organizations are best shown by diagrammatic presentation. In the accompanying schemes the movement of the ware in each trade is indicated by arrowheads, and agency is shown by having the lines cross the rectangles. The vertical sections show the five-fold succession of middlemen mentioned. Fitters, Manchester men, mealmen, and clothiers do not fit in the scheme. The first were factors, not buyers; the second were producers, manufacturers, and wholesale merchants at the same time; the mealmen were both wholesalers and retailers; and the clothiers were a class of manufacturing merchants having peculiar relations to the rest of the trade, since they bought from and sold to the same factors.

Coal had the simplest and most dissevered organization; it moved directly, without change of form, from one specialized middleman to the next specialized middleman, or to the consumer. The middleman functions were clear-cut; there was little integration. Pools took the place of integrated business. The trade had two sets of factors—the fitters and the crimps; the latter were agents between the travelling and the resident merchants. The explanation of these peculiarities of the coal trade subsists, as shown in Chapter IV, in the localization of production and consumption of the ware, in the single method and route of transport, the freedom allowed to all ship-masters to trade at Newcastle, the distance between the places of production and consumption, the itinerancy of the merchant requiring agents at both points, the durability of the ware, the gild and town monopoly system, and the nature of coal-mining, requiring continuous operation.

The live-stock and meat trade was but slightly more complex. The breeder and grazier sold to the drover and jobber, who through the agency of the salesman sold to the wholesaling carcass butcher, and he to the retailing cutting butcher. But this simplicity was disturbed by the very general practice of the salesmen and butchers buying directly from the breeders and graziers, especially in the vicinity of the City. The jobbers, salesmen and butchers, wholesale and retail, competed in buying, and caused a confusion of their several functions. Such over-lapping and elimination of businesses was a prominent feature of the live-stock and meat trade. The cause of this feature lay in the wide distribution of stock-raising. Nearly every county of the British Isles contributed to London's meat supply, and the animals were driven on foot towards the metropolis. In these two particulars, viz., the dispersion of production and the number of routes and directions of movement, the coal and live-stock trades differed radically. In the former there was little or no opportunity for fusion of businesses; in the latter the prosecution of a single business was rare. It followed that the latter was less given to monopolies, and that where any arose it was temporary and depended upon the largeness of the buying; if jobbers or salesmen gained a monopoly of any market it could only be maintained by continued large buying; competition among the businesses was rife and took the direction of integration at every opportunity. There was also more variaton in the commodity of this trade. The animals and the meats differed but were consumed for the most part in a single form. This variation made possible a specialization among the dealers,—some handled sheep, some mutton,—some handled pigs, some pork and bacon,—etc. In this trade there were therefore specializations in a horizontal as well as a vertical manner. The extent of this specialization depended upon the volume of the consumption of each kind of meat.

The organization of the corn and corn products trade resembled that of live stock to a considerable degree. The chief differences were introduced by the facts that there was a large exportation abroad both of the raw and the manufactured product, and that corn was consumed in two forms—as bread and as drink. The two forms of consumption created three classes of manufacturers—the miller, the malster, and the brewer or distiller; and each class of manufacturer discharged its products through different middlemen. Not like the crimp and salesman, the Bear Key corn factor sold to four distinct sorts of buyers —the exporting merchant, the wholesaling miller, the wholesaling malster, and the brewer and distiller. The malster was also an exporter. The trade thus had two classes of exporting merchants. It appears that the differentiating element, which worked the higher complexity of the corn and corn products trade, was the variety of manufacture. For there was the same tendency of the businesses to integrate, i.e., of the millers, malsters and distillers to buy from the producers directly rather than through the factors; and for the same reasons apparently—the wide dispersion of production and the variety of routes by which corn came to market. Neglecting the fact that the wholesalers were manufacturers, the corn trade reduced to the simple five-fold type remarked above: the mealman was the exception, being both retailer and wholesaler.

The wool and woolens trade was the most complex in mechanism. The causes of this complexity were many. In the first place, the wool-growing was somewhat sectional: certain districts of England produced greater supplies than others and particular qualities; in the woolens these grades of wool were mixed. Besides certain fine wools were imported from abroad. The manufacturers were localized not only as to kind of cloth produced but also as to process of manufacture; a certain section produced bayes, another kerseys, another Spanish cloths; certain sections specialized in spinning, others in weaving, others in dyeing cloth. This localization of the production of wool and of kinds of cloth and of processes of manufacture rendered the whole kingdom mutually interdependent, required an extensive and complicated mechanism of interchange, and gave origin to many specialized businesses, such as yarn-merchants, wool-staplers, etc. Three contemporary systems of distribution arose—that of the Manchester men, that of the Leeds Market, and that of Blackwell Hall; all three systems had interrelations and used sometimes the same agents for the same or different functions: the Manchester men employed the same retailers, the Leeds factors employed the same wholesalers and merchants and sometimes the same Blackwell factors as were used in the Blackwell Hall system. The western clothier was a phenomenon peculiar to this trade; likewise the Blackwell factor's relations to the other middlemen, since he dealt in both the raw and manufactured ware. A large proportion of the woolens were exported and consequently the merchant played a more important part in woolens than in other trades. The wholesale draper was differentiated from the exporting merchant. There were both an itinerant retailer and a resident retailer—the chapman and the shopkeeper. Some opportunity though not the same degree of advantage as in the corn trade existed for the integration of businesses; and to some extent the clothier did buy wool directly from the grower or yarn from the yarn-merchant and refrain from employing the jobber, stapler and factors. These many circumstances introduced elements which worked very great complexity in the organization of this trade.

Viewing severally the five successive groups of middlemen above remarked, it will be noted that the coal trade lacked the buyer and had instead the fitter who was factor. In the live-stock trade the grazier was not only buyer but fattener, i.e. a sort of producer; whereas in the corn and wool trades the buyers did not improve or change the ware while in their hands. In the wool trade the buyer was eliminated in two of the three methods of marketing.

In the coal trade the ship-master operated in both the domestic and foreign trade, but the cattle drover and jobber, the corn jobber, and the wool jobber and stapler were particularly engaged in the domestic trade. The middleman quality of the drover was ephemeral; he was successively agent of the grazier, middleman, and servant of the salesman. Several middlemen existed in the wool-jobbing group on the basis of source of supply and form of the ware; the foreign wool came through the hands of merchant importers, the domestic through jobbers and staplers; the stapler was also an assorter; the yarn-merchants dealt in a partly-manufactured form of the ware.

The functions of the factors were similar, except that they dealt between different parties. The live-stock salesman sold to a wholesaler-butcher who changed the form of the ware; the crimp sold to a pure wholesaler; the corn factor sold to domestic manufacturing wholesalers and to exporting merchants; the Blackwell factors sold to three classes—purely wholesale drapers, exporting merchants, and domestic manufacturing tradesmen, the clothiers. The Blackwell factors were factors for the Leeds factors, and entertained a double relation to the western clothiers.

The corn wholesale group embraced a variety of manufacturers, differing in this respect from wool which was manufactured either in the household before it passed into the hands of middlemen, or by the clothiers. The malster dealt wholesale with the brewer and also acted as exporting merchant. The differentiation of the woolens draper from the merchant was a specialization peculiar to this trade. There was a greater variety of retailers in the corn trade than in the other trades for the reason that the ware was transformed into a variety of forms in the hands of the manufacturing wholesalers and specialized retailers arose to handle each form.

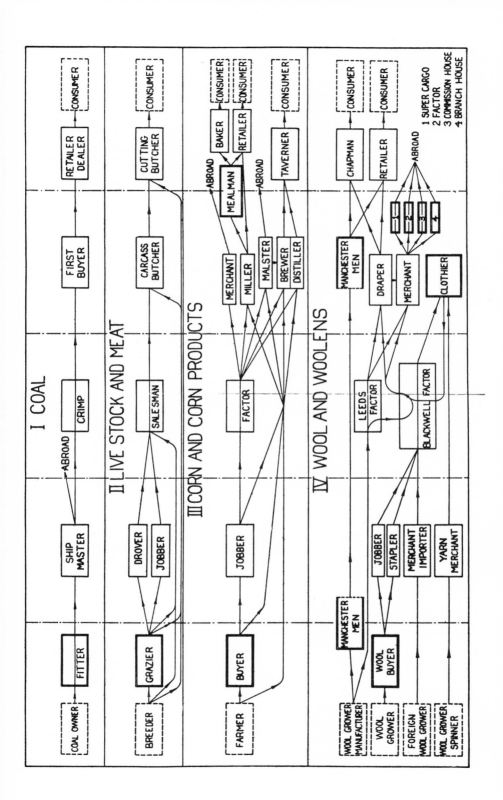

CHAPTER VII.

The Tradesman and the Merchant—The Commercial Population

In the preceding chapters the technique of particular trades has been presented. The middleman organization of the English business world before 1760 has been outlined in four groups of trades, the trades within each group having similar characteristics respectively. The treatment has been specific with respect to the ware handled; the business world was quite arbitrarily separated into these four divisions; and in the last chapter the separation was further emphasized by a summary statement of "contrasts and comparisons." Unless the reader of those chapters consciously guards himself against it, he is likely to think of the business world as actually existing in this disjointed state; whereas it is a unit of interdependent parts. The empire of business is a unitary organism of men having economic, social, political, and other connections. In this last chapter it is proposed to consider more *general* aspects of the middlemen.

The progress of the several wares has been traced in two directions: in the direction of the wholesaler or exporting merchant and in the direction of the consumer. The degree of specialization with respect to wares was, in general, not so marked in the case of either the merchant or the retailer as it was in the case of the intervening handlers: that is, both the merchant (the wholesaler and the exporter) and the retailer tended to handle a variety of goods rather than one particular good. The retailer commonly functioned as *general* grocer, provision dealer, mercer, dry-goods dealer, etc.; and the merchant did not confine himself to a single ware but exported mixed cargoes. This mingling of wares in the stocks of the retailing tradesman and of the exporting merchant tended to bind together the middlemen of the four general groups discussed above. Each group had common interests with the others through these distributors. For this reason, even if it were possible, no particular advantage could be realized by differentiating the cloth merchants, for example, from the merchants dealing in general merchandise; nor the retailer of cloth from the more general dry-goods tradesman. With minor exceptions, the business operations of the specialized and general merchants were alike; and the same was true of the specialized and general tradesmen. What particularity has seemed necessary has been presented in the previous chapters, and the following pages will be devoted to some general considerations with respect to the tradesman and the merchant, or grouped together, to the commercial population.

The history of the concept attaching to the word "merchant" shows that the merchant's relation to the organization of business varied in the several economic stages in the evolution of commerce. The term has continued in use while its concept varied with time and place. Under the Merchant Gild it embraced all in any way concerned with buying and selling, be they craftsmen or shopkeepers.[1] In the Companies of Merchants in the fifteenth and sixteenth centuries[2] it applied to a strictly middleman class who bought to sell again. Thereafter, represented in the Staplers and Merchant Adventurers,[3] it gained the meaning of extensive dealer, wholesale trader, especially those having dealings with foreign countries.[4] The first line of demarcation was drawn to distinguish craftsmen who made marketable commodities from those whose occupation it was to buy and sell such goods, not manufactured or produced by themselves, for profit. This line was traced by the elements that dissolved the Gild Merchant. The second line of demarcation separated the retailer and tradesman from the wholesaler and trader to foreign ports. This line was traced by the very extension of commerce beyond seas and in greater mass. It had become well recognized by 1631, when a writer said, "He is

[1] Ashley, Ec. Hist., I, 80, discusses the character of the merchant in the Merchant Gild; see also Ibid., II, 168, where he shows that the trading class was a fruit of the gilds.

[2] During these centuries "merchant" was used with the modern meaning of exporter and importer. The business of the Ipswich cloth merchants in 1282 appears to have been transmarine: "cloth of Cogeshale, Maldon, Sudbury, and of other clothes that ben bought in the cuntre and comyn into the town in to merchauntz handys for to pass from the cay to the partys of the see." Black Book of the Admir., Rolls Series, II, 187; V. C. H., Suffolk, II, 255. Cf. the following quotations, as listed in the New Dict.: in 1400, Mandeville, XI, 122, "Thidre comethe Merchauntes with Marchandise be See;" in 1513, More, in Grafton. Chron. II, 776, "A wise Marchant neuer aduentureth all his goodes in one ship;" in 1596, Dalrymple, tr., Leslie's Hist. Schtl., IX, 252, "In the meine tyme our Marchantes quha feiret na Ill . . . sayled . . . to France."

[3] The Merchant Adventurers would not admit shopkeepers to join their Company in 1634: Macpherson, II, 381.

[4] Gross, I, 157, points out these three stages.

properly called a Merchant . . . who passeth ouer the Seas
. . . and from thence transports merchandise."[1]

This concept wherein the merchant was conceived as doing a transmarine business carried with it several accessory notions. In the
first place, the merchant might sail the seas as supercargo. The
above-quoted definition holds clearly this content. Other references
might be cited to the same effect.[2] In the early seventeenth century
the merchant had not generally differentiated from the itinerant class
who carried their goods in person; the supercargo was not general.
In the second place, the merchant might have connection with the
ownership and direction of the ships employed. He sometimes was
captain, owner and merchant at once, or he united one of these
functions with that of merchant. During the seventeenth century
particularly, he specialized as merchant resident and used agents as
carriers and buyers and sellers abroad. Thirdly, he might be a member of an association of merchants incorporated by royal or municipal
charter, and engage with his fellows in the organization and dispatch
of trading expeditions and in the establishment of factories and trading stations in foreign lands. He was one of a Company of Merchants
Adventurers. Lastly, he might be dealer with certain countries and
in certain commodities, in some of which he became expert. In other
words, there was a two-fold basis[3] of specialization and classification
developing: (a) the commodity dealt in, and (b) the country dealt
with. There were, for instance, "the marchans of cloth lynnen and
wollen," and the Muscovy and Levant merchants.

But foreign trade was divided into an "active" and a "passive"
class; in the former the English merchants were the initiators, the
undertakers, and conductors of the traffic; in the latter the merchants
of Flanders, of the Italian cities and France brought their wares to
England, established business relations, and carried products away.
The "passive" commerce, among other things, required a wholesaler
or big dealer who in short time and at short notice could dispose of
and fit out whole cargoes. It was equally needful that some big
dealer assemble the wares from and distribute into the interior parts

---

[1] Weever, Auc. Fun. Mon., 341.

[2] See Raleigh, Hist. of World, I, IV, II, Sec. 18, 204 (1614), "Hee . . .
pretending the death of his Marchant besought the French . . . that they
might burie their Marchant in hallowed ground." Ditto (1681), R. Knox, Hist.
Rel. Ceylon, IV, I, 118, "My Father the Captain ordered me with Mr. John
Loveland, Merchant of the Ship, to go on shore." (See New Dict.)

[3] The same classification was the most common in 1747; Campbell, 288.

of the Isle.   The execution of this inland circulation of trade did not fall within the proper province of the merchant who did the maritime branch of wholesale purchases and sales.   It was the particular employment of the tradesman to distribute imports from the metropolis and outports throughout the Kingdom and to collect and convey thither the surplus products for exportation to other distributing points.   During the period under study, this distinction between "merchant" and "tradesman" was (except in Scotland and Northern dialect) well understood.[1]

The merchant's business consisted in four branches—(a) buying and selling for himself or for others on commission, (b) speculating in time and place on merchandise, (c) dealing in money and credit, and (d) insuring goods and ships in transit.[2]   Originally the merchants —the Merchant Adventurers—performed all four.   By 1760 the merchant might do one, two, three, or four, of these businesses at the same time, as might suit his interests.

The tradesmen embraced the wholesalers and retailers of the inland trade.   One set assembled and another dispersed the wares: the movement was toward the merchant and wholesaler on the one hand and toward the consumer on the other.   The collectors were the buyers, jobbers, clothiers, carriers, etc.; the distributors were the warehousekeepers, the shopkeepers, wholesalers and retailers, factors and carriers, etc.   The lines of cleavage for classification of tradesmen were (a) the commodity handled, (b) the manner of sale, (c) the residence of the tradesman, and (d) agency.   For example, there were (a) grocers, mercers, linen and woolen drapers, tobacconists, hosiers, booksellers, etc.; (b) there were wholesalers and retailers; (c) there were London tradesmen, West-of-England clothiers, Manchester Men, Leeds factors, etc.; and (d) there were factors and principals.   Some of the tradesmen were interested in the manufacture of their wares.   Some kept shop, some were itinerant; some were exclusive wholesalers, some mingled wholesaling and retailing; some were carriers of their wares, some depended on others for carriage;

[1] Compare the definitions given by Postlethwayt, Dict., I, in the Dedication (1774) and Defoe, Com. Eng. Tr., I, 2 (1745); II, 207–12, with Roberts, Map of Com., 3 (1638).   In Scotland retail shopkeepers were called merchants.   In 1733 ("Interest of Scotland," 122), "The Business of a retailing shopkeeper, whom we call a Merchant, is to buy Goods in large Quantities from the Merchant, or the Manufacturer, or, by Commission, from their Factors, and to sell them out in small Quantities to the Use for Home-consumpt."   See also Burt, Lett. N. Scotl., (1730), I, 66, and (1798) Monthly Mag., VI, 437 (cited in New Dict.).

[2] Ricard, II, 443; Molloy, De Jure, 419; Defoe, Plan of Eng. Com. (preface), IV.

some dealt coastwise, others made use of land and river carriage. The vast variety of commodities and methods and directions and agents gave an intricacy which only its common-place quality suffered to be unnoticed in the organization of the trade.

To round out the historical and descriptive treatment of the marketing methods before 1760 there are needed yet the operations of the general tradesman and the general merchant, the retailer and the exporter class. For instance in the case of wool and woolens the study of the organization of the middlemen has, on the one hand, carried the woolens into the hands of the merchant exporter. He has been shown to buy his goods in person or by the agency of the factors and packers (a) at Blackwell Hall or (b) at the packer's house, or (c) at the draper's house, or (d) at the Leeds' market, or (e) directly at the clothier's house in the country; and his cargo was put into portable state by the packer. The operations by which he reached the foreign consumer have not been presented. On the other hand, the distribution to the domestic consumer has not been completely followed out: the wholesale or jobbing draper disposed of his cloth to retailers; the business of these general retailers is to be considered. The genesis of these tradesmen was by way of the fair, market, shop, and store.

FAIR AND MARKET.

Throughout this period the chief medium of commerce for the great mass of the population was the weekly market in the market town and the less frequent fair. Taken together these means of exchange did such a volume of business as rendered that done at the shops and stores comparatively unimportant. A major fraction of the goods handled at the latter passed, at one or more stages in their preparation or carriage, through the markets or fairs. But this disparity grew less as the period progressed. At the beginning of the eighteenth century there were permanent, fixed stores and shops only in the considerable towns and cities; a gradual increase obtained in their number, variety and service in the decades following.

England was served by many extensive fairs. The most renowned and greatest was at Stourbridge. Those of Bristol, Exeter, Westchester, and Edinburgh were famous. They were held at various seasons of the year, some having more than one session in that time. The fairs tended to specialize and handle chiefly one commodity. There were fairs for sheep at Weyhill and Burford; for horses at Pancrass; for cattle at Bartholomew, London; for fish at Yarmouth;

for butter at Ipswich; for cheese at Atherston and Chipping-Norton, etc.[1]

The medieval fairs were important events. They represent the occasion of greatest freedom known in medieval economy. In towns, where gild control of trade so dominated economic life at other times, during fair time exchanges and sales might be freely carried on among all the inhabitants, whether gildsmen or not, and strangers and travelling merchants were welcomed for their wares. The presence of chapmen and traders gave the countrymen new opportunities of selling their surplus local produce and of buying goods manufactured outside their neighborhood.[2]

The weekly markets were as widely dispersed as the market towns and their number exceeded the number of the latter, some towns having special markets for particular things. London had about thirty-five public markets besides the many coal-wharves which amounted to markets, though not public.[3] Market privileges were granted by the crown to individuals. The period from 1200 to 1500 covered their most rapid development. Between the dates 1199 and 1483 over 2800 grants of markets and fairs were made and a majority of these during the first seventy-four years.[4] The total number of market towns in England and Wales in 1720 was reported at 758; and in 1741 at 786.[5] This averaged 16 per county. At the first date there were about 1,300,000 houses in England and Wales,[6] consequently each market town supplied on an average 1700 houses or 8500 people (allowing, as usual in that period, five persons to the house). These numbers must be considered only as approximations.

The markets, like the fairs, specialized in certain commodities, and soon became famous for their wares. The cloth market at Leeds has been mentioned;[7] other cloth markets of wide local importance were

[1] An extensive list of fairs is given in the Atlas Mar. et Com., 1728, 112; a weekly list was published in Owen's Weekly Chronicle, 1758, giving location, dates, and goods handled. The most general work on the subject is the large report by the Market Rights and Tolls Commission.

[2] See V. C. H., Hants, V, 417.

[3] See lists in Defoe, Tour, II; 172; Maitland, London, II, 728.

[4] Rew, 46.

[5] Smith, Memoirs of Wool, II, 399; the latter number is gotten by summation of the towns per county as given by Ogilby, Br. Dep. (In 1676 there were 641, according to Speed, 6.)

[6] By a like computation from Ogilby's data.

[7] A traveller in 1777 remarked that "at Leeds the clothing trade . . . may be seen in all its glory," attesting the fact that the market was maintaining itself in the throes of the Industrial Revolution. Mavor, Br. Tours, II, 245.

at Halifax, Norwich and Exeter; the great broadcloth market was Blackwell Hall, London; Shrewsbury was the greatest provision market in the West of England;[1] Cirencester the greatest wool market, outside Stourbridge;[2] Farnham the greatest corn market, after Bearkey and Marklane; Smithfield the greatest cattle and sheep market, etc. In London[3] the largest markets for corn were Bearkey, Marklane and Queenhite; for fish and coal, Billingsgate; for cloth, Blackwell Hall; for meats Leaden Hall, Newgate, Honey Lane, and Fleet Market; for cattle and sheep and horses, Smithfield; for hay Hay Market and Bishop's Gate. Other markets were devoted to more general business and on certain days or in certain sections of the market certain goods were handled. Leaden Hall was a composite market of this sort. It contained three large squares opening into each other and into divers streets. In one square were handled meats, hides, leather, and shoemaker's tools, and Colchester bayes were sold upstairs. In a second square were the fish and provision markets, and the mutton and veal markets. And the third supported four markets, viz. for butter, poultry, bacon and herbs.[4] In all the considerable towns the markets tended toward specialization of ware. In Worcester in 1781 there were a "Corn Market" and "Grass-cross" market for butter, cheese and fruit, and "Beast-market" for cattle.[5] The rural town markets were more likely for general merchandise, especially food. The tolls register, for instance, of Winchcombe in Gloucester in 1327—about the time when markets and fairs were at their best—reports the following in the list of wares coming into town: herrings, sea fish, salmon, cattle, skins, hides, corn, salt, butter, tallow, wax, cheese, pepper, onions, almonds, figs, raisins, cinnamon, wire, coal, lead, pitch, oil, and tar.[6] The list indicates an exchange of local extractive products for exotic goods.

"In certain of the (London in 1419) Markets, such as those of

[1] Defoe, Tour, II, 314.

[2] Ibid., 36; Com. Eng. Tr., II, 192.

[3] "Shall the large mutton smoke upon your boards?
Such, Newgate's copious market best affords.
Wouldst thou with mighty beef augment thy meal?
Seek Leadenhall; St. Jame's sends thee veal;
Thames Street gives cheeses; Covent Garden fruits;
Moorfield old books; and Monmouth Street old suits."

Gay's Trivia, 1716.

[4] For fuller description see Defoe, Tour, II, 173–4.

[5] Nash, Worces., II, App. XCVI.

[6] V. C. H., Glouces., II, 154 n; Landboc, Introd. XXXI.

'Chepe' or 'Westchepe' (Cheapside), and Cornhill . . . the sellers of bread, cheese, poultry, fruit, hides, woolfels, onions, garlic and other small wares, stood in the main road, between the kennels; while in others again, as at Graschirche, and before the Convent of the Friars Minors, at Newgate, the extensive pavements, . . . seem to have been appropriated to the sellers. In other markets, stalls were permanently erected for their convenience, as at the market of St. Nicholas Flesh Shambles, for butchers, . . . and 'Stokkes' Market on the site of the present Mansion House: the stalls in which were appropriated to the fishmongers on fish days, and to the butchers on flesh days."[1] There were no night markets "by reason of (the) . . . great peril of felonies, as well as other trespasses, may in process of time in divers ways arise."[2]

For the marketing of cloth halls were more necessary to protect the ware against the weather. Early in each town's industrial career there was erected a cloth-hall. Colchester had its "Dutch Bay Hall;"[3] Ipswich its "Motehall;" Witney its "Blanket Hall;" London its "Blackwell Hall;" Halifax its "Cloth Hall;" etc. Oswestry had no special hall and the trade in Welsh webbings was confined to one or two streets, the inconvenience of which method was expressed by a writer who complained that the goods had to be sought "in any garret, stable, parlour, or kitchen."[4] In the latter half of the eighteenth century cloth-halls were erected in the north district at Bradford, 1773; "Piece Hall," Colne, 1775; "Tanney Hall," Wakefield, 1776; "Manufacturers' Hall," Halifax, 1779.[5] The Halifax "Manufacturers' Hall" is representative. It consisted of 315 rooms, in three stories, built on three sides of a square. About five-sixths of these rooms were tenanted by Halifax burgesses and the rest by traders from the neighboring towns of West Riding.

These halls and the exchanges therein were under a severe discipline. The very early systems of regulation agree quite exactly with those of the eighteenth century.[6] It was ordered at Ipswich that all fullers and clothiers of that town and country should market their goods at Motehall all on market days on pain of forfeiting every cloth sold outside. At Shrewsbury purchase of undressed cloth was lim-

---

[1] Lib. Alb., I, XLV.

[2] Lib. Cust., XCIX.

[3] V. C. H., Essex, II, 388.

[4] Plymley, Agric. of Shrops, 334.

[5] V. C. H., York, II, 419.

[6] Cf. those of Colchester, 1373, V. C. H., Essex, II, 383, and of Ipswich 1447, V. C. H., Suff., II, 256, and of Halifax, 1779, V. C. H., York, II, 420.

ited to property-holding and tax-paying burgesses; none was to be
bought at markets in Oswestry Pool, or the Marches adjoining; only
the drapers who had served seven years at apprenticeship could buy
and only at specified times.[1]   In Halifax at the ringing of the bell at
ten o'clock each Saturday the merchants buyers were admitted into
"Manufacturers' Hall;" the market lasted two hours.   In the after-
noon a one-hour market was opened in one room for worsted yarn.
Cloth-sellers other than the occupiers were admitted to do business
if they paid one penny per piece sold.[2]   The regulation of Blackwell
Hall has been described.[3]

Born of the medieval theory of town policy and perpetuated by
legislation for the government of markets and against ingrossers, forestallers and regraters, existed a general body of law and custom
designed to thwart the rise and operations of the middleman.   The
most common, as in the case of the cloth-halls, was the prohibition to
buy anywhere but in a market.[4]   If corn, for instance, was not brought
to market the consumer or a middleman would have to seek it from
the producing farmer.   In general it was too troublesome for the
consumer to make a canvass of the rural parts in search of his supply
of corn.   The legislator therefore had the alternative of forcing the
farmer to bring his surplus corn to market himself or to permit an
intermediary to do the marketing.   But to intrust a middleman with
the privilege of engrossing the corn and exacting a profit, which might
be arbitrary, and exorbitant, depending on the people's necessity,
was dangerous to the common weal.   The legislator therefore acted
on the principle that victual being a necessary sustenance for the body
should not be esteemed at the seller's liberty,[5] and required two things,
first, that no one should buy or sell except at open public market on
known days, hours, and place,[6] and secondly, that fixed prices should
be set on all provisions, as by assizes of bread, beer, etc.

It has been said that "the true spirit of this law . . . . was
an intelligent glimpse, but imperfect in several respects."[7]   It rested

---

[1] V. C. H., Shrops., I, 429.

[2] V. C. H., York, II, 420.

[3] Cf. Clothier, above.

[4] For treatment of this prohibition see "Leg. and Com. of Corn," 287 et seq.

[5] Schanz, I, 622, quoting Henry VIII.

[6] Cantillon held it was "*more natural* that Farmers should bring the Produce of
the Land, as being a certain Market or Place to find Vent, than that Chapmen
should go about the Country, where they could not well agree for the purchase of
what they wanted." Cantillon, Analysis, 9.

[7] Leg. and Com. of Corn," 293.

on the general proposition that production, manufactures and commerce only existed for the benefit of the *whole* community—the "poor commons of the realm." The main object of the regulation of the markets was "to promote fair dealing, and to prevent and punish chicanery."[1] It gave publicity of sale and credible witnesses of the transfer of the goods. The hours and places and persons trading were carefully prescribed with this end in view; as were also special pie poudre courts provided. Other less generous ideals moved the legislator, no doubt; for instance, the town dealers were hostile to the intervention of country-buying competitors; and "no trifling part or the town revenue came from fines paid yearly by nonfreemen for the privilege of holding a stall in street or market."[2]

But the principle of the prohibition was defective. It did not prevent the rise of speculator merchants on the public market, and it cramped commerce in places where it would have been useful to the public welfare; pressing needs in local parts could not be expeditiously supplied if large supplies carried by a dealer in ready stock could not be shipped directly and not delayed by passing through a public market; besides the very publicity of considerable purchases on the market caused a fluctuation of price which the merchant would care to conceal or prevent if he were free to buy in private.

The occasion and necessity of fairs and markets obtain where agriculture has progressed but little and population is scattered and sparse. Here continuous trade is impossible and buyers and sellers must arrange a common periodic assemblage. The less frequent assemblages and, at the same time, drawing from a wider area, are fairs. Fairs antedated markets both in origin and decline.[3] They presuppose a slighter intercommunication of regions and a greater local and domestic economic self-sufficiency, than are characteristic of conditions when markets prevail. There are fewer people, having fewer and simpler wants, practically self-sufficing, and separated by want of facilities of transport and travel. Most necessaries of life are produced on the manors; many are bought from one another; so

---

[1] Rew, 48–9.

[2] Green, Town Life, II, 35.

At times the protective policy of the towns was carried to great extremes. There was a severe curtailment of the privileges enjoyed by markets which existed just outside London's bounds, for instance: "They went so far as at one time to prohibit any one from going out of the city for the purpose of buying corn, cattle, or any other merchandise, with the single exception of timber from Southwark." (Munimenta Gildhallae Londoniensis, ed. Riley, Rolls Series, I, pp. LII, 273.

[3] Green, Town Life, II, 25–6.

there is little need for a place of frequent resort for purchase or sale. The exotic supplies can be procured by occasional resort to periodic fairs. For example in Lincoln in the thirteenth and fourteenth centuries about Ingoldmells there were bakers and tipplers on every manor and the tenants bought from one another malt, beans, flour, corn, timber, nails, and divers "marchandise."[1] They bought robes, wine, and the best cloth at Boston Fair. Often times the canons of the abbeys would buy at the fairs as agents for their parishioners.[2] The fair was "superannuated" and "was already falling into a slow decrepitude" in the fifteenth century.[3] It tended toward toys, baubles, knickknacks, and amusements, as it lost, comparatively, its former economic significance and thus perpetuated itself till the present day. The causes of its comparative decline were chiefly the changed social and economic conditions.[4] Population had grown denser per square mile, land[5] and river and coastal traffic had extended, towns had developed, and production increased. The town economy yielded to the regional; the domestic and local self-sufficiency of the former age had grown less pronounced; surplus produce of farm and manufacture moved greater distances. It had become possible for a more frequent or even continuous exchange, which was realized in the weekly or daily market.

But the same changes when developed on a larger and more complete scale tended in turn to superannuate the market. This movement was noticed in the century under study. The result was a gradual transfer of business from the periodic to the continuous market represented in the shops and stores. The advent of these media of commerce premise a volume of trade, and a specialization of industry, and an ease of communication, and a density of population, far greater than was existent in times when fairs and markets featured prominently. Exchange was undergoing a transformation. Producers no longer met consumers. Intermediaries and agents of consumers and producers conducted the exchange and transportation and storage of wares.

Besides the general, many specific agencies operated to effect this transition. It has been shown that the practice of forestalling, in-

---

[1] V. C. H., Lincoln, II, 386.
[2] Whitaker, Craven, 458, 472.
[3] Green, Town Life, 25-6.
[4] See discussion in Cunningham, Growth, I, 451, of the decline of fairs, 1461 to 1485.
[5] Smiles, Lives, I, 191

grossing and regrating increased rapidly, and that the laws against the practice fell into desuetude.   The essayist mourns the decline of the country markets wrought by the ambulant jobbers and ingrossers; places where from one to four hundred loads of corn were wont to come were at that date, 1718, "entirely left off and disused"— and "the Tolls sunk to nothing."[1]   The "Engrossing Farmer" was equally destructive; he reduced the country population; he sent his produce to the larger, more distant markets.   It was prophesied in 1758 that if the then present rate of decline continued for two decades more, "half the shops in the market towns must be shut up."[2]   Sale by use of samples was a great injury to the markets, for it reduced the "concourse of people and horses, and carriage to the place."[3] Fairs became places where orders were taken by wholesale-men who transacted their business "wholly in their Pocket-books, . . . meeting their Chapmen from all parts" and making "up their Accounts, receive(d) Money chiefly in Bills," and took orders.[4]   Such sales at Stourbridge in 1722 were said to "exceed by far the Sales of Goods actually brought to the Fair and deliver'd in Kind."   The London wholesalers, frequently from their customers at the Fair, took orders for £10,000 worth of goods or more per man.   Especially the dealers in heavy goods, "as wholesale grocers, salters, braziers, iron-merchants, wine merchants and the like," did their business in this way.[5]   The fairs thus lost another characteristic feature, the exchange and display of things in kind.

SHOP AND STORE.

The relative decline in the market's importance was accompanied by the relative rise of the shop's and store's.   It has been opined that the licensing of pedlars may have furthered this change.[6]   The disintegration of the household economy made more business necessary. The decay of the insistence on apprenticeship allowed the less active

---

[1] "Essay against Forestallers, 18, 20.

[2] Gent. Mag., 1758: 509.

[3] Defoe, Com. Eng. Tr., II, 183.

[4] Strype commenting on the Great Fire of 1666 said "it was in the long vacation, being that particular time of the year, when many wealthy citizens and tradesmen were wont to be in the country at Fairs and getting in of Debts, and making up accounts with their chapmen."   Besant, Stuart London, 248.

[5] For these operations of the London wholesalemen, see Defoe, Tour, I, 94.

[6] See Chapman, above.

and unskilled to enter the retail business.[1]   The slighter taxes (there
was no tax on stock-in-trade in shops, the taxes being levied on land)[2]
likewise inclined the people to the tradesman's life.   All these general
and particular cases effected the rise of the shop and store in the city,
town, and country village.

The store sprang from the shop and stall.   In 1189 in Fitz-Alwyne's
Assize stalls are mentioned in London.   They appear to have been
wooden frameworks projecting from the gables facing the street and
used as places for the exposure of various articles for sale.   Civic
ordinance limited them to two and a half feet in depth, moveable
and flexible, and varying with the width of the street or lane.[3]   All
the articles sold were very likley made by the artisan displaying them
for sale.   During the next two centuries shops of this kind must have
become usual: ordinances are extant which state the legal position of
women renting shops,[4] and others excluding non-freemen from trading as retailers.[5]   Poles and signs of wine-taverns are mentioned.[6]
But by far the most common method of sale was at market places in
certain portions of the streets.

In Tudor times street criers became common: Besant quotes a
ditty which mentions hucksters of sand, brooms, oysters, cockels,
herrings, straw, kitchen "stuffe," pippins, and cherries, and "pouch-
rings, bootes, and buskings;" some of these were bartered for things,
such as old shoes.[7]   The "shopae" at this date "were probably mere
open rooms on the ground floors, with wide windows, closed with
shutters   .   .   .   these rooms being enlarged, no doubt, in some
instances, by the extra space afforded by the projecting and moveable stalls."   .   .   .   "Seldae, selds, or shealds, are occasionally
mentioned as places for the stowage or sale of goods;" they were
likely large sheds used as warehouses and belonging to the gilds or
richest citizens.[8]   These structures were built irregularly and with
little alignment to the street.[9]

[1] Schmoller, Grundriss, II, 37–38; "Trade of England revived," 28.

[2] Dowell, Taxation, III, 14–15, tells of an effort in 1759 to make shopkeepers
bear a part of the burden of taxation, and how the bill failed through offensive
details contained in it.   A tax was laid in 1785: Macpherson, IV, 72.

[3] Lib. Alb., I, XXXII.

[4] Lib. Alb., I, 205 (III, 39).

[5] Time of 14 Edward II, Lib. Cus., 312.

[6] Lib. Alb., I, LXV.

[7] Besant, Tud. Lon. 198.

[8] Lib. Alb., I, XXXVIII.

[9] Besant, Eighteenth Century London, 126–9.

About 1600 the stalls had become sheds (roofed stalls) with "solars" over them; and then they were becoming enclosed stalls, i.e., shops. The shops were open in the lower part and protected with a shutter or glass which was closed up at night; the upper part was provided with glass windows.[1] Goldsmith's row had "the most beautiful frame of fair houses and shops that be within the walls of London, or elsewhere in England. It containeth in number ten fair dwellings houses and fourteen shops, all in one frame, uniformily builded four stories high, beautiful toward the street with the Goldsmith arms and the likeness of Woodmen."[2] It was "beautiful to behold the glorious appearance of Goldsmiths' shops in the South Row of Cheapside."[3] A German traveler in 1598 said there were "to be seen in this street, as in all others where there are goldsmiths' shops, all sorts of gold and silver vessels exposed to sale, as well as ancient and modern medals, in such quantities as must surprise a man the first time he sees and considers them."[4]

Another very common shop was the tobacconist's. Barnaby Rich in 1614 estimated that there were over 7000 such shops in London.[5] Tobacco was also sold by apothecaries.[6] Paternoster Row was occupied chiefly by mercers, silkmen and lacemen, and shopping was a popular pastime for the women, gentry and nobility.[7] Book-stores were very numerous.[8] Delaney probably gave a picture of his day 1632 when he tells the sightseeing trip his clothiers made in London, as follows: "Now when they were brought into Cheapside, there with great Wonder they beheld the Shops of the Goldsmiths; and on the other Side, the wealthy Mercers, whose Shops shined with all Sorts of coloured Silkes; in Watling-street they viewed the great Number of Drapers; in Saint Martins, Shoemakers; at Saint Nicholas Church, the Flesh Shambles; at the End of the Old Change, the Fish-mongers; in Candleweeke-street, the Weavers."[9] There appears to have been a considerable increase in the number of shops in London in the cen-

---

[1] Besant, Tudor London, 199–200, 191, 276. See description of butchers' shops of fifteenth century in Shrewsbury; Abram, 92–3.

[2] 1598, Stow.

[3] Maitland, I, 301.

[4] Besant, Tudor London, 191, quoting Paul Hentzner.

[5] Rich, Honestie of this Age, 26.

[6] Dekker, Gull's Horn Book, quoted by Fairholt, Tobacco, 49, 56.

[7] Besant, Tud. Lond., 269, 290; Stuart Lond., 251.

[8] Besant, Tud. Lond., 272–3.

[9] Deloney, Thomas, Ch. VI.

tury preceding this date. Stowe ascribed the extravagant spending, of which he complained, to the fact that display windows "made such a show in passengers' eyes, that they could not help gazing on and buying these knickknacks."[1]

The Great Fire in 1666 caused a dispersion of the shops. New streets became shopping districts. Shopkeepers who had erected temporary quarters in these new streets found it convenient to stay here.[2] Suburban shops were also arising quite fast.[3] The specialization of shops according to wares gave a wide variety to the eighteenth century retailing places. On Fleet Street forty-seven kinds were listed: the more numerous were those of the booksellers, goldsmiths, printers, drapers, hatters, and clockmakers.[4] In the coffee-houses auction sales were conducted by the assembled traders. It was the custom of the tradesmen to board their apprentices and assistants.[5]

A foreign shopper in 1715 described the mercer's shops as "perfect gilded theatres," and the mercers as "the sweetest, fairest, nicest, dished-out creatures" with "elegant address and soft speeches;" ushers "completely dressed at the door" bowed to all coaches that passed and handed the ladies out and in. This tendency to cater to the public was so extravagant that this visitor somewhat with disgust pronounced the mercers "the greatest fops in the kingdom." Display of goods was a more important part in retailing than formerly.[6] Defoe in 1745 said it was "a modern custom, and wholly unknown to our ancestors . . . to have tradesmen lay out two-thirds of their fortune in fitting up their shops;" the sum thus spent in decorations, fine shelves, shutters, glass windows, columns. etc., was frequently in excess of £500.[7] The modern principle of display had been caught. The newspaper, which had been but recently begun, gave opportunity for advertisements and the stores published their stocks of goods. These advertisements often took a very modern tone, and they also promoted the adoption of the method of fixed

---

[1] Besant, Stuart London, 195–6.

[2] Ibid., 250–1.

[3] Ibid., 196.

[4] Besant, Eighteenth Century London, 96–8. See list in Campbell, 128–30, 177–8, 199, 200, 202, 215, 283.

[5] Ibid., 249.

[6] Cf. Mantoux, 98, for the opinion that the seventeenth century shop was without windows and display of goods. Citations have been given above showing this was not the general condition.

Defoe, Com. Eng. Tr., Ch. XII.

prices for all comers in the place of higgling always.[1] Another instance of the effort to make display was the vieing of shopkeepers at pushing their bow-windows out into the street, even to the great inconvenience of traffic.[2]

In many respects the smaller shops of 1750 had kept their early characteristics. In a list of nuisances which a reformer proposed to remove and amend are named "Sheds for shops placed against the walls of churches," and "Streets blocked up with sheds and stalls."[3] Not all shops appear to have had glass windows, some were open with a pent-house above.[4] Every shop had its conspicuous and significant signboard. The shopkeeper stood at his door and solicited business from passers-by.[5] Some shops had manufacturing rooms in connection, which furnished part or all the wares.[6] Others bought their wares from many sources, all over England and abroad, and sometimes there was coöperative buying.[7] In 1747 there were 175 trades or different kinds of shops at which things were sold. The trade and the craft continually overlapped. The draper, the grocer, the mercer, the glover, and the hosier had shops which were solely for the sale of goods.[8] By 1791 the Directory adds nearly two hundred trades to the 1747 list. The common retail stores were mostly general stores.[9]

There was and had been a growing distinction between the goods usually handled in shops and those usually handled in markets; in 1695 the shops were reported as wont to handle mercery wares, lace, linen, groceries, confections, hardware, glass and earthenware, cutlery, draperies, etc.,[10] while the markets handled raw produce and materials and provisions. The division turned to a considerable extent on the degree of perishability.[11]

[1] See an advertisement, quite typical, quoted from the "Postboy," 1712–13, of a drygoods and clothing house, mercer and draper, in Martin, Grasshopper, 215. Of course, resort to the files of these old newspapers where accessible gives a more general notion of contemporary methods of advertising. See Sampson, History of Advertising.

[2] Besant, Eighteenth Century London, 90.

[3] Gwyn, Essay on Improvements, quoted in Besant. Eighteenth Century London, 89.

[4] Ibid., 78.

[5] Mantoux, 98; Besant, Tudor London, 273.

[6] Campbell, 177–8, 215.

[7] Ibid., 188.

[8] "General Description of All Trades," 1747, cited in Besant, Eighteenth Century, London, 248.

[9] Campbell, 283; Mantoux, 98.

[10] Maitland, London, I, 499.

[11] Cf. conditions at Worcester; V. C. H., Worces., II, app. XCVI.

Besant has portrayed the daily life of certain tradesmen of the eighteenth century as taken from their diaries. One was Thomas Turner of East Hothley, Kent, a general dealer and storekeeper, who lived from 1728 to 1789. "He was prosperous in his business, . . . read a good deal, . . . was much respected for his knowledge, . . . enjoyed the company of his friends" and drank considerably. Tradesmen were members of several clubs usually and frequenters of the taverns for social purposes. They often had country houses on suburban roads and fitted them up quite elaborately. They sent their children to good schools, and were acceptable in the best society of the country families.[1] Some metropolitan tradesmen encouraged manufactures in the country towns. For example, one Greaves of London fostered the production of tameys and prunellas and various kinds of figured and flowered stuffs of Kidderminster in the period about 1717.[2]

With few exceptions until the thirteenth century no permanent shops were to be found in the country market towns. Commodities were bought and sold almost exclusively at public markets. This was true of Hants in the far south[3] and of Lincoln of the far north.[4] William of Malmesburg (time of Henry I) called Lincoln "an emporium of men coming by land and by sea"[5] and some shops of a more or less permanent character are reported there in 1231–4.[6] In Nottingham at this time practically everybody lived by agriculture. The population was sparse. At Blyth there were fifteen tradesmen, owning on an average about £5 worth of merchandise but they too were engaged in agriculture and sheep farming. In other parts the same conditions prevailed. Tax returns indicate that only about a fifth of the population in 1327–8 had property valued above 10*s.*[7] In Colchester, Essex, the woolmen and clothmen appear to have had some shops during the fourteenth century.[8] During this century also shops and solars arose in Gloucester for a regulation in 1346 prescribed that weavers' looms should stand neither in solars nor in cellars, but only in halls and shops next the road, in sight of the people.[9]

---

[1] See Besant, Eighteenth Century London, 240–45.
[2] Nash, Worces., II, 43.
[3] V. C. H., Hants, V, 417.
[4] V. C. H., Lincoln, II, 386.
[5] R de Hoveden, Rerum Angl. Scriptores post Bedam, 290.
[6] "Final Concords," 245, 259; V. C. H., Linc., II, 386.
[7] V. C. H., Nott. II, 272–3.
[8] V. C. H., Essex, II, 383.
[9] V. C. H., Gloucester, II, 152.

With the rise of manufactures in England it was possible through division of labor to have concentration of population in towns. The denser population and its dependence upon exchanges made permanent country shops possible, though not necessary: a direct barter economy at periodic public markets continued to be the prevailing system. But in the larger towns permanent shops did arise. The gild regulations of the villages deal much with buying and selling in shops. Every master who kept shop or who made a business of buying, wholesale or retail, anything which he did not produce above a certain amount, was constrained to contribute and enroll as a merchant gildsman.[1] In 1650 there were butchers' shops in Wirksworth, Derby. This was a lead-mining town, and in the moot hall (lead-mining court hall) under the court room were built six butchers' stalls and two butchers' shops for rent.[2] Here again the concentration of population and specialization of industry occasioned permanent shops. As in London, the shopkeepers in the country towns confined themselves to distinct streets and the streets were usually named from the predominant occupation.[3] Sometimes they were grouped about or under the churches and public buildings, and the rentals were used for the upkeep of these.[4]

During the period of prosperity following the Restoration shops tended to gain on markets in the ascendency of importance to trade. By 1760 it was said, with much exaggeration, that there were "hardly any markets in our country towns," and that country shopkeepers and hucksters bought of the farmer and sold again at an advanced price.[5] Pococke's characteristic description of a good town contained five elements—"good shops," "manufactures," "considerable markets," "a thorough-fare," and "public houses."[6] The shops are said "to supply the country, the markets and fairs." An example of how necessary a larger population is for the maintenance of permanent stores is cited by the traveler at Lanidlos on the Severn in 1750, "a small poor town, in which most of the shops are kept by the tradesmen of Newtown, and are open'd only by market days, which

---

[1] See regulations at Beverley in sixteenth century; Selden, XIV, 415.

[2] Houghton, Comp. Miner; V. C. H., Derby, II, 339.

[3] For example, at Worcester; Nash, Worces., II, app. XCVI.

[4] Note the above case at Wirksworth; see the illustration at Kendall; Pococke, II, 2.

[4] "Thoughts on Public Reg. Gran.," 33–4.

[5] See, for instance, Pococke, I, Totness, p. 105; Truro, p. 110; II, Kyneton, p. 222; Hereford, p. 227; Badminster, p. 250; Bendley, p. 272; Warwick, p. 284; and Abergaveney, p. 29.

are kept for the sale of meat, bread and cattle."¹ The concentration of the population depended upon the division of labor, the division of labor upon the facilities of transportation. As will be shown elsewhere, the carriage of goods, persons and information was much improved during the century 1660 to 1760. The rise of permanent shops was concomitant and causal to the relative decline of the public market and the travelling merchant and chapmen. Middlemen increased in number and became sedentary.

Retailing and wholesaling were always under close municipal supervision and regulation. Buying to sell again in the same town was permitted to gildsmen alone. The purchase of raw materials, the keeping of wine-taverns, the retailing of certain commodities as cloth, corn, etc., were, likewise, competent only to gildsmen. The qualities of the wares were prescribed and inspectors executed the regulations.² Traders were constrained to contribute to the gild merchant if they made it a business to buy and sell, or dealt, wholesale or retail, in any thing they did not produce themselves. There was usually some sum of money specified as the maximum amount above which a burgess dare not trade without enrolling as a merchant.³ All persons who bought at markets and fairs to sell again retail or wholesale in towns were constrained to be merchant gildsmen.⁴ If the ware was manufactured or converted into new form while in the hands of the middleman he was not necessarily a merchant.⁵ Retailers of cloth paid license fees for setting-up shop.⁶ A frequent regulation was to limit the number of tradesmen per town or commodity. At Lyme Regis about 1600 the purpose of the limitation of the number of tradesmen that had "liberty to use their trade" seems to have been to prevent excessive competition from making too many of them chargeable to the town.⁷ At Woodstock the number of buyers any glover could engage was limited to two, a larger number being dangerous to the competition deemed best for the public market.⁸ All such medieval regulations were gradually discarded and the business of the tradesmen became very free during the seventeenth and eighteenth centuries.

¹ Pococke, II, 20.

² In illustration see Davies, Southampton, 139; V. C. H., Hants, V, 415.

³ Instance Beverley in 1503 with 5m. as the limit and in 1582 £10: Selden, XIV. 81, 90.

⁴ Ibid., 75.

⁵ Ibid., 93.

⁶ Ibid., 100.

⁷ V. C. H., Dorset, II, 249.

⁸ V. C. H., Oxf., II, 257.

The Royal Exchange.

The shops in the Royal Exchange[1] had a peculiar relation to trade and commerce. The celebrated merchant and citizen of London, Sir Thomas Gresham, in 1566, erected at his own expense "a commodious Edifice for the Convenience of Merchants to meet in." At his death he willed a moiety to the corporation of London and a moiety to the Mercers' Company.

The building's interior was laid out in "walks" or paths on either side of which were stalls or shops, the whole forming a sort of bazaar.[2] The merchants of each nation had their particular "walk," e.g. those trading to Italy had the "Italian Walk," where they met each other and the alien Italians who came for business. These "walks" in the second story were sometimes called "pawns," from the German "Bahn," and Dutch "Baan."[3]

At the opening of the exchange in 1570, Gresham rented out the shops to merchants and shopkeepers. They were furnished with the wares peculiar to shops in those days—"mousetraps, bird-cages, shoeing-horns, lanthorns, and Jews' trumps," and the second story was given over to armourers, apothecaries, booksellers, goldsmiths, and glass-sellers. By 1631 these shops had become the elite of the city and were resorted to by "many foreign princes daily to be best served of the best sort."

The Exchange was burned in the Great Fire 1666 and was rebuilt on the former plan. It was a quadrangular building, 203 by 272' feet, and contained 160 shops, 100 being above stairs, besides the "fine vaulted cellars." These shops were renting at £20 and £30 in the first quarter of the eighteenth century,[4] and produced a rental of £4000, "one of ye Richest Spots of ye dimension in ye whole World." These shops were designated by sign-boards, but the "walks" could be distinguished by the costumes of the alien merchants.

The Exchange was primarily a meeting place of merchants and the shops appear to have been a device whose rental paid the expense of

---

[1] For the founding and early history of the Exchange, see Stow, Survey, 202; Maitland, London, I, 256–7, II, 898–902; Howe's edition of Stow, Survey (1631), 869; Wheatley and Cunningham, London, III, 183; Hazlitt, Liv. Cos., 183; Besant, Tudor Lond., 219–2.

[2] For diagram, see Maitland, II, 901. For pictures, see Besant, Stuart London, 197.

[3] Another derivation is from "Pannus" or cloth, commonly pledged on the Exchange.

[4] Obilby, Br. Depicta, 77 (1720). Burgon, II, 513 (1712).

the upkeep. Here the merchants managed, negotiated and began business with one another. It was a great resort for brokers of exchange and of merchandise. The crowd that congregated here was very motley in nationalities and costumes, and was a seething mass of business.[1] The other larger trading cities of England erected buildings of like character and purpose as soon as they acquired a considerable body of merchants and bulk of foreign trade.[2]

FUNCTIONS OF THE MERCHANT AND TRADESMAN.

The world appreciates but little the transcendent advantage it has enjoyed through the agency of the merchant and tradesman. A few observers have at times recognized "The Merchant . . . . as the Life, Spring, and Motion of the trading World," and as giving "Life and Vigour to the whole Machine."[3] Limited locality and ignorance of men and places, as well as pecuniary inability, render manufacturers and farmers incapable, generally, of acting in the additional character of merchants. Their surplus products would perish and decline or fail to arise were it not for a vigilant, active class either devoting their own property, time and abilities to traffic or devoting their time and abilities to the sale and despatch of goods on the accounts of these producers. Commerce consists in the equalization and distribution of surplus goods as between persons in different places and different times. These ends are accomplished by carriage, storage, foresight, communication and exchange. The agents of these acts are the merchants, tradesmen and brokers. Of two persons, or of two places, the one receives a succor which is relatively necessary to it, by exchanging a surplus which is relatively useless to it, against the goods of which it is needy.

These functions may be grouped in two classes. The middleman buys with some distant or future market in view. As far as the future market is the objective one, the business is purely speculative and rests on the control of capital. This dealing in time-markets may be regarded as the "capitalistic" function. But when this future market is also a geographically distant one, a second function is called into

---

[1] Addison was a great lover of the place and has given an exquisite description of the confusion and crowd there during business hours. Spectator, No. 69. The English merchants dressed very soberly. Besant, Tudor London, 197. The reader will find pictures of the dress of the wealthy merchants of London, ibid., 308, taken from a "Collection of Ancient and Modern Dresses, 1772."

[2] At Bristol their exchange was called "Tolsel;" at Newcastle, "Maison-Dieu."

[3] Campbell, 284; Dobbs, Essay on Trade, II, 18.

play, namely, the discovery, study and fostering of that market and the connecting of the local and distant markets. This dealing in place-markets may be called the "connective" function. It is concerned with the methods of business connection and the means and use of communication.

(A). The Connective Function and the Facilities for its Performance.

The merchant developed connections. The status and conditions prevalent in a country with no, or an inactive, merchant class found illustration in Turkey in the eighteenth century. An author in 1728 said the Turks had no course of exchange between the Capital and other parts of the world; that they had no correspondence to the distant parts of the world nor traded with merchants anywhere except such as came immediately and directly to them; that they had no postal system internal or foreign; and that they gave no credit in trade.[1] But the very success of a merchant hinged upon his ability as a "commercant," i.e., his ability to develop connections, relations, organizations and dependencies in the empire of business.[2] English merchants studied the manufactures and methods of foreign lands, studied the wares desired by foreign markets,[3] and introduced these exotic things into the domestic production. The rise of a merchant and tradesman class always preceded that of a manufacturing class.[4] Foreign luxuries became home necessities. The merchant was cosmopolitan, travelled widely, came from his voyages full of new ideas, with new customs, new goods; he initiated wants and a higher scale of living.[5]

This establishment of relations whereby things foreign were got for the surplus of home industries was the most peculiar function of the merchant. He pierced the unknown seas, discovered new realms, set up factories and secured custom in the remote corners of the earth. No less in deed than name was he a "Venturer." He ventured against stiff opposition at home, en route, and abroad. Public opinion was long opposed to him; his foreign wares competed with home wares; he exported bullion; he practiced usury; his profits were condemned as unjustifiable and as the wages of iniquity. Pirates were

---

[1] Atlas Mar. et. Com., 173.

[2] Mantoux explains Boulton's success at exploiting Watt's engine thus. See Mantoux, 89.

[3] Postlethwayt, Dict., s. v. Manufacturers.

[4] Ashley, Ec. Hist., I, 77.

[5] Houghton, Collection, IV, 62–6, discusses the reaction of exotic luxuries on the life of the Kingdom.

teeming on the seas; his craft was warlike but frail; the knowledge and aids of navigation were meager. Abroad he was a suspected stranger, confined to limited quarters and privileges, subject to arbitrary imposition by foreign princes. It was no wonder that any trader who triumphed over the hostility of opinion, seas, and princes, and the risks of distant markets was hailed as an object of national pride, the "loadstar and chief chosen flower" of Albion!

Five methods of marketing abroad were devised by the merchant: (a) travelling merchant, (b) supercargo, (c) factor, (d) foreign resident commission house, and (e) branch house. This is roughly the historical order by which they rose to relative importance.

Supercargo. The earliest merchants either were sea-captains and masters of ships or were merchants who accompanied their goods the cargo of another's ships. As such they attended and did their own buying and selling abroad. The differentiation of the merchant function and the ship-master function, and, further, the ship-owner function was in process during the seventeenth and eighteenth centuries. So long as the practice was for the merchants to accompany their cargoes very strait limitations were thus put to the volume of business that could be done; few voyages could be made in a year; foreign connections had to be made each time; few markets could be reached; business abroad was spasmodic; business at home was interrupted by their going away; and so forth. By reason of such inconveniences a recourse was had to the supercargo.

"Supercargo" is defined as an agent "confined to the sale of goods under direction on some voyage, and it may be the purchase of others, in conformity with the orders his employer may give him."[1] The merchant prepared and shipped the cargo in his own or another's ship and sent a supercargo to conduct the sales abroad; the return cargo was bought, prepared, shipped and accompanied by the supercargo. This system of agency was necessitated in the period before international bills and machinery of exchange had been instituted between the countries trading. For example, in Turkey as late as 1728 the Imperial City had no course of exchange with the outside world; if any merchant bought a cargo of goods at some Mediterranean or Western port he could not remit the money for payment by bills of exchange, but had to send a supercargo with it in the ship to buy, pay for, and bring away the lading.[2] For this reason the first ventures of

---

[1] Beawes, Lex Mer. Red., 43.
[2] For this practice, see Atlas Mer. et Com., 173.

commerce in any new field were generally made by the merchant himself or a supercargo. A good instance is related by Bourne describing the use of supercargoes by the earliest Glasgow tobacco merchants in 1707. In this case the company of merchants sending him appointed the captain of the vessel as supercargo. In later voyages one of the partner merchants acted in this capacity.[1] The supercargo was paid by salary or commission, usually the latter. The East India Company paid its supercargoes 5 per cent for managing their effects.[2] The merchant principal made out an invoice of the goods in the cargo sent; it contained a particularized "account of the whole prime cost and charges attending such merchandizes, for the government of his . . . supercargo, in the sale thereof."[3] The invoice gave assurance to the supercargo that he was disposing of the goods so as to leave a reasonable profit for his principal on the money invested. Oftentimes the merchant would add 10 per cent or 15 per cent to the amount of the bill and obtain thus a greater profit if the supercargo made sale at the higher figure.[4]

A peculiar instance of the use of the supercargo, and, at the same time, of the combination of the functions of the supercargo and factor, occurred in the practice of the South Sea Company in their Assiento "annual Permission Ship." Spain, in the first quarter of the eighteenth century, began to enforce more rigidly her monopoly of trade with her West India colonies. The "English Merchants perceiving that they could not with any safety trade directly to the Spanish West Indies, settled Correspondents at Cadiz, 'and Employed Spanish Factors, to whom they consigned great quantities of our Manufactures, which Factors went in the galleons and sold the said Manufactures, and brought back the returns in their own names, which upon their return to Old Spain, they found means to remit privately to their principals in England."[5] By the treaty of Utrecht the English South Sea Company had permission to send an annual ship to Porto Bello and other West India ports. The supercargo method was begun in 1721, at the instance of Sub-Governor Sir John Eyles, by this Company; in that year their annual Permission Ship was laden with a cargo of £250,000 worth of foods and four supercargoes were dispatched to manage the Company's sales.[6] Two classes of

[1] Bourne, Eng. Mer., 392–3.
[2] Lockyer, 17.
[3] Postlethwayt, Dict., s. v. Factor.
[4] Ibid., s. v. Invoice.
[5] Allen, Essay on Methods, 17.
[6] "An Inquiry into the Misconduct," 7–8.

supercargoes were therefore in use in the West Indies trade; first, those of Cadiz who were resident and native factors of Cadiz, serving English merchant principals, but who were willing to do a clandestine trade to the Spanish West Indies in the capacity of supercargo, apparently for native Cadiz houses but in reality in the employ of English merchants. This class was instituted for the very purpose of evading Spain's restrictions on the West Indies' trade, and they served well their purpose. The other class were those employed directly and openly by the South Sea Company; they were Englishmen and ostensibly did and were sent to do open and honest business, but, although agents of the Company they were implicated in various fraudulent deals in collusion with other officers of the Company both against the Company and against the Spanish traders.[1] The institution of the supercargo method had been designed as a corrective of frauds heretofore committed by the Company's factors against the Company itself; however it opened the way to greater misconduct. The tendency of both classes was, therefore, to further the extravagant smuggling trade in Spanish America, which reached its climax in the "Merchants' War" with Spain in 1739.

The Cadiz supercargoes were in touch with the whole Spanish American trade.[2] Cadiz was the "Embarcardero of the Spanish Indies; from the Port of Cadiz the Galleons and Flota set out and thither they returned again loaden with all the Riches of the Indies."[3]

The French conducted a like commerce through Cadiz.[4] The French did not even discharge their goods at Cadiz but transferred their French ships to the Galleons of Spain. They paid their Cadiz "Correspondents" as commission £8 per pack of merchandise, not a percentage rate on the selling price. In a calculation given for the "annual Permission Ship," 1733, it appears that the annual adventure amounted to £350,000 sterling, of which £20,000 or nearly 6 per cent was paid as commission to the supercargoes, but on the basis of cost of the cargo the commission was 10 per cent.[5]

---

[1] Templeman, South Sea Co.; the whole pamphlet, sixty-two pages, is an exposition of their frauds; "An Inquiry into the Misconduct," is devoted to the same purpose; Anderson, Origin, III, 166.

[2] For an excellent description of the distribution of the goods shipped from Cadiz to Spanish America, see Allen, Essay; Allen had resided for some years in Peru. See also, Anderson, Origin, III, 165.

[3] Allen, 9.

[4] Savary, II, 174–82.

[5] Anderson, Origin, III, 198.

Factor. A factor is a merchant's agent, residing abroad, constituted by letter of attorney, to transact the business of purchasing, selling, transporting, and exchanging, that shall be committed to his care by his principal. A factor differs from a supercargo in the fact that he is resident abroad, whereas the supercargo comes and goes, travelling with cargoes. He differs from a servant in the particulars that he is made by merchants' letters, receives a percentage factorage, is answerable for acts *ultra vires* of his commission, may act for several principals simultaneously, is under the bond, and is responsible personally for goods in his trust, whereas a servant acts without letters of attorney, is paid a salary or wages, serves one master unless directed to serve others by this one, and is more irresponsible. his credit being merged in his master's.[1] Nor are they the same as brokers-of-merchandise, or "courtiers de marchandises," as the French call them. The broker is a local man who facilitates exchange i.e.,, contrives, proposes, makes, and concludes bargains between merchants and merchants, etc. His profession is indispensable to trade and commerce; he studies the mutual wants of merchants and eases their barter. He, like the factor, receives a percentage commission.[2] But he lacks the foreign residence, the financial responsibility, the consignee and other qualities characterizing the factor. Brokers were usually licensed and limited in number;[3] no such restraint was put on factors, and it generally happened that factors employed brokers themselves in their buying and selling in the cities abroad.[4] The factor acted on authority of a letter of attorney, a commission.[5] This determined his rights, powers, and duties. These commissions were either absolute or limited. The former as early as 1682 generally contained these words: "Dispose, do, and deal therein as if it were your own;" which words excused the factor from responsibility if the transaction turned out a loss, the presumption being that he did it for the best and according to his discretion.[6] The merchant

---

[1] For definition, see the following authorities: Hatton, Mer. Mag., 204; Postlethwayt, Dict. s. v. Factor; Beawes, Lex. Mer. Red., 43; Schönberg, II, 237-8.

[2] The business and classifications of brokers are outlined in: Postlethwayt, Dict. s. v. Exchange Broker; Savary, Par. Neg., II, 293-4; Hatton, Mer. Mag., 208; Ricard, I, 71; Schmoller, Grundriss, II, 35; Schoenberg, II, 237-8.

[3] 10 Ric. II, Cap. 1; 8 and 9 Wm. III, Cap. 32; 3 Geo. II, Cap. 3.

[4] See an instance in Davidson, 402, where the factor was to deduct the broker's commission from his own factorage.

[5] See copy of a commission in use during the eighteenth century, in Postlethwayt, Dict., s. v. Factor.

[6] Molloy, de Jure, 421.

sometimes instructed his factor to buy up to a certain amount, and inclosed a "closed end" bill of exchange on a banker.[1] The limited commission bound the factor to buy or sell at or within specified prices, or not at all.[2] The absolute commission was more common and convenient, and increasingly so as commercial honor and worth grew.

The chief functions of the factor were stated in the definition of the term: he cared for the commercial interests of his principal in the port where he resided. The sale of the cargoes consigned to him and the purchase of return cargoes were his prime business; but scarcely less important were the accessory business of insurance, exchange, packing and lading, paying customs, etc., collecting debts due his principal, securing and maintaining the favor of foreign princes and mercantile houses, and the various other business attendant upon foreign negotiation. His functions differed somewhat with the place in which he acted, for instance, at Havana, the sole business of the South Sea factors was to sell slaves and make returns of the ready money received, while at Panama and Porto Bello they had also the care for the collection of debts.[3] A factor was free to serve several merchants principals simultaneously, in which case the risk of his actions was joint.[4] By means of factors the merchants were enabled to negotiate with the whole world without leaving their stores or accounts; by correspondence they learned the relative dearth and abundance of goods in its different parts, and by correspondence the principal directed a consignment of goods from one of his factors to another.[5] The settled residence of the factor in the section in which he operated was a distinct advantage over the supercargo system; he had opportunity for furthering his principal's interests without interruption; his residence gave him credit and clientele as well as better insight into the needs of the people and methods of dealing with them; and in many places he was able to effect political changes in his district highly beneficial to his business.[6]

The pay of a factor was called commission or factorage and was a percentum allowance on the selling and cost prices of the goods sold

[1] Savary, Par. Neg., 286.

[2] Hatton, Mer. Mag., 204.

[3] "Inquiry into Misconduct," 32.

[4] Molloy, De Jure, 422; see also Postlethwayt, Dict., s. v. Factor, for the legal relations between factor and principal.

[5] Savary, Par. Neg., II, 250.

[6] A good instance is Sir Dudley North's activities while at Constantinople; see Bourne, Eng. Mer., 224; North, Lives, II, 375 et seq.

and bought. The rates paid varied with the distance from England, being highest in the West Indies, the Plantations, and the Western world in general, medium in the Levant, and lowest in Holland.[1] Various reasons may be assigned for the higher pay at the farther points, such as (a) the risk due both to the longer course by sea and to the smaller degree of protection afforded by the home government; (b) the less desirable habitation in the outskirts of civilization, and (c) the smaller volume of regular dependable traffic from which commission was to be drawn.

The constant residence of the factors abroad rendered it comparatively easy for them to escape the consequence of their frauds. Distance and the weakness of international law made them more or less irresponsible. The most difficult and, at the same time, important thing in the employ of factors was the consideration of their honor and integrity; and various devices were effected for their control abroad, devices such as the bonds or "caution" into which they entered; the organization of the government of a factory abroad whereby their business was supervised by the governor and board; the prescribed systems of accounting and reporting; the rigid qualifications required of those elected to the position of factor, etc.

But despite all efforts at preventing misconduct and frauds they were prevalent. Some of the more common may be specified. One was effected by marriage to foreign women. This act made them foreign subjects and two evils resulted; they pretended bankruptcy[2] and the goods in their hands were fraudulently paid over to confederates from whom later they were received again; and also upon their death all goods in their hands were seized by the foreign women, as in Turkey, where there was no way of making a written will.[3] For these reasons the merchants and companies wanted only unmarried

---

[1] The following schedules illustrate this point; the first column is taken from Hatton, Mer. Mag., 1712, 207; the second from Postlethwayt, Dict., 1774, s. v. Factorage:

Places	1712 Rates per cent	1774 Rates per cent
Barbadoes, West Indies.....	5	8
Levant....	3	
Italy,...		2½
France, Spain, Portugal, etc.........................	2	2
Hamburg, etc......................................	2	
Holland, etc.......................................	1½	1½

[2] Davidson, 391.

[3] North, Lives, II, 452.

men as factors and regulations were laid to effect this end.[1] The inadequacy of the law of inheritance made it necessary in some places to have the factors act in partnership, so no seizures of goods by local authorities were possible.[2]

Another common fraud was false accounting and reporting to the principal. They stuffed the expense account especially for local hire and customs paid at the port. The selling price and the cost price of the cargoes received and sent were falsified to the factor's profit.[3] By such and other frauds the principal's money was embezzled. No better corrective was found for such misconduct than a prescribed system of accounting and provisions for close inspection of accounts.[4]

A very peculiar fraud was operated by the factors in the Plantations and Colonies of America. It is asserted that here they connived at depreciating the currency during the time they held the goods on hand and made returns to the English merchant on the basis of the cheap currency. Or to procure large business they sold at high prices in consideration of very long credit given, and the returns of exports were never shipped off till after a long period, in which interim the colonists had purposely inflated and depreciated the currency.[5]

Throughout their history the most general evil done by the factors against their principals issued from their practicing the merchant's business in conjunction with that of factor. Possession of goods of their own which they purposed to sell always biased the factors in favor of their own goods; they sold these first or on the best markets to the evident prejudice of the principal. Collusions of various sorts and with various parties were resorted to whereby they heaped the expense of their own merchant business on the account of their principal or engaged in direct competition with them.[6] These abuses were very prevalent among the officers of the East India and other companies. A trader in India wrote in 1711: "All private trade,

[1] North, Lives, II. 452. This sort of regulation was laid by the Scots at Veere, 1630–1649, requiring factors to be unmarried persons, factorage to expire at marriage, and the merchants to be paid all debts due them before the factors dare marry. See Davidson, 398–400.

[2] Dudley North had his brother Montagu join him at Constantinople for this reason; North, Lives, II, 401.

[3] Illustrative examples of these frauds at accounting are given in Savary, Par. Neg., II, 450–2.

[4] For example in 1629, see Davidson, 400–1.

[5] Douglas, Discourse concerning currency, 22, 32–33.

[6] For early practices, 1624, of this kind, see Davidson, 397, quoting from C. R., III, 164–5.

either in Europe or Country ships, has been so long ingrossed by the Company's servants, that they really think they have a right to it at their own rates. The Agent at Ispahan is concerned one-third, the chief of Gombroon one-third, and the rest of the factors of Persia the other third in all investments; so that here's scarce an Englishman in place, will give a true account of the value of goods against his own interest."[1] Against such a general collusion the Company was quite helpless; each factory was managed by Governors and a Council who passed upon all orders, general letters, and monthly accounts, and signed them or ordered the Secretary to sign them.[2] Yet in spite of this elaborate machinery for securing true accounting the abuses of the officers in doing private trade continued notorious, all being interested.

Factors were trained for their work by a practical business apprenticeship. In France they first served a retail tradesman, after which "les garçons facteurs" or "commis" apprenticed themselves to a "negociant" or "marchand grossier" doing a large foreign and domestic business.[3] Having acquired a knowledge of the theory and practices of merchandizing he was held competent to ship as factor. The English laid less exaction or emphasis on apprenticeship, but more on actual experience in foreign fields. For this reason most factors were great travellers in their early years. Henry Gerway,[4] successively a Levant factor, Levant merchant, and Governor of the Levant Company, boasted that he had been "an experienced traveller" and had been "in all parts of Christendom," an invaluable training for his business. Part of this experience abroad was gained in the capacity of supercargo; a voyage gave the candidate opportunity to show his talents and recommend himself to his principal. The South Sea Company practiced a method of grading their servants on the basis of seniority and in this way arrived at their choice of factors.[5] The colonies offered great chance for young merchants who lacked capital of their own; they settled in the colony and received consignments from their friends in England which they sold on commission; having gained a training and a fund of capital they returned to England and set up as merchants to the same colony.[6]

---

[1] Lockyer, Trade in India, 225.

[2] Ibid., 5.

[3] Savary, Par. Neg., 121.

[4] Bourne, Eng. Mer., 222.

[5] "Inquiry into Misconduct and Frauds," 32.

[6] "Trade and Navigation," 100. The dearth of capital in the Colonies was a fundamental reason why sales abroad were more usually done by resident factors than by domestic merchants. See treatment by Craik, Hist. of Com., III, 107.

Commission House. The line of demarkation between factor and commission house cannot be absolutely drawn, because a commission merchant is a factor. A commission house buys and sells in foreign trade, in its own name, for a number of principals a variety of goods, on commission. It receives the goods by consignment from a merchant or manufacturer. It is entrusted with the possessions, control, management, and disposal of the goods sold. It does business in its own name but on the account and at the risk of the principal.

These houses are houses of reputation, capital and credit. They allow the consignor to draw on them for a large per cent of the value of the goods consigned, immediately upon receipt. Such advances require large capital on the part of the consignee. They store the goods, sell them in their own name, and guarantee payments of the accounts to the consignor. They carry out the shipping details, caring for lading, shipping, insurance, commercial papers, etc. They also buy goods upon order from foreign houses, and finance and ship the order, collecting their outlay from the consignee. Their profits arise from the commission paid, interest on their outlay, insurance, profits, etc.[1]

The advantages that are realized by a foreign firm in buying through a commission house are first, that all orders may be forwarded and all payments made to one person instead of dealing with various firms; and that likewise all shipments are received on one bill of lading; and secondly that larger credit is likely to be got from a commission house, it being acquainted with the general condition of trade and having wider banking connections. Ricard declared it to be "le plus advantageux de toutes les branches de commerce."[2] It is equally advantageous for the producer to dispose of his goods through the commission house, for the house carries out the details of shipping and procures lower freight rates on the large bulk shipments than can be had on the small quantities the manufacturer would have to ship; and further the commission house is a home firm whose financial strength is easily investigated, against which suits for the recovery of debts are made according to home laws, whereas if the dealing was done directly by the producer, collections would be made abroad.

The obvious disadvantages engendered in the dealing through the commission house are that the house handles a variety of goods and

---

[1] Description of the business of the commission house may be found in Savary, Par. Neg., II, 130; Mod. Bus., II, 75, 100, 102–5; Schmoller, Grundriss, II, 35–6; Manes, Lehr. Hand., 215, 229, 230.

[2] Ricard, II, 443.

is not specialist in any, and that the house usually wants an exclusive agency for the principal and the granting of this monopoly may result in limiting the market for the principal's goods.

Increasingly during the period under study did the merchants of Europe act mutually as factors for each other, until by 1774 it was asserted to be "the universal custom of Merchants of the highest credit, throughout Europe."[1] The growth of this system depended upon the development of an international reputation for honor, integrity and worth by the merchants. In the early part of the eighteenth century, note was taken of the great number of merchants in London "who were solely maintained by Foreigners in Holland, France and other Nations by Factorage" at $2\frac{1}{2}$ per cent.[2] And in 1747 Campbell[3] said, "Most Merchants are Factors for one another in this" consignment business. These references are indicative of a progress toward confidence and credit among the merchants of the several nations. It became the custom of commerce among these merchants of established reputations to have current and commission accounts constantly between one another, and they consigned to, drew on, remitted to, and sent commissions to, one another by letter.

Thus during the century the foreign connections were developed and extended. The merchants began to differentiate, some serving themselves only, others acted as factors and merchants and still others pursued the pure commission house business. The increase of communication and mutual understanding among the merchants, the specialization of commission merchants, and the very variety of merchants all tended to a larger commerce.

A difference in the method of doing the American business developed along this line, during the century, between London and the outports. The generality of the London merchants became consignees of the American planters and sold their produce on commission; with the proceeds they bought East India goods and English manufactures on commission and shipped them as return cargo. In other words, the Londoner became a pure commission house. But in the ports the merchants continued to carry on their commerce with America on their own accounts, and employed factors in the colonies to buy their

[1] Postlethwayt, Dict., s. v. Factors.

[2] "Letter to Maxwell on the Bank," 11; it was the opinion of the writer of the "British Merchant," XXXVI–XXXVII, that the merchants of England, more than of other nations, did business on their own capital and less as factors.

[3] Campbell, 288.

produce and sell their consignments of East India goods and English wares.[1]

Branch House. A merchant firm may conduct other houses, of like kind, abroad and use these as means of carrying on their foreign business. Such branch houses have distinct advantages which recommend them to modern business. A branch house permits foreign customers to fill orders without delay or the formalities connected with long distance ordering, and to order small quantities; it impresses the customer with a feeling of security in the responsibility of the distant firm; by it mistakes and disputes are easily adjusted and redress effected without delay which a long tedious correspondence entails; and it may carry a limited stock of goods, and quote two prices, one for prompt shipment from the branch, the other for shipment from the home office.[2]

The English merchant made use of the branch house.[3] His sons and servants were trained up in these houses abroad. It was advantageous to have one or more members of the firm live abroad and conduct the branch house; the purchases could be made at first hand and the course of foreign business more successfully provided for.[4] For this reason "the most capital houses of mercantile trade throughout Europe" were generally composed of several partners; either a partner resided abroad, or travelled abroad, "in order to make the better judgment of the credit and fortune of their correspondents, cement ties of commercial friendship with others, and extend their traffic in general."[5]

Conclusions. By these four means of connection, viz., supercargo, factor, commission house, and branch house, the mercantile world was put in close and intimate touch, one part with another. The larger merchants effected a universal correspondence; "universal Merchants" became common.[6] The intensity of mutual interdependence grew apace; the world of commerce became more sensitive, but at the same time its general tenor became more stable and dependable. The

[1] "Increase and Decline of Trade," 31-2.

[2] The above advantages are discussed in Mod. Bus., IX, 108.

[3] See Savary, Par. Neg., II, 525; Defoe, Com. Eng. Tr., I, 164.

[4] Savary, Par. Neg., II, 134; points out the advantages of resident partners at Amsterdam, 1673.

[5] Postlethwayt, Dict., s. v. Mercantile College.

[6] Postlethwayt, Dict., s. v. Invoice; particularizes Sir John Lambert as l'exemple par excellence of business connections and said his mercantile negotiations were almost beyond the pitch of credit, having accounts with every conspicuous merchant of Europe contemporary with him.

operations of business abroad were more easily done; there was a vast economy of time and expense.   The Post Office became a chief avenue of commerce, and dispatch its watchword.   In the more portable and durable commodities a world market was being realized.   The merchant was acceding to a wider empire of business.

The Carriage of Goods, Persons, and Information.

Domestic carriers.   The market area for any commodity varies with the nature of that ware, the extent of the demand for it and its qualities of portability and durability.   But the importance of each of these characteristics is affected by the state of the facilities of communication and transport.   The degree to which these facilities were developed and the degree to which the system of marketing was perfected in organization, in other words, the extent of the market area and the volume of business, depended much upon the initiative of merchant and tradesman.   It has been shown in previous chapters that the middleman rather than the producer or consumer effected the organization of sales before the Industrial Revolution; he was also active in fostering better facilities of transport and communication.

Some of the *connective* features of the *merchant* have been treated under the preceding captions, supercargo, factor, etc.   The corresponding features of the *tradesman* have in part been considered in Chapters II–V.   The development of the vehicles of inland land- and water-carriage, the rise of the turnpike and the canal and canalized river, and kindred topics have received extensive treatment by numerous writers; and are accordingly passed here, although the progress in these different lines was due in no small part to the agency of the tradesman.[1]

The effect of these improvements was to call forth a specialized class of carriers, to reduce the costs of carriage, make possible larger loads, increase the speed of transit, and add to the safety, comfort and convenience of travel and traffic.   It also broke down the local prejudices and customs, travel became less an adventure among unknown peoples, news travelled more quickly, England became more metropolitan, sensitive, united.

The carriers were composed of various elements and were employed by different parties.   The London and Bristol wholesalemen maintained a set of carriers to distribute their goods among their country customers.[2]   Under the old market system the farmers did their own

[1] Illustrated by "Sentiments of a Corn Factor," 10–1.
[2] Atlas Mar. et Com., 14.

carrying to market. A very good description of the method of carriage is given by Henry Best in 1641. The custom was to dispatch a train of eight horse-loads at a time under the charge of two men. A load consisted of two three-bushel sacks of oats. The trip required a long day.[1] A like system of horse-pack carriers was used by the Staffordshire potteries to distribute their products and to bring fuel.[2] The Manchester men employed horse-pack trains in their own charge or in that of their agents.[3] The petty chapmen and travelling merchants were carriers as well as tradesmen.[4]

Carriage by wagon and cart increased as the roads were improved. Wagoners brought wool and cloth to London by regular time-schedules[5] in 1706 and this was spoken of as a "wonted" practice.[6] In 1745 many farmers and others kept teams and carriages for hire to others to bring corn, meal and malt to London, and carry back coal, groceries, wine, salt, iron, cheese, and other heavy goods for the shopkeepers and tradesmen of the country.[7] It was said that there were in London in 1770 a hundred and fifty inns at least for the reception of such commodities and provisions as were brought thither by land in wagons out of the country, and that these returned at stated times with London commodities.[8]

A kind of stage-coach was introduced into London in 1608. This hackney-coach soon acquired a "general and promiscuous use"[9] in the city and spread into the country. By 1685 there had become established a system of stage-coach service between London and important termini scattered over England, and even Edinburgh. Schedules of times and rates were published.[10] Many private parties took up the occupation of common carrier; they owned stage-coaches of their own, had regular places and times of departure and arrival,

[1] Surtees, 33:100. The "cadgers" who carried corn for the millers are treated under that caption in Chapter II.

[2] Meteyard, Wedgewood, I, 267.

[3] Defoe, Tour, I, 94; Com. Eng. Tr., I, 260; Atlas Mar. et Com., 108. For a recent authority see Bourne, Eng. Mer., 354. The Manchester Men are discussed in Chap. V.

[4] See descriptions in Chap. V.

[5] An Act in 1662 prohibited the carriage of wool except by day. 13–14 Chas. II, Cap. 18, Sec. 9.

[6] Haynes, View of the Present, 87, 90–1.

[7] Defoe, Com. Eng. Tr., II, 176.

[8] "New Present State of G. B.," 173.

[9] Rymer, Foedera, XIX, 721. "A Proclamation for the restraint of the multitude and promiscuous uses of coaches about London and Westminster," 1635.

[10] See an extensive advertisement quoted in Sampson, 71.

and sought public patronage by advertising.[1]   The "Stage-coachmen upon the grand roads of England" were derived from and fostered by other trades, such as the innholders, the coach and harness makers, and the licensed coachmen of London.[2]   The rise of the stage-coach was opposed by a large part of the people on the grounds that it would destroy the breed of good horses, destroy good horsemanship, lessen the king's revenues, etc.;[3] but it became the most common means of travel in the eighteenth century.[4]

Post Office.   Another line of carrier activity pushed by the trading classes was the postal service.   The early English Post Office had a political and military origin, but the carriage of mail for private parties was used to help defray the expense of the royal mail.

In 1638 Thomas Withering laid the basis of modern postal systems; his reforms were to provide for the carriage of private letters at fixed rates, to increase the speed of the posts, and to put the Post Office on a successful financial footing.   The Civil Wars worked a general confusion and disorganization of postal carriage.   Under the Commonwealth the Post Office was farmed out.   In 1657 one general Post Office of England was established and put under one Postmaster General nominated and appointed by the Protector for an indefinite term not exceeding eleven years.[5]

The postal system was highly centralized.   London was the point all letters passed.   Rates were imposed in 1660 on the assumption that all letters passed to, from or through London.   A letter, instead of going directly from Bristol to Exeter, 80 miles apart, went first to London and then to Exeter, travelling 300 miles.[6]   In 1661 Bisshopp reported eight "Clerks of the Road"—men who had care of the dispatching of mail by each of the four great Roads—two of the Northern, two of the Chester, two of the Eastern, and two of the Western Road; in 1677 the Kent and the Bristol Roads were added.[7]   Cross-post

---

[1] Sampson, 77, 80, contains exemplary advertisements of their services in 1672–3.   See descriptions of the service in "Grand Concern," 25 et seq.

[2] "Grand Concern," 40.

[3] Ibid., 25 et seq.

[4] The government of London and of England regulated the prices, number of horses, width of tires, size of loads, etc.; see 3–4 W. & M., Cap. 12; 9 Anne, Cap. 18; 5 Geo. I, Cap. 12.

[5] For full account see Hemmeon, 14–24.

[6] Hemmeon, 138–9.   Roads between Dover and Portsmouth, Portsmouth and Salisbury, London and Yarmouth, and London and Carlisle through Lancaster were established in 1652.   See Cal. S. P. Dom., 1652–3: 312.

[7] Tombs, 22; Hemmeon, 27, 101.

roads were introduced in 1696. And in 1711 sub-centers of the postal system were established in Edinburgh, Dublin, New York, the West Indies and other American colonies.[1] The same year the Scotch Post Office, which had been established in 1695, was united with the English under the one London Postmaster General.[2] Packet service to Ireland was started in 1653,[3] to the West Indies in 1702,[4] and that to Holland, France, Flanders and Spain was improved.[5] The mail service in 1691 has been summarized as follows: "On Monday and Thursday letters went to France, Italy, and Spain, on Monday and Friday to the Netherlands, Germany, Sweden, and Denmark. On Tuesday, Thursday, and Saturday, mails left for all parts of England, Scotland, and Ireland, and there was a daily post to Kent and the Downs. Letters arrived in London from all parts of England, Scotland, and Ireland, on Monday, Wednesday, and Friday, from Wales every Monday, and from Kent and the Downs every day."[6]

A most important extension of service was made by the bye-posts and cross-posts. Posts between the market towns and the nearest post towns were called "bye-posts." They were introduced in 1689. The success of the Exeter-Bristol cross-post led to their further establishment by the government and by private individuals.[7] In 1721 Ralph Allen was given a lease of the cross- and bye-posts for seven years at £6000 rental a year;[8] he furnished a thrice-a-week service during the next two decades and a daily service in the east and southwest directions from London after 1741.[9] The most important crosspost was that established in the west of England. Branches from Plymouth, Exeter, Taunton, Bridgewater and Bristol joined and followed the Severn through Gloucester, Worcester, Shrewsbury, Chester, Liverpool, Warrington, Manchester, Bury, Rochdale, Halifax, Leeds, York and Hull. The provision of this road was "to maintain the Correspondence of Merchants and Men of Business, of which

---

[1] Hemmeon, 34; 9 Anne, Cap. 10, Sec. 4.

[2] Ibid., 32, 34.

[3] Cal. S. P. Dom., 1652–3: 312, 449.

[4] Cal. T. P., 1702–7: 64.

[5] A sketch of international postal relations is given in Hemmeon, 111–17.

[6] Hemmeon, 31. A like summary is given, page 38, for the service in 1750; by which date daily mails were provided to the south and midland counties; the service to Ireland, Wales and Scotland, and to the Continent was practically the same.

[7] Cal. T. P., 1657–96: 55; 1697–1702: 56.

[8] Cal. T. B. and P., 1731–4: 539.

[9] Ibid., 1739–41: 449–50.

all this Side of the Island" was full.[1] It afforded the Hull merchants
with a more expeditious advice of the arrival of their ships in the
Channel, and a direct correspondence was made possible between the
dealers, shopkeepers, and manufacturers of these western and nothern
towns; whereas all correspondence heretofore passed tardily through
London and paid double postage.

The tradesmen found several particular uses for the mails besides
their regular correspondence. One was the carriage of certain light
goods by post, such as laces, diamonds, etc.[2] Another was the device
introduced by the Bank of England in 1738 to facilitate the transmission of large sums of money by post called "Bank Post Bills;"[3]
the notes were payable at seven days' sight so that in case the mail
was robbed the parties might have time to stop payment of the bills.
Still another use was the transmission of mercantile papers and bills
receivable and payable.[4] Special forms of assignation or indorsement
were invented to insure against robberies or loss of the mails.[5] Lastly,
a very important usage was the sending of patterns and samples by
mail.[6] It is probable that the franking privilege as it was abused in
the eighteenth century was of itself a considerable inducement for a
merchant to enter public life.[7]

Newspaper. A final method of mercantile communication must be
mentioned, viz., the newspaper. The first *Weekly Newes* appeared in
1621. The first business advertisement in a newspaper dates from 1658.
The rise of the coffee-house into popular favor promoted the newspaper by creating a desire for news; it was the custom, according to a
censor, for "the meanest of shopkeepers and handicrafts" to spend
"whole days in coffee-houses to hear news and talk politicks." The
first daily newspaper was printed in 1702. In spite of a stamp tax,
levied in 1712 and continued, with alterations, for a century and a half,
and ruining the lower class of newspapers, there were printed in London in 1724, the following numbers of newspapers—dailies three, week-
lies five, thrice-a-week seven, thrice-a-week half penny posts three,—
eighteen in all. The first provincial newspaper started in Norwich,
1706, and was followed by York and Leeds in 1720, Manchester 1730

---

[1] Defoe, Tour, III, 72–3.

[2] Cal. T. B. and P., 1731–4: 223, 234, 242.

[3] Bisschop, Rise, 141–2; Gilbart, I, 41, 138.

[4] 12 Chas. II, Cap 35 allowed them to be carried at the same rates as letters.

[5] Some of these methods are given facsimile in Gent. Mag., 1731: 120.

[6] J. H. C., 1745–50: 751–2; 26 Geo. II, Cap. 13. Sec. 7–8.

[7] See sketch of abuses in Hemmeon, 159–67; and in Macaulay's and Lecky's
histories.

and Oxford 1740.[1] The average number of newspapers sold annually in England 1751–1753 was 7,411,757, and in 1760 it was 9,464,790.[2] This was surely a prodigious increase in the circulation of news over what it was a century earlier.

The commercial and business uses of newspapers consisted in diffusing the political events of the day at home and abroad; in communicating consular letters and essays on trade, as well as reports of the markets and the movement of ships; and, lastly, in advertising. The newspapers grew in public influence and political power in this century. They were subsidized by political parties and used as tools of criticism and defense of the administration; while the stamp tax had the effect of purging the newspaper press and confining it to men of substantial character and respectability. Essays on trade are well illustrated in Houghton's Collection, or the articles in the magazines.[3] They are a veritable, though diffuse, mine of economic literature. Houghton's also contains weekly reports of the custom-house, of the imports by the several merchants, of the prices of the stocks on the Exchange, etc. Advertising in newspapers after its start in 1658 made rapid progress. In 1675 a mercury was devoted to "Advertisements Concerning Trade," and was followed in 1679 by a gratuitous sheet of advertisements for "promoting Trade," trusting for profit to the payments for insertions only.[4] The increase in the number and influence of the newspapers improved their value as means of advertising. The advertisements lacked the attractive qualities of the modern type, but related to a wide range of subjects and interests.[5] The 1712 stamp tax also applied to advertisements and checked the number appearing.[6] By the middle of the century advertising in newspapers had become quite the universal practice of the merchant, trading and moneyed classes.[7] In 1745 the *General Advertiser* proved to be "the first successful attempt to depend for support upon the advertisements it contained, thereby creating a new era in the newspaper press. From the very outset its columns were filled with them, between fifty and sixty, regularly classified and separated by

[1] Sampson, 6.

[2] Ibid., 4.

[3] This was the period of the Review, Tatler, Spectator, Freeholder, Gentleman's Magazine, etc.

[4] Sampson, 78–9 puts the dates several years earlier.

[5] The range of advertising is well stated in the various categories named in an advertisement by a publisher in 1675, quoted in Sampson, 79–80.

[6] Sampson, 8, 180.

[7] See Postlethwayt, Dict., s. v. Advertise, Affiche.

rules, appearing in each publication; the advertising page put on for the first time a modern look."[1] The affairs of trade hereafter superseded those of society life as the most numerous branch of advertisements.

Summary and Conclusions. In the foregoing paragraphs effort has been made to demonstrate that between 1660 and 1760 in particular, extensive developments were made in the means of communication and transport; that these means were of increasing service to the trading class; and that they were fostered by this class. Land and water vehicles, by 1760, were larger and some were, in construction, specialized for particular trades. The use of the wagon and stagecoach increased. In the latter part of the period there was a general good-roads movement and a turnpike system was inaugurated. At the same time the canalization of rivers and the digging of canals to connect natural waterways extended the internal navigation of the Kingdom. The charges for carriage fell precipitately. A specialized class of carriers arose, running schedule lines of vehicles, at reduced rates and greater speed, for the transport of travellers and merchandise. The general Post Office was established and extended by byeposts, cross-posts and foreign connections. The rapidity of transportation and the general serviceability of the mails were bettered. The newspaper was founded and arose to what was, considering the age, an immense circulation; it was devoted increasingly to the service of trade. Abroad, the system of agency was developed and the universal merchant became common. The government extended its consular service and took a more vigorous interest in the welfare of foreign trade.

One result of this general progress in communication and transport was to widen the market area. The transport of goods, people and news was the basal and causal element in the expansion of business before 1760. The means of production in workshop and farm were practically unchanged. The increase in the volume of products was in response to the larger market, made possible by better communication, and stimulated by lower prices, larger variety, and suggestive advertisements. But the larger volume of goods passing from producer to consumer wrought not only a greater occasion for the middleman, but also effected a further differentiation of the middleman: branches of the trade which hitherto could not support a specialized agent could now afford a profitable employment for him.

[1] Quoted by Sampson, 191, from some authority not specified.

A second result was to concentrate trade in the most convenient ports and inland markets, and cause a decline in the local market town and fair. London, Bristol, Liverpool and Leeds became wholesale centers, discharging goods to provincial retailers. They also became centers of a more general trade, places of mutual exchange of goods from all parts of the kingdom. The mechanism of trade became most complex at these points, and the larger volume of wares that came thither furthered the complexity by enabling the middlemen to differentiate. Warehouses became a necessary complement to these wholesaling centers; and the capitalistic, speculative middleman played a larger rôle. Factors became a common class seated in the Exchanges of these cities.

A third result was to render commerce more sensitive and more responsive to local or individual needs. Local dearths and surpluses were more readily equalized. Differences in prices were reduced by the fall in the price of carriage. Business arose where none heretofore could exist. More rapid and reliable information about methods of production, markets, changes in price and trade reduced distances practically. Sectionalism and local jealousies and customary self-sufficiency were supplanted by commercial unity. The nation became metropolitan. The business men of the cities controlled the pulse of a trade that flowed to and from all parts of the kingdom.

(B) Capitalistic Function, and the Financial Facilities for its Performance.

This function has been explained to mean dealing in time-markets. It consists in the use of capital and credit instruments as means by which the supply of goods is made to fit the demand. Given a seasonal or erratic supply and a steady demand, or given a steady demand and a seasonal or erratic supply, the equalization of demand and supply requires foresight, storage facilities, organized market, and business capital. The equalization is effected by speculation, insurance, credit, capital. Whether farmer or manufacturer or miner, whether tradesman or merchant, that is, whether producer or middleman essays to equalize supply and demand the possession or control of capital is necessary. In the study of the middleman of the corn, textile, mineral and animal industries in the earlier chapters it was repeatedly shown that the producers did not turn out their products at what times and in what quantities they were needed, and that this adjustment of need and provision was performed by the middleman class. The uses of capital in the possession or control of middlemen are, then, the subject matter of this section.

Capital—its Sources and Distribution. Before the Industrial Revolution the moneyed men were the merchants, the goldsmith-bankers, the tradesmen and the Western clôthiers, but the merchant and not the manufacturer represented the most advanced stage of capitalism. Among the men of commerce capital consisted, for the most part, of large stocks of raw or manufactured goods. They represented the investments of the merchant, who, in the operations of his business, had to be a proprietor of money and credit. During the interim of his purchases and sales his property was hazarded in the fickle balance of commerce. While the goods were in transit or in storage his capital was invested and bound and subjected to the contingencies of carriage, spoliation, and market. But in so far as he equalized the relative supply of the markets, and consequently of prices on the markets, both as between places and as between times, he was performing an invaluable function to consumers and producers. As a capitalist he advanced money to the producer, relieved him from risks, steadied the price, and assured a market; to the consumer he assured a constant supply at a uniform price and to be procured with more ease by him. By the economies he could effect he could pay the producer a higher price, charge the consumer a lower, and as the volume of his business and the rapidity of his returns increased a smaller amount per unit would be taken as his share of the profit, and therefore he would serve producer and consumer the more. This would encourage industries at home by keeping up markets abroad; lower prices would stimulate a larger consumption and a higher standard of living. These were the opportunities which capital afforded to the merchant, and the competition with his fellows was a compellent force pressing him to the service.

It is quite beyond the scope and proportions of this volume to cover with much detail the rise of commercial capital and commercial uses of capital. At various points in the discussions of the activities of particular middlemen some attention has been given to their capitalistic function. Now, in a more general manner, may be presented the rise in the volume of capital handled in commercial transactions, the rise of a specialized class of financial middlemen, and the rise of modern business methods with respect to commercial paper. The capitalistic quality so permeates the middlemen's business that some attention to this phase is required in a treatment of their work. The most characteristic thing of modern industrial and commercial life is the dominant importance of capital and credit. Quite the opposite fact characterized the medieval market system. A momentous transition in the nature of commercial and manufacturing activity was in progress in the two centuries preceding the Industrial Revolution in which event the capitalistic régime was established.

One of the familiar comments of political, financial and economic writers of the period 1660 to 1760 concerned itself with the obvious increase in the volume of material wealth in England. Davenant estimated that about 1688 the average annual increase in the wealth or general stock of England was at least £2,000,000.[1] The same year King put the yearly increase in general at £2,401,200.[2] This increase in stock appeared "in the extensiveness of our traffic abroad, richness of our apparel and household furniture, variety of new manufactures, and in the increase of our cattle, buildings, shipping, plate, jewels,, bullion and ready money, and in the vast stores . . . . of our own native goods, and of foreign commodities."[3] The total stock in 1660 was estimated at £56,000,000 and in 1688 at £88,000,000.[4] This accession of thirty millions in as many years was made in the face of contrary circumstances; the plague and fire of 1665 and 1666, and the Dutch War reduced the increase by twenty millions. It was agreed that the Revolution, the War with France, and the expense of the recoinage cost the nation forty millions of stock and profits, and a couple of decades were required to recuperate the same volume of stock as was held in 1688.[5] The losses during this war fell chiefly on the trading classes, especially the merchants and insurers.[6] However, the Hanoverian establishment created a firm confidence in public faith.[7] Business was sound at bottom though troubled on the surface, and recovered quickly on the conclusion of the war. By 1738 the plenitude of money for investment raised the 3-per cent government funds to a premium.

Geographically this wealth was much concentrated in the counties about London, and the northern counties were relatively poorest, in the seventeenth century. The counties about London also increased

---

[1] Davenant, Works, I, 93–4, 374.

[2] Ibid., II, 184.

[3] Davenent, Works, I, 377.

[4] Ibid., I, 375.

[5] Ibid., II, 277.

[6] Defoe, Projects, 32.

[7] A good test was the subscription of £2,000,000 to the capital of the "General Society," 1698. See Anderson, II, 637–8.

[8] Chalmers, Estimate, 114.

in wealth fastest. These facts are evident from comparisons of the apportioned tax assessments[1] of 1660, 1672, and 1693. The rank of the richest counties during this interim shows some remarkable shifts. Surrey rose from fifteenth to second place; Oxford from sixteenth to eighth; Berks from fourteenth to sixth; and Bucks from ninth to fourth. Suffolk and Kent declined most. The distribution of wealth agreed with the distribution of people,[2] Middlesex being densest and Surrey second.

The commercial and industrial capital accumulated from various sources. Davenant allotted the £2,000,000 annual increase into three parts, £900,000 from the manufactures and home product disposed of in the plantations and the re-exportation of part of the returns; £500,000 from sales on the Continent; and £600,000 from the East India trade.[3] Trade, manufacture and agriculture were the great sources.[4] In each there were prodigious growths. Another source was the English interests in the Spanish plate fleets, both from their contributions towards the charges of these Spanish expeditions[5] and from the piratical successes of English privateers. Foreigners purchased large holdings in English national debt.[6] The Dutch in particular bought up the debt. As Holland declined through losses by wars, the burden of taxation, and the rivalry of other nations, her capital, heretofore invested in commerce, was loaned to foreign states and enterprises.[7] England was also the recipient of much capital by having Irish and colonial absentees reside on her soil, as well as by salaries paid to Englishmen in official capacity in Ireland and the colonies. Calculations made in 1728 put the flow of Irish wealth to England annually at between £400,000 and £622,000.[8] One very lucrative place of invest-

---

[1] Rogers, Ag. and Pr., V, 118–19, see also his Eco. Interp. of Hist., 153–7; the same situation existed in 1736, apparently, for the rate of interest bears, other things being equal, a reciprocal relation to the volume of loanable capital, and at this date the rate was lower in the maritime counties than the inland, and lower in London and vicinity than elsewhere. Allen, Ways and Means, 8–9.

[2] Rogers, Ag. and Pr., V, 78.

[3] Davenant, Works, I, 93–4.

[4] Compare with Gibbin, Ind. in Eng., 304.

[5] Justice, Gen. Treat., 106.

[6] In 1728 they were said to hold seven or eight millions. See "Wealth and Commerce," 4; compare Anderson, III, 318.

[7] See Yeats, Growth, 237–43. The difference in the rates of interest in Holland and England was the attraction. Barbon, Discourse, 85.

[8] Browne, Reflections, 47–8; Dobbs, Trade of Ireland, 51; Prior, List of Absentees, 1–14.

ment was in the Barbadoes' and other West Indies' sugar plantations.[1] Englishmen stocked plantations of their own or loaned freely to resident planters at high rates. The accounts of tradesmen and shopkeepers in England show that they made much money by lending at usury during the sixteenth and seventeenth centuries.[2]

The English merchant was not satisfied with the rate of profit which the Dutch merchant made.[3] The Dutch did a big business for a small profit, the English preferred to do a smaller business at a large profit.[4] English merchants professed "to trade for profit and withdrew from any trade which did not keep up to their standard of profit;" for instance, the Turkey trade declined because the merchants regarded it as not worth pursuing.[5] The English merchant had an opportunity which the Dutch did not, in that he could invest his surplus in land in his native country, whereas the Dutch soil was so limited that the Dutch merchant had to re-invest his earnings in commerce or in enterprise abroad.[6] The large profits of English trade made it very difficult to recruit the army and navy and to supply the colonies with settlers.[7] The standards of gross profits in England had become rated at about 25 per cent, which included the ship's freight and the merchant's expense and net profit: of this 5 per cent was allowed for freight alone.[8] But English merchants in the colonies would not deal for as little profit as they would at London.[9]

It was generally conceded that the merchant should make a greater profit than the prevailing rate of interest, because of bad debts and other risks.[10] The rate of interest, however, in Holland, was until the fourth decade of the eighteenth century from 2 to 3 per cent lower than in England. For instance, in 1722 the following rates were given[11] as the ruling rates for public and private loans:

[1] Houghton Collection, II, 321–3; Legion, Hist. of Barbadoes; Cunningham, Growth, II, 473.

[2] See exposition in Hall, Eliz. Soc., 48–53.

[3] Gent. Mag., 1737: 715.

[4] Culpepper, Plain English, 14; Besant, Tud. Lon., 238; Malyns, Center of the Circle of Commerce; Anderson, Origin, III, 149, 185; cf. Harris, Collection of Voyages.

[5] Horsley, on Maritime Affairs, 30–1.

[6] Culpepper, Plain English, 14.

[7] Defoe, Com. Eng. Tr., 250–1.

[8] "Tracts on Irish Wealth," 56, 59–60; compare with Prior, List of Absentees, 61.

[9] "Letter from a Merchant," 74.

[10] Barbon, Discourse, 32.

[11] Hatton, Comes, Suppl., 3.

	per cent
Italy	3
Holland	3
Barbadoes	10
Ireland	7
Sweden	6
France	7
Spain	10
Scotland	10
Turkey	20
England	5 and 6

This disparity was a marked disadvantage to the English merchant and tradesman, and statesmen sought to remedy it.[1] A common theory was that the commercial rate was determined by the legal rate.[2] The power of the legislature over the rate was a question of much debate. Some caught the truth that trade made low interest, and that legislation would be ineffectual, either lopping off trade or causing evasion.[3] The interests vested in the public debt after the Revolution prevented reductions as far as they could.[4] But the increase of trade, wealth and capital lowered the commercial rate in England to 3 and 4 per cent before 1740, and the English merchant enjoyed more of an equality of competition.[5]

The actual disadvantages under which the English merchant labored during the greater part of the period studied, from this disparity of interest rates, had several direct effects. In the competitive markets the Dutch could undersell the English by the difference in the amount of interest.[6] The higher rate made English merchants do business on a smaller scale,[7] and invest in business which made a

[1] Interest on money was first allowed in 1546, and again in 1571; the maximum rate was 10 per cent. The legal rate was reduced to 8 per cent in 1624, and to 6 per cent in 1651 and 1660, and to 5 per cent in 1714. See 37 Hen. VIII, Cap. 9; 13 Eliz., Cap. 8; 21 Jas. I, Cap. 1; 12 Chas. II, Cap. 13; 12 Anne, Cap. 16; 23 Geo. II, Cap. 1.

[2] Very full discussions of the principles are given in Gent. Mag., 1737: 717–36; 771–788; Dobbs, Essay on Trade, 18–29; Gilbart, 165–170.

[3] North, Discourse, 4, 7–8; Pollexfen, Discourse, 60. Gilbart, 165 thinks there was much propriety and justification in the passage of the early laws fixing the commercial rate of interest. See his reasons.

[4] See Barnard's efforts to reduce the interest on the public debt 1737 and 1750. Bourne, Eng. Mer., 294–5.

[5] Gent. Mag., 1739: 10; "Wealth and Com.," 1; Chalmers, Estimate, 98; Allen, Ways and Means, 9.

[6] Barbon, Discourse, 79.

[7] Culpepper, Plain Eng., 15.

quicker return.[1] The high interest tempted merchants to retire early and become "usuers;"[2] whereas in Holland these experienced merchants continued at commerce to the advantage of the nation. The unequal rates made Holland a storehouse of foreign goods and the site of vast warehouses and an entrepot.[3] The more extensively business was done on credit the greater the advantage of the Dutch who could borrow at three and loan at six in the English market.[4] In those trades particularly in which the margin of profit was small, such as ship-building, fishing and the carrying trade, the difference in the rate of interest worked against the English.[5] Finally, the high rate of interest discouraged the young from entering the mercantile life, since it made it difficult to secure credit enough to start business.[6]

In the middle of the eighteenth century the stock necessary for a graduate apprentice to set up in business as master varied widely with the trade.[7] For instance, a woolen or linen draper required from £1000 to £5000; a mercer, from £1000 to £10,000; a packer, from £300 to £500; a coal-crimp, from £1000 to £10,000; a butcher, from £20 to £100; a brewer, from £2000 to £10,000; and a banker, at least £20,000. To obviate the difficulties young merchants had to meet in securing such provisions of capital, it became common for successful merchants to make bequests, in the trust of gilds, cities, or other foundations, to supply young merchants with loans without interest.[8] Appointments to positions, of tythemasters or tax-collectors were usually turned to pecuniary advantage by the incumbents. The opportunity of turning over the lord's or government's money in half yearly intervals left a considerable sum in the officers' hands the greater part of the time; and it was common for them to use the funds meanwhile in trade. For instance, during the reign of Charles II one John Curtis—a land

---

[1] Barbon, Discourse, 83–4.

[2] Culpepper, Tract against Usurie, 1; Gent. Mag., 1737: 714.

[3] Coke, Discourse, 62; "Way for Enriching," 2, 4; Barbon, Discourse, 81. See discussion under "Corn Merchant," above.

[4] "Abstract of Grievances," 9. The system of long credit introduced by the Blackwell Hall factors induced foreign factors to come and operate in London. Smith, Memoirs, I, 393.

[5] Culpepper, Tract against Usurie, 4; Gent. Mag., 1737: 715.

[6] Gent. Mag., 1737: 734.

[7] See Campbell, 331 et seq. for extensive statistics.

[8] For examples of this sort of bequests see Brand, II, 238. See treatment in Leonard, Early Hist., 233. Other examples are given in V. C. H., Worcester, II, 292; Assoc. Archit. Society, Rep. and Papers, XV, 331; V. C. H., Surrey, II, 346; Manning and Bray, Surrey, I, 76.

reeve by homage—did a large business in lead ore and smelted lead.[1] Many other examples might be cited. The fact that any one who chanced to have capital under his control, given the least opportunity, invariably made mercantile use of it indicates how important a factor capital was to early business when credit facilities were meager.

Commercial Credit. Men of trade and commerce who lacked gold and silver resorted to and developed credit. With minor exceptions the great system of modern credit in the business life of the English people arose in the century before 1760. International exchange, book-credit, promissory notes and a few other representatives of credit had a meager use before 1650, but the real age of credit was inducted by the goldsmith banker during the Civil War and the Puritan régime.

Book-credit was the simplest, earliest, and most general form of credit. Nearly every seller was likely to grant credit of this kind occasionally or customarily to buyers. Traders bought on time rather than borrow money directly at interest; in fact the two practices were alike, except that book-credit usually drew a higher but implicit rate of interest,[2] double or more. Shopkeepers and larger tradesmen and merchants carried running accounts with one another and with their customers. The clothier was a considerable giver and taker of this sort of credit. He bought his materials on time and allowed the cloth merchant or draper time. In 1745, an ordinary clothier was generally owing £4000 or £5000 in debt.[3]

Loans attested by promissory notes were facilitated in two respects about 1700. Greater security was provided by the introduction of fire-insurance.[4] It at once became the practice to refuse to lend money upon houses unless they were first insured; by 1723 it was said that not one in a hundred would lend otherwise.[5] A means of greater security was also procured by the initiation of a system of public registry of deeds, mortgages, and conveyances.[6] The country gentle-

---

[1] V. C. H., Somers, II, 377.

[2] North, Discourse on Trade, 7.

[3] Defoe, Com. Eng. Tr., I, 272.   See chapter on Textiles and Textiles Materials.

[4] After the Great Fire there was much talk of fire insurance.   London started municipal insurance against fire in 1680.   In the last decades of the century joint stock and mutual insurance arose.   See Sharp, London, II, 425–6; Defoe, Projects, 78.

[5] Hatton, Comes, 300.

[6] In 1702, for West Riding, 2–3 Anne, Cap. 4; 1708, for East Riding, 6 Anne, Cap. 25; 1709, for Middlesex, 8 Anne, Cap. 12; and 1735 for North Riding, 8 Geo. II, Cap. 6.

men had suffered many inconveniences and abuses in borrowing
money on their land's security.[1] The passage of this law gave a legal
standing to a registered mortgage which made it sound collateral for
loans.

But the nucleus of modern commercial credit is the bank. Banking
serves commerce and trade extraordinarily. Banks are places of
security for the deposit of money, thus providing against the contingencies of the honesty and ability of servants, and of theft, fire and
loss. Depositors are allowed interest on deposits. The floating idle
credit of the community is collected and employed in large sums to
facilitate trade. The productive capital of the nation is increased,
and economized; its rapidity of circulation is furthered. The bankers
employ their own credit as capital; their note issues. however fictitious
a credit it may be, are a stimulus to trading activity. Banks provide
advances to persons who want to borrow. Those engaged in trade are
enabled to augment their capital and extend their operations and their
wealth. The transmission of money is another benefit performed for
society; the hazards and expense of actual carriage of money are reduced. Banking methods economize the time required in financial
bargaining: the counting and assaying of coins are eliminated. The
tradesman is relieved from the care of presenting and collecting bills
receivable; the custody and care of these are left to the banker. The
standing of a dealer is established by his credit and respectability at
the bank; the banker is the constant referee as to the financial responsibility of commercial houses.

Banking was inaugurated by the goldsmiths. They had long done
a pawnshop business in connection with their smith work.[2] In 1638
Charles I established a register of pawns and sales and allowed fees in
proportion to the size of the loan on the pawn.[3] The pawn-broking
was continued along with their banking business as late as 1690.[4]
About 1645 they became buyers and exporters of bullion.[5] During
this period of insecurity due to the Civil Wars the merchants deposited their cash and plate with the goldsmiths for safe keeping.[6] By

[1] "Grand Concern," 9–11.

[2] Pawnbroker's shops were first opened in England during the reign of Elizabeth
and were known as "Banks for the Relief of Common Necessity," which loaned
money on pledges. Besant, Tud. Lon., 238. There was little borrowing for purposes of trade evidently. Cunningham, Growth, 325.

[3] Royal Charter of London, in Maitland, I, 316, 319.

[4] Price, Handbook, 63.

[5] "Mystery," 4.

[6] Ibid., 3; "Appeal to Caesar," 22, quoted in Martin, Grasshopper, 117–18.

an inducement of four pence a day interest paid on deposits they soon acquired large holdings, and set up "running cashes," making loans to merchants and others for weeks and months and trusting "some to come as fast as others was paid away." By discounting merchant's bills of exchange at high interest they made a considerable profit.[1] They loaned to Cromwell and Charles II; loaned on pawns and bottomry; loaned on "notorious Contracts, or upon personal Securities from Heirs whose Estates" were "in expectancy;"[2] the rates in these cases were exorbitant.[3] The goldsmith bankers were favored by Cromwell and they grew in number and power. Charles II also borrowed heavily from them.[4]

The banking business was checked by the Great Fire and by the Dutch exploit at Chatham.[5] The first commercial panic of English history occurred in 1667.[6] It was repeated in much worse form in 1672 when Charles closed the Exechequer and refused to pay the principal of the bankers' loans. "The whole nation was panic-struck; the bankers stopped payment; few merchants were able to meet their bills they accepted; trade was paralyzed; and the very ships could not be cleared at the custom-house for want of money."[7] The business organization had already become extremely dependent upon credit.

In 1677 the list of all the goldsmiths keeping "Running Cashes" numbered forty-four.[8] From this time to 1690 there was a progressive differentiation between banking, pawn-broking and goldsmithing. Francis Child, "the Father of the Profession," was the first to devote himself exclusively to banking.[9]

It seems that the fundamental purpose or function of banks was the transfer of ownership of money by the assignation of deposits,

---

[1] "Mystery," 4.

[2] Ibid., 5.

[3] Pollexfen, Discourse, 68.

[4] Burnet, I, 204. Charles paid 8 per cent interest. Pepys' diary from 1662 to 1667 contains numerous references to his banker, one Stokes of the "Black Horse." 1662–3, 1/22; 1665–6, 1/10; 1666, 3/30, 7/6, 7/11, 8/13, 8/17, 11/12; 1667, 9/27, 12/16. Edward Backwell was the most eminent goldsmith and banker before 1672, at which date he was ruined. He did business with Charles and many prominent people and companies. He had accounts with all the goldsmiths and acted as a clearing house. Price, Handbook, 3–5, 29.

[5] Pollexfen, Discourse, 73.

[6] Anderson, Origin, II, 483.

[7] Burnet, I, 205 note.

[8] "London Directory, Addition."

[9] Price, Handbook, 27.

"without the danger and trouble of keeping, carrying, or telling it."[1] The original of this was likely the use of safety deposit vaults as depositories for valuables.[2] The goldsmiths performed both these services. They received on deposit gold and silver plate and coin, as well as government tallies, and gave the depositors book credits and notes.[3] The earliest known record of a goldsmiths note issued for an amount of money deposited with him dated from 1667.[4] These were the original of the modern bank-note. The principle of the check and check-system was also devised at this time by the goldsmiths. Loans to goldsmiths for their notes was practically limited to the depositor's needs of running cash; loans for other purposes were generally backed by mortgages.[5] This fact made the rapidity of the circulation of the notes very great. In 1672 it was reported that "the same mony was transmitted nine times in one morning . . . and the mony in specie was left untouched at last."[6] In 1691 North said the goldsmiths held less than one-tenth of their deposits as cash reserve.[7] Nevertheless their notes commanded a premium over the other existing currency.[8] All these facts attest the invaluable service afforded to trade by goldsmith banking.

The goldsmiths made great profits. They never paid more than 6 per cent on deposits, but often charged 20 or 30 per cent for loans.[9] Their very low reserves must have increased this difference immensely. They rapidly accumulated fortunes and became the most influential capitalists.

Throughout the latter half of the seventeenth century there was a growing demand for a commercial bank as an aid to merchants.[10] It appears that the merchants resorted to the goldsmiths with reluctance;[11] but the dispatch of trade forced them, in spite of extensive

---

[1] Hartlib, Essay, 28–9.

[2] Beawes, Lex Mer. Red., 364.

[3] Bisschop, Rise, 62.

[4] Price, Handbook, 41.

[5] Pollexfen, Discourse, 73.

[6] Lewis, Proposals, 2.

[7] North, Discourse, 21.

[8] Hodges, Groans, 13–14; Barbon, Discourse, 19.

[9] Martin, Grasshopper, 117; Price, Handbook, 63.

[10] See writings of Hartlib, Benbridge, Lambe, D'Ouvilly, Houghton, Patterson, Barbon, Chamberlain, Murray, et al.

[11] Barbon, Discourse, 19. The big merchants and dealers appear not to have been the goldsmiths' best customers. Chamberlayne, Several Objections, 18. The bankers solicited the merchants personally on the Royal Exchange for the

losses, to use goldsmiths' notes. In 1653 Hartlib pointed out as defects of the system of banking by the assignation of deposits, as then in use, (a) that it was used by merchants only, (b) that it did not increase the circulation for the volume of currency equalled the volume of silver deposited, and (c) that the accummulation of so much money in one place was a temptation to seizure by the crown.[1] But within the next few decades the first two of these objections were corrected, for all classes began to deposit with the goldsmiths and the circulation was increased by the banknotes backed by small reserves. The latter objection proved too true in 1672. Thereafter, public opinion increasingly favored the projects for a municipal or national bank.

In 1676 there was formulated a plan for a "Bank of Credit" and proposed to the Mayor, Aldermen, and Common Council of London. After several examinations it was undertaken as a project "highly conducing to the general good."[2] It provided for a subscription to a fund under the care and management of trustees chosen by the subscribers; and "many Considerable and Wealthy Inhabitants" subscribed a "Fund more Substantial than any Bank abroad."[3] Subscriptions were paid in kind, e.g., tin, lead, copper, iron, raw silk, wool, cotton, etc. These wares were put in warehouses provided for the purpose, for one year, and substitutions of other goods were allowed during the year. Credit was allowed on such deposits up to two-thirds or three-fourths of their market value, depending on the durability of the goods and the stability of price. This credit was transferable on the books of the "Bank" and redeemable. The depositor paid 6 per cent per annum for the credit, warehousing, salvage and bookkeeping.[4] Thirty-five advantages were particularized which it was expected would be realized from this bank;[5] the fundamental consideration was that "by the help of this Bank" production and trade could be made less subject to stops and starts. The makers and dealers might "deposit their Goods, . . . and by

privilege of keeping their cash. North, Lives, II, 103. Banking was opposed by some prominent merchants on various grounds, not commercial particularly. See North, Lives, III, 148; Anderson, II, 507, 519–20; Child, Discourse, Preface.

[1] Hartlib, Essay, 29.

[2] Houghton, Collection, IV, 145; "England's Interest," 3; Murray, Corp. Cr., 3–4.

[3] "England's Interest," 3; "Bank Credit," 4, names several subscribers "considerable for Reputaion and Estates."

[4] Murray, Corp. Cr., 5–6; "England's Interest," 3–4.

[5] "England's Interest," 6–8.

raising a Credit on their own dead Stock, . . . increase their Trades until they [got] a good Market."[1] It was held that credit to three or four times the value of the goods deposited might be had in this manner by successive deposits. The "Bank" failed in 1683.

It was also frequent for merchants about 1670 to enter into partnerships among themselves and give joint bonds for security to all persons who offered to deposit money with them.[2] With these deposits they ventured in all sorts of undertakings. The above-cited Thompson, for example, dealt in wine and silk, was an interloper in the India trade, traded to Russia, and ventured in mines, Irish manufactures, and international exchange.[3] This firm failed in 1675. The business world had learned a lesson. The charter of the Bank of England prohibited it from trading directly or indirectly.[4] To allow the bank to merchandize would not only lessen the stability of the bank, but permit it to monopolize the trade in what commodities it pleased.[5] It was, however, authorized to make advances on the security of merchandise lodged with it or pledged to it by written documents.[6] This part of the business, it was thought, would furnish a principal source of profit.

The Bank of England was founded in 1694 primarily as a revenue measure[7] to sustain the government of the Revolution in its foreign wars. It was a Whig institution.[8] Its foundation was opposed by the goldsmiths and other private bankers, by the landed interests, and by those jealous of the new king and the purse; and was supported by the Whigs and the commercial interests. Prominent merchants like Godfrey and Herne[9] were zealous supporters of Patterson's new system of banking. Forty merchants subscribed five-twelfths of the loan which formed the corporate fund.[10] The national advantages, advertised as about to accrue from the bank, included the revival and expansion of public credit, the extension of the circulation, and the improvement of commerce.[11]

[1] "Bank-Credits," 6.
[2] "Case of Richard Thompson," 3.
[3] Ibid., 3–4.
[4] H. M., England's Glory, 90, 93; 5 W. & M., Cap. 20, Secs. 27–8.
[5] "Remarks upon the Bank," 18.
[6] 5 W. &. M., Cap. 20, Sec. 28.
[7] 5 W. &. M., Cap. 20.
[8] Rogers, Ec. Int., 214–15; Macaulay, IV, 454–5.
[9] "London Directory," Editor's Introduction, IX.
[10] Lawson, 40.
[11] Macpherson, Annals, III, 660.

The Bank at once became "the very heart of the economic life of the country," and performed invaluable functions with respect to commerce. Not least of these was the separation of the finances of the government from the trading companies.[1] Heretofore trading companies like the East India Company were forced to become financial supports of the government. These sudden and irregular diversions of capital from trade interrupted commerce and caused wide fluctuations in the rate of interest. Hereafter government financing was handled independent of trade.

The Bank added to the available capital of the country and gave wider opportunity for trading on borrowed capital.[2] In conjunction with the reform of the currency in 1696 it corrected the disadvantageous rate of foreign exchange.[3] But it did not perform as many functions as commercial banks might and many extensions of service were suggested,[4] such as advances to importers to pay duties, loans on landed security, etc. By the middle of the eighteenth century, however, it was agreed that the methods of business employed by the Bank of England were more satisfactory to the commercial world than those of any foreign country.[5]

Banking institutions extended themselves very little in the first half of the eighteenth century. The following numbers of banks existed:[6] in 1677, 44; 1738, 21; 1754, 18; 1763, 23; 1736, 21; 1740, 28; 1759, 24; the fluctuations were caused by failures, amalgamations, and foundations.

Country banks were very slow to arise. The first was founded at Gloucester in 1716. It was the only one of its kind as late as 1737. By 1750 there were twelve, and 1772 twenty-four country banks.[7] Their development coincided with the improvement in the means of communication and the development of the North after 1750. The Bank of England made no extension of its business after 1742 except in the immediate vicinity of London, and country banks took the initiative in country financial operations. Some London private banking firms established country connections by delegating a junior

---

[1] See treatment by Scott, III, 199–200.

[2] Cunningham, Growth, II, 442. For contrary opinions by contemporaries, see Defoe, Projects, 46–7, and "Against the continuance," 11–12.

[3] Scott, III, 200–1.

[4] See, for instance, Defoe, Projects, 48–53; and a quotation from London Magazine in Gilbart, II, 35–7.

[5] Beawes, Lex Mer. Red., 365.

[6] See lists in Price, Handbook, 158–161.

[7] Bisschop, Rise, 150.

partner to some provincial town to open a bank in connection with the metropolitan one;[1] but the greater part of the country banks were instituted by merchants and tradesmen to facilitate their business.[2]

Country tradesmen who had frequent correspondence with London found it to their advantage to establish special accounts current with some London firm, for the adjustment of their bills drawn with respect to Londoners. They soon began to accept country bills from their friends and sent them up to London with their own, against their current account. With the multiplication of such services it became profitable for the merchants to deal in internal exchange, paying money for bills and bills for money, and charge for the accommodation. To draw trade to their doors they posted the signboard "Bank:" banking and merchandizing were done together. They had vaults and accepted funds belonging to their customers, for safekeeping. They soon began to employ such funds in their own business and allow interest, as well as lend it out to other parties at better rates. They thus came to buy and sell domestic exchange, receive deposits and make loans, discount bills and notes, and deal in general in commercial paper. As business increased they dropped merchandising.

Meanwhile banking was done in a meager way by other agents. The tax collectors had difficulties in transmitting their moneys to London and held them on hand a while, till they could buy bills from the merchants if possible. Manufacturers paid their employees in scrip or "promises to pay," i. e., a kind of banknote, which became current locally.[3] Some of these merchant bankers were employed as agents of the Scottish banks to distribute their notes, e.g., the Couttses and Campbell and Carr. The traveling merchants gave credits to and took money from their rural customers and charged and allowed interest on such funds. The "Mine Adventurers of England" and

---

[1] Bisschop, Rise, 149.

[2] See discussion of this feature in Bisschop, Rise, 146–8, Phillips, Banks, 9–10, 22–23; Thornton, Paper Cr., 237–8, 241; Lawson, II, 148 et seq. The gist of these references is given in the following paragraph. See also Cunningham, Growth, III, 824; 7 Geo. IV, Cap. 46.

[3] During the seventeenth century "tradesmen's tokens" were frequently issued either by towns or by private tradesmen. Between 1650 and 1700 the Hants towns and villages—at least forty-five—issued them freely; there are over two hundred known kinds. They bore the name and occupation of the issuer. A large majority bear the arms of grocers; others were issued by tallow-chandlers, mercers, vinters, bakers, drapers, brewers, etc. V. C. H., Hants, V, 428. Similar forms of credit tokens were very common in other counties. Nash, Worcester, XC.

the "British Linen Company" did a banking business alongside, or to the exclusion of, their mining, mercantile and manufacturing operations.[1]

The prevalent custom of country merchants assuming the banking function was illustrated in divers businesses. Mansfield was a linen-draper, Cuming a cloth dealer, Alexander a tobacconist, Coutts a corn dealer, etc.[2] The first country bank was the Old Gloucester bank founded by James Wood, a soap and tallow chandler.[3] Another great London banking firm owes its origin to one Smith, a Notting-ham draper, who developed a local banking business, extending to Preston, Hull, Lincoln, and finally London.[4] The Liverpool bankers were originally general merchants, tea-dealers, linen merchants, and one was a watch and clock manufacturer.[5] The first country bank to be regularly established as such was at Newcastle in 1755.[6]

In the light of their mercantile origin, it is apparent that the country banks performed an important service for country industry and trade. Their rise is one phase of the provincializing tendency of English commercial life after 1720. Their services consisted in the ordinary services of commercial banks.[7] They entertained business relations with the London banks and transmitted and received specie. By discounting bills in the industrial sections they supplied capital. In the rural parts they afforded loans for capitalistic agriculture. They afforded accommodation to many classes, but particularly those engaged in commerce. Their very close relation to the industrial and commercial expansion was revealed during the Industrial Revolution, in the first five decades of which the number of country banks rose from twelve to nearly four hundred.

It was alleged in 1689 that the increase in the volume of money in the two previous decades had curtailed the practice of doing business on time.[8] At the same time it was also said that not one-tenth part of the "moneys imployed at interest" were loans to trading people for purposes of trade.[9] Two decades later an observer opined that credit was used in no other trading nations as it was in England and

---

[1] Phillips, Banks, 8; Rep. Com. of H. C., 1710.

[2] Bourne, Eng. Mer., 337.

[3] Ibid., 333; Lawson, 150.

[4] Lawson, 151; Bourne, 333.

[5] Hughes, Liv. Bks., 38, 49–50.

[6] Lawson, 149.

[7] See Thornton, ch. VII; Bisschop, Rise, 156–7.

[8] "Discourse about Trade," pref., 4.

[9] North, Discourse, 6–7.

particularly by the inland traders.[1] And in 1745 it was estimated that two-thirds of the total trade of England was done on credit, and in some trades four-fifths or more.[2] On the basis of such testimonies it appears that from 1690 onward the English tradesman did business on a relatively smaller capital and larger credit. A long chain of credit was introduced into the wool and woolens business by the Blackwell Hall factors. In other trades the same tendency appeared. The recoinage of 1696 and the consequent stability in the value of the currency promoted the use of credit.[3] A century later England suffered a panic and depression of unwonted severity, and financial writers agree that the occasion and cause was the rise of country banks and their large banknote circulation.[4] Manufacturers did most of their business on borrowed capital.[5]

Goods could be held for a rising market by means of credit. Tradesmen borrowed "to shun the precipice of selling."[6] The goldsmiths aided importers by advancing the customs duties, and taking into their care and custody the imported goods until they could be sold. This function was not performed well by the Bank of England.[7] Goods for exportation were bought for credit and repaid by the imports received in exchange; but this sort of trade was hazardous and subject to forced sales abroad and at home.[8] The foreign factors had to trust the purchasers abroad and often bought on time. In the northern trade the division of the year into the summer and winter season forced the giving of six months' credit.[9] The Merchant Adventurers at the beginning of the seventeenth century had forbidden their members to borrow on note or pawn from foreign merchants;[10] and to give credit on sales for longer than six months or offer more than 7 per cent discount for cash payments.[11] By 1650 the merchants of Ipswich allowed their Elbing customers "15 or 18 moneths day of payment for their Clothes," and those of Hull, York and Newcastle

[1] "Vindication," 83, 85.

[2] Defoe, Com. Eng. Tr., I, 274.

[3] A. V., Regulating of the Coin, 5–7. Cf. "Currency in Leeward Islands," 58.

[4] Chalmers, Hist. View, 229; Macpherson, Annals, IV, 266.

[5] Craik, III, 136–9, using as authority the hearings by special committee investigating credit conditions 1793.

[6] Culpepper, Plain English, 8; "Vindication of the Bank," 78.

[7] Defoe, Projects, 51–2.

[8] "Vindication of the Bank," 81–2; "Way for Enriching," 11.

[9] Ricard, I, 388–9; J. B., Interest, of Gt. Br., 17.

[10] Lingelbach, Mer. Ad., 126.

[11] Ibid., XIX.

got "20 dayes or a moneths respite" in their purchases abroad.[1] The English sugar merchants loaned to the planters at a lower rate than could be procured in the West Indies, and thus gained such an economic control over them as to force their trade to English ports.[2] The English had a similar dominion over the Portugese trade by keeping the merchants of that country constantly in debt to them to the amount of 2,500,000 reis.[3]

Another common use of credit was to increase the stock of young merchants and tradesman as they started in business.   It was almost impossible for a young man without capital to get a start except by borrowing.   In Scotland a system of "cash credits" was developed for this purpose.[4]   The increase of stock by credit, or the doing of business on borrowed funds, made business more speculative,[5]   but was the basis for a great increase in the volume of trade done.[6]   The Bank of England did not accomodate the small tradesman as much as was designed in this respect,[7] and the business was done by private bankers.

Another and most important use of credit is the transmission of money.   To the merchant and trading class this service has become a thing indispensable in their business activity.   The development of the transmission of money depended upon the amount of this kind of business done.   Exchange did not give rise to trade, but trade gave rise to exchange; after trade was established, however, the introduction of exchange extended trade.   To the degree that English commerce, foreign and domestic, increased in any period it may be assumed that exchange, after it was originated, increased.

Exchange is the most intricate part of commerce—"the greatest and weightiest Mystery that is found in the whole Map of Trade."[8] Yet it was introduced into English foreign commerce in the early days while its volume was small.   Bills of exchange were apparently introduced from abroad before the fifteenth century.[9]   The Merchant

---

[1] "Way for Enriching," 11–12.

[2] "State of the Sugar Trade," 6, 14.

[3] Beawes, Lex Mer. Red., 624.

[4] See advantages pointed out by Hume, Essays, I, 339.

[5] "Vindication of the Bank," 85.

[6] Defoe, Com. Eng. Tr., I, 267-8; H. M., Eng. Glory, 27, 65; "Credit of our Government," 4.

[7] Defoe, Projects, 47; "Reasons of the Decay," 15–6.

[8] Scarlett, Stile, preface.

[9] Cf. Lawson, 23–4. The various operations of the exchange business of the Mérchants of the Staple are illustrated in the Cely Letters between 1475–88.

Adventurers employed foreign exchange at the opening of that century, and enacted strict regulations for its conduct. A stringent ordinance enforced, under severe penalties, the due payment of bills of exchange.[1] All bills had to be drawn on the staple town and there only.[2] A maximum rate of exchange was prescribed.[3] In 1638 it was observed that a specialized class[4] was arising who "in many places" found "the excellence" of "the art and mysterie" of exchange "more profitable and beneficial" than "the art of Merchandizing it selfe."[5] At that time the "Exchanges practised in England, and principally in London" were "but as a Rivolet issuing out of the great streame of those Exchanges that" were "used beyond the Seas," and "limited but to some few places, as to Antwerpe for Flanders, to Roven and Paris for France, to Amsterdam and Rotterdam for the Netherlands, to Dansicke for the East Country, to Venice for Italie, to Edenburgh for Scotland, to Dublin for Ireland," and all other parts were reached by secondary exchanges from these centers.[6] By 1682 it was pronounced so necessary an appendix to commerce "that without it Trade (could) scarcely subsist, . . . the soul and life . . . the very Essence of all Commerce."[7]

The reasons for this rapid extension were (a) primarily its usefulness in transmitting money, (b) its facilitation of usurious contracts and the evasion of the laws against usury,[8] (c) its being a ready means of procuring credit and tiding accounts,[9] (d) the favor of princes who wanted to stay the outward flow of specie,[10] and (e) its employment as a way of shifting the risks in shipping.[11]

Attention is called to the following pages which contain points illustrative of these operations: XIII, 3, 15, 17, 18, 25, 34, 45. The letters are replete with such data.

[1] Lingelbach, Mer. Ad., 117.

[2] Ibid., 54, 109.

[3] Ibid., 109.

[4] Cf. 2 Jas. I, Cap. 21.

[5] Roberts, Map. 47.

[6] Ibid., 256. See Scarlett, Stile, 364 et seq. for a list of countries and cities with which London did exchange business in 1682.

[7] Scarlett, Stile, pref.; a like statement in Savary, Par. Neg., 127 (1679).

[8] Beawes, Lex Mer. Red., 412; Scarlett, Stile, pref.; Robinson, Eng. Saf., 38–9.

[9] See discussion of dry exchange in Beawes, Lex Mer. Red., 413–452, and Savary, Par. Neg., 236–242; Ricard, I, 202, and "State of the Pub. Cr.," 7, contains special instances of this means of raising credit.

[10] Beawes, Lex Mer. Red., 411; Savary, Par. Neg., 127.

[11] Scarlett, Stile, 251, 253.

London from the first was the center of exchange with respect to the Isles.[1] During the last century under study the financial center of Europe tended to shift from Amsterdam to London, but at the close of the eighteenth century Amsterdam was still paramount.[2] Many Dutch Jews had migrated to London and brought along their business of exporting and importing specie and of exchange.[3]

The banks of London took care of all bills made payable at the banks, or in London and indorsed to the banks and deposited with them.[4] This relieved the merchants from much business detail. Another agency, which antedated the banks,[5] and which was of marked assistance to the merchants in procuring and selling exchange, was the brokers.[6] Brokers of merchandise contrived, made and concluded bargains and contracts between the merchants English and merchants strangers. In the early seventeenth century they began to negotiate exchanges.[7] The Lombards and goldsmiths did likewise. Brokers of exchange were defined by Scarlett as "Persons . . . to inquire of Persons that have any monyes to remit or to draw, and to agree such persons concerning the Conditions."[8] Because they lent themselves to usurious bargaining they were at first rather disreputable, but by the middle of the eighteenth century they had established themselves as a "considerable Body of Men and of vast Credit" and the word of some would "pass upon the 'Change for some Hundreds of Thousands."[9] Their particular service to commerce was to reduce the rate of exchange below what it would be if merchants were to transact the business directly with one another; for, being interested in concealing their transactions from one another, they could not so well understand the situation of the market.[10] The number of brokers on the Royal Exchange was unlimited and their

---

[1] Roberts, Map, 256; Scarlett, Stile, 363; Justice, Gen. Tr., 90; Browne, Appeal, 15; La Touche, Letters, 5; "Interest of Scot," 100; Defoe, Com. Eng. Tr., I, 282–5; Bisschop, Rise, 31–6, 43, 68–138, 139–40.

[2] Ricard, I, 199.

[4] "Further Considerations," 47–8.

[3] Beawes, Lex Mer. Red., 363–4.

[5] 2 Jas. I, Cap. 21.

[6] At the opening of the fifteenth century ordinances were laid against fraudulent brokers of exchange. Lib. Alb., I, 368.

[7] 2 Jas. I, Cap. 21, Sec. 1; Roberts, Map, 47.

[8] Scarlett, Stile, 8.

[9] Cf. Liber Albus, III, 145 with Campbell, 296, for social position of brokers.

[10] Alldridge, Uni. Mer., 93, 125–6, 199–200; Lawson, 28.

bidding for business competitive, but they were licensed by the government and put under bond.[1] Their brokerage in the middle of the period ranged from one-quarter to one per cent;[2] the settlement of the Dutch Jews in London had the effect of reducing the rates.[3] Foreign bills of exchange were from their very beginning the most binding and most effectual paper-security in use amongst merchants.[4] They derived their force, not from statutory law, but from the general practice and consent of merchants. A sort of recognized universal law of exchange rendered them the most obligatory commercial paper. The obligation of inland bills of exchange depended more upon legislative enactments.[5] In England the common law did not fully accord foreign bills that high regard which they enjoyed abroad and in 1755 it was said to be no extraordinary thing to see merchants at law for a year or two about the payment of exchange.[6] The most advantageous form of bills of debt was the bill of dry-exchange (cambia sicca), and it was used much in the seventeenth century by merchants. It contained no mention of the sum loaned, only of the sum to be paid, and therefore lent itself to usury. The sum was to be repaid at a certain time and place, and, if not paid punctually, it, being a bill of exchange, had preference before all other papers. It was negotiable.[7] There was, therefore, a legal reason for the rapid rise of foreign exchange in the century studied, i.e., *foreign* bills were drawn for use in the *domestic* trade because of their good quality as commercial paper.

Beyond doubt, the dangers besetting the carrying of money on English roads promoted the rise of inland exchange.[8] The rise of banks, especially country banks, aided the transmission of money: they transmitted money by means of agencies, branches, and the circulation of their notes. The country banker kept a reserve with his London correspondent against which and into which bills were drawn. London firms established branch banks in the country and made use of their common fund to receive or pay out at either main

---

[1] Beawes, Lex Mer. Red., 455; Postlethwayt, Dict., s. v. Royal Exchange, Broker; Scarlett, Stile, 10; Justice, Gen. Tr., 19; 8–9 Wm. III, Cap. 32.

[2] Justice, Gen. Tr., 28.

[3] "Further Considerations," 50–1.

[4] Scarlett, Stile, 266 et seq.; Justice, Gen. Tr., 66; Hewitt, Treatise, 44.

[5] Forbes, Bills, 2–3.

[6] Hewitt, Treatise, 44–5.

[7] Scarlett, Stile, 266 et seq.; see Molloy, De Jure 287, for negotiability.

[8] H. M., Eng. Glory, 11–12.

or branch bank.[1]   If a bank had credit for its notes over a wide area, money could be transmitted by these notes within that area.   For safety the notes were often cut into two parts, one of which was held until the receipt of the other was acknowledged.   Bank-post bills drawn at seven days sight performed the same function.

After 1697 inland bills of exchange enjoyed all the power and validity of the most formal commercial instrument.   At the same time they were the most easily negotiated and transmitted.   No cumbrous deeds, lawyers, witnesses, or special securities were attached or required.   Their security increased with every indorsement. They were used to transfer debts; to provide extra credit; to fix the time and conditions of the payment of a debt in a form least apt to litigation; and to afford an easy way of giving a guarantee.   They were drawn by the wholesalers upon retailers, by producers or manufacturers upon wholesalers, by retailers upon consumers, and against consignee factors.[2]

Inland exchange promoted commerce in two ways: (a) it reduced the price of goods indirectly by reducing the cost of conveying back the money received in return.   This reduction exceeded the simple cost of carriage by the amount of the premium to cover the risks of transporting specie.   The cost of bringing back this money must be regarded as a part of the cost of production, and in that way influenced price.   (b) It increased the rapidity of the circulation of capital. Payment could be realized at once by discounting bills received drawn on the consignee and further business be done while the consignment was in transit; otherwise, in the interim of transit of the consignment and of the return money business would suffer a lapse.

Inland bills were not properly supported by law till the enactments of William and Anne.[3]   These acts were forced by the exigencies of commerce, for inland bills had lost their force and were not punctually and regularly paid.[4]   English tradesmen had long suffered from the weakness of their law for the transference of bills of debt,[5] and put forward strong arguments for making all bills of debt assignable,[6] as

[1] Inland exchange was done with difficulty before country banks arose; see Cary, Discourse, 28–9 and Essay on Nat. Cr., 173. See examples of drafts drawn by provincial manufacturers on London bankers about 1690, in V. C. H., Durham, II, 315–6.

[2] See Defoe, Com. Eng. Tr., I, 278–82.

[3] 9–10 Wm. III, Cap. 17; 3–4 Anne, Cap. 9; 7 Anne, Cap. 25.

[4] Forbes, Bills, 170; Justice, Gen. Tr., 67–73.

[5] Child, Brief Observations, 2.

[6] For example, see "Grand Concern," 56–8; Pollexfen, Discourse, 66.

an aid to the conduct of business. Relief was given to bills of exchange in 1698, when the law defined a way for protesting bills.[1] In 1704 promissory notes were made assignable by indorsement and given the same legal standing as bills of exchange. The old question, whether bills of exchange and promissory notes were assignable or indorsable over, within the custom of merchants, to any other person, or whether the person to whom a bill or note was payable or to whom such bill or note was assigned could maintain an action against the person who first made or assigned it, was definitely determined in the affirmative. This legislation was of infinite value to the rising commerce of the eighteenth century.

Another financial means which served the merchant's needs in the line of credit and security was marine insurance. A statute, the first bearing upon the subject of insurance, dated 1601, declared in its enacting clause that the insurance of ships and cargoes had "been Time out of Mind an Usage amongst Merchants, both of this Realm and of foreign Nations."[2] This act established a court "for the hearinge and determynynge of causes arisinge from policies of assurance." The court was a failure from defects in its composition.[3] The 1601 statute mentions an "Office of Assurances within the City of London" in which the business seems to have been concentrated and policies of insurance registered. Brokers of insurance existed at this date, "concerned . . . in the Writing of Insurances and Policies" and having "Dwellings near the Exchange." The institution of coffee-houses was a great convenience to underwriters; "Hains," "Garraway," "Thomas Good" and "Lloyd's" were particularly used by the mercantile classes; although the "Insurance Office" at the Royal Exchange remained the headquarters until the eighteenth century.

The seventeenth century witnessed the specialization of a class of underwriters who made insurance their sole business. Heretofore marine insurance was done as a part of the general mercantile and financial business of merchants or goldsmiths. The merchants did a sort of mutual insurance of each other's ships and felt an obligation "in honor" as a "generous Merchant" to assist "Ensuring of others, . . . the Premio running reasonable."[4] Some merchants continued

---

[1] The act was strengthened by 3–4 Anne, Cap. 9, with respect to non-accepted bills.

[2] 43 Eliz., Cap. 12.

[3] 13–14 Chas. II, Cap. 23, Sec. 1.

[4] Molloy, De Jure, 297.

to do this sort of mutual insurance alongside the specialized under-writers.[1]

There were two classes of specialized underwriters—the private and the public. The former were unincorporated, had private offices, and if their contracts were registered at all it was in these offices. The latter were members of the two great insurance companies and their policies were registered in due form in a public office, as at the Royal Exchange.[2] In 1720 charters were issued to two marine insurance companies giving them the exclusive privilege of insuring with respect to other companies but not exclusive with respect to private persons.[3] The companies were one phase of the speculative mania of the day and were the saner representatives of about a hundred insurance projects brought forward. Their incorporation was opposed by the private underwriters, but in vain; in the end it proved a great benefit to them by protecting them from the possible competition of many marine insurance companies.

A coffee-house proprietor named Lloyd established a newspaper for his patrons in 1696. It was published thrice a week and contained news from the various ports at home and abroad relative to shipping. "Lloyd's News"[4] during the six months of its existence was a medium of communication for merchants, captains, shippers, and under-writers. It was suppressed by the government, and seems to have been succeeded by "news-letters" furnishing shipping and commercial intelligence to the guests at Lloyd's. These were either passed from hand to hand or were read from a "pulpit." Meanwhile this hostelry was becoming the center of all manner of maritime business. In 1726 "Lloyd's List"[5] began to be published, and the underwriters developed a special intelligence department of their own. The "List" contained the rates of London exchange on foreign markets, the current prices of stocks and funds, a tide-table, news of the arrival and departure and accidents of ships, both foreign and domestic, etc. Such news was of first importance to merchants and underwriters.

Loaning on bottoms—bottomry—was a common method of procuring capital, of making loans at usurious rates, and of shifting or

---

[1] Forbonnais, II, 23.

[2] Postlethwayt, Dict., s. v. Assurance; Hatton, Comes, 289.

[3] 6 Geo. I, Cap. 18; 7 Geo. I, Cap. 27, Sec. 26. See discussion in Anderson, Origin, III, 99–102; Cunningham, Growth, II, 491–2; Scott, III, 402–3; Martin, Lloyd's, Ch. VI.

[4] Martin, Lloyd's, 66.

[5] Ibid., 76.

distributing risks.[1] In the latter sense it was a form of insurance or substitute for it. One form called "insuria marina" had many advantages over direct borrowing for adventures—it saved brokerage, interest, other insurance, renewals, obligation of insuring others, and at the same time insured against the risks of seas and enemies, and the rates however high were not regarded usurious. The East India Company employed "bottomry bonds" because they afforded at the same time insurance and capital, and were attractive to investors by reason of their speculative quality.[2] Loans at bottomry were widely used and were procurable even in distant Madras.[3]

The rise of insurance promoted commerce by lessening the risk to each individual and making him more ready to invest in commercial undertakings. A larger fraction of the total available capital was devoted to trade and industry; hoarding cash reserves against contingencies was less necessary. Commerce became more calculable and reliable, and business confidence increased. The total number of persons engaged in commerce was enlarged; the man of small means could adventure as underwriter or as lender on bottomry or as merchant of part of a cargo. All its effects in promoting commerce were indirect and not measurable in figures; but they were none the less powerful. For chance it substituted reasonable foresight; for apprehension and sense of hazard it gave confidence. Except in some ephemeral abuses[4] it repressed and tended to destroy the gambling spirit in mercantile affairs. Marine insurance was originated under the pressure of need, and its theory was evolved long after its practice was prevalent. Its volume necessarily depended upon the volume of imports and exports and on the size of the merchant marine.[5] But through the improvement in its organization it increased faster than the volume of trade.

Summary and conclusions. In conclusion and summary of the capitalistic quality and functions of the middleman class, it has been shown that the fundamental justification of the class obtains in the equalization of supply both in time and place; that to perform this function capital was indispensable; that the middleman buys in times of plenty

[1] Molloy, De Jure, 294–7; Postlethwayt, Dict., s. v. Bottomry.

[2] Scott, II, 172.

[3] Lockyer, Trade, 17.

[4] One of these abuses was jobbing in insurance, taking risks to sell to subscribers at higher premiums; another was gambling on vessels in which no interest was owned; another was overvaluation and purposed destruction for the sake of the principal. See 19 Geo. II, Cap. 37; Cary, Discourse, 93–4.

[5] See statistics in the Introduction, Chapter 1.

and stores the wares for times of dearth; that he buys in places of plenty and carries to places of dearth; that these two major operations rest upon the possession of capital and a developed system of commercial credit. Following this theme a number of pages have been devoted to outline the character of the capital and credit technique, through which the business of the time was done. The volume of commercial capital was found to commence to increase during the Elizabethan reign and to accelerate rapidly after the Restoration. Until about 1720 there was a concentration of this capital and wealth about the metropolis and the counties of the Thames valley soared in riches; after 1720 there was a provincializing tendency in wealth, business and industrial life. The wealth accrued from the profits of trade, colonies and home industries; the English merchant was handicapped by higher rates of interest and, therefore, labored for higher rates of profit than the Dutch merchant; as business was done increasingly on a credit basis this handicap would have proved insuperable had not the volume of capital and the credit organization been wonderfully improved and caused the rate of interest to fall. The mercantile classes devised and fostered commercial institutions. Their efforts to institute commercial banks were supplemented by the rise of goldsmith banks and the national bank, and during the eighteenth century they developed the system of country banks with metropolitan connections. These banks conducted the business of transmitting money by domestic exchange and international exchange. The early merchants did a more complex business: they were relieved by the specialization of special classes of financial men, like the exchange brokers, bankers, and the marine insurance brokers. All these functions were parts of the medieval merchant's business: they are branches of the capitalistic part of mercantile life. Some analysis of the process by which these differentiations of functions were worked out has been given. This sketch of the evolution of business classes based upon operations in capital and credit is meant to bring out the importance that must be accredited to these phases of middleman activity.

CHARACTER AND TRAINING.

A writer posited, as a prime maxim relating to trade, that the constant support of trade and navigation greatly depended upon the judgment, skill, and address of the merchants and traders in general.[1] Another prized "trading merchants that lived abroad in most parts of the world, who have not only the theoretical knowledge, but the practical expe-

---

[1] Postlethwayt, Dict. s. v. Trade.

rience of trade."[1]   Another valued "die kaufmännishen Grund-
sätzen der Ehrlichkeit, der Ordnung und der Sparsamkeit." Burke
ascribed the success of traders to "sharp and vigorous understandings"
and "the virtues of diligence, order, constancy, and regularity" and
to having "cultivated an habitual regard to commutative justice."[2]

These quotations agree in assigning the merchant special qualities
of mind and temperament and broad experience with the world.   It
was then a contemporary opinion that the English merchants were
more educated and cultivated than foreign merchants.[3] Defoe, in
explaining why banks, stocks, insurance, etc., were originated by the
merchant·class, held the "true-bred merchant the most intelligent
man in the world, and consequently the most capable when urged by
necessity to contrive new ways to live."[4]   This vigor of mind and daring spirit was evident in the fact that "the richest, most active, indus-
trious, thriving part of the Tradesmen" were of the non-conformist
type in the seventeenth century.[5]   Travel, experience with men,
and ventures in commerce, stimulated "sharp and vigorous understandings."   Mercantile life required broad learning, acute judgment
and reflective mind.[6]   The subjects in which proficiency of knowledge
and use was essential were many.[7]   He had to be able to use commercial papers, as bills of exchange, bills receivable and payable, policies
of insurance, letters of attorney, receipts, protests, charter-parties,
contracts of partnership, charters corporate. Bookkeeping and
accountancy and accessory branches of mathematics; local and foreign weights, measures and coins; commercial law and customs;
technical knowledge of commerce and banking facilities; physical and
commercial geography; processes, methods and materials of production; statistics; knowledge of public affairs and public law; sound
knowledge of English and commercial correspondence; acquaintance
with the best markets for particular goods; factorage and commission;
navigation; etc., etc.,—all these but intimate how comprehensive
must be the learning and interests of the "Universal Merchant" and
"Complete Tradesman."

[1] Child, Brief Observations, I.

[2] Burke, Works, VI, 218.

[3] Br. Mer., XXXVII–XXXVIII.

[4] Defoe, Projects, 33.

[5] "Et a dracone," 9; Petty, Pol. Arith., 26 (I, 263, Hull ed.).

[6] See Richard, II, 441–2, for the merchant's mental outfit.

[7] The fullest discussions of the proper education of a merchant are given in
Postlethwayt, Dict., s. v. Mercantile College; Roberts, Map, 17–18; Levi, Education of the Merchant; Defoe, Com. Eng. Tr., I, 3.

The training for these functions was acquired in three ways: apprenticeship, business college, and travel. The earliest merchants travelled with their goods and knew their markets first hand. In the sixteenth century the supercargo arose and relieved the merchant;[1] thereafter the travelling supercargo was a merchant at training. The merchant of the seventeenth and eighteenth centuries gained his foreign experience as supercargo and factor for London principals. The regular course of training consisted of (a) attending a grammar and writing school, (b) serving an apprenticeship to some London merchant, (c) shipping as supercargo, (d) acting as resident factor abroad, and (e) doing private business out of the factory abroad; after which the trained merchant-elect returned to London and set up as merchant to those parts of the world with which he had gained acquaintance.

Many illustrations from life might be cited. Sir Dudley North attended a grammar school, and a writing school,[2] where he learned "good hands and accounts;" he was then apprenticed to a Turkey merchant in Threadneedle Street; shipped to Archangel as supercargo; was agent for several Turkey merchants of London; became partner of one Hodges living at Constantinople; and finally returned to London and set up as Turkey merchant.[3] Edward Colston of Bristol was educated in London, and served as factor in Spain.[4] Sir John Barnard attended school and passed straightway to a responsible position in the counting-house.[5] William Patterson of Dumfries spent a few years of wandering life in the American Colonies and West Indies, and engaged in a clandestine and piratical business in West Indies, and engaged in trading voyages between the Bahamas and Boston before returning to England and setting up as full-fledged merchant.[6] It was the practice throughout the seventeenth and eighteenth centuries for the Newcastle Merchant Adventurers to send their enfranchised apprentices abroad, sometimes "even during

[1] Schmoller, Grundriss, II, 31.

[2] There were elementary business schools in London; e.g. Richard Hayes, author of "The Negociator's Magazine," 1730, ran one. See Preface, N. 13.

[3] North, Lives, II.

[4] Bourne, Eng. Mer., 248.

[5] Ibid., 285.

[6] Ibid., 254–5. See the account of the great trading traveller Anthony Jenkinson, 1546–1572, in Hakluyt; also, of Humphrey Chetham, in Fuller, Worthies of England.

their apprenticeship, to increase their knowledge and to improve their efficiency." They lived abroad from six to eight years and acted as factors for the home merchants.[1] Josiah Child was of the opinion that English merchants in his day did not give their sons and daughters a sufficient training in writing, arithmetic and accounting,[2] and ascribed Holland's ascendancy over England in commerce partly to this cause. The same opinion was expressed by Postlethwayt a century later.[3] It is important to note, therefore, that the English emphasized rather practical experience than scholastic training in preparation for the mercantile life.

The Elizabethan Statute of Apprentices[4] required a seven year apprenticeship of all who aspired to exercise the craft or mystery of merchandizing. It specified that no apprentices could be taken by merchants whose parents could not dispend 40 *s* yearly income from landed estate, and, if they lived in a market town not corporate, £3 sterling. Again in 1638 in the Royal Charter which Charles I gave to London a full seven years' apprenticeship was insisted upon for merchants of London and the environs within ten miles.[5] The French had a very detailed and extensive system of mercantile apprenticeship.[6] The "Mystery of this Trade" consisted in knowing the "difference in the qualities of wares,"[7] the prices and profits that were customary with respect to each, and all the matters and practices of commerce in general.

The apprentices and journeymen to a tradesman lived in their master's home. The parents of the candidates were required by the master to give bonds for the good conduct of their children, and also a premium at the time of entering. The premiums increased in amount during the century, especially in the last quarter of the seventeenth, when it was said they increased a third. The premium which parents were willing to pay varied not only with the calibre of the merchant-master and the training given, but also with the chance the master gave the apprentice to make money for his own account

---

[1] Surtees, 101: XXIV.

[2] Child, Brief Observations, 1–2.

[3] Postlethwayt, Dict., s. v. Mercantile College.

[4] 5 Eliz., Cap. 4, Secs. 27, 29, 31.

[5] Maitland, I, 315.

[6] See expositions of it in Savary. Par. Neg., 50–63, 118–121, 291–5; Postlethwayt, Dict., s. v. Apprenticeship.

[7] Barbon, Discourse, 12 Savary, Par. Negoc., 58–63.

while yet in the master's service. The law of supply and demand likely determined somewhat the rate of premium.[1]

After the apprenticeship of seven years was completed the enfranchised usually served the master a few years abroad as factor before they began buying and selling on their own account.[2] Those who did not go abroad moved to the suburbs of London and set up as retailing shopkeepers.[3]

The rigidity in the practice and the insistence upon apprenticeship in the mercantile world declined in the eighteenth century.[4] This was particularly true among the tradesmen. Campbell, writing in 1747, scorned the idea of asking learners to serve seven years' apprenticeship in such simple trades as retail shopkeeping, and names many in which it was entirely unnecessary. Defoe also noticed that the old-time sense of duty that existed between master-merchant and apprentice was decadent.[5] Fewer noblemen's sons were apprenticed in the midst of the century than in former times: contemporaries ascribed this to the lower profits realized in general by merchants—causing a decline in the attractiveness of the occupation—and to the influence of the standing army, whereby the fashion changed and the noble families put their sons in the army rather than into merchandizing.[6] This trend toward freedom and accommodation of practice to actual commercial advantage and away from the arbitrary interference of government in trade was in line with the general tendency of the century.

In the quotation from Burke above, a virtue ascribed to the merchant was a deep sense of commutative justice. An international code of commercial law had arisen and was founded on the practices of honor and justice to which the mercantile world had been accustomed. An early writer ascribed the same importance that Burke did to the fairness and squareness with which the English merchants treated their foreign customers and for which they endeavored to establish and maintain a reputation.[7] The same idea was the root of the use of trade-marks, so prevalent among the early merchants, and of the high respect which the civil and common law accorded to

---

[1] For the above data, see, J. B., Interest of Gr. Br., 83; Defoe, Com. Eng. Tr., 107–8, 111–13; "Discourse about Trade," 87.

[2] North, Lives, II, 349; Savary, Par. Negoc., 118–121.

[3] "Advantages of Enlarging Towns," 9–10.

[4] Besant, Tudor London, Ch. V.

[5] Defoe, Com. Eng. Tr., I, 10.

[6] Gent. Mag., 1732: 1015, 1021; 1733: 1014–15.

[7] Roberts, Map, 258–62.

these marks.[1] The merchants of any considerable value in commerce were known internationally by their "Marks." Dudley North, though he exercised some of the most indirect practices, always gave the most careful consideration to prevent frauds and cheats. "No solicitation or means whatsoever could prevail with him to cover or connive."[2]

However, already in the sixteenth century the merchant and trades- man had acquired a notorious name for fraudulent business habits. Piers Ploughman assigned his selling powers to "the grace of guile gone among" his wares.[3] "To play the Merchant with" was synon- ymous with cheating, and "to have Merchant's ears" meant to affect not to hear when the terms of bargains proved disadvantageous.[4] That such reputation should attach to the tradesman class is not strange when the whole medieval theory of life and public opinion were adverse to their business. The frauds of the worse elements of the class were sufficient cause to perpetuate the epithet long after the maxim of honor and honesty had come to prevail among the better.

The merchants aided their fellows and descendants by their practical and theoretical writings on trade and commerce. It is impossible and not desirable to make an inclusive list of the valuable publica- tions of English merchants: a few illustrations only are to be men- tioned. In 1638 Lewis Roberts, a merchant of wide experience and secretary of the Levant Company dedicated his "Map of Commerce" to the Harveys, five of the seven Harveys being merchants and his patrons in his early life. The tributes paid to Roberts by his con- temporary merchants and men of the world signify the great use of his "Map." It was replete with the most useful data, giving the detail of the technique of commerce, the products and wares, and maps of a high degree of excellence. Thereafter the geographical contour of the world of trade was pretty well determined. John Scarlett, a Merchant of the Eastland Company, in 1682 published his "Stile of Exchanges, containing both their Law and Custom as Practiced now in the most considerable places of Exchange in Europe," especially written for the direction and convenience of the merchant classes.

---

[1] Molloy, De Jure, 420.

[2] North, Lives, II, 147, 150.

[3] Langland, Piers Ploughman, Pass. VII, 213–14. (Citation given in the New Dictionary.) Much of the fortune of such renowned and philanthropic merchants as Sir Thomas Gresham was gained by fraud, usury and high finance. His busi- ness methods were none too honorable. Hall, Eliz. Soc., 58, 63–7.

[4] For these uses see Nash, Christ's Tears, 83; Rowley, New Wonder, IV, I, 51; Lyly, I, I., 169; Rojas, II, 7. (Citations given in the New Dictionary.)

This was the most elaborate work on Exchanges in English to date, and has been quoted by all subsequent treatises. International exchange had come to play increasingly a prominent rôle in business, and this book did invaluable service. Alexander Justice in 1707 seconded this "Stile" by a "General Treatise on Monies and Exchanges:" he had had "Yeares Experience . . . in that way of Business."

Another kindred class of books was published by such writers as Hatton,[1] Hayes,[2] Webb,[3] Fisher,[4] and others. These were every-day business guides more serviceable to the tradesman than the merchant. They contained systems of bookkeeping and accounting, forms of commercial paper, summaries of commercial law, examples of business correspondence, etc. Another class of writers catering to the tradesmen were the newspaper and magazine publishers, such as John Houghton in his *Husbandry and Trade*, 1688–90, which contained weekly reports of the custom house, of merchants and their imports, of prices of stocks on the Exchange, etc.

Such theoretical merchant writers as Mun, North, Child, Cary, Cantillon, Postlethwayt, Defoe and numerous others created a national and international interest in commerce, raised the merchant to a sphere of political importance, secured governmental coöperation, and were the most influential agents in fixing international policy. The theory and practice of Mercantilism took their finest touches through these writers' pens and ships.

SOCIAL POSITION.

In the medieval period the landed interests predominated in wealth, influence and respectability. The tradesmen's business, in this age of direct exchange at public markets, was regarded in some cases as parasitic and sinful.[5] There was generally in public opinion and esteem a predisposition in favor of the agricultural folk and the hereditary landed gentry and nobility. The merchant class were generally outside the pale of the highest social recognition.[6] From

[1] Hatton, Merchants' Magazine.

[2] Hayes, Negociator's Magazine.

[3] Webb, The Complete Negociator.

[4] Fisher, The Instructor.

[5] See Ashley, Ec. Hist., I, 144, for an exposition of the public opinion of that day with respect to the tradesman class.

[6] A curious but interesting remark by Pococke, about 1750 with respect to Preston brings out this prejudice: "This town subsists . . . by many families of middling fortune who live in it, and it is remarkable for old maids, because these families will not ally with tradesmen, and have not sufficient fortunes for gentlemen." Pococke, I, 12.

the fifteenth century onward commercial magnates strove for social prestige against this all-pervading sentiment. There was likewise a common sentiment that wholesale merchandizing was more honorable than retail.[1] This distinction likely found its basis in the natural admiration elicited by wealth, power, largeness of business. There were exceptional cases where small tradesmen attained social distinction.

The effect which these popular prejudices had on commerce cannot be determined. They stimulated while they discouraged. Commerce opened a way to social rank and respect, and this chance tempted its undertaking; but during the attempt the stigma of the cast was upon the undertaker, and many would be deterred from it. In the philosophy of the weak-spirited, it would be better to live an obscure freeholder or a needy nobleman's son than dabble in the despicable business.

The way to social prestige was by wealth. The financial status of merchant princes appealed to the scions of a needy aristocracy. Emulation provoked the merchant to settle the accumulations of his business in landed estates. He bought land, and retired to the leisure becoming to a country gentleman,[2] hoping that the quality of leisure and land ownership would avail socially. Trade was the surest way to riches,[3] and the rich trader stood some chance of honor and preferment. Wealth tended to make trade detract less from gentility. By marriages, elevations to peerage, and apprenticeships a nobility of wealth arose.

The ancient families recruited their wasted and exhausted estates by marrying their sons and daughters to rich merchants and tradesmen.[4] The list of great merchants who had marriage relations with

[1] This opinion was common in France and England: cf. Savary, Par. Neg., II, 19, 84, and Postlethwayt, Dict., s. v. Anonymous.

[2] La Touche, Letters, 4–5, points out the evil effect the retirement of these experienced and competent merchants had on business. See also Gibbins, Ind. in Eng., 278–9. See tradesman Stoddard's investments in land: Hall, Eliz. Soc., 56–7.

[3] Locke, Works, II, 8. The desire for wealth as a means of gratifying the desire for social distinction became an important economic factor between 1377 and 1485. Cunningham, Growth, I, 465; II, 10.

[4] Defoe, Plan of Eng. Com. 81–2; Com. Eng. Tr., I., Ch. XXIV; Postlethwayt, Dict., s. v. Commerce; Anderson, Origin, III, 373–4; Hazlitt, Liv. Cos., 8; Lecky, Hist., I, 209. See plea for the honorableness of the life of the merchant in Besant, Stuart London, 193, quoting Howell. The money lender did not realize as high recognition generally: for his social position and business activities refer to Hall, Eliz. Soc., 48–53; Besant, Tudor London, 48–53.

the peerage in the eighteenth century was long.   A most notable instance of the espousal of a merchant's daughters to noblemen was that of Sir William Cockaine who placed his six daughters in marriage with peers or their immediate kindred.   Sir Josiah Child, merchant, married one of his daughters to the Duke of Beaufort, another to the Duke of Chandos, another to Lord Granville, and his son became Lord Tilney.   By such prudent alliances social distinction was bought and later inherited.

The Crown also acquired immense strength under the Stuarts and Hanoverians by the elevation of merchant princes to the peerage. Men of eminent usefulness and capacities were called to share the highest distinctions of rank.   The goldsmith Duncomb, the hosier Furnese, the tradesman Child, the scrivener Lownds, and scores of other men of the lower mercantile sphere were entered into a mercantile aristocracy alongside the one of birth and land.   Such knighted merchant princes as Smythe, Garway, North, Child and Barnard became not only the ablest champions of the trading interests in the halls of Parliament, but also the chief advisers of the Crown on all commercial matters.

In a third way was the man of commerce sometimes elevated to a social parity with the peer.   By the English law of primogeniture, the younger sons of a noble family were without title or estate.[1]   It early became the custom for noblemen to put these into apprenticeship to the eminent merchants of the ports near at hand or of London.[2] In 1699 Liverpool had "many gentlemen's sons, of the counties of Lancaster, Yorkshire, Derbyshire, Staffordshire, Cheshire and North Wales . . .   put to apprenticeship in the town."[3]   The most of the Levant merchants were men "of fortune and family . . . very considerable, as well in point of birth as riches."[4]   The French commercial writers cited with admiration this practice of the English noble-born entering commerce and emulated it.[5]   Defoe summarized the situation in this way: "The rising Tradesman swells into the

[1] Compare the Dutch law of gavelkind with English primogeniture with respect to getting sons into business; see Child, Brief Observations, 1.

[2] Defoe, Com. Eng. Tr., I, 246.   This practice became the practice after the Commonwealth; see, Hume, Hist. of Eng., V, 526; Chamberlayne, Angliae Not. 1673: I, 320–2.

[3] "Moore Rental," 77, quoted in Bourne, Eng. Mer., 311.

[4] Beawes, Lex Mer. Red., 628.

[5] Savary, Par. Neg., 19–20; Coyer, Nobl. Com., is an extensive argument in favor of the participation of the French nobility in commerce as the English were doing.   Louis XIII admitted some merchants into the nobility in 1627.

Gentry, and the declining Gentry sinks into Trade . . . Thus Tradesmen become Gentlemen, by Gentlemen becoming Tradesmen."[1]

The results of these shifts in gentility were, in the first place, to originate "a new species of gentlemen", as Dr. Johnson called the English merchant; but the merchant was new only in the sense of being more generally recognized. In 1640 it was said that "Marchaundes & Franklonz . . . may be set semely at a squyers table."[2] The compiler of the *London Directory*, 1677, made "a passing reflection" as to the dignities of the merchants of London as follows: "Some are knights and baronets; some are alderman; the mass are plain John or Thomas, with a considerable sprinkling of Misters."[3] But these knights, baronets and aldermen differed from their colleagues so titled in one essential particular, viz., that they were men of wealth. They spent freely, lived luxuriously, and in equipage, display, estate and mansion outshone the landed gentry.[4] The splendid homes of Sir John Eyles, Sir Gregory Page, Sir Nathaniel Mead, the Earl of Tilney, and many more such merchant princes were looked upon with envy by the nobility of hereditaments.[5] These princes were buying up the estates and ancient possessions of the English gentry, and by power of purse were dispossessing them from their time-honored realms.[6] Probably the greatest result, therefore, of the shift in social prestige was to erect an aristocracy of wealth and set it in antagonism to the ancient aristocracy of birth. This rivalry in France broke into the passion of the Revolution in 1789. In England it was constantly tempered by the admissions of merchants of wealth into the ranks of the peerage; the peerage was democratized; the spirit of destruction was thus tempered, and, though conquered and subjected, the nobility of birth still holds a high respectability in eminently commercial England.[7]

[1] Defoe, Plan. of Com., 12.

[2] The quotation is cited in the New Dict., s. v. Merchant, from Russel, Bk. Nur. 1071, Babees Bk. Mrs. Green found that the merchants and traders during the fifteenth century were beginning to rise by their wealth to prominence socially and politically. See Green, Town Life, II, 68–9, 78–9.

[3] "London Directory," XV.

[4] Instance Sir Dudley North's luxurious way of living: Bourne, Eng. Mer., 228; also the references from Defoe, cited in the following note; Chamberlayne, Ang. Not., 1673, II, 212.

[5] Defoe, Com. Eng. Tr., I, 243–5; Plan of Com., 100.

[6] Defoe, in 1728, claimed he could name five hundred such estates within a hundred miles of London. Defoe, Plan of Eng. Com., 80–84.

[7] Similar observations are found in Toynbee, Ind. Rev., 63; Lecky, Hist., I, 170 et seq.; Gibbins, Ind., 324.

The second great result of the rise of men of commerce to social recognition was the favorable reaction this very recognition had on commerce itself. When wealth became a recognized source "of civic distinction, of power in the state, of social position and consideration," commerce received an invaluable aid.[1] There came a stimulus in two ways—men of noble rank and education were encouraged to enter trade with hardy spirit—and the intermixture of the higher and lower classes, i.e., the gentry with the mercantile folk, animated the lower by emulation and the higher by pride to do a more extensive commerce.[2] A still more general stimulus came indirectly by the national concernment given to commerce in Parliament Hall and Council Chamber. When merchants became legislators and councilors, the interest of commerce found champions, even to the degree of provoking a "Merchants' War."

PUBLIC LIFE.

This entrance of the merchant and tradesman into public life may be regarded as the third great consequence of his rise in wealth. The last century of the Stuart régime was politically checkered and ended in the Revolution but was on the whole a century of material prosperity. Particularly did England grow in wealth after the Commonwealth period.[3] In the midst of the growing commercial resources the trading and moneyed classes were rising to a place of high importance in the counsels of state. Their opportunity came by the vices of the last two Stuarts. The Revolution was effected by an alliance of certain of the aristocracy, of the non-conformists, and of the commercial classes—embraced in the Whig party. The Hanoverian dynasty was thus dependent upon the maintenance of the support of the merchants and men of wealth. William at once entered upon a European war: the government suffered from financial difficulties; every sort of taxation was attempted, but proved insufficient; the exigencies led to the adoption of a new system of public finance—that of a public funded debt. By acquiring public funds a permanent interest was established by the monied class in the perpetuation of

---

[1] The ambition for acquisition of wealth was stimulated by the possibility of purchase of civil public office. See Von Ruville, Pitt, I, 113.

[2] These ideas are suggested in Mahan, Sea Power, 55, and Chalmers, Estimate, 46.

[3] See Chap. I; also Child, Discourse on Trade; Petty, Pol. Arith., 170–1; Davenant, Dis. on Pub. Rev.; Macpherson, Annals, II, 629–30.

the new ruling House. The establishment of the Bank of England in 1694, the recoinage in 1696, the operations of the great trading companies for charters and favors—all these financial events intertwined the monied interest with the government interest, as opposed to the landed and Tory interest, in an almost indissoluble union.[1]

From the Revolution till 1760 the Whigs were almost continuously in the ascendancy and waged the long drawn struggle with the landed interest. The Tories insisted that land and a majority of landholders ought to be regarded with more concernment than trade and traders. To this end in 1712 a temporary Tory government tried to pass the Landed Property Qualification Act; it aimed at keeping from Parliament men whose wealth was ventured in trade and stock.[2] The monied interest held the government loans and threatened the government's policies and ministries.[3] The Bank and East India Company exercised such an influence in Parliament as to be declared dangerous by the opposition.[4] The commercial element became very conspicuous in legislation and administration. Patterson, Godfrey, Barnard and others championed bills and carried them through Parliament. Commercial and financial questions, especially during the long administrations of Walpole and Pelham, excited most interest. Debates were concerned in the national debt, the rate of interest, the sinking fund, the excise, bounties and subsidies, the land- and shop-tax; even religious questions, and questions of foreign policy and immigration turned upon their commercial aspects. In brief, it may be said that the merchants in general held as legislative objectives among others the following: The establishment of a National Bank,[5] reduction of the rate of interest on the public debt,[6] maintenance of the balance of trade by legislative prohibitions and support, reform of the currency, transferability of bills of debt, establishment of a merchant court, opposition to the naturalization of the Jews, registry of deeds, mortgages, etc., increase in the convoy service, colonial enterprise, maintenance of the tax on land as opposed to the taxes setting hard upon trade as excises, shop-taxes; etc. In many matters

[1] Very ample treatment of these combinations may be found in Von Ranke, Hist., V, Ch. X; Postlethwayt, Dict., Moneyed Interest; Lecky, Hist., IV, VI; Cunningham, Growth, II, 404–5.

[2] Lecky, I, 217.

[3] Defoe, Essay on Loans, 10, 14.

[4] Cf. "Reasons of the Decay of Trade and Private Credit," 36–7, and "Vindication of Bank of England," 37, et seq.

[5] For example, consider the efforts of William Patterson and Michael Godfrey.

[6] John Barnard made this his task, 1757.

their interests were widely opposed; for instance, the interloper merchants opposed the chartering of exclusive trading companies; but where there was agreement, these legislative measures were realized.

The most influential merchant in political affairs before the Revolution was Sir Josiah Child.[1] He was the autocrat of the East India Company, and favorite at the court of Charles II. Child made Charles many private loans, and, though a Whig and raised by Whig influence to the governorship of the East India Company, he was made a baronet by Charles. James II hated Child while Charles was living, but Child turned Tory when James came to the throne and became, as was said, "an abject slave of the Court, for purposes of his own aggrandisement."[2] His Toryism caused a schism in the Company and Papillon led the opposing faction and interlopers during the next decade. The Revolution of 1688 left him but little influence at Court; the outward management was entrusted to other hands, the real direction, however, remained covertly in his hands. Child's secret in securing favor at Court with the Stuarts was the giving of presents to all who could help or hurt at Court. He distributed bribes judiciously and prodigally and mastered the situation.

After the Revolution the mercantile element, representative of the monied interests, found their opposition not in the Court but in the landed nobility and interests. The struggle centered in parliamentary elections; the control of the Commons was the all important objective. Money became the means. The borough system of representation and representatives' playing for local interests made Parliament peculiarly adapted for plutocratic intervention. No less did the exaggerated esteem for wealth and riches easily gained that prevailed among the upper classes contribute to the success of monied men. Besides the conduct of the State devolved more fully into the hands of the sovereign and his ministers than it could in a more democratic government. The sovereign and ministers could be kept in subjection to the monied class by a venal control of the House of Commons. Accordingly, an all-pervading system of bribery and corruption was developed, and reached amazing proportions under Walpole's masterful hand. Plutocracy prevailed almost everywhere in the government.[3] A renowned statesman expressed the situation by his confident statement, "All these men have their price," referring to

---

[1] Consult Bourne, Eng. Mer., 240 et seq.; Scott, II, 128–189.

[2] See Macaulay, VI, 142; Bourne, 241; Scott, II, 145–167.

[3] See such contemporary writings as "Collection of Debates;" Davenant, Works IV, 128; Burnet, Hist. of his Own Time, IV, 362; and such recent works as Cunningham, Growth, II, 404–5; Macaulay, Hist., IV, 385–6, 498.

his mercenary associates and henchmen. A contemporary wrote: "Bank bills, Places, Lyes, Threats, Promises, Entertainments are everywhere employed to corrupt Men's Affections, and mislead their Judgments. Boroughs are rated on the Royal Exchange, like Stocks and Tallies; the Price of a Vote is as well known as an Acre of Land; and it is no secret who are the monied Men and consequently the best Customers."[1] The Septennial Act by extending the length of Parliaments from three to seven years gave the monied interests more opportunity to effect their organizations. During their parliamentary careers, Osborne, Churchill, Walpole, and a dozen others built up fortunes.[2] Efforts were made to stem the tide of corruption but in vain: the legislative inquiry in 1694-5 unearthed many monstrosities in the relations of the officers of the trading companies to those of the government; Leeds, Cooke, and others were disgraced; but the same course of operations continued. The property qualification of members of Parliament aimed at reducing corruption and bribery[3] by keeping out the monied class; but the law only caused perjury and evasion.

There were many obvious tests of the power of the mercantile and financial interests. In the last decade of the seventeenth century they had such dominion as to be able to submit to the House of Commons the greatest part of the "Ways and Means."[4] In 1732 Walpole sought to conciliate the landed interests by enacting a system of excises and of bonded warehouses: but the power of the mercantile class was unequivocably demonstrated by their successful resistance to these measures.[5] They showed their irresistibility by forcing the Walpole government, contrary to his pet and long used policy of peace, to enter upon a war with Spain, a war rightly denominated the "Merchants' War."[6] And Mahan says, "It was the boast of London Merchants that under Pitt commerce was united with and made to flourish by war; and this thriving commerce was the soul also of the land struggle, by the money it lavished on the enemy of France."[7] So, then, it is evident that in all the great economic events of the century the influence of the merchant and tradesman was second to none.

[1] "English Advice," 4.
[2] Rogers, Ec. Int., 466.
[3] Coad, Trade and Plantations, 40-1.
[4] Defoe, Projects, 34.
[5] Smith, Wealth of Nations, preface, XXXIX.
[6] See Latimer, Mer. Ad. 188-9; "A Short Account," 50 et seq.
[7] Mahan, Influence, 297. This is a paraphrase of a verse on a monument erected to Pitt in London.

Laboring under the doctrine of the Balance of Trade it was long debated whether it was desirable to have merchants in Parliament and Council. It was observed that a merchant might have an interest distinct from that of his country. If the Balance were unfavorable, the merchant could nevertheless gain the difference between the cost and the selling price. The merchants gained while the nation was losing: the loss was supposed to be drawn from the landholders and laborers.[1] The practice of the merchant followed his interests and yet as a whole he did it in direct opposition to the prevailing theory of commerce.

The private interests of the merchants were likewise suggested as unfitting them for legislators and counsellors. Contrariety of interests would result in mutual opposition and "rather puzzle than give light to the argument in debate." Each particularized his own interest and had too little concernment in what had respect to the advantage and disadvantage of the whole public.[2] The merchants in Parliament did represent local interests, and sometimes personal interests. For instance, Thomas Johnson, a merchant of Liverpool, was "a devoted friend to his native town" and "made it his chief business to promote the commercial and municipal importance of Liverpool . . . both by his speech and vote in Parliament."[3] The Bristol merchants secured favorable legislation by way of sugar bounties and opposed the Excise of 1732.[4] William Patterson was the Scotch merchant who contributed most to effecting the union of England and Scotland.[5] William Beckford, a prominent merchant and planter was Pitt's advisor in the West Indies' situation in 1759.[6] These are but illustrative of the sectionalism and private or local interests of the merchant representation in Parliament.

In the country towns the clothiers and other tradesmen were rising into public office in their localities. In the second quarter of the seventeenth century the worthies of the cloth trade began to be elected Treasurers of their counties, displacing knights and esquires.[7] In the towns the merchants had held the magistracy under the gild system and continued to hold office under the competitive system.

[1] See, for example, the discussion in "The British Merchant," II, 141–2.

[2] See Gee's opinion in his Trade and Navigation, 239.   For a contrary opinion see Gent. Mag., 1739: 131, 158.

[3] Bourne, Eng. Mer., 307, 311–14.

[4] Latimer, Mer. Ad., 187, 189.

[5] Bourne, Eng. Mer., 173–6.

[6] Von Ruville, Pitt, II, 222–3.

[7] Roberts, Soc. Hist., I, 368.

PEDIGREES OF THE COMMERCIAL CLASSES.

The merchants were derived from various sources. The differentiation of the merchant and tradesman from the craftsman of the early gilds appears to have been on the basis of gild master and gild yeomen. The master had to care for the disposition of the manufacture and was the most likely to be drawn into trade. This is illustrated by the drapers and merchant tailors,[1] the masters of which companies, even in the time of Edward III, were the great importers of woolen and linen cloth. The increase in the wealth and the number of the people required a greater division of labor, and the freemen, having become rich, gave themselves over exclusively to trade and left way for a further differentiation among the yeomen into small masters and journeymen. And with these latter the same process of differentiation repeated itself, resulting finally in three classes, (a) journeymen craftsmen, (b) retail shopkeepers, and (c) large masters, to which rank some arose, and small masters.

The master of the gild, who gave up the manual side of the business, became either a shipping merchant or an employing merchant. The earliest shipping merchants were at once ship-owners, ship-masters, and exporters of goods; these three branches became specialized in whole or part before 1760. The exporting merchant either travelled abroad with his cargo or employed agents to accompany it or to receive it by consignment: these agents specialized as supercargoes and factors. The merchants separated their multifarious employments—some became bankers, some insurers, some speculated in stocks and commodities, some became commission-house factors, and others remained exporters of merchandise and used these other parties in the prosecution of exporting.

The employing merchants distributed themselves into three categories—becoming wholesalers, retail shopkeepers, or large masters, such as the western clothiers. As has been shown elsewhere, the clothiers were related to the wholesalers and merchants by factors, and the wholesalers sold to the retailers. From the journeymen differentiated a class of small masters, some of whom became large masters and others shopkeepers. These differentiations are shown in the accompanying outline.

---

[1] See Brentano in T. Smith, Eng. Gilds, CVII; Unwin, Ind. Org., 44–5; Herbert, I, 29; Hazlitt, 265–6.

CRAFT GILD.
- *1. Master*
  - 1. Shipping Merchant
    - 1. Ship-Owner
    - 2. Ship-Master
    - 3. Exporting Merchant
      - 1. Itinerant
        - 1. Supercargo
        - 2. Travelling Merchant
        - 3. Factor
      - 2. Resident
        - 1. Banker
        - 2. Insurer
        - 3. Speculator
        - 4. Commission House
        - 5 Exporter
  - 2 Factor
  - 3 Merchant Employer
    - 1. Wholesaler
    - 2. Factor
    - 3. Large Master
    - 4. Shop-keeper
- *2. Journeyman*
  - 1. Small Master
    - 1. Large Master
    - 2. Shop-keeper
    - 3. Small Master
  - 2 Journeyman
    - 1. Shop-keeper
    - 2. Journeyman

While these differentiations were in progress the trading population was being recruited from various trades and places.   Inside the gilds was arising a middle class, which was to transform feudal society into the society of modern times.[1]   During and after the sixteenth century various causes were operating to force the urbanization of the rural folk.   Enclosures and sheep-farming were reducing the chances of livelihood in the country.   As the urban population increased the middlemen increased the faster in both numbers and activities, and drew a large proportion of their tale from the peasant freeholders and the gentry.   "The progress of discovery and the increase of international trade were offering new opportunities for wealth to the mercantile class, and the sons of the English gentry were impelled or drawn towards those favored seaports which had chartered or statutory trading facilities.   There they became apprentices, as their only available means of entering the trading community, whose status they

---

[1] Ashley, Ec. Hist., II, 168.

raised by their rank and whose influence they increased by their energy."[1] As early as 1633–5 there were nine hundred families within the walls of the City of London who were descended from the country gentry and had preserved proof of their descent. The great majority of these were engaged in trade, and nearly every kind of trade was represented.[2]

This practice of apprenticing rural folk infringed the townsmen's monopolies, and Parliament sought to restrain it. In 1405 only those were allowed to apprentice their children whose lands afforded them a spending capacity of 20s. per year. The Elizabethan Statute of Apprentices, 1562, declared it to "be unlawful to any Person dwelling in any City or Town Corporate, . . . exercising any of the . . . Crafts of a Merchant . . . Mercer, Draper, etc. . . . to take any Apprentice . . . except . . . the Father and Mother of such Apprentice . . . shall have . . . Lands . . . of the yearly value of forty shillings."[3] The Act probably confirmed the practice of merchants apprenticing freeholders' sons.

The relative numbers of these recruits drawn from the different districts roundabout a seaport varied, other things being equal, inversely as the economic conditions of those districts respectively were good. Newcastle drew apprentices from Durham, York, Northumbria, Cumberland, Westmoreland and other places. The total number of apprentices enrolled, during two and a quarter centuries, into the Merchant Adventurers of that city, and the percentage enrolled from each source are indicated in the following table:[4]

Recruits of Newcastle Merchants.

SOURCES	1579–1699	1700–1800	1800–1900	UNIT
Total Enrollments	936	631	160	Persons
From Newcastle	20	60	73	Per cent
" Durham	30	15		"
" Northumbria	15	15		"
" York	15	2		"
" Cumberland	6	2		"
" Westmoreland	5			"
" Other places	3	5	2	"
" Not Recorded	6	1	25	"

[1] Surtees, 101:XXII.
[2] "Visitation of London," 1633–5; Besant, Stu. Lond., 176.
[3] 5 Eliz., Cap. 4, Sec. 27.
[4] Data taken from Surtees, 101:XXIV.

It appears that during the last quarter of the seventeenth century four-fifths of the apprentices were recruited outside the Newcastle population, and two-fifths during the eighteenth century. This is telling evidence of the process of urbanization. The rural folk of Durham, Northumbria and York were entering largely into mercantile life. Mantoux has shown also that in the Industrial Revolution after 1760 the capitalist-manufacturer class was likewise recruited, not particularly from the "industriels" of the first half of the century, but from these rural people and gentry.[1]

The conclusion is that the trading population was not only differentiating from the crafts and within itself, but was being recruited in numbers, capital, energy and respect by increments of the best English stock—the freeholders of the country.

THE COMMERCIAL POPULATION—ITS NUMBERS.

It appears that the commercial population of England was increasing both relatively and absolutely during the century preceding the Industrial Revolution. Although the Mercantile Theory and Policy emphasized the importance of a large population to the national strength, there was no consensus of opinion as to whether it was desirable or not to have a relative increase in the commercial population. Coke in 1671 set it down as the thirty-sixth of his prefatory petitions that the retail trade of England was managed by many more persons than were necessary.[2] He claimed that though the trade of Amsterdam handled ten times the value of goods that the trade of London did, yet the retailers of London were twenty times more numerous.[3] Somewhat the same conviction was expressed by another observer who said there were in 1673 "five times as many of most trades as were   .   .   .   twenty or thirty years agoe   .   .   .   and thereby   .   .   .   trade   .   .   .   [was] more diffused."[4] Apparently the Civil War and Revolution had shaken up the whole industrial order and broken the restraints of trade.

Fifty years later the same phenomena were noticed and commented upon. A writer in 1721 declared that in his opinion England had two-

---

[1] Mantoux, 380–2.

[2] Coke, Treatise, (Preface).

[3] Coke, Treatise, 69. Coke cited Sir Charles Harbord as authority, but further said: "I   .   .   .   am content to make good all which is said hereon, before any legal Judicature," 112. The statement appears to be an exaggeration; but shows the conviction of a contemporary observer.

[4] "Grand Concern of England," 50.

thirds as many merchants "as all the rest of Europe put together;"[1] that there was no nation that had "so many true downright Merchants," who drove "all their trade upon their own Capital, as the English."[2] And during the next twenty years, according to another writer, the number of merchants in London, Bristol and Liverpool trebled.[3] Defoe was very profuse in relating how different trades had "monstrously increased" in London, causing such "alterations in the trading places in London" that, if one "recollected how things stood in London about fifty years" before, he would "be struck with surprise at the changes made in the time."[4] And it was to this increase in the number of manufacturers and shopkeepers that he ascribed the increase of trade "up to such a prodigy of magnitude."[5]

For want of census statistics the truth of these opinions cannot be surely tested. The evidence is cumulative, however, and to one general tenor, viz., that the commercial population was rapidly increasing. Some statistical estimates were made. In 1677 there were in London 1786 merchants at least.[6] In 1688 King estimated the commercial population of England at 246,000; in 1769, Young allowed 700,000 as engaged in commerce.[7] Defoe thought the total tradesman population of Great Britain in 1745, including their servants, apprentices, and journeymen was nearly two millions.[8] The most definite and specific, as well as the most probable, results in a statistical way may be had by comparing the estimates of population by King in 1688 and those by Postlethwayt in 1750.

The first of the accompanying Tables[9] gives the number of families, the average number of persons per family, and the total number of persons, in each of three classes into which they divided the commercial population. The Table concludes with the total number of persons in Great Britain.

[1] Brit. Mer., **XXXV**.

[2] Ibid., **XXXVII**.

[3] "Late Improvements," quoted in Smith, Mem., II, 314; also paraphrased in Gent. Mag., 1739: 478.

[4] Defoe, Com. Eng. Tr., II, 235–9 (1745).

[5] Defoe, Plan of Eng. Com., **101–3**.

[6] "London Directory;" see also, Br. Mer., **XXXV**.

[7] See Hobson, Mod. Cap., 22, for his opinions on the distribution of the population among the industries.

[8] Defoe, Com. Eng. Tr., II, 210.

[9] King's estimates are given in Davenant, Works, II, 184; Prothero, Eng. Agr., 453–4; Chalmers, Estimate, 203. Postlethwayt's estimates are given in his dictionary, s. v. People.

The second Table consists of results obtained by computations with the data of the first Table, namely, the percentum increases from 1688 to 1750 in the number of families and of people in the three respective classes and in the total population.

Obviously little dependence can be placed upon computations from data which only purport to be personal estimates, made by two different men, in different times and circumstances. The Tables are only drawn up to add to the other evidence what little they may. Discounting, therefore, the validity of these conclusions by a wide margin, the following are tentatively proposed: (a) That the mercan-

Table A. Table of Population of England.

CLASSES	NO. OF FAMILIES		PERSONS PER FAMILY		TOTAL NO. OF PERSONS	
	1688	1750	1688	1750	1688	1750
Eminent Merchants and Traders..............	2,000	2,900	8	9	16,000	26,100
Lesser Merchants and Traders..............	8,000	11,100	6	6	48,000	66,600
Shopkeepers and Tradesmen.................	50,000	59,190	4½	5	225,000	295,950
Total.................	1,349,586	1,472,339			5,500,520	6,000,000

Table B. Showing Comparative Increases, 1686 to 1750

	FAMILIES	PEOPLE
	per cent	*per cent*
Total Population...	9.9	9.8
Eminent Merchants...	45.0	63.0
Lesser Merchants..	39.0	39.0
Traders, Shopkeepers...	18.0	32.0

tile and trading part of the population were becoming an increasingly larger per cent of the nation; the total population had increased less than 10 per cent, whereas the commercial classes had increased variously from 32 to 63 per cent. (b) That the eminent merchants were increasing at a faster rate than the lesser, and far more than the tradesmen; this means that business was concentrating in the hands of the bigger merchants. (c) That there was arising a greater commercial interdependence among the parts of the Kingdom and between England and the nations beyond seas.

On a priori grounds one would conclude that the commercial population was increasing faster than the rest of the people. As the density of population increased, the need of and opportunity for middlemen were accelerated. The denser the population the more complex was the technique of trade, but the degree of complexity outran the relative degree of density of population. The larger and concentrated consumption caused a greater dependence upon commercial agents. Local specialization of industry caused a like dependence. More frequent and easier communication was wrought by the denser population and occasioned a larger use of business men. Viewed in whatever light, the 10 per cent increase in population would call for a higher per cent increase in the commercial population.

In the second place, the knowledge of commerce was cumulative. The experiences and practices of the preceding generations fructified in the next. The ratio of daring and adventure might be constant or decreasing, yet the commerce done be increasing. Furnished with the data of past efforts and experiments at commerce, the less skillful and venturesome could conduct a business which only the best and elect could do heretofore. In other words, a larger per cent of the people were assisted to the training requisite to the tradesman and merchant and the doors of trade and commerce flung wide for them to enter.

A further opportunity for a larger commercial life consisted in the greater freedom of trade. The medieval system of town monopoly, town protection, gild control, and "well-ordered" market, was dissolving. The custom of "foreign bought and foreign sold" was evaded or abandoned. The insistence on a term of apprenticeship weakened and was neglected. The shopkeeper in his shop was supplanting the periodic direct exchange on the public market. The license system for drovers, badgers, and pedlars, did not withstand the movement toward freedom. The old restraints which hedged about the alien merchants were removed.[1] The monopolies of the Tudors and early Stuarts were abolished. In nearly every respect it was easier for the people to move into the sphere of commerce.

Lastly, the foreign market was greatly extended by commercial wars and treaties. Cromwell initiated the policy of extension, and the century and a half that followed was a succession of wars with a commercial motive. Portugal was transformed into an economic dependency of England. India and America were added as colonies. These fields of operations and of opportunity called forth a larger merchant marine and a larger commercial population.

The personnel of this commercial part of the people and its distribu-

[1] 25 Chas. II, Cap. 6; Cap. 7; 1 Wm. & Mary, Cap. 32.

tion by classes on the bases heretofore suggested would be interesting if data existed, but it is very fragmentary. In 1733 there were 30,000 tobacconists in Great Britain, an average of three in every parish.[1] About the same time there were said to be 200,000 alehouses and innkeepers who sold alcoholic beverages.[2] Out of 96,000 houses in London in 1732 Maitland found 16,000 were hostelries and drinking places, while less than 5,000 were devoted to the sale of provisions. The following table is made from his data:[3]

Breweries	171	Bakers	1,072
Brandy Shops	8,659	Butchers	1,515
Alehouses	5,975	Cheesemongers	411
Taverns	447	Fishmongers	159
Inns	207	Poulterers	217
Coffee-houses	551	Herbstalls	1,214
Total	16,010	Total	4,588

In such western clothing towns as Trowbridge, Bradford and Melsham, with populations of three thousand or less, there was an average of about fifty clothiers in each in 1739.[4] It was estimated in 1753 that the Jews had nearly two-thirds of their money invested in commerce, and one-third in money, and that they did one-twentieth part of the foreign commerce of the nation, and the greatest part of the West Indies trade.[5]

THE COMMERCIAL POPULATION—ITS DISTRIBUTION.

The mercantile population centered in London. Bristol was the most extensive outport in commerce; Liverpool grew very fast during this century, faster than Bristol, and was becoming the second port after London. Each port of importance had its local celebrity of commerce who especially interested himself in the industries at hand in these places.[6] Norwich manufactured a kind of cloth—worsteds—especially destined for a foreign clientele; Yarmouth was interested in fish, malt and coal, Hull in corn, Bristol in Irish and West Indian products. But from very early times it could be granted to London that "Here have their residence, the rich and most eminent merchants

---

[1] "The Late Excise Scheme Dissected," 78.

[2] Defoe, Com. Eng. Tr., II, 217.

[3] Maitland, II, 719; cf. 735.

[4] Gent. Mag., 1739: 205.

[5] "Further Considerations on the Act," 16, 36, 42ff, 46–7.

[6] See Mantoux's treatment of this theme in his "Industrial Revolution," 88.

of this Island."[1]   In the Directory of 1677 a list of nearly two thousand merchants was drawn up; a great many of them had houses in the suburbs of London and did business from their homes; they dwelt at Highgate, Newington Green, Islington, Clerkenwell Green, Hackney, Hogsden, Bethnall Green, Kingsland, Moorfields, Spitalfields, and Mile-end.   The capital accumulated by commerce in the city spread itself out over Surrey, Middlesex, Essex, and Kent in mansions and estates, the envy of the landed gentry.   Provincial towns like Derby were yet at the end of the seventeenth century without a wholesale tradesman.

London was the center of the commerce of Great Britain.   The metropolis of the Isles, of Europe, of the world; centrally located with respect to the Kingdom and to western Europe; a port with a commodious harbor—in all it had a commanding position for land and maritime commerce.

A large fraction of the population of England was concentrated in this city.   A decade before the close of the seventeenth century the number of its people was put at 696,000.[2]   A calculation based on the imports of sea-coal gave for 1690, 530,000, and for 1716, 630,000.[3] An estimate of the population of England and Wales, based on the returns from the hearth duties, was 8,000,000 for 1690.[4]   Chalmers put it at 7,000,000,[5] and King at 5,500,000.   It appears that about one-tenth of the people were Londoners in 1690.   An estimate in the third quarter of the eighteenth century distributed a population of 6,000,000, allowing 750,000 to London and 950,000 to all the other market towns with more than 150 houses each, and the remaining 4,300,000 to the country.[6]   This gave London one-eighth of the people of England and Wales.

The concentration of trade was still more marked, as will appear from the Table[7] below for 1685–6:

	London	*Outports*	*Total*
Imports into	569,126 (45%)	715,293	1,284,419
Exports	409,563 (80%)	105,665	515,228

---

[1] Roberts, Map, 234.

[2] Anderson, Origin, II, 578; IV, 690.

[3] Gent. Mag., 1736: 355.

[4] Anderson, Origin, II, 594.

[5] Chalmers, Estimate, 48–59.   See the estimates given in Macpherson, Annals, II, 68, 634, 674; III, 134.

[6] Postlethwayt, Dict., s. v. People; cf. estimates by the census authorities, 1801.

[7] Data from Br. Mer., I, 282–305.

Eighty per cent of the exports passed through London.[1] They consisted of manufactures and minerals carried to London by internal and coastwise traffic, and of colonial and foreign goods re-exported: the concentration was of both foreign and domestic trade. Only about half as large a per cent of the imports came to London, but still it was 45 per cent of all the imports.[2] It was Maitland's opinion 1732 that London did one-fourth of the foreign commerce, since she paid that proportion of the customs duties.[3]

As to shipping, in 1702 London had 560 ships averaging 151 tons each, a total of 84,560 tons; while the total for all England was 3281 ships averaging 80 tons, or 262,480 tons. London had 18 per cent of the ships and 40 per cent of the tonnage.[4] The status in the middle of the century is shown by the following Table:[5]

DATE	PORT	TONNAGE ENTERED	TONNAGE CLEARED	TRAFFIC
1750	London	511,680	240,000	Coastwise
1751	"	234,369	173,843	Foreign
		746,049	413,843	Both
1751	Outports	245,485	522,802	"
	Both	991,534	936,645	"

Of the total tonnage entered 75 per cent came to London, and of the total tonnage cleared 44 per cent went from London. Of the entries into London 69 per cent were from the outports, and of the clearances 58 per cent were to the outports.

It, therefore, appears that London was predominant in population, trade, and shipping, and that no other ports approached it in these respects. Commerce focussed upon the capital and metropolis. During the seventeenth century the continental influence waned and

---

[1] Statisticians have calculated that from the midst of the reign of Henry VIII till the second quarter of the eighteenth century London port paid yearly between 70 and 90 per cent of the customs duties of England.

[2] The character of the goods exported and imported via London is shown in a statistical chart for 1730 in Anderson, Origin, III, 162–3; the statistics of re-exported American goods are given, III, 176.

[3] Anderson, Origin, III, 300; compare with Davenant's opinion, 1711, ibid., III, 41.

[4] Based on statistics given in Macpherson, II, 719 note.

[5] Based on statistics given in Rep. from Com. H. C., XIV, 353, 441, 501. A slight discrepancy enters from the fact that the statistics for the coastwise traffic of London for 1751 are not at hand, and those for 1750 are used.

the metropolitan waxed. London towered in the commerce of the Isles.[1]

There were slight internal migrations of the population in England in the early eighteenth century.[2] The poor law and the law of settlement restricted the urbanization of the people. A tendency existed, however, for the artisan, trading, and official classes to drift toward London. It was also the common opinion of the time that people propagated faster in cities than in the country.[3] These two causes tended to perpetuate and accelerate the momentum of an early start whereby London had its predominance in population.

The ascendancy of London in foreign trade rested on a long-standing record of actions and reactions. As the seat of the government, as the best central port, as the largest city, etc., it attracted most trade; but the increases of trade reacted on the size of the city, prosperity prospered by prosperity. It owned the most shipping, had the most merchants, could fit out the best cargoes, and secure the most convoys.[4] It had a prodigious home consumption, was a center of internal distribution, and had the largest market. More moneyed men resided here, bills of exchange and insurance were more easily and cheaply negotiated, and credit more readily procured. It was more influential in Parliament, was the seat of the foreign trading companies,[5] and the center of the financial operations of the government. Goods could be bought here for the best sorted cargoes, at lower prices, more easily and expeditiously, than in any other port.[6] So that unless some very great advantage was found in a particular outport, London was resorted to, and its commerce accelerated accordingly. By the force of these advantages London effected such an economic dominance over the American colonies that it was used as an argument that they never would or could rebel.[7]

It has been shown that the postal system was one radiating from London by five or more great roads, and that rates were charged on the theory that all letters went to, from, or through London. The

[1] See V. C. H., Suff., II, 249.

[2] Chalmers, Estimate, 219.

[3] "Advantages of Enlarging," 7; Chalmers, Estimate, 218–19.

[4] In time of war more ships used London port than in time of peace relatively by reason of convoy service. Houghton, Collection, II, 324.

[5] "Opening the Turkey Trade," 4–10; "Essay on Causes of Decline," 41–5.

[6] Many of these advantages were appreciated at the time: See "Increase and Decline," 4–5.

[7] "Atlas Mar. et Com.," 329–30, shows in detail the conduct of the New England commerce and its relations to London.

introduction of bye-posts did not change this system, and cross-posts were tardily develoved.   The post was one of the agents effecting the concentration of commercial interests in London.[1]

It early became the center of the circulation of the manufactures and agricultural products of the several counties.   A kind of emulation arose among the cities in the amount of goods they sent up to London.[2]   The city controlled the wool and woolens trade, the corn trade, the coal trade, and the live-stock trade, and affected considerably the trade in butter, cheese, fish, poultry, wine, horses, tin and linen.[3]   It was the most complete entrepot that had yet graced the train of commercial progress.

In the period studied, London acquired an ascendancy in money, wealth, and finance.   In 1698 Davenant estimated that London owned seven-ninths of the new coinage whereas its "usual and former proportion" was less than one-third.[4]   He noticed that a concentration of wealth had been under foot since 1660; formerly it had been more equally dispersed among the counties of the Kingdom.   Many causes operated to effect this concentration.   The residence of landlords,[5] members of Parliament, and officers of the government and army in the metropolis caused a flow of money for rents and salaries toward the metropolis.[6]   It was claimed by Child that the payment of interest on deposits by the goldsmith bankers drained the country parts of ready money.[7]   The financial operations of the government concentrated money upon the capital city.   The public funds were floated here, and interest on them paid out here; taxes were paid directly or ultimately into the London coffers; the government's mints were located here; bonds for customs duties were procured here; and the financial men of London were in better favor with the government.[8]   In internal and foreign trade London was the "grand warehouse," the "grand treasury of the nation."   The commission and brokerage business done by the London agents for the merchants and tradesmen of the provincial towns and outports brought large sums

---

[1] "Grand Concern," 30 shows that the stage-coach business had like effect.

[2] "Atlas Mar. et Com.," 109.

[3] See previous chapters.

[4] Davenant, Works, I, 158–9.

[5] Macaulay, I, 315 comments that before the Revolution of 1688 the country gentleman seldom went with his family up to London and that the county town was his metropolis.

[6] Gent. Mag., 1735: 355.

[7] Child, New Discourse, 18.

[8] Cary, Essay on Nat. Cr., 187–9; "Increase and Decline," 35–7; Gent. Mag., 1735: 355.

to the city.[1]   The convenience of drawing all exchanges domestic and foreign on London led merchants to establish reserves with their agents there.   It was the seat of the national bank.   Through these and other influences London became the financial center of Great Britain and succeeded Amsterdam as that of the world.[2]

The results of this concentration of people, commerce, trade, wealth and finance in the city London showed chiefly in the degree to which the economic organization was developed.   A city by the mere fact of its collected body of people renders particular assistance to trade.   But London—capital, metropolis, port and entrepot, all in one— afforded unusual advantage to the commerce of the English people. Its magnitude influenced the inland trade as a receiving and distributing point for the whole kingdom, as consumer of the produce of the whole country, and as the general money center.   It was said in 1745 that every shopkeeper in the remotest town of England, unless unusually mean, had correspondence with the London tradesmen.[3]   It was the entrepot of the nation.[4]

An entrepot serves commerce by reducing the costs of carriage, since it makes possible the carriage of large loads in one direction instead of parcels in many directions.   It is a convenient place to procure sortable cargoes which are necessary in the trade to certain parts.   Special economies are developed by the rise of brokers and agents who make it their business to promote mutual exchanges at the entrepot.[5]   Besides it concentrates the commercial interests of the nation, making a more effective and favorable public opinion with respect to commerce.

The influence of the London market on absolute prices throughout England is shown in the accompanying Table.   The Table consists of data gathered and tabulated by Arthur Young in several journeys in the third quarter of the eighteenth century; several of his tables are here condensed into one.   It will be observed that prices generally decreased as the distance from London increased; that the more transportable any ware was the less the variation in price (compare butter and meat); that the price of bread and cheese was uniform over

---

[1] "Increase and Decline," 32–3.

[2] For complete treatment see Bisschop, Rise.

[3] Defoe, Com. Eng. Tr., II, 78.

[4] It was questioned at the time whether the kingdom was not "like a rickety body, with a head too big for the other members."   See discussion in Anderson, Origin, II, 617.

[5] See Savary, Par. Neg., II, 284–5, for discussion of such agents, and "Reflections and Considerations," 7–9, for the need of sortable cargoes.

all England, regardless of distance; and that the price of meat fell most regularly with distance. The range of prices of meat was one penny: this represented the expense of driving to market and the waste of flesh upon the road. The uniformity in the price of bread depended upon the universality of the culture of wheat and its portability. The uniformity of the price of cheese was due to the fact that it could be transported easily in bulk.

Table Showing Influence of London Market on Prices.[1]

DISTANCE FROM LONDON	BREAD			BUTTER		
	Northern[2]	Eastern[3]	Southern[4]	Northern	Eastern	Southern
Miles	*d.*	*d.*	*d.*	*d.*	*d.*	*d.*
0– 20			2			8
0– 50	1½	1¼		6¾	7¾	
20– 60			2			6¾
50–100	1½	1¼		6	6¼	
60–110			2			6
100–150		1¼		6	6¼	
100–200	1¼					
110–170			2			5½
150–170		1⅛			7⅛	
200–300	1			6		
300–				5		

DISTANCE FROM LONDON	CHEESE			MEAT[5]		
	Northern	Eastern	Southern	Northern	Eastern	Southern
Miles	*d.*	*d.*	*d.*	*d.*	*d.*	*d.*
0– 20						4¾
0– 50	4	4¼		3¾	4	
20– 60						4⅙
50–100	3¾	3½		3¼	3½	
60–110						3¾
100–150	3¼	3½		3	3¼	
100–200						
110–170						3½
150–170		3½			3¼	
200–300	2			2¾		
300–	2½			2½		

[1] For corn prices, see Chapter on Corn and Corn Products.

[2] Young, Six Months Tour, IV, 274 et seq.; covers 65 towns.

[3] Young, Eastern Tour, IV, 306–7; covers 37 towns.

[4] Young, Six Weeks Tour, 315 et seq.

[5] The price of meat used is an average of beef, veal and mutton; all prices in the table are stated in pence per pound.

The capital that converged upon London was devoted more to the operations of commerce and financial institutions than to manufactures. The tradesman or merchant of the country town could not compete with the one of the metropolis. The concentration of commercial capital in London established more fully the merchants of that city in their superior position with respect to the country merchants. The capital of the country parts, therefore, tended to become industrial capital, devoted to manufactures rather than commerce; and became dependent to a considerable degree upon the commercial capital of the metropolis. The great manufactures sprang up far from London. Only when and where it became more convenient to market these manufactures elsewhere than at London did commercial capital and commercial interests evolve from or converge upon the outports. Fish, coal, and corn gave employment to some commercial capital in the North Sea ports. Bristol traded to the American colonies and plantations. But the rise of manufactures in the north checked London's supremacy in commerce. After 1720 the rise of the outports into commercial activity and into competition with London was very evident.[1]

There were very obvious changes in the local distributing of industry and population in England. Observers like Harrison, Leland Fuller, Defoe, Richardson, Fiennes, Pococke, and Young noted them. The drift was northward. The causes were fundamentally economic: water power was more plentiful, the rainy climate was more apt for textile manufactures; coal and iron fields were nearer. The population of Devon and the "cider counties" seemed to migrate to York.[2] The migration became quite general during the latter part of the eighteenth century from the south, east and west toward the north and northwest.[3]

Meanwhile a shift or variation in the character of London's business was noticeable.[4] London became more a financial center, and less a mercantile center. It was a transition from merchandizing proper to agency, factorage, brokerage, speculation, insurance, banking, etc. The merchant lost his preëminence in the commercial activities of the city:[5] stock-jobbers and bankers acquired greater fortunes with

---

[1] This phenomenon was observed contemporaneously. See Gent. Mag., 1739: 478; Smith Mem., II, 314; Atlas Mar. et Com., 109.

[2] Massie, New Cider Tax, No. 4.

[3] Toynbee, Ind. Rev., 32–8; Gibbins, Ind. in Eng., 332–3, 349–50.

[4] "Increase and Decline," 34–5.

[5] Municipal honors and duties devolved upon others than the heads of princely commercial houses. Macaulay, I, 327–8.

more ease, and in less time;[1] the brokers on the stock-, corn-, and coal-exchanges, and the underwriters at Lloyd's eclipsed the merchant exporter.   The financier outran the merchant.

Roughly speaking, the latter and greater part of the eighteenth century was one of decentralization with reference to English commerce.   It was the period of the rise of provincial towns and outports, especially in the north, into commercial importance.   According to a calculation by the Census of 1801 the population of London was practically constant from 1700 to 1750, rising from 674,350 to 676,250 only; whereas most of the other towns and cities grew by leaps and bounds.[2]

One cause of this decentralization was the natural limitation of growth.   The expenses attaching to the London trade increased faster than the facilities for profit.   The carriage of goods; the gains of factors packers, porters; the charges for hallage, lighterage, wharfage; and the port charges, were higher in London than in other ports. It likewise cost more to victual and man ships in the port of London.[3] The cost of living was higher there.[4]   The port became crowded and many inconveniences were engendered.[5]

A second cause was that the customs duties were unequally collected.   Smuggling was connived at by customs officials in the outports while there was a more vigorous enforcement of the customs laws in London.   This was said to cause a migration of merchants and traders to the outports, and retailers bought rather from the outport merchants since they could offer lower prices.[6]   It was alleged that the administration enforced customs laws more strictly in some ports than in others so as to procure parliamentary influence.[7]

The conveniences of navigation were better in some outports. Some were situated advantageously for trade to particular parts, as Hull to Holland, Bristol to America, etc.[8]   The passage of the English Channel and the demurrage in the Thames were undesirable.   In time of war, the ships sailing from London were much exposed to the enemy.[9]

[1] Gent. Mag., 1748: 10 is one of a host of references that might be given to show that stock-jobbing detached London from the mercantile interest.

[2] Anderson, III, 298.

[3] "Opening the Trade," 4.

[4] "Increase and Decline," 17; Gent. Mag., 1748: 408–10.

[5] Capper, Port and Trade, 143 et seq.

[6] Gent. Mag., 1748: 408.

[7] "Increase and Decline," 21.

[8] Capper, Port and Trade, 117.

[9] Ibid., 21.

A large part of the London trade was conducted by monopoly companies. This circumstance led the American, African and West Indian trade to establish itself in ports where it could be conducted by individual traders.[1] Monopolies freed these companies of London from competition and the stimulus that attends it; they did not conduct their commerce with the same economy that private adventurers did.[2] The outports became the seats of interlopers who succeeded in wresting commerce from London.

In the period of the Industrial Revolution the most potent factor in provincializing both foreign and domestic commerce was the development of the canal system. Many intermediary tradesmen were eliminated, and foods passed directly from Birmingham or Manchester to the foreign user.[3]

The relative rank of the ports in 1702 is shown by the distribution[4] of shipping:

London	84,560 tons	Liverpool	8,670 tons
Bristol	17,325 tons	Whitby	8,250 tons
Ipswich	11,154 tons	Hull	7,590 tons
Newcastle	10,899 tons	Exeter	7,139 tons
Yarmouth	8,866 tons	Scarborough	6,900 tons

Their relative importance is also indicated by their populations. The changes occurring in these proportions are roughly shown by comparisons of their relative growths in the first half of the eighteenth century. While Bristol was doubling, Liverpool increased five- or six-fold, and London remained practically constant.

	1685-1700	1700-1760
London	530,000[5]	725,903[10]
	550,000[6]	676,250[9]
	670,000[7]	
	696,000[8]	
	674,350[9]	

---

[1] Capper, Port and Trade, 117.

[2] "Increase and Decline," 8; "Opening the Trade," 4–6.

[3] See treatment in Mantoux, 118. This practice was arising in 1728; see "Atlas Mar. et Com.," 109; Defoe, Tour, III, 93.

[4] Based on data from Macpherson, II, 160–1 note.

[5] Gregory King.

[6] Davenant.

[7] Petty.

[8] Anderson, Origin, II, 578: IV, 690.

[9] Report, Census, 1801. (See Enc. Brit., 11 ed. XVI, 965.)

[10] Maitland, 1737.

	1685–1700	1700–1760
Bristol	29,000[2]	95,000[3]
	48,000[1]	100,000[3]
Liverpool	4,000[4]	30,000[5]
	6,000[4]	35,000[5]
		25,787[7]
Dublin	69,000[1]	94,000[6]

The provincial manufacturing towns of the north were making very rapid progress after 1700. The estimates of the population indicate that they grew much faster than the old manufacturing towns like Norwich.

	1685–1700	1700–1760
Manchester	6,000[8]	40,000[8]
		50,000[8]
		40,000[9]
		45,000[9]
Leeds	7,000[10]	
Sheffield	4,000[10]	40,000[9]
Birmingham	4,000[10]	30,000[9]
Norwich	28,000[8]	56,000[8]
	29,000[8]	58,000[8]
		60,000[9]

Bristol had long enjoyed the second position among the British cities with respect to trade. In 1760 it had about one-seventh the population and trade of the metropolis.[11] It was the most independent and developed entrepot, except London.[12] The consumption by its large population and extensive commerce to the interior rendered it a port where merchants could dispose of their whole cargoes in bulk; all other ports, Liverpool excepted, had to divide the return cargoes of their merchants with London, and make up part of their export cargoes there.[13] The shopkeepers of Bristol did a great wholesale trade among the western counties and Wales. They distributed over a region extending from Southampton to the Trent, and including

[1] Anderson, Origin, II, 578: IV, 690.
[2] Macaulay, I, 314.
[3] Macpherson, III, 322.
[4] Macaulay, I, 320; Lecky, I, 324.
[5] Lecky, I, 214; Macpherson, III, 323.
[6] Macpherson, III, 323.
[7] Bourne, Eng. Mer., 331.
[8] Lecky, I, 214.
[9] Macpherson, III, 322–3.
[10] Macaulay, I, 315, 318, 319.
[11] Compare Owen, Br. Depict., 141 with the above tables of population.
[12] "Atlas Mar. et Com.," 14.
[13] Defoe, Tour, II, 249.

Wales and Ireland. They used the sea, the Wye and the Severn. In 1764 two hundred sail were used in this inland navigation. The Severn was navigable for vessels of large burden 160 miles from sea. The goods shipped upstream were coal, manufactures, and American products; great quantities of grain, iron, earthenware, wool, hops, cider and provisions were sent down-stream. The African and American trade was particularly developed by the Bristol merchants.[1]

The port next in size and fast becoming greater was Liverpool. The rise of Liverpool was the most phenomenal of any port. In six decades it increased seven-fold in population.[2] "The decade following the Restoration may be described as the most momentous in the whole history of Liverpool. After centuries of comparatively quiet vegetating the town suddenly began to expand, and entered on a career of development and increase that has few parallels in history."[3] In 1702 it had one-thirtieth of the shipping of England,[4] in 1716 one-twenty-fourth, and in 1792 more than one-sixth.[5] This rapid expansion resulted from many causes. It was well situated for the Irish and American trade. It had a good harbor.[6] It received initial stimulus from the Irish Rebellion of 1641, the favor of Cromwell, and the damper put on London's trade by the Great Fire in 1665–6. It was fortunate in having "several ingenious men settled in Liverpool" from London; the Moore family was, in particular, one of promoters.[7] The two great causes were the growth of manufactures in Lancashire and Yorkshire, and that of the American trade.[8]

The most obvious peculiarity of the ports on the east side of Britain was that there were three capital ports, each having a "singular and particular trade" to itself, in which the others were scarcely at all concerned.[9] Newcastle supplied coal and grindstones and salt, Hull exported corn to Holland, and Yarmouth conducted the whole herring fishery on the east coast.[10] The Humber was the passage by which

---

[1] See Hurt, Bristol, 170; Latimer, Mer. Adv., 169, 179–183; 3 Geo. II, Cap. 31; "Present State of sugar," 16–7 and 22–3 Chas. II, Cap. , Sec. II, for factors promoting Bristol's foreign commerce.

[2] Anderson, III, 143, 261, 325, 461; see above table.

[3] Moore, Liverpool, XXXI.

[4] Macpherson, II, 160–1 in note.

[5] Bourne, Eng. Mer., 320.

[6] It was improved in 1710: Anderson, III, 36.

[7] Bourne, Eng. Mer., 300–1; Moore, Liverpool, XXXI.

[8] Moore, XXVII, quoting Blome, 1673; Defoe, Plan, 84–5.

[9] "Atlas Mar. et Com.," 2.

[10] These trades were discussed in the Chapters above. Yarmouth's commerce is treated in Anderson, III, 454–5, and Defoe, Tour, I, 73.

Leeds' cloth was shipped abroad.[1] Some private merchants procured an Act of Parliament for making the rivers Aire and Calder
navigable at their own expense. By this means Leeds and Wakefield
were put in communication with York and Hull. Hereafter merchants from Holland, Bremen, Hamburgh and the Baltic bought Leeds
products through commission agents at Leeds and shipped them from
Hull.[2] Hull became the receiving and distributing point for all the
commerce of the Humber system—of the Trent, Don, Idle, Aire,
Calder and Ouse.[3] Defoe was of the opinion that "in proportion to
its dimensions" there was "more business done in Hull than in any
town in Europe."[4]

Lynn Regis resembled Hull in location with respect to rivers, and in
handling corn, and in being a receiving and distributing point.[5]

Other groups of towns made comparatively little advance in trade
and commercial population after 1700. One such was York, Exeter,
Nottingham, Derby, Shrewsbury, Gloucester and Worcester.[6] By
1750 some had actually retrogressed. The decline of the manufacturing districts of the east and west of England was most marked.

The movements of the general population and of the manufacturing
and commercial populations are, of course, one. Under exceptional
circumstances a town may have had a large mercantile class although
it had a small population and commerce itself. It has, for instance,
been remarked above that the merchants of the Newcastle coal-trade
came at one time principally from Ipswich. But as a general premise
manufacturing is both cause and effect of a dense population, a large
fraction of which is commercial. The English people became one-
tenth metropolites during the seventeenth century, and until the
Industrial Revolution a large fraction of the remainder were agriculturists. It has been shown above that after 1720 especially there was
an urbanization toward the outports and the industrial towns of the
north and the northwest. The fraction at agriculture decreased.
These movements were decentralizing and provincializing portions of
the trade and commerce that centered in London. Less unity and more
variation, more entrepots and more directions, characterize the organization that was arising after 1720. The factory system was working a
reorganization in the mechanism and technique of English business.

---

[1] Anderson, III, 459.

[2] Defoe, Tour, III, 93; "Atlas Mar. et Com.," 4, 109.

[3] Defoe, Tour, III, 147; Anderson, III, 459–60.

[4] Defoe, Tour, III, 144.

[5] Defoe, Tour, I, 83–4 contains an excellent account of the trade.

[6] See their numbers as estimated by Macaulay, I, 316, about this date.

LIST OF WORKS CITED.

A. V. An essay for regulating of the coin, etc. 2d. ed. London, 1696.

ABRAM, A. English life and manners in the later middle ages. London, 1913.

————— An abstract of the grievances of trade, etc. London, 1694.

————— Abuses relative to the articles of provisions, etc. A letter in which is set forth the nature of certain. London, 1765.

————— An account of some transactions . . . relating to the East India Company. London, 1693.

ADDISON, J. Spectator, No. 69. London, 1711.

————— Advantages that new buildings, and the enlargement of towns and cities, etc., A Discourse showing the great. London, 1678.

————— Against the continuance of the Bank, etc., Reasons offered. London, 1707.

————— Aggravii Venetiani, On the Venetian and other grievances, together with a proposal for raising the price of tin. 1697.

AIKIN, A. Journal of a tour through Wales and part of Shropshire. London, 1797.

AIKIN, JN. A description of the country from thirty to forty miles around Manchester. London, 1795.

ALDRIDGE, W. The universal merchant, in theory and practice, etc. Phila., 1797.

ALLEN, R. An essay on the nature and methods of carrying on a trade to the South Sea. London, 1712.

ALLEN, W. Ways and means to raise the value of land, etc. London, 1736.

————— The ancient trades decayed, repaired again, etc. London, 1678.

ANDERSON, A. An historical and chronological deduction of the origin of commerce, etc. 4 Vols. London, 1801.

ANDREWS, A. The history of British journalism. 2 Vols. London, 1859.

————— An appeal to the common sense of Scotsmen, etc. Edinburgh, 1747.

ASHLEY, W. J. English Woolen Industry. In the publications of the American Economic Assoc., Vol. 11.

" An introduction to English economic history and theory. London, 1888.

————— Atlas maritimus et commercialis. See Halley, Ed.

B. E. A new dictionary of terms, ancient and modern, of the canting crew. London, c 1696.

B. M. Reasons offered by the Merchants Adventurers and Eastland Merchants. London.

BABBAGE, C. On the economy of machinery and manufactures. London, 1832.

BAINES, TH. History of the commerce and town of Liverpool, etc. London, 1852.

————— Bank-Credit: or the usefulness and security of the Bank of Credit, etc. London, 1683.

BARBON, N. A discourse about trade. London. 1690.

BARTLETT, TH. Treatise on British mining. London, 1850.

BAXTER, R. Baxterianae reliquiae; or, Mr. R. Baxter's narrative of the most memorable passages of his life and times. London, 1696.

BEAWES, W. Lex mercatoria rediviva, etc. London, 1752.

BENHAM, W. Winchester. London, 1884.

BESANT, W. London in the eighteenth century. London, 1902.
"   London in the time of the Stuarts. London, 1903.
"   London in the times of the Tudors. London, 1904.
BEST, H. Rural economy in Yorkshire in 1641, being the farming and account books, etc. Publications of Surtees Society, Vol. 22. Durham, 1857.
BILLINGSLEY, JN. General view of the agriculture of the county of Somerset, etc. 3d ed. London, 1798.
BISSCHOFF, JAS. Comprehensive history of the woolen and worsted manufacture, and of sheep. 2 vols. London, 1849.
BISSCHOP, W. R. The rise of the London money market. London, 1910.
BLACKNER, JN. History of Nottingham. Nottingham, 1815.
—— BLACKWOOD'S Edinburgh Magazine. Edinburgh, 1817–1914.
BORLASE, W. The natural history of Cornwall. Oxford, 1758.
BOURNE, H. R. F. English merchants, etc. New ed. London, 1886.
BRAND, JN. History and antiquities . . . of Newcastle upon Tyne. 2 Vols. London, 1789.
BRERETON, W. Notes on a journey through Durham and Northumberland, 1635. (Reprint.) London, 1847.
BREWER, J. S. Letters and papers, foreign and domestic, London, 1852–1910.
—— British Merchant. A collection of papers, etc., The. 3 Vols. London, 1743. (Note: citations in Arabic numerals.)
—— British Merchant; or, Commerce preserved. (C. Kind ed.) 3 Vols. London, 1721. (Note: citations in Roman numerals.)
(BROWNE, JN.) An appeal to the Revd. Dean Swift, etc. Dublin, 1728.
"   Reflections, little to the purpose, on a subject less to the purpose. Dublin, 1728.
BURGON, J. W. Life and times of Sir Thomas Gresham. 2 Vols. London, 1839.
BURKE, ED. The works of the right honorable Edmund Burke. New ed. London, 1803.
BURNET, G. History of his own times. 4 Vols. London, 1818.
BURT, Ed. Letters from a gentleman in the North of Scotland. 5 ed. 2 Vols. London, 1818.
BUSCHING, P. Die Entwickelung der handelspolitischen zwischen England und seinen Kolonien. Stuttgart, 1902.
BUTTERWORTH, JAS. An historical and descriptive account of the town and parochial chapelry of Oldham. Oldham, 1817.
Calendar of Patent Rolls. Lyte edition.
Calendars of State Papers. (Domestic, Treasury, Ireland and Foreign).
CAMDEN, W. Magna Britannia et Hiberna. Gough ed. London, 1789.
CAMPBELL, R. The London Tradesman, etc. London, 1747.
CANTILLON, PH. The analysis of trade, commerce, coin, bullion, banks and foreign exchange. London, 1759.
CAPPER, C. The port and trade of London, etc. London, 1862.
CAREW, R. Survey of Cornwall. London, 1602.
CARY, JN. A discourse on trade, etc. 2d ed. London, 1745.
"   An essay towards the settlement of a national credit, etc. London, 1696.
—— Case of the bakers in Dublin, etc., Considerations on the. Dublin, 1757.

CARRY, JR. Case of Messieurs Brooke and Helier. ca 1700.
——— The case of Richard Thompson and Company. London, 1678.
——— Causes of the decline of the foreign trade, etc., An essay on the. 2d ed. London, 1750.
CELY. The Cely Papers, selections from the correspondence and memoranda of the Cely family, Merchants of the Staple, 1475–1488. Malden ed. Royal Historical Society. London, 1900.
CHALMERS, G. An estimate of the comparative strength of Great Britain. London, 1802.
CHAMBERLAYNE, ED. Angliae notitia; or, the present state of England. 2 parts. 1673 ed. London.
CHAMBERLAYNE (or CHAMBERLEN), H. Several objections sometimes made against the office of credit, fully answered. London, 1682.
CHAPMAN, S. J. The Lancashire cotton industry—a study in economic development. Manchester, 1904.
CHILD, JOS. Brief observations concerning trade, and the interest of money. London, 1668.
" A new discourse of trade, 2d ed. London, 1693.
——— The clothiers complaint: or, reasons for passing the bill, against the Blackwell Hall factors, etc. London, 1692.
COAD, G. A letter . . . wherein the grand concern of trade is asserted, etc. London, 1747.
COKE, R. A discourse of trade. London, 1670.
" A treatise wherein is demonstrated, etc. London, 1671.
——— Collection of the debates and proceedings in Parliament, in 1694 and 1695, upon the inquiry into the late briberies and corrupt practices. London, 1695.
CONGREVE, T. Scheme . . . for making a navigable communication, etc. London, 1717.
——— Considerations on the present dearness of corn. London, 1757.
——— Considerations on the present high prices of provisions and the necessaries of life. London, 1764.
COOKE, C. W. R. Cider and Perry. London, 1880.
——— County curiosities, or a new description of Gloucestershire. Gough ed. London, 1757.
——— Coventry Leet Book. Dormer Harris ed.
COX, T. Magna Brittania et Hibernia, antiqua et nova. London, 1720.
COYER, G. F. La noblesse commercante. London, 1756.
CRAIK, G. L. History of commerce. 3 Vols. London, 1844.
——— Credit of our government, etc., A Letter . . . . relating to the. London, 1705.
CULPEPPER, TH. Plain English . . . concerning the deadness of our markets. London, 1673.
" A tract against usurie, etc. London, 1641.
CUNNINGHAM, W. Growth of English industry and commerce. 3d ed. 3 Vols. Cambridge, 1896.
" AND MACARTHUR, E. A. Outlines of English Industrial History. London, 1895.

CUNNINGHAM, W.   Currency in the Leeward Islands, Two Letters to Mr. Wood on the coin and. London, 1740.

DALRYMPLE, J. (tr.) The historie of Scotland . . . by . . . Jhone Leslie, etc. London, 1596.

DAVENANT, C. The political and commercial works. Whitworth ed. 5 Vols. London, 1771.

DAVIDSON, J. The Scottish staple at Veere, etc. London, 1909.

DAVIES, J. S. A history of Southampton. London, 1883.

DEERING, CH. Nottinghamia vetus et nova; or, an historical account of Nottingham. Nottingham, 1751.

DEFOE, D.   The complete English Tradesman. Scott ed. 2 Vols. Oxford, 1841.
    "   An essay upon loans, etc. London, 1710.
    "   An essay upon projects, etc. London, 1697.
    "   A plan of the English commerce. London, 1728.
    "   Some thoughts upon the subject of commerce with France. London, 1713.
    "   A tour thro' the whole island of Great Britain. 2d ed. London, 1738.

DELONEY, TH.   The history of John Winchomb usually called Jack of Newberry, the famous clothier, 1597. Hallwell ed. London, 1859.
    "   Thomas of Reading; or, the sixe worthie yeomen of the west. 6th ed. London, 1632.

──────   Description of England and Wales. London, 1769.

──────   Discourse about trade, wherein the reduction of interest . . . is recommended. London, 1690.

──────   Discourse concerning trade and that in particular of the East Indies. London, 1689.

DOBBS, A.   An essay on the trade and improvement of Ireland. Dublin, 1729.

──────   The domesday of St. Paul of the year MCCXXII—and other documents. Hale ed. Camden Society. London, 1858.

DOUGLAS, W.   Discourse concerning the currencies of the British Plantations, etc. London, 1751.

DOWELL, S.   A history of taxation and taxes in England, etc. 4 Vols. London, 1884.

DYSON. All such procolamacions . . . of Queen Elizabeth, etc. London, 1600.

Early Chancery Proceedings. P. R. O.

EARWAKERS, J. P.   Local gleanings relating to Lancashire and Cheshire. Manchester, 1875.

(CHANDLER), Edward Bp. of Durham, A charge . . . concerning engrossing of corn and grain, etc. London, 1756.

──────   England displayed. London, 1769.

──────   England's interest, or the great benefit to trade by banks, etc. London, 1682.

──────   English advice to the freeholders of England. London, 1714.

──────   English Dialect Society. Printed glossaries, 18–22, old country and farming words. Publications. Vol. III. Nos. 23, 30. London, 1879–80.

──────   Enquiry into the misconduct and frauds committed by several of the factors . . . of the S—S— Company. London, 1736.

──────   Essai sur l'état du commerce d'Angleterre. London, 1755.

(CHANDLER), Edward Bp. of Durham, An Essay on the causes of the decline of foreign trade, etc. 2d ed. London, 1750.

——— An Essay to prove that regrators, engrossers, forestallers, . . . are destructive to trade, etc. London, 1718.

——— Et a Dracone, or some reflections upon a discourse, etc. London, 1668.

FABER, R. Die Entstehung des Agrarschutzes in England. London, 1888.

FAIRHOLT, F. W. Tobacco; its history and associations. London, 1859.

FAREY, JN. General view of the agriculture and minerals of Derbyshire. London, 1811.

FELKIN, W. History of machine-wrought hosiery and lace manufactures. London, 1867.

FIENNES, C. Through England on a side saddle. London, 1888.

FISHER, GEO. The instructor; or, the young man's best companion. London, 1735.

FISHER, JN. Book of John Fisher. Kemp ed. London.

FITZHERBERT, A. The Boke of Husbandrie. English District Society. London, 1882.

——— Flour trade and dearness of Corn, Two Letters on the. London, 1766.

FORBES, W. A methodical treatise concerning bills of exchange. 2d ed. Edinburgh, 1718.

(FORBONNAIS, F.) Elements du commerce. Leyden, 1754.

FRAME, R. Considerations on the interest of the county of Lanark, etc. Glasgow, 1769.

FRENCH, G. J. The life and times of Samuel Crompton, inventor of the spinning machine called the Mule. London, 1859.

FULLER, TH. The church history of Britain. London, 1685.

" The history of the worthies of England. London, 1662.

——— Further considerations on the act to permit persons professing the Jewish religion to be naturalized, etc. London, 1753.

GALLOWAY, R. L. History of coal mining in Great Britain. London, 1882.

GEE, J. Trade and navigation considered. London, 1729.

——— The Gentleman's Magazine; or, Monthly Intelligencer. London, 1731 et seq.

GIBBINS, H. Industry in England, etc. London, 1896.

GILBART, J. W. A practical treatise on banking. (Part I.) London, 1827.

——— The golden fleece. London, 1737.

GOUGH, R. Antiquities and memoirs of the parish of Myddle. London, c 1833.

GRAFTON, R. A chronicle at large, and meere history of the affayres of Englande, etc. London, 1568.

——— Grand concern of England explained, in several proposals, etc. London, 1673.

GREEN, R. A brief history of Worcester, etc. Worcester, 1802.

GREEN, MRS. T. R. Town life in the fifteenth century. 2 Vols. London, 1894.

GREY, W. Corographia; or, a survey of Newcastle upon Tine, etc. Newcastle. 1694. In Harleian Miscellany, III, 267.

GROSS, C. The gild merchant, etc. 2 Vols. Oxford, 1890.

H. M. England's glory; or, The great improvement of trade, etc. London, 1694.

HABINGTON, TH. Survey of Worcestershire. Worcester Historical Society. 2 Vols. Worcester, 1893.

HALL, H. Society in the Elizabethan age. 2d ed. London, 1887.

HALLEY, E. Atlas maritimus et commercialis. London, 1727.

HARRIS, JN. Navigantium atque itinerantium bibliotheca; or, A complete collection of voyages and travels, etc. 2 Vols. London, 1705.

HARRISON, W. A description of England. In Hollinshed, R., Chronicles of England, Scotland and Ireland. 6 Vols. London, 1807–8.

HARTLIB, S. An essay upon . . . Potters designe; concerning a bank of lands, etc. London, 1653.

HATTON, ED. Comes commercii: or, the trader's companion. 4th ed. London, 1723.

"   The merchants' magazine; or, tradesman's treasury. London, 1712.

"   New view of London, etc. London, 1708.

HAY, A. The history of Chichester, etc. Chichester, 1804.

HAYES, R. The negociator's magazine. London, 1730.

HAYNES, JN. View of the present state of the clothing trade in England, etc. London, 1706.

HAZLITT, W. C. The livery companies of the city of London. London, 1892.

HEMMEON, J. C. The history of the British Post Office. Cambridge, 1912.

HENRY, R. The history of Great Britain, etc. London, 1796.

HERBERT, W. The history of the twelve great livery companies of London, etc. 2 Vols. London. 1837.

HEWINS, W. A. S. English trade and finance, chiefly in the seventeenth century. London, 1892.

HEWITT, JN. A treatise upon money, coins and exchange, etc. London, 1755.

Historical Manuscripts Commission. Reports.

———— The History of the ancient town of Cyrencester, etc. Cirencester, 1800.

HOBSON, J. A. Evolution of modern capitalism. London, 1896.

HODGES, W. The groans of the poor, the misery of traders, etc. London, 1696.

HOLLAND, H. General view of the agriculture of Cheshire. London, 1808.

HOMER, H. The enquiry into the means of preserving . . . the publick roads, etc. Oxford, 1767.

HORN, T., AND ROBOTHAM, JN. Janua languarum reserata, etc. London, 1643.

HORSELEY, W. (tr.) Deslandes' An essay on maritime power and commerce. London, 1743.

HOUGHTON, JN. Husbandry and trade improved; being a collection of many valuable materials relating to corn, etc. 4 Vols. London, 1728.

HOUGHTON, T. The Compleat miner, etc. London, 1688–9.

HOUSMAN, JN. A Topographical description of Cumberland, Westmoreland, Lancashire, and a part of the West Riding of Yorkshire. Carlisle, 1800.

HUGHES, JN. Liverpool banks and bankers. Liverpool, 1906.

HUME, D. Essays moral, political and literary. London, 1875.

"   History of England, etc. New ed. Boston, 1849.

HUMPHREYS, A. L. The materials for the history of the town of Wellington, etc. London, 1889.

HUNT, W. Bristol. London, 1887.

———— Increase and Decline of trade in London and the outports, An essay on the. London, 1749.

HUNT, W.   Interest of Scotland considered, with regard to its police, etc.   Edinburgh, 1773.

J. B.   Interest of Great Britain considered, etc.   London, 1707.

JAMES, G. C.   Pseudo-cost-book mines.   London, 1855.

JAMES, JN.   Continuations and additions to the history of Bradford and its parish.   Bradford, 1866.

JARS, G.   Voyages metallurgiques, ou recherches et observations sur les mines et forges, etc.   Paris, 1774–81.

———   Journals of the House of Commons.

JUSTICE, A.   A general treatise of monies and exchanges.   London, 1707.

KENNET, W.   Parochial antiquities.   In Publications, English Dialect Society, No. 23.   London, 1879.

KNOX, R.   An historical relation of Ceylon, etc.   London, 1681.

LANGLAND, W.   The vision of William concerning Piers Ploughman, etc.   W. W. Skeat ed.   London, 1867–85.

———   The late excise scheme dissected, etc.   London, 1734.

LATIMER, JN.   The history of the society of Merchant Adventurers . . . of Bristol, etc.   Bristol, 1903.

LA TOUCHE, J. D.   Letters on trade.   Dublin, 1747.

LAWSON, W. J.   The history of banking, etc.   Boston, 1852.

LECKY, W. E. H.   A history of England, etc.   New York, 1878.

(NECKER, J.)   Legislation and the commerce of corn, On the.   (Transl.)   London, 1776.

LELAND, JN.   The Itinerary of John Leland the antiquary.   Hearn ed.   9 Vols.   Oxford, 1710–2.

LEONARD, E.   Early history of English poor relief.   Cambridge, 1900.

L'ESTRANGE, R.   Seneca's Morals.   London, 1702.

(BINDON, D.)   Letter from a merchant who has left off trade, etc.   London, 1738.

———   A letter to Henry Maxwell, Esq., plainly showing if a bank had been establish'd, etc.   Dublin, 1721.

———   A letter to Sir William Strickland . . . relating to the coal trade.   London, 1730.

LEVI, L.   Education of a merchant.   London, 1868.

"   History of British commerce.   2d ed.   London, 1880.

LEWES, W.   Her Majesty's mails, A history of the Post Office, etc.   London, 1865.

LEWIS, M.   Proposals to the King and Parliament of a large model of a bank, etc.   London, 1678.

LEWIS, S.   A topographical dictionary of Wales, etc.   2 Vols.   London, 1833.

———   Liber Albus.   See Riley.

———   Liber Custumarum.   See Riley.

LINGELBACH, W. E.   Internal organization of the Merchant Adventurers of England.   In Transactions of the Royal Historical Society, XVI, 1902.

LOCKE, J.   The works of John Locke.   3d ed.   London, 1727.

LOCKYER, C.   An account of the trade in India, etc.   London, 1711.

———   The London Directory of 1677.   (Reprint.)   1878.

LYLY, J.   The woman in the moone.   London, 1595.

LYSONS, D.   London and its environs described.   6 Vols.   London, 1761.

MACAULAY, T. B.   History of England.   5 Vols.   New York, 1871.

McCulloch, J. R. Literature of political economy—a classified list. London, 1845.

Macpherson, D. Annals of commerce, manufactures, fisheries and navigation, etc. 4 Vols. London, 1805.

Madox, Th. The history and antiquities of the Exchequer of the kings of England. London, 1711.

Mahan, A. T. The influence of sea power upon history. Boston, 1892.

Maitland, W. History and survey of London, etc. 2 Vols. London, 1756.

Malynes, G. England's view in the unmasking of two paradoxes. London, 1603.

Mandeville, Jn. The voiage and travaile of Sir John Mandeville. (J. O. Halliwell reprint.) Lumley ed. 1907.

Manes, A. Lehrbuch der Handelswissenschaft. Leipzig, 1907.

Manning, O. The history and antiquities of the county of Surrey, etc. Continued to the present time by W. Bray. 3 Vols. London, 1804–14.

Mantoux, P. La revolution industrielle au xviiie siecle. Paris, 1905.

Marshall, W. The rural economy of Gloucestershire. 2 Vols. Gloucester, 1789.

Marshall, W. H. Provincialisms of East Norfolk. 1787. In Publications of English Dialect Society, No. I. London, 1873.

Martin, F. The history of Lloyd's and of marine insurance in Great Britain. London, 1876.

Martin, J. B. The Grasshopper in Lombard Street. London, 1892.

(Massie, J.) Orders . . . for preventing and remedying the dearth of grains, 1630. (Reprint.) London, 1758.

Massie, Jos. Observations on the new cider tax, etc. London, 1764.

Mavor, W. British tourists: or, traveller's pocket companion, etc. 6 Vols. London, 1814.

Meteyard, E. Life of Josiah Wedgewood. 2 Vols. London, 1865–6.

Middleton, Jn. View of the agriculture of Middlesex. 2d ed. London, 1807.

(Miege, G.) Brittania fortior; or the new state of Great Britain and Ireland, etc. London, 1709.

Misselden, E. Free trade. Or, the means to make trade flourish. 2d ed. London, 1622.

——— Modern business, the principles and practices of commerce, accounts and finance. Johnson, J. F., ed. New York, 1910.

Molloy, C. De jure maritimo et navali, etc. 8th ed. London, 1744.

——— Monthly magazine: or British Register. 60 Vols. London, 1796–1826.

Moore, F. Considerations on the exorbitant price of provisions. London, 1773.

Moore, Ed. Liverpool in the reign of Charles II. Liverpool, 1899.

Morant, P. The history and antiquities of the town and borough of Colchester, etc. London, 1748.

Mortimer, Th. Every man his own broker; or, a guide to Exchange–Alley. 6th ed. London, 1765.

Morton, Jn. The natural history of Northamptonshire. London, 1712.

Mun, Th. England's treasure by foreign trade. London, 1664.

(Murray, R., or Moray) Corporation credit, or, a bank of credit made current, by common consent in London. London, 1682.

" Proposals for the advancement of trade, etc. London, 1676.

(MURRAY, R., or MORAY) The Mystery of the new-fashioned goldsmiths or bankers, etc. London, 1676. (In Martin, Grasshopper, Appendix E.)

NASH, TH. Christ's tears over Jerusalem. London, 1593. (In Brydge's Archaica.)

NASH, T. R. Collections for the history and antiquities of Worcestershire. 2 Vols. London, 1781–9.

NAUDÉ, W. Die Getreidehandelspolitik der Europaeischen. Berlin, 1896.

———— Le negoce d'Amsterdam, etc. Amsterdam, 1694.

NEILSON, N. Economic conditions on the manors of Ramsey Abbey. Philadelphia, 1899.

———— A new English dictionary of historical principles. Oxford, 1888 et seq.

———— The new present state of Great Britain, etc. London, 1770.

NICHOLLS, H. G. The forest of Dean; an historical and descriptive account. London, 1858.

NICHOLSON, J. S. The history of the English corn laws. London, 1904.

NOAKE, JN. Worcestershire in olden times. Worcester, 1849.

NORDEN, J. The surveyor's dialogue. London, 1607.

NORTH, D. Discourses upon trade, etc. London, 1691.

NORTH, R. Lives of the Norths. 3 Vols. New ed. London, 1826.

ODDY, J. J. European Commerce, shewing new and secure channels of trade, etc. 2 Vols. Philadelphia, 1807.

OGILBY, JN. Britannia depicta: or, Ogilby improved, etc. London, 1736.

"   Itinarium Angliae. London, 1765.

(CHAMBERLEN, H.) Office of credit fully answered, Several objections sometimes made against the. London, 1682.

(TUCKER, J.) Opening the trade to Turkey, Reflections on the expediency of. London, 1753.

OWEN, H., AND BLAKEWAY, J. B. A history of Shrewsbury. 2 Vols. London, 1825.

———— OWENS' Weekly Chronicle. London, 1758.

PALGRAVE, R. H. J. Dictionary of political economy. 3 Vols. London, 1894–9.

PALLISER, F. B. History of lace. London, 1865.

———— The parliamentary history of England from the earliest period to the year 1803; continued as Hansard's parliamentary debates.

Parlimentary Rolls. Rotuli parliamentorum.

PARIS, M. Chronica majora. 7 vols. Luard, ed. Rolls Series. London, 1872–83.

"   Historia Anglorum. 3 Vols. Madden, ed. Rolls Series. London, 1866–9.

Patent Rolls. 38 Vols. London, 1891–1908.

PEPYS, S. Diary and correspondence. 5 Vols. London, 1848–1849.

PETTY, W. Economic writings of Sir William Petty. 2 Vols. Hunt ed. Cambridge, 1899.

PHILLIPS, M. History of banks, bankers and banking in Northumberland, etc. London, 1894.

PICTON, J. A. Selections from the municipal archives and records, etc. Liverpool, 1883.

PIKE, J. R. Britain's metal mines: a complete guide to their laws, etc. London, 1860.

PINNOCK, W. History and topography of England and Wales. 6 Vols. London, 1825.

PLOT, R.   The natural history of Oxfordshire, etc.   Oxford, 1677.
"   The natural history of Staffordshire.   Oxford, 1686.
PLYMLEY, J.   General view of the agriculture of Shropshire.   London, 1803.
POCOCKE, R.   The travels through England of Dr. R. Pococke.   2 vols.   Camden Society   (ns.), XLII, XLIV.   London, 1888–9.
POLLARD, A. F.   England under the Protector Somerset.   London, 1900.
(POLLEXFEN, J.)   Discourse of trade and coyn.   London, 1697.
———   The Post Boy.   With foreign and domestic news.   (Periodical.)   London, 1695–1710.
POSTLETHWAYT, M.   The universal dictionary of trade and commerce.   2 Vols.   4th ed.   London, 1774.
———   The present state of the sugar colonies, consider'd.   London, 1731.
PRICE, F.   Handbook of London bankers.   London, 1876.
———   Prices of provisions, etc., Three letters concerning the.   London, 1766.
(PRIOR, T.)   A list of the absentees of Ireland, etc.   Dublin, 1729.
Privy Council Register.   Acts of the Privy Council.   1542–1604.   Dasent, ed.   London, 1890–1907.
———   Proposal to cause bankrupts to make better and more speedier payments, etc., An humble.   London, 1779.
PROTHERO, R. E.   English farming past and present.   London, 1912.
PRYCE, W.   Mineralogia Cornubiensis: a treatise on minerals, mines and mining, etc.   London, 1778.
———   The Public Register: or, the weekly magazine, etc.   London, 1741 et seq.
RADCLIFFE, W.   Origin of the new system of manufacture, commonly called "Power-loom Weaving."   Stockport, 1828.
RALEIGH, W.   The historie of the world.   London, 1614.
RAMSAY.   Cartularum Monasterii de Ramesia.   3 Vols.   Hart, ed.   Rolls Series.   London, 1884–93.
RASTALL, W. D.   The history and antiquities of Newark, in the county of Nottingham.   Newark, 1805.
RAY, JN.   A collection of English words   . . .   proper to the northern, the other to the southern counties.   London, 1674.
———   Reasons for a limited exportation of wool.   London, 1677.
———   The reasons of the decay of trade and private credit.   London, 1707.
———   Reflections and considerations occasioned by the petition   . . .   for taking off the drawback on foreign linens, etc.   London, 1738.
———   Remarks upon the Bank of England, with regard more especially to our trade and government.   London, 1706.
———   Report from the committee on the woolen manufacture of England, 1806.   Parliamentary Papers, 8440.
———   Reports from committees of the House of Commons.   Vol. 14, 1772, 1773; Vol. IX, 1774, 1783, 1795–6, 1800, 1802; Vol. X, 1785, 1786, 1798–9, 1800, 1802; Vol. XIV, 1796, 1799, 1800, 1801.
———   Reports of cases in the Courts of Star Chamber and High Commission.   Gardiner, ed.   Camden Society.   London, 1886.
———   A review of the evils that have prevailed in the linen-manufacture of Ireland.   Dublin, 1762.

REW, R. H. An agricultural faggot. A collection of papers on agricultural subjects. Westminster, 1913.

REYCE, R. Suffolk in the XVIIth century: the breviary of Suffolk, etc. Harvey ed. London, 1902.

RICARD, S. Traité du commerce. 2 Vols. Amsterdam, 1781.

RICH, B. The honestie of this age: etc. Reprint, Percy Society. London, 1844.

RILEY, H. T. Munimenta Gildhallae Londoniensis: Liber Albus, Liber Custumarum, et Liber Horn. 3 Vols. London, 1854–1860.

ROBERTS, G. The social history of the southern counties of England, etc. London, 1856.

ROBERTS, L. Merchants mappe of commerce. London, 1636.
"   Treasure of Trafficke. (In Political Economy Club, Collection of early English tracts on commerce.) London, 1856.

ROBERTSON, W. Phraseologia generalis. Cambridge, 1693.

ROBINSON, H. England's safety in trades encrease. London, 1641.

ROGER DE HOVEDEN. Rerum Anglicorum scriptores post Bedam. London, 1596.

ROGERS, J. E. T. Economic interpretation of history. New York, 1888.
"   A history of agriculture and prices in England. 7 Vols. Oxford, 1902.

ROJAS, F. DE (tr.) Aleman's life of Guzman d'Alfarache, or the Spanish rogue. 2 Vols. 1622.

ROWLEY, W. A new wonder, a woman never vext, etc. London, 1632.

RUSSEL, JN. The babees book . . . the bokes of nurture of Hugh Roberts and J. Russel. T. J. Furnivall ed. London, 1868.

RYMER, TH. Foedera, conventiones, Litterae, etc. 30 Vols. London, 1703–5.

SAMPSON, H. History of advertising. London, 1874.

SAVAGE, J. The history of the hundred of Carhampton, in the country of Somerset. Bristol, 1830.

SAVARY, J. Le parfait negociant, etc. 2d ed. Paris, 1679.

SCARLETT, JN. The stile of exchanges, etc. London, 1682.

SCHANZ, G. Englische Handelspolitik gegen Ende des Mittelalters, etc. 2 Vols. Leipzig, 1864.

SCHMOLLER, G. Grundriss der allegemeinen Volkwirtschaftslehre. 2 Vols. Leipzig, 1904.

SCHOENBERG, G. F. Handbuch der politischen Oekonomie. 3 Vols. Tuebingen, 1896–8.

SCOTT, W. R. The constitution and finance of English, Scottish, and Irish joint-stock companies to 1720. 3 Vols. Cambridge, 1911.

Selden Society, Beverley town documents. Leach, ed. Vol. XIV. London, 1900.

———— Sentiments of a corn factor, on the present situation of the corn trade. London, 1758.

SHARPE, R. R. London and the Kingdom. 3 Vols. London, 1894–5.

———— A short account of the late application to Parliament . . . upon the neglect of their trade, etc. 3d ed. London, 1742.

Shropshire Archaeological and Natural History Society, Transactions. 8 Vols. Shrewsbury and Oswestry, 1878–85.

SMILES, S. Lives of the engineers. 3 Vols. London, 1862.

SMITH, A. An inquiry into the nature and causes of the wealth of nations. Rogers ed. 2 Vols. Oxford, 1869.

SMITH, C. A short essay on the corn trade, and the corn laws. London, 1758.
"   Tracts on the corn trade and corn laws. London, 1804.
SMITH, JN. Chronicum rusticum commerciale, or, memoirs of wool, woolen manu-
facture and trade, etc. 2 Vols. London, 1747.
"   A review of the manufacturer's complaints against the wool grower.
London, 1753.
SMITH, T. English Gilds. London, 1870.
——— Social England, a record of the progress of the people, etc. 5 Vols.
Trail, ed. London, 1895.
——— Some reasons humbly offered for establishing a yarn market in the city
of Dublin. Dublin, 1895.
Somersetshire Record Society. Sessions Records Book. London, 1887–1914.
SPEED, JN. The theatre of the empire of Great Britaine. London, 1676.
——— State of the public credit, A true. London, 1721.
——— The state of the sugar trade, etc. London, 1747.
——— State papers: domestic. treasury, Ireland, and foreign.
——— Statutes at large.
STEER, G. Complete mineral laws of Derbyshire. London, 1734.
STEVENS, J. A parochial history of St. Mary Bourne. London, 1888.
STEVENSON, W. H. Records of the Borough of Nottingham, etc. Nottingham,
1882.
STOW, JN. A survey of London. Morley ed. London, 1890.
STRYPE, JN. Memorials of Archbishop Cranmer. 3 Vols. Oxford, 1848.
Surtees Society, Publications: London.
Vol. 33, Best's farming book, 1857; Vol. 101, Newcastle Merchant
Adventurers, 1899; Vol, 105, Newcastle Hostmen's Company, 1901.
Sussex Archaelogical Society, Sussex archaelogical collections. London and
Lewes, 1848 et seq.
TAYLOR, JN. The carriers cosmographie, etc. London, 1637.
TEMPLEMAN, D. The secret history of the late directors of the South Sea Company.
London, 1735.
THORESBY, R. The diary of Ralph Thoresby, F.R.S. 1674–1724. Hunter ed.
2 Vols. London, 1830.
THORNTON, H. An enquiry into the nature and effect of the paper credit of Great
Britain. London, 1802. (In McCulloch, Select Tracts, 11.)
——— Thoughts on the utility of publick register granaries, The humble as-
dress of a true Briton . . . with his. London, c 1765.
TOMBS, R. C. The King's Post. Bristol, 1905.
TOOKE, TH. History of prices and the state of the circulation—from 1793–1837.
6 Vols. London, 1838–57.
TOYNBEE, A. Lectures on the industrial revolution in England. London, 1884.
——— Tracts, concerning the present state of Ireland, . . . its riches,
revenue, trade and manufactures, A collection of. London, 1729.
——— The trade and navigation of Great Britain considered, etc. London,
1729.
(NEWMAN, D.) Trade of England revived, and the abuses thereof rectified, etc.
London, 1681.
——— A treatise of wool and cattell. London, 1677.
——— A treatise of wool and the manufacture of it. London, 1685.

TUCKER, JOS. Instruction for travelers. London, 1757.

TUKE, J. General view of the agriculture of the North Riding of Yorkshire. London, 1794.

TURNER, W. H. Selections from the records of the city of Oxford, 1509–1583. Oxford, 1880.

——— Universal Magazine of knowledge and pleasure. (Periodical). London, 1747–1803.

——— Universal British directory. London, 1793.

UNWIN, G. The gilds and companies of London. London, 1908.

" Industrial organization in the sixteenth and seventeenth centuries. Oxford, 1904.

URE, A. The cotton manufacture of Great Britain systematically investigated. London, 1836.

USHER, A. R. P. The history of the grain trade in France, 1400–1710. Cambridge, 1913.

——— The Victoria histories of the counties of England. Doubleday and Page, ed. Westminster, 1900 et seq.

——— View of the advantages of inland navigation, etc. London, 1785.

(POWELL) A view of real grievances, with remedies proposed for redressing them. London, 1772.

——— A vindication of the Bank of England. London, 1707.

——— Visitation of London, 1633–5 (In publications, Harleian Society). London, 1869 et seq.

VON RUVILLE, A. William Pitt, Earl of Chatham. 3 Vols. London, 1907.

WATSON, J. Y. A compendium of British mining, etc. London, 1843.

——— Way for enriching the nations of England and Ireland, etc., A clear and evident. London, 1650.

——— The wealth and commerce of Great Britain considered. London, 1728.

WEBB, B. The complete negociator. London, 1767.

(WEBBER, S.) The consequences of trade; as to the wealth and strength of any nation. 3rd ed. London, 1740.

WEEVER, JN. Ancient funeral monuments within the united monarchie, etc. London, 1631.

WELCH, C. History of the worshipful company of the Pewterers of the city of London. 2 Vols. London, 1902.

WELDON, W. Hints for erecting county granaries, etc. Dublin, 1757.

WHEATLEY, W. B. AND CUNNINGHAM, P. London past and present. London, 1891.

WHITAKER, T. D. The history and antiquities of the deanery of Craven, county of York. Leeds and London, 1878.

WOOD, A. The life and times of Anthony Wood, antiquary of Oxford, 1632–1695, described by himself. Clark, ed. Oxford Historical Society, XXVI, 5 Vols. Oxford, 1891–1900.

WOODCROFT, B. Brief biographies of inventors of machines for the manufacture of textile fabrics. London, 1863.

WORLIDGE, J. Vinetum Brittanicum; or, a treatise of cider and other wines and drinks. London, 1676.

YARRANTON, H. England's improvement by sea and land. 2 parts. London, 1677, 1682.

" Extract from a dialogue. London, 1677.

YEATS, JN. The growth and vicissitudes of commerce, etc. London, 1872.

YOUNG, A. The farmer's tour through the East of England. 4 Vols. London, 1771.

    "   General view of the agriculture of the county of Suffolk. London, 1797.

    "   General view of the agriculture of the county of Sussex. London, 1808.

    "   A six months tour through the North of England, etc. 2d ed. 4 Vols. London, 1771.

    "   A six weeks tour through the southern counties of England and Wales. 2d ed. London, 1769.

APPENDIX.

Table showing products by counties.

Thames Counties:

COUNTIES	YEARS	Corn	Malt	Hay; Pasture	Cattle	Sheep	Horses	Cheese; Butter	Fish	Poultry	Wool	Woolens	Linens	Coal	Iron	Salt	Other mineral	Other mfg.
Essex	1676								x									
	1720	x			x				x	x		x						x
	1762								x			x						
Kent	1676	x		x	x							x			x			
	1720	x			x				x	x			x					
	1762	x											x					x
Hertford	1676																	
	1720	x	x		x				x									
	1762	x	x		x													
Middlesex	1676																	
	1720																	
	1762																	
Surrey	1676	x		x	x													
	1720	x																x
	1762																	
Buckingham	1676	x		x	x	x												
	1720	x			x	x												
	1762				x	x						x						x
Berks	1676																	
	1720	x			x				x	x	x							x
	1762	x	x															
Oxford	1676																	
	1720	x	x		x													
	1762											x						x
Wilts	1676					x												
	1720					x					x	x						
	1762											x						
Northampton	1676											x						
	1720	x			x	x						x						
	1762	x	x				x					x						x

Severn Counties:

COUNTIES	YEARS	Corn	Malt	Hay; Pasture	Cattle	Sheep	Horses	Cheese; Butter	Fish	Poultry	Wool	Woolens	Linens	Coal	Iron	Salt	Other mineral	Other mfg.
Shropshire	1676	x												x	x			
	1720	x			x									x	x			
	1762	x										x		x	x			x
Worcester	1676	x		x	x				x			x				x		
	1720							x	x			x				x		
	1762	x			x	x			x			x				x		x
Hereford	1676								x	x								
	1720	x							x	x								
	1762	x							x	x								x
Gloucester	1676	x				x			x	x			x					
	1720	x				x				x					x	x		x
	1762	x				x		x		x					x			x
Monmouth	1676	x		x	x				x									
	1720	x			x	x			x									
	1762	x										x		x	x			
Somerset	1676								x								x	
	1720	x			x	x			x	x							x	
	1762	x			x	x		x				x					x	

443

Appendix

Table showing products by counties—Continued.

Region	Counties	Years	Corn	Malt	Hay; Pasture	Cattle	Sheep	Horses	Cheese; butter	Fish	Poultry	Wool	Woolens	Linen	Coal	Iron	Salt	Other mineral	Other mfg.
Trent Counties	Lincoln	1676	x		x	x				x	x								
		1720				x		x		x	x	x							
		1762		x											x				
	Nottingham	1676	x		x	x									x				
		1720	x	x						x	x				x				
		1762	x	x		x						x	x		x				x
	Leicester	1676	x		x	x									x				
		1720	x			x	x					x			x				
		1762	x			x	x					x	x						
	Derby	1676													x	x		x	
		1720	x												x	x		x	x
		1762	x	x								x			x	x		x	x
	Stafford	1676	x		x	x	x								x	x	x	x	x
		1720	x		x	x	x								x	x	x	x	x
		1762	x		x	x	x								x	x			x
	Warwick	1676	x		x	x													
		1720	x	x		x										x			
		1762													x	x			x
Southern Counties	Sussex	1676	x		x	x				x	x					x			
		1720	x	x		x				x	x	x				x		x	
		1762	x	x												x			x
	Hampton	1676																	
		1720	x			x				x		x	x						
		1762	x									x	x			x			
	Dorset	1676	x		x	x												x	
		1720	x		x	x				x			x	x					
		1762	x			x	x							x					
	Devon	1676			x							x	x					x	
		1720	x			x				x	x		x					x	x
		1762											x					x	
	Cornwall	1676			x					x								x	
		1720	x							x	x				x			x	
		1762																x	
Eastern Counties	Norfolk	1676	x			x	x			x									
		1720	x				x					x	x						
		1762	x									x	x						x
	Rutland	1676	x			x	x												
		1720	x			x	x			x		x							
		1762	x			x	x												
	Suffolk	1676	x		x	x	x		x										
		1720							x				x	x					
		1762	x			x			x				x	x			x		
	Cambridge	1676	x		x	x				x	x								
		1720	x							x	x								x
		1762	x		x	x													
	Huntingdon	1676	x		x	x													
		1720																	
		1762	x		x	x													
	Bedford	1676	x																
		1720	x						x			x							
		1762	x				x												x

Table showing products by counties—Continued.

	COUNTIES	YEARS	Corn	Malt	Hay; Pasture	Cattle	Sheep	Horses	Cheese; butter	Fish	Poultry	Wool	Woolens	Linens	Coal	Iron	Salt	Other mineral	Other mfg.
Northern Counties	Cumberland.......	1676	x		x	x				x	x				x			x	
		1720	x			x				x	x				x			x	
		1762	x			x									x			x	
	Northumberland...	1676													x				
		1720													x				
		1762													x			x	x
	Westmore.........	1676			x	x													
		1720	x		x	x							x						x
		1762											x						x
	Durham..........	1676													x	x		x	
		1720	x			x				x					x	x		x	
		1762							x					x	x	x		x	
	Lancaster.........	1676	x		x	x				x	x								
		1720	x			x				x	x		x						x
		1762	x	x									x	x	x				x
	York..............	1676	x		x	x							x						
		1720	x			x	x			x			x		x	x		x	x
		1762	x			x	x			x			x		x	x		x	x
	Chester..........	1676			x	x			x								x		
		1720	x			x			x	x	x						x	x	
		1762	x			x			x								x		
Wales	Glamorgan........	1676																	
		1720	x			x	x			x	x				x				
		1762													x			x	
	Cardigan, Carmarthen, Pembroke	1676	x			x									x			x	
		1720	x			x	x			x	x				x			x	
		1762	x			x				x					x			x	
	Brecknock.........	1676																	
		1720	x		x					x									
		1762	x			x				x			x						
	Radnor............	1676																	
		1720																	
		1762	x	x		x													
	Montgomery.......	1676																	
		1720	x				x	x		x	x								
		1762										x							
	Denbigh & Flint	1676	x					x											
		1720	x				x												
		1762					x								x			x	x
	Carnarvon, Merioneth	1676	x	x		x													
		1720				x	x			x	x								
		1762				x	x												

Authorities for above table:
1762, Anderson, Origin, III, 449–63.
1720, Ogilby, Brit. dep.
1691, Miege, Brit. fort., Chs. III–IV.
1676, Speed, Theatre, Books I and II.
  In these authors the products of the counties are severally named; they are indicated in this table by the X's.
Miege used Speed as a source-book.